The European
Women's Almanac

**Other Columbia University Press
Reference Books**

The Columbia Dictionary of European Political
History since 1914, *John Stevenson, ed.* (1992)

The Columbia Dictionary of Political Biography,
The Economist (1991)

The Concise Columbia Dictionary of Quotations,
Robert Andrews, ed. (1989)

The Concise Columbia Encyclopedia, Second Edition
(1989)

The Columbia Granger's Index to Poetry, Ninth
Edition, *Edith P. Hazen and Deborah J. Fryer, eds.*
(1990)

The Concise Columbia Book of Poetry,
William Harmon, ed. (1990)

Paula Snyder

The European
Women's Almanac

Columbia University Press
New York

Columbia University Press
New York

Published in Great Britain by Scarlet Press 1992
5 Montague Road, London E8 2HN

Copyright © Paula Snyder 1992

Library of Congress Cataloging-in-Publication Data
The European Women's Almanac
Snyder, Paula

Snyder, Paula, 1954 –
The European women's almanac / Paula Snyder.
p. cm.
ISBN 0-231-08064-6 (c) : $35.00 – ISBN 0-231-08065-4 (p)
1. Women – Europe – Handbooks, manuals, etc. I. Title.
HQ1587.S69 1992
305.4'094 – dc20 92-13451 CIP

Typesetting by Kathryn Holliday
Cartography by Mike Shand
Printed in the United States of America

Acknowledgements

The debt of gratitude *The European Women's Almanac* owes to women and women's
organisations across the continent is immense. My heartfelt thanks are given to all those
who helped me to contact sources of information, to the women who wrote to me giving
freely of their thoughts, and to all the organisations who supplied me with information.
The *Almanac* could quite simply not have been written without them. My thanks are also
due to all the other people researchers depend on, but who tend to be forgotten – the
librarians who helped track down elusive information, the postal workers who delivered
all the bulky documents.

Finally I must thank all the women involved with Scarlet Press for their help taking the
idea of the *Almanac* and turning it into print: Belinda Budge, Christine Considine, Avis
Lewallen and Victoria Wilson; Kathryn Holliday for the long hours she spent artworking
the pages; and to my editor Ann Treneman for sharing my tiredness as well as my
excitement, for her skilful editing, and for being on the other end of a phone when I
needed her. P.S.

Contents

Foreword

The information, statistics and commentaries on the socio-economic position of women in Europe, presented in *The European Women's Almanac,* provide without exception a picture of inequality, gender and wage discrimination. Women's earnings are often 25% to 30% less than those of men doing the same jobs; legislation to protect women's health and safety is woefully inadequate. Women are everywhere under-represented in national parliaments, as well as in the European Parliament, where they still have to overcome the 40% hurdle. Perhaps it is hardly surprising, therefore, that legislation reflects male ideas of what issues should be addressed, and that even legislation purporting to deal with matters of concern to women has a male bias and narrow vision.

What legislators fail to appreciate is that the various economies could not survive without the contributions made by women working inside and outside the home: unlike many men, no woman 'works' only outside the home. This book shows that women everywhere shoulder an unequal economic and domestic burden, and have unequal life chances because obstacles are placed in their paths. There are exceptions, but a picture emerges of women having to fight every inch of the way.

The data in the *Almanac* gives lie to the concept of the 'new man'. Progressive social legislation is often weak, a small nod in the recognition of a problem but often appallingly inadequate. It defies understanding that governments can with one voice commend even higher female participation in the workforce and with the other deny the provision of proper child-care facilities for children and other dependants. Clearly legislators still think largely in terms of the nuclear family with wife at home – an image that often corresponds to reality in less than 10% of families.

The *Almanac* presents the data that shows conclusively that attitudinal and legislative changes are long overdue. Finding best practices in individual countries might help to identify a standard that all should meet. This book is a valuable tool in helping us to do this. Women need to make common cause in Europe to promote change for the betterment of society: everyone would gain as a result.

Juliet Lodge
Professor of European Politics, University of Hull, and
the UK's 1992 Woman of Europe

Introduction

The idea that gave birth to *The European Women's Almanac* was of a single and affordable source of information on women, summarising where they stand and how they live in a Europe that stretches from Iceland in the north, across the European Community states, to Romania and Bulgaria in the east and to Malta in the south. In the first attempt to pull together this enormous range of information, women in 26 countries would have access to how they fared in education and employment; their legal rights; what health care could offer them, and much more. They would also be able to look at the provisions affecting them more than men in a world where traditional roles remain the greatest inequality of all: parental leave and benefits, child-care facilities, and such life-shaping 'little' things as the structure of the school day.

Our coverage in this edition does not include the newly independent Baltic states. Nor have we included other countries from the former Soviet Union – a decision taken after lengthy discussions with Scarlet Press. Where Europe ends, Russia raises imponderable questions and we did not want to include some European Soviet women and exclude others. As the Soviet Union fell apart, the European Community came together. The Social Charter that is part of the European Single Market will extend valuable rights to millions of women in 11 of the member states, but not, it seems, in the United Kingdom – already the odd one out in providing no statutory rights for workers – which may not sign it. Among the most glaring problems to be redressed across Europe are the plights of part-time workers and the poverty of female pensioners, who are everywhere more likely to live on only a basic pension. Some changes will come about more quickly than others, but there are no revolutions in the offing for women waiting for equality.

The practical difficulties of putting the idea of the *Almanac* on to the printed page were great. With the exception of reports such as the meticulous European Community states and Nordic Council studies in certain areas, facts on women's rights are not generally easy to track down. Most of the published work on Europe ignores the very existence of women and the sources that do exist vary enormously in approach. The result was that some sections of the book had to be pieced together from a sentence here and a reference there.

Although the countries are arranged alphabetically, useful comparisons can be made between various groups of countries. The most obvious is of the 12 member states that make up the European Community – Belgium, France, Denmark, Germany, Greece, Ireland, Italy, Luxembourg, Netherlands, Portugal, Spain and the UK. However, in looking at trends in specific areas of women's rights, Denmark could equally be grouped with the other Nordic countries of Finland, Iceland, Norway and Sweden.

The countries of eastern Europe share a broad legacy in terms of provision such as maternity leave and women's participation in employment, though all data on eastern Europe should be used in the knowledge that societies there are undergoing rapid change or even, in the case of Yugoslavia and to a lesser extent Albania, disintegration.

My starting point in gathering information was women themselves. Something like 1,200 letters were written: to women's organisations and groups, women's studies departments, trade unions, employers' organisations, embassies, government ministries and, of course, to individuals.

A central aim was to present not the promises of where women ought to be, but the facts of where they are. I reasoned, for example, that women would be more interested in what they actually earned compared with men, than in what the law said they ought to be earning; that the numbers of pre-school children in publicly funded child-care places were more relevant than a government's target for nursery provision. So disappointment was inevitable when large, weighty documents arrived through the post, only to be discarded because they contained nothing more than recommendations of what ought to be done to bring about equality. But perseverance paid off, and gradually the figures came together for this first reference book for Europe's 250 million women.

Facts alone, however, do not tell the full story of women's lives. Greater participation in employment does not necessarily mean that women have an easier time finding nursery places, that their standard of living is any higher, that food is any easier to buy. In the eastern states, but also in such places as Greece, statistics conceal major economic and social issues, such as the existence of second economies. From the very beginning, the *Almanac* aimed to include the thoughts of women actually living in the countries.

Long letters began to arrive from all over Europe, each with a life to share. There are no statistics that could reflect Roumy Slabakova's explanation of the need for elderly women to queue for food in the bitter cold of a

Bulgarian winter or Vlasta Jalusic's frightening analysis of how the disintegration of Yugoslavia is in turn destroying women's rights.

Despite their willingness – and that of so many others – to tell their stories, the pace of political change in eastern Europe has left a gap both in the statistics and in providing an accurate picture of daily life. Women's lives were almost immediately affected by the revolutions of 1989 and one of the sadnesses of the statistics that do exist is that, in some cases, they represent what women have lost or may be losing: maternity rights, child-care facilities, the right to control their own fertility.

German unification saw women in the former East Germany fighting to preserve their rights to abortion, also under threat in Poland and parts of old Yugoslavia, and wondering what to do as nurseries closed around them. In Hungary women have lost the right to have their jobs kept open for 3 years after giving birth. And everywhere in the east, unemployment is rising. There is hope that the changes will also bring positive opportunities for women, including access to safe, modern methods of contraception. And while women may be enjoying greater freedom of expression, they are also questioning why one of the products of Western-style democracy has to be a highly visible and growing trade in pornography.

Examples like these show how necessary it is to listen to the voices of individuals, as well as to the chant of documented information. Throughout the *Almanac,* the picture that emerges from countries as diverse as Sweden and Hungary is of women exhausted by the burden of running a home and shouldering the main responsibility for children on top of a full-time job. While equal rights legislation strives to chip away at the stubborn inequalities of the workplace, education and government policies, it does not reach very far into the sensitive area of the home. Women in Europe, both in and out of work, are the main providers for their families, in terms of time and skills invested. Bringing home the bacon depends only on the salary attached to a job – turning it into a meal requires ability, imagination and, most of all, time. We can only hope that, by the next edition, all of us women in Europe will have more of it.

Paula Snyder
Brighton, March 1992

If you would like to contribute to the next edition of the *Almanac,* either by sending us sources for information or by contributing your own experiences, please write to: *The European Women's Almanac,* Scarlet Press, 5 Montague Road, London E8 2HN.

How to use this book

The 26 countries covered in the *Almanac* have been listed in alphabetical order. The information in each chapter is presented in the same order and, as much as possible, in the same way. For each country, there is:

- An introductory snapshot of the country, including general facts and map
- A short description of the country's political and cultural status
- A statistically based reference section outlining rights and benefits under the headings of:

Immigration and residence rights

Equal rights

Birth, life and death
Includes marriage and divorce trends
Tables may include:
Breakdown of population by sex and age group
Population density by region
Births and deaths per 1,000 population

Lesbian rights

Women and health care
Includes abortion and contraception
Tables may include:
Major indicators for women's health

Parental pay, leave and benefits
Includes data on maternity and parental leave and pay, nursing mothers, paternity leave, maternity benefit, right of return to work, and time off to care for sick children

Child-care provision
Includes data on 0–6 year olds, primary school, outside school hours care and contributions to child-care costs

State benefits
Includes data on retirement pensions, survivors' pensions, disability, sickness and unemployment benefits, family and child benefits

Women and employment
Includes data on statutory rights, part-time work, working mothers and unemployment

Tables may include:
Women in employment trends
Employment by industrial sector
Most common occupations by sex
Women's earnings compared to men's

Women in trade unions

Women and politics

Women and education
Tables may include:
Pupils and students by school type and sex
Women students by subject studied

Women and detention

● **Sources**

● **Letters**
Individual contributions from women in the country

● **Addresses**

While every effort has been made to include as much information as possible for each country, in many cases it was not possible to find reliable facts and figures. Indeed, in some cases they simply do not exist, and this is particularly true of the eastern European countries of Albania, Bulgaria, Czechoslovakia, Hungary, Poland, Romania and Yugoslavia.

In addition to the country-by-country information the *Almanac* provides a range of comparisons between countries in the areas of population, health and maternity, marriage and divorce and education. These tables start on page 393.

Albania

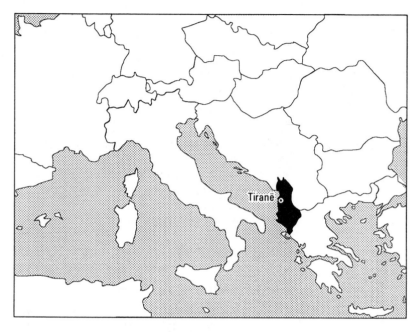

Tiranë

- **Population** 3.2 million, 48.5% female
- **Area** 28,748 sq km
- **Population density** 110.7 people sq km
- **GNP per capita** $930 (1986)
- **Public spending as % of GNP:** defence 4% (1986); health 2.3% (1987)
- **Currency is the lek:** official exchange rate 1989 £1 = LEK8.4; US$1 = LEK5.2

The president is head of state and chairs the Council of Ministers, which holds executive authority. The single-chamber People's Assembly is made up of 250 deputies elected every 4 years. Local government is based on 26 districts with people's councils elected every 3 years. The right to vote comes at age 18.

The state owns 70% of all urban housing, with the waiting period for an average apartment 3 years

In 1967 Albania became the world's first atheist state. At the end of World War Two, 70% of the population was Muslim and 20% Albanian Orthodox.

Almost half of Albania is forested and in 1988 more than half the population (51.7%) were employed in agriculture with 22.9% in industry. The most densely populated parts are Tiranë (293.3 people/sq km) and Durrës (286.0). The least populated are in Kolonjë (30.5), Përmet and Tropojë (both 42.4). The Greek population is estimated at 60,000.

BIRTH, LIFE AND DEATH

Annual average resident population

	total pop (1000s)	female (%)	male (%)	urban (%)	rural (%)
1950	1,215.2	48.7	51.3	20.5	79.5
1960	1,607.3	48.5	51.5	29.5	70.5
1970	2,135.6	48.6	51.4	31.8	68.2
1980	2,671.3	48.4	51.6	33.6	66.4
1985	2,962.2	48.4	51.6	34.2	65.8
1989	3,182.4	48.5	51.5	35.5	64.5

Source: data from Valentina Leskaj, from official government statistics

High birth rates have resulted in the youngest population in Europe – approximately 40% are under 15 – and although the birth rate is slowing it will remain high in the future. The number of deliveries grew from 76,400 in 1986 to 82,150 in 1990. In addition, there has been a fall in infant mortality rates. The natural increase in population is higher in rural areas – 21.9 for every 1,000 inhabitants in 1987 compared with 17.2 in urban areas.

Population density by region (1988)

region	area sq km	population	pop density per sq km
Berat	1,027	173,700	169.1
Dibër	1,568	148,200	94.5
Durrës	848	242,500	286.0
Elbasan	1,481	238,600	161.1
Fier	1,175	239,700	204.0
Gramsh	695	43,800	63.0
Gjirokastër	1,137	65,500	57.6
Kolonjë	805	24,600	30.5
Korçë	2,181	213,200	97.8
Krujë	607	105,300	157.2
Kukës	1,330	99,400	74.7
Lezhë	479	61,100	127.5
Librazhd	1,013	70,800	69.9
Lushnjë	712	132,200	185.7
Mat	1,028	75,900	73.5
Mirditë	867	49,700	57.3
Përmet	929	39,400	42.4
Pogradec	725	70,500	97.2
Pukë	1,034	48,200	46.6
Sarandë	1,097	86,800	78.9
Shkodër	775	45,800	59.1
Skrapar	2,528	233,000	92.2
Telepenë	817	49,100	60.1
Tiranë	1,238	363,100	293.3
Tropojë	1,043	44,200	42.4
Vlorë	1,609	174,000	108.1
total	**28,748**	**3,138,300**	**109.2**

Source: *Europa World Year Book 1990* (31st edition)

Natural movement of population per 1,000 inhabitants

	live births	natural increase	marriages	divorces
1950	38.5	24.5	10.1	0.8
1960	43.3	32.9	7.8	0.5
1970	32.5	23.3	6.8	0.7
1980	26.5	20.1	8.1	26.5
1985	25.9	19.6	8.9	0.8
1989	24.7	19.0	8.6	0.8

Source: data from Valentina Leskaj, from official government statistics

Analysis of marriages by age of women (%)

age group	1942	1950	1960	1970	1980	1986
under 20	38.0	47.7	46.7	41.3	27.0	21.0
20–24	43.4	34.0	41.0	45.5	56.3	56.9
25–29	12.3	11.2	8.3	8.3	12.3	17.7
30–34	3.9	3.5	2.2	2.5	2.1	3.2
35+	2.4	3.6	1.8	2.4	2.3	1.2
total	100.0	100.0	100.0	100.0	100.0	100.0

Source: data from Valentina Leskaj, from official government statistics

Average number of family members

	total	urban	rural
1950	5.8	4.6	6.1
1960	5.8	5.3	6.1
1969	5.9	5.0	6.1
1979	5.9	4.6	6.2
1989	4.7	3.9	5.3

Source: data from Valentina Leskaj, from official government statistics

The chronic shortage of housing means that young couples often have to live with parents or other family members. The figures that follow show that most families are made up of one couple living with their unmarried children. However this figure includes couples who are legally separated but, because of the lack of housing, are still living together with other family members, usually parents or grandparents.

Family structure according to number of couples in each home (% of all families)

no of couples	1950 urban	1950 rural	1969 urban	1969 rural	1979 urban	1979 rural
1 couple	74.3	54.8	76.3	59.0	81.0	65.0
2 couples	21.4	30.1	21.3	30.0	18.0	29.2
3 couples	3.5	10.3	2.2	8.3	0.9	4.9
4 couples	0.6	3.0	0.2	2.2	0.1	0.8
5 or more couples	0.2	1.8	–	0.5	–	0.1

Source: data from Valentina Leskaj, from official government statistics

Life expectancy

	women	men	total
1950–1951	54.4	52.6	53.5
1960–1961	66.0	63.7	64.9
1980–1981	72.2	67.7	70.2
1985–1986	75.5	68.7	71.9
1988–1989	75.5	69.6	72.4

Source: data from Valentina Leskaj, from official government statistics

Births and deaths for every 1,000 population (1988)

birth rate (1987)	25.5
death rate	5.4
infant mortality per 1,000 live births	39.0
marriage rate	8.3
life expectancy (women)	74.2
life expectancy (men)	69.2
fertility rate per woman	3.0

Sources: data from *Demographic Statistics 1990* (Eurostat); *Europa World Year Book 1990* (31st edition)

LESBIAN RIGHTS

The common age of sexual consent for lesbians, gay men and heterosexuals is 14, the second lowest in Europe. Same-sex relationships were illegal until 1977 and, despite legal equality, they still suffer from strong social taboos.

WOMEN AND HEALTH CARE

Medical services are free, and medicines are free for babies under 1 year. In 1988 there was 1 doctor for every 671 people.

Abortion and contraception: The distribution of contraceptives is very limited, and abortion is used as a method of birth control. Very few couples use modern family planning methods. There is a critical need for information: a questionnaire found that 76% of women had insufficient information on contraception.

PARENTAL PAY, LEAVE AND BENEFITS

Maternity leave and pay: 180 days at 80% of salary.

Time off to look after sick children: 10 days' paid leave every 3 months.

CHILD-CARE PROVISION

Primary school: In 1988 the pupil to teacher ratio in primary schools was 20:1.

Contributions to child-care costs: The state pays 65% of kindergarten charges.

STATE BENEFITS

State benefits are financed through a non-contributory state social insurance system which covers all workers.

Retirement pensions: Women retire between 45 and 55 (men between 50 and 60). Pension is 70% of the average monthly pay for any 3 consecutive years during the last 10 years of employment.

Sickness benefit: Paid at 70%–100% of salary.

WOMEN AND EMPLOYMENT

Women make up 46.7% of the working population, though the figure is higher for the food industry, light industry, education and culture, and the health service, where almost 4 in 5 workers are women. Workplace meals are state subsidised by 18% to 35%.

% of workforce who are women (1989)

industry	44.5
construction	8.9
agriculture	52.4
transport and communication	16.0
trade stockage	53.1
education and culture	52.7
health	78.8
others	38.5

Source: data from Valentina Leskaj, from official government statistics

In June 1991 average pay was £10 a month

Over the past 20 years, as more women took up higher education, the number of women in jobs requiring specialist qualifications increased. 47.3% of workers with secondary education and 38% of workers with higher education are women.

Women in specialist jobs requiring higher education (1989)

	%
electrical and electronic engineers	23.9
construction engineers and architects	32.3
mechanical and metallurgical engineers	13.8
industrial chemists	49.2
agronomists	22.2
veterinarians	20.5
doctors	45.3
dentists	51.9
pharmacists	71.6
economists	53.4

Source: data from Valentina Leskaj, from official government statistics

WOMEN AND POLITICS

Women have had the vote since 1958. After the 1991 elections only 3.6% of elected deputies in the People's Assembly were women.

WOMEN AND EDUCATION

The percentage of pupils and students who are women has risen from 40.6% in 1960 to 45.6% in 1970, 46.7% in 1980 and 47% in 1986.

Although primary and secondary education is free, students in higher education pay fees which vary according to family income. Secondary school graduates must spend a year working on collective farms or in factories.

SOURCES

Doing Business with Eastern Europe: Albania; Demographic Statistics 1990 (Eurostat); *Europa World Year Book 1990* (31st edition); *Out In Europe* (Peter Tatchell, for Channel 4 Television); *Third World Guide 91/92* (Instituto del Tercer Mundo); Valentina Leskaj.

LETTER FROM ALBANIA

Valentina Leskaj, family planning expert, Tiranë

There have been achievements in the field of legislation concerning mother and child. As well as maternity leave and sick children's leave, women are guaranteed light work during pregnancy and free medicines for a child under 1 year of age. There is a network of creches and kindergartens in the towns and the countryside, although sometimes not enough and lacking in quality.

A survey found that 70% of all women were against continuing high birth rates. This is because, with the coming of a child, there are immediate barriers and economic difficulties.

In our country women are faced with another day's work at home where three fundamental conditions are lacking – food, running water (including drinking water) and heating. These problems have become worse during this transitional period, but they are also connected with out-of-date technology in the energy industry, and the lack of decent quality children's clothing.

Women are also facing problems not known before to do with the changing role of the state with the introduction of a market economy that does not guarantee women's place in the labour market. Finally, there is the migration phenomenon which adds to the familiar burden. There still exist inequalities in home responsibilities within the family, especially in the countryside, although many backward customs and mentalities have gone.

These factors restrain the active participation of

women in social and political life, and prevent a solution to the problem of how to be a working woman and a mother. This explains why women want to reduce the number of children they have. This is even more marked in the countryside, where there are 2.35 times as many deliveries as in the towns. 60% of the population lives in rural areas, where women have children at a younger age, and where they generally have more children and with shorter intervals between.

Contraceptives have a very limited distribution in Albania which is why abortion is practised as a means of birth control. Providing women's health information is one way of solving the problems of birth control. The low level of family planning information is the result of the paternalistic policy followed by the government, and of sex education being considered taboo until recently.

The high natural growth in population has most affected women who bear the burden as mother, wife and worker for dealing with economic, social and health problems.

The women work 8 hours a day all week except on Sunday which is a holiday. The resulting state of fatigue has a major effect on women and their children, especially when women have sole responsibility for the family. There is no difference in law between pay for men and women, but men are more qualified than women and so our pay is lower. The economic and social status of women is lower than for men.

ADDRESSES

Ambassade de l'Albanie, 131 Rue Pompe, Paris 16, France

Bashkimi te Grave te Shqiperise (Women's Union of Albania), Tiranë

Central Council of Albanian Trade Unions, Këshilli Qëndror i Bashkimere, Profesionale të Shqiperisë, Bulevardi Dëshmorët e Kombit, Tiranë

Austria

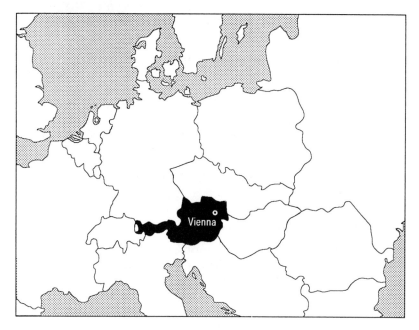

- **Population** 7.6 million, 52.4% female
- **Area** 83,853 sq km
- **Population density** 90.6 people sq km
- **GDP 1988** Austrian schillings 1,567 billion (£79 billion)
- **GDP per capita** £10,339
- **GDP per capita in purchasing power parity** (UK=100) 100
- **Public spending as % of GNP:** defence 1.3% (1986); education 6% (1986); health 5.3% (1987)
- **Consumer price index** 1980 = 100; 1989 = 138
- **Currency is the schilling** 1989 £1 = AS19.1; US$1 = AS11.82

The Federal Republic of Austria is made up of 9 provinces, each with its own provincial assembly and government. The Federal Assembly has 2 chambers: the National Council (Nationalrat) and the Federal Council (Bundesrat).

The social budget represents roughly 27% of the Gross National Product The Nationalrat has 183 members and is elected for 4 years by proportional representation. The Bundesrat has 63 members elected by provincial assemblies for varying terms. Head of state is the federal president who is elected every 6 years. The Council of Ministers, led by the chancellors, is responsible to the Nationalrat. Voters must be 19.

99% of Austrians speak German, and there are small Croat and Slovene speaking minorities.

IMMIGRATION AND RESIDENCE RIGHTS

Applicants for permanent residence visas, which are granted through the Federal Ministry of the Interior, must show proof of support and accommodation. Austrian employers must apply for work permits for foreign nationals. Applicants must know German well.

Teachers in state schools are civil servants and must therefore be Austrians. Setting up a business requires a separate permit from the provincial government.

EQUAL RIGHTS

The constitution contains a general provision that there should be equality in law without discrimination on the grounds of sex. A legal basis for positive action has not yet been enacted, but because Austria has ratified the UN convention on positive action, the constitution is held to allow for this.

More than 50% of women over 70 live alone compared with 17% of men The Secretary of State for Women's Affairs is responsible for labour market policy on equality, and the Commission for Equal Treatment, which is part of the Ministry of Labour and Social Affairs, deals with equality in the workplace and cases of discrimination.

BIRTH, LIFE AND DEATH

Breakdown of population by sex and age group (1000s) (1988)

	all		women		men		% of women in age group
	no	%	no	%	no	%	
0–14	1,330.8	17.5	650.0	16.3	680.8	18.8	48.8
15–24	1,209.1	15.9	592.1	14.8	617.0	17.1	49.0
25–39	1,692.5	22.3	845.9	21.3	846.7	23.4	50.0
40–59	1,820.5	24.0	917.6	23.1	902.9	25.0	50.4
60–74	1,009.1	13.3	610.3	15.3	398.8	11.0	60.5
75+	534.1	7.0	363.8	9.1	170.2	4.7	68.1
all	7,596.1	100.0	3,979.7	100.0	3,616.4	100.0	52.4

Source: data from Central Statistical Office, Vienna

Distribution of population by province, sex and age group (1988)

	% of total pop	% of women in pop	% of under 35s in pop	% of over 75s in pop
Burgenland	3.5	51.8	25.0	6.9
Kärnten	7.1	51.8	26.3	6.3
Nieder-österreich	18.8	51.8	24.5	7.3
Ober-österreich	17.1	51.8	26.5	5.9
Salzburg	6.1	52.2	27.0	5.6
Steiermark	15.6	52.1	25.5	6.6
Tirol	8.1	51.8	27.8	5.6
Vorarlberg	4.2	51.1	29.4	5.1
Wien	19.5	54.6	19.8	9.9
Austria	**100.0**	**52.4**	**25.0**	**7.0**

Source: data from Central Statistical Office, Vienna

Births, deaths, marriages and divorces (per 1,000 of population)

	1970	1975	1980	1985	1987
birth rate	15.0	12.5	12.0	11.6	11.4
fertility rate per woman	2.29	1.82	1.65	1.47	1.43
life expectancy (women)	73.38	74.70	76.08	77.36	78.13
life expectancy (men)	66.46	67.66	69.01	70.40	71.53
death rate	13.2	12.7	12.2	11.9	11.2
marriage rate	7.1	6.2	6.2	5.9	10.1
average age at marriage (women)	22.3	22.1	22.6	23.9	24.1
average age at marriage (men)	25.5	25.4	25.6	26.6	26.5
divorce rate (%)	18.1	19.8	26.3	30.8	29.5

Source: data from *Disparities of Living Conditions Among Women and Men in Austria* (Inge Gross, Austrian Ministry of Labour and Social Affairs)

The average size of household was 2.6 people in 1990, compared with 2.8 in 1971. The abolition of the marriage allowance for first marriages in 1988 resulted in a big jump in marriages in 1987; between 1986 and 1987 the increase in first marriages was 80.1%.

30% of all families are headed by 1 parent who, 87% of the time, is a woman. 34% of single parents are women who have brought up their children alone for more than 5 years. Until 1989, when the Parent and Child Law gave parents equal rights, the guardianship of the children of unmarried mothers went automatically to the district youth welfare offices.

LESBIAN RIGHTS

Same-sex relationships were illegal until 1971. The lesbian age of consent is 14, the same as for heterosexuals (18 for gay men). Lesbian organisations and publications are illegal under Sections 220 and 221 of the penal code. All cases, however, have eventually been dropped. In addition, homosexuals in danger of persecution because of their sexual orientation have been granted asylum.

WOMEN AND HEALTH CARE

Compulsory health insurance provides cover for the insured person, their spouse and children, plus other relatives in the household. Children are covered up to 18 unless in full-time education (then up to 27). Children who cannot earn a living because of illness or disability are covered for life. Young people aged 15 to 19 must have a medical examination every year.

60.2% of callers to the Austrian Family Planning Association's helpline are boys

People can visit any doctor affiliated to the health insurance scheme. They may also visit non-affiliated doctors, but insurance will only cover the fee up to the level of an affiliated doctor. Health insurance organisations pay fees directly to the doctors, though the patient pays the first 20% under the insurance schemes for civil servants, the self-employed and farmers. Health insurance covers ante-natal, delivery and post-natal care up to 10 days in a hospital or maternity home (longer if necessary).

Doctors are free to choose treatments within regulations to keep costs within 'tolerable limits'. Free hospital treatment is provided without limit, provided the patient chooses a general ward. Each prescription cost AS24 in 1988, but they are free in cases of extreme hardship and for certain infectious diseases. Most dental treatment is free but payments are sometimes required for orthodontic treatments and full sets of dentures.

22% of practising doctors and 28% of dental surgeons are women. In 1988 there was 1 doctor for every 517 people.

Major indicators for women's health (1989)

maternal deaths (all causes) per 100,000 live births	7.89
maternal deaths (abortion) per 100,000 live births	1.13
% of all live births to mothers under 20 (1985)	8.59
% of all live births to mothers aged 35+ (1985)	5.28
deaths from cancer of the cervix (age 0–64) per 100,000 women (1988)	3.18
deaths from malignant neoplasm female breast (age 0–64) per 100,000 women	19.02
deaths from trachea/bronchus/lung cancer (age 0–64) per 100,000 women	6.04
deaths from trachea/bronchus/lung cancer (age 0–64) per 100,000 men	31.45
deaths from diseases of the circulatory system (age 0–64) per 100,000 women	36.26
deaths from diseases of the circulatory system (age 0–64) per 100,000 men	114.38
deaths from suicide and self-inflicted injury per 100,000 women	12.49
deaths from suicide and self-inflicted injury per 100,000 men	35.57

Source: data from Health for All 2000 Indicator Presentation System (World Health Organisation Regional Office For Europe)

Abortion and contraception: Abortion was illegal until 1975, when women won the right to abortion on request up to about 15 weeks (12 weeks' implantation) after consulting a doctor. It is available up to the second trimester if the woman's physical or mental health is at risk, if the foetus's health is at risk or in cases of foetal handicap. For this, girls under 14 need parental consent. Abortion is not normally covered by health insurance and services are not widespread because of conscientious objection by hospitals and medical staff. Public information on abortion is scarce and no statistics are available.

PARENTAL PAY, LEAVE AND BENEFITS (1988)

Maternity leave and pay: Women are banned from working 8 weeks before and 8 weeks after giving birth (12 weeks after for premature, multiple or Caesarean births). Maternity leave pay is provided through health insurance and is 100% of net earnings over the previous 3 months. Mothers are not paid while in a hospital or maternity home on health insurance. Under self-employed and farmers' health insurance schemes maternity pay is AS250 a day.

The Parent and Child Law bans the use of violence in child-rearing

Optional parental leave and allowance: This can be shared by both parents and is available from the end of protected maternity leave until the child's second birthday. Or, if employers agree, parents can reduce their hours of work until the child's third birthday. A monthly allowance is claimed which is higher for single mothers and those on low incomes. Adoptive parents may also take optional parental leave. Single mothers, and mothers whose partners are on low incomes or who cannot work because of lack of child care can claim special relief of 92%–95% of unemployment benefit until the child is 3. Foreign women with a work permit exemption certificate can also claim this benefit.

Maternity allowance: Paid to Austrians and women who have been permanent residents for the previous 3 years. AS2,000 is paid at birth (AS5,000 if recommended medical examinations have been done); AS5,000 at age 1; AS3,000 at age 2; and AS2,000 at age 4 if the child has been medically examined.

Right of return to work: Under arrangements for optional parental leave, jobs are held until the child's second birthday.

Nursing mothers: Breastfeeding women are entitled to a 45-minute break in a working day of 4–8 hours, and two 45-minute breaks (or one of 90) in a working day of more than 8 hours, without loss of pay or deductions from other breaks.

Special nursing leave: One normal working week on full pay is given to nurse a close relative or dependant in the same household (covers all children including adopted or foster). Women and men workers in the same family may alternate their special nursing leave.

CHILD-CARE PROVISION

Under 7s: One-third of women who do not return to work after having a child would like to work but can't because of the lack of child-care facilities. Although the worst shortage is for 1–3 year olds, there are also not enough child-care places for older pre-school children. 85% of creches and 64% of day-care centres are in Vienna. Kindergartens in Vienna are also much more likely to stay open during lunch break (92% compared with a 53% average nationally).

I in 5 women who give up work after having a child don't go back to work because their husbands don't want them to

Primary school (7 years up): Most schools are half-day and after-hours care is almost non-existent outside major cities. The school year runs from September to June. In 1988 the pupil to teacher ratio in primary schools was 11:1.

Contributions to child-care costs: Child-care benefit, based on income, is paid to women who would have to give up work if they had no assistance with child-care costs and to women looking for a job or on training courses. It is paid until a child is 12.

STATE BENEFITS (1988)

Social insurance is compulsory under 4 separate schemes: health, accident, pensions and unemployment. Not everyone has to contribute to all these schemes – for example pensioners need only contribute to the health scheme and students only to the accident scheme.

Contributions are not required during some periods,

including time spent in education and, for women, the 12 months after giving birth. Those on sickness or unemployment benefit or maternity pay are exempt.

Austria has bilateral agreements covering health, accident, pensions and unemployment insurance and family allowance with Belgium, Finland, Germany, Italy, Luxembourg, Netherlands, Spain, Sweden, Yugoslavia and the UK.

The Austrian Institute for Economic Research estimates the value of housework done by women at AS400 billion a year

Pensions insurance: Pensions were generally paid at 60 for women (65 for men) until 1990, when the Supreme Court ruled that different retirement ages were unconstitutional. The retirement system is now under reform.

To qualify for an old age pension, you must have paid 180 monthly contributions in the 30 previous years. For disability or incapacity benefits, you must have paid 180 monthly contributions or, if under 50 (55 for men) paid 60 monthly contributions out of the previous 120 months.

Pensions are based on an 'assessment' period according to age: after 45 years of insurance cover the pension is 79.5% of the assessment basis; for 1–30 years of cover it is 1.9% for each year; for 31 to 45 years it is 1.5% for each year. In May and October an extra pension payment is made, each equal to a full month's pension, making a total of 14 monthly payments a year. A children's increment of 3% of the assessment basis is paid to mothers for each child.

Pensions are adjusted at the start of each year in line with incomes. In December 1989 women's average pension compared to men's was 52% for retired manual workers and 61.5% for non-manual.

Adjustment payments: While there is no minimum level a nominal level is set, and if a person's pension plus any other income falls below this the difference is covered by an adjustment payment.

Survivors' pensions: A widow's pension is 60% of the insured person's pension (the widower's pension is two-thirds of this amount until 1995 when it will be paid at the same rate). Children are paid 40% of the widow/widower's pensions if they have lost 1 parent (and 60% if they have lost both) until the age of 18, or longer if they are students or trainees or incapable of earning a living.

Health care: An additional payment equal to 50% of the pension is paid to pensioners, widows/widowers and orphans (under 14) who require constant care. Pensions institutions also run health spas and sanitoria and may pay for cures as part of their health-care programmes.

Health insurance (see also Women and Health Care): Sickness benefit is paid from day 4 of illness up to 78 weeks, excluding periods covered by normal wage. It is paid at 50% of last income (up to a maximum) for the first 42 days, then at 60%.

A contribution of up to AS6,000 may be paid towards the funeral expenses of an insured person or to his or her family.

Accident insurance: The scheme, whose main aim is to prevent occupational accidents and diseases, runs 7 hospitals for accident cases, 1 for occupational diseases and 4 rehabilitation centres reserved for accident victims.

Disability allowance: Paid to insured people incapacitated by at least 20% because of an occupational disease or accident. The full allowance is two-thirds of the assessment basis, normally the previous year's earnings.

Rehabilitation: During rehabilitation training an allowance of 60% of previous income is paid.

Survivors' allowances: Spouses of those who die from an occupational disease or accident are paid an allowance of 20% of the assessment basis. On remarriage, the allowance is paid off with a lump sum equal to $2\frac{1}{2}$ times the yearly total. Children who have lost a parent are paid 20% of the assessment basis, and 30% if they have lost both. The total paid to dependent survivors cannot be more than 80%. Help with funeral expenses may also be given.

Unemployment insurance: Every employee automatically receives this and anyone receiving unemployment benefit is covered by health insurance.

Pay: To qualify, individuals must be unemployed but willing and able to work, and must have paid unemployment insurance contributions for a minimum period. The pay is for a minimum of 12 weeks and a maximum of 30, based on average income for the last month of work (between AS45.50 and AS345.10 a day). There are extra allowances for dependants.

Emergency relief: If entitlement to unemployment pay or special maternity allowance runs out, emergency benefits based on financial circumstances are paid. There is no time limit, but eligibility is reviewed every 26 weeks.

Optional parental leave allowance: See section under Parental Pay, Leave and Benefits.

Interim help in advance of pensions: From the age of 54 women (59 for men) are entitled to special interim aid until they receive their pensions if they lose their jobs before retirement age.

Family benefits: Family allowance is paid to all permanent residents for children under 19 living at home. It is also paid for unemployed children up to the age of 21 and those undertaking vocational study up to the age of 25. Monthly payments are AS1,300 for each child under 10, and AS1,550 for each child over 10. Payments are doubled for each severely disabled child. For low-income families there is a supplement of AS200 per child. People on family allowance also qualify for half-price rail travel.

Child-rearing benefit: This is paid in some provinces, under varying conditions, to low-income families with small children.

Maternity allowance: See section under Parental Pay, Leave and Benefits.

Maintenance: May be paid by a court if the person responsible has failed to pay and payment cannot be legally enforced.

Special assistance: In cases of emergency such as death of main earner or natural disasters, special allowances can be paid to those receiving family allowances, and to expectant mothers (Austrian citizens, or stateless and permanently resident in Austria, or refugees).

WOMEN AND EMPLOYMENT

Equal rights: The Equal Treatment Act as amended applies to employment, termination of employment and career promotion. Since 1990 the burden of proof lies equally with both sides in cases of violation.

60% of Austrian women want men to share housework equally but a study has shown only 1 in 50 husbands does half the housework

Statutory rights: Employers must pay the minimum wage agreed under collective bargaining. If no collective agreement exists the Federal Arbitration Board must set minimum wage scales if asked by an employee.

The standard working week is 40 hours, spread usually over 5 days. Hours may be extended by 5 hours a week but total overtime cannot be more than 60 hours a year. A working day of more than 6 hours must include a half-hour break.

Working on Sundays is forbidden, though where special arrangements apply (such as in transport or catering) extra payments are normally made. Workers must be paid a 100% supplement to normal wages for working on public holidays. All workers are entitled to a 36-hour break every week, which must include 1 full working day. There are 13 statutory public holidays.

Every employee is entitled to 28 days of paid annual leave (rising to 36 days after 25 years of service). It is illegal for employers to offer extra pay in place of annual leave. If a worker falls ill for over 3 days during holiday, the time is not counted as holiday.

Women's hours: Generally women are not allowed to work between the hours of 20.00 and 6.00, though there are exceptions such as jobs in transport, broadcasting, cleaning and nursing.

Part-time workers: Generally they have the same rights as full-time workers, though the number of hours can affect certain rights.

Sick leave: Employers must grant paid sick leave of between 4 and 10 weeks on full pay depending on length of service (see also Health insurance section under State Benefits). Sick leave on half pay is granted for every additional 4 weeks. Full entitlement to sick leave is restored 6 months after returning to work.

Maternity: Expectant mothers cannot be employed in work that might endanger their health. After the fifth month of pregnancy women may only spend 4 hours a day on their feet. Pregnant women are banned from tasks including lifting and carrying, those involving hazardous substances or extremes of temperature, piecework, work paid by results and anything that entails a risk of accident. A woman cannot legally be dismissed during pregnancy, or for 4 months after delivery or 4 weeks after the end of special maternity leave, except in extreme cases. This also applies to adoptive mothers.

Economic activity and unemployment (1987)

	% women	% men
economic activity rate	34.6	57.0
labour force who are employees	84.1	86.8
labour force who are self-employed or unpaid family workers	15.9	13.2
labour force working part-time	16.9	1.4
unemployment rate	5.6	5.1
all unemployed by sex	43.4	56.6

Source: data from Central Statistical Office, Vienna

Employment by industrial sector (1987)

	women no (1000s)	%	men no (1000s)	%	women as % of workforce
agriculture and forestry	137.7	10.0	152.6	7.5	47.4
energy and water	5.5	0.4	34.6	1.7	13.7
mining and quarrying	4.1	0.3	22.4	1.1	15.5
manufacturing	329.0	23.9	710.2	34.9	31.7
construction	26.2	1.9	266.6	13.1	8.9
wholesale and trade	249.2	18.1	205.5	10.1	54.8
hotel and catering	112.9	8.2	61.0	3.0	64.9
transport and communications	38.6	2.8	181.1	8.9	17.6
finance and insurance	97.8	7.1	93.6	4.6	51.1
social and public service	375.9	27.3	309.3	15.2	54.9
total	**1,376.8**	**100.0**	**2,034.8**	**100.0**	**40.4**

Source: data from *Disparities of Living Conditions Among Women and Men in Austria* (Inge Gross, Austrian Ministry of Labour and Social Affairs)

Women's median net income as a percentage of men's by occupation (1989)

unskilled workers outside agriculture and forestry	83.6
semi-skilled manual workers	75.9
skilled manual workers	70.5
supervisors and craft workers	61.4
all manual workers	74.0
unskilled non-manual workers	79.4
semi-skilled non-manual workers	82.9
medium-level non-manual workers	84.0
very highly qualified non-manual workers	86.6
all non-manual workers	72.7
low-graded civil servants	89.4
medium-graded civil servants	92.4
very highly qualified civil servants	78.3
all civil servants	93.3
all workers	**82.5**

Source: *How Much Less? Earnings Disparities Between Women and Men in Austria* (Irene Wolf and Walter Wolf, Austrian Federal Ministry of Labour and Social Affairs)

Women's occupations: 66% of working women were concentrated in this table's 7 occupational groups, taken from a total of 75 in the Austrian classification system. By comparison 45% of working men were concentrated in the 7 groups where male employment is most concentrated.

Women's share of occupational groups (%) (1987)

auxiliary, clerical and administrative	19
retail and wholesale trade	13
farmers	10
medical workers	7
teachers	7
building cleaners	6
bookkeepers, cashiers and related	5

Source: *Disparities of Living Conditions Among Women and Men in Austria* (Inge Gross, Austrian Ministry of Labour and Social Affairs)

Working mothers:

Labour force participation rates for women aged 15–59 by number of children (1987–88)

	activity rates (%)
all women	57.7
without children	63.2
with children	53.0

	activity rates (%)	
	women with partners	women without partners
number of children under 15		
1	56.8	80.7
2	41.4	70.4
3 or more	38.1	57.8
age of youngest child		
less than 2	41.4	72.6
3–5	46.3	82.2
6–14	50.3	80.9
total	**49.5**	**71.3**

Source: *Disparities of Living Conditions Among Women and Men in Austria* (Inge Gross, Austrian Ministry of Labour and Social Affairs)

Taxation: In 1988 a children's allowance of AS1,800 for each child was deductible. Some income tax deductions can also be claimed for children – for extra expenses such as housing, insurance, illness and maintenance payments. A non-taxable single-income allowance is given where only 1 marriage partner is being paid.

WOMEN IN TRADE UNIONS

Just over 30% of the members of the Austrian Trade Union Federation (ATUF) were women in 1989. More than half of them belonged to just 3 unions: the white collar workers' union, local government employees' union and public service employees' union. The 2 unions with the highest proportion of women members are the Union for Hotel, Catering and Personal Services, and the Union for Textile, Garment and Leather Industry workers.

Women accounted for 10.3% of the delegates to the 1987 ATUF congress, 9.2% of its national executive (6.8% of voting members and 17.6% of members acting as advisers).

WOMEN AND POLITICS

Women won the vote and the right to stand in elections in 1918, when they were elected for the first time to the national assembly and the Vienna city council. 1918 also saw the end of the ban on women attending political meetings.

Two of the 16 federal ministers are women: Johanna Dohnal (women's affairs), and Dr Marilies Flemming (environment, youth and family affairs). One of the 4 ministers of state is a woman, Dr Maria Fekter (construction and tourism).

Most local councils have departments dealing specifically with women's issues.

Women elected to the Nationalrat in 7 October 1990 election

political party	total no of seats	no of seats held by women	% of seats held by women
Sozialistische Partei Oesterreichs	80	21	26.3
Oesterreichische Volkspartei	60	7	11.7
Freiheitliche Partei Oesterreichs	33	7	21.2
Gruene	10	5	50.0
total	**183**	**40**	**21.9**

Source: Austrian Embassy, London

WOMEN AND EDUCATION

In 1922 Elise Richter became the first female professor in Austria. She died in 1942 in the Theresienstadt concentration camp

61% of teachers (excluding universities) are women. The number of university and art college students has tripled since 1960. Then, 27% of new students were women and by 1987–88 the figure had increased to 49%. Thirty years ago 6 times as many men as women graduated from university. By 1987, the number of women had increased so that 4 graduated for every 7 men (1.75 times as many men as women).

Subjects that attract the highest proportion of new women students are: translation and interpretation (92.5% of new entrants), philology/culture (79.6%), pharmacy (78.5%) and philosophy/humanities (69.8%). Lowest proportions of women among new entrants are in mining (13.5%), engineering (18.9%), soil science (36.0%) and theology (37.4%).

Pupils and students by school type and sex (1987)

	female %	male %
general schools	48.3	51.7
higher general schools	50.7	49.3
technical colleges	44.1	55.9
elementary vocational training schools	34.6	65.4
medium-level vocational training schools	46.0	54.0
higher-level vocational training schools	46.4	53.6
vocational training colleges	76.4	23.6
teacher training colleges	71.5	28.5
universities and art colleges	44.0	56.0

Source: *Disparities of Living Conditions Among Women and Men in Austria* (Inge Gross, Austrian Central Statistical Office)

Domestic science, which used to be obligatory only for girls, was made compulsory for all secondary pupils by an amendment to the 1987 School Organisation Act

Equal opportunities: From 1990 all universities are required to have equal opportunities commissioners. Two national commissioners for equal opportunities will be employed full time by the Ministry of Science and Research.

Allowances: Schoolchildren and students under the age of 27 receive travel allowances. Textbooks are provided for the first 8 years, after that vouchers are given for exchange in bookshops. Education allowances are based on family size and income and the progress of pupils, and are paid from class 10 to encourage continuing education. Students in boarding schools or hostels receive an accommodation allowance. University education is free but student allowances are paid only in certain circumstances, including for academic achievement.

WOMEN AND DETENTION

In September 1988 the women made up 4% of all prisoners; minors (age 18) and young adults made up 1.6% and foreigners 10.9%.

SOURCES

Austrian Embassy, London; *Abortion Laws in Europe, Planned Parenthood in Europe,* Vol 18 No 1, Spring 1989 (Supplement, amended April 1990); *Disparities of Living Conditions Among Women and Men in Austria* (Inge Gross, Austrian Federal Ministry of Labour and Social Affairs); *Europa World Year Book 1990* (31st edition); Health For All 2000 Indicator Presentation System (World Health Organisation Regional Office for Europe); *How Much Less Earnings Disparities Between Women and Men in Austria* (Irene Wolf and Walter Wolf, Austrian Federal Ministry of Labour and Social Affairs); *Les Actions Positives en Faveur des Femmes en Europe Occidentale* (Institut Syndical Europeen); *Out In Europe* (Peter Tatchell, for Channel 4 Television); *Planned Parenthood in Europe* (Vol 19 No 3) (International Planned Parenthood Federation); *Pocket World in Figures* (The Economist); *Positive action and the constitutional and legislative hindrances to its implementation in the member states of the Council of Europe* (Council of Europe); population statistics from the Central Statistical Office, Vienna; *Prison Information Bulletin* June 1990 (Council of Europe); *Social Security in Austria* (Federal Press Service); *The Woman in*

Austria (Austria Documentation); *Third World Guide 91/92* (Instituto del Tercer Mundo); *Women in Austria 1985–90*

ADDRESSES

Austrian Embassy, 18 Belgrave Mews West, London SW1X 8HU. Tel: 071 235 3731

State Secretariat for Women's Affairs, Bundeskanzleramt, Ballhausplatz 1, 1014 Wien. Tel: (43 1) 22 25 35 03 38

Bund Osterreichischer Frauenvereine, Austrian Council of Women, Wilhelm Exnergasse 34–36, 1090 Wien

Bundesministerium für Arbeit und Soziales (Federal Ministry for Employment and Social Affairs), Stubenring 1, 1011 Wien. Tel: (43 1) 22 27 11 00

Bundesministerium für inners (Federal Ministry of the Interior), Herrengasse 7, 1014 Wien

Landesarbeitsamt für Niederösterreich (employment office in Vienna), Hohenstauffengasse 2, 1013 Wien

Österreichische Gesellschaft für Familienplanung, Üniversitätsfrauenklinik II, Spitalgasse 23, 1090 Wien

Österreichischer Gewerkschaftsbund (Austrian Trade Union Federation), Hohenstanfengasse 10–12, 1011 Wien 1. Tel: (43 1) 22 25 34 44

Hosi Wien (Homosexuelle Initiativ Wien), Novaragasse 40, 1020 Wien. Tel: (43 1) 26 66 04

ÖKISTA (Austrian Committee for the International Exchange of Students), Türkenstrasse 4, 1090 Wien

Belgium

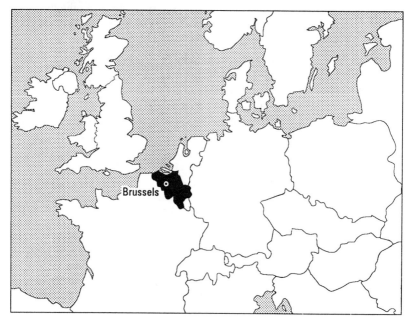

- **Population** 9.9 million, 51.2% female
- **Area** 30,519 sq km
- **Population density** 323.6 people sq km
- **GDP 1988** Belgian francs 5,604 billion (£95 billion)
- **GDP per capita** £9,544
- **GDP per capita in purchasing power parity** (UK=100) 98
- **Public spending as % of GNP:** defence 3.1% (1986); education 5.6% (1986); health 5.6% (1987)
- **Consumer price index** 1980 = 100; 1989 = 153
- **Currency is the Belgian franc** 1989 £1 = BFR57.7; US$1 = BFR35.8

Belgium is a monarchy made up of 9 provinces. In 1963 4 linguistic regions were established: French, Flemish, German and Brussels, which is bilingual (Flemish and French). 57% of the population speak Flemish, 42% French and 0.6% German.

Women's day is celebrated on 11 November

Legal power is held by the monarch and the 2-chamber parliament: the 182-member Senate and 212-seat Chamber of Representatives. In the Senate 106 are elected directly, 50 by provincial councils and 25 co-opted by elected members. One is a senator, by right the heir to the throne. All members in the Chamber are elected by proportional representation. While executive power is nominally held by the monarch, in practice it is exercised by the cabinet. The monarch appoints the prime minister. Voting is compulsory from age 18. All members of the government must be 25 and all senators 40.

Local government is based on the linguistic regions. The Flemish, French and German-speaking communities and the Flemish, Walloon and Brussels regions each has a legislative council, executive and civil service.

IMMIGRATION AND RESIDENCE RIGHTS

Citizens of the EC (excluding Spain and Portugal) and Monaco do not need work or residence permits, but must register at their local town hall within 8 days of arriving. Spanish and Portuguese citizens need work permits until January 1993. Citizens of other countries need a work permit for employment, a professional card if self-employed, or a residence permit.

Immigrants, mainly Italian, Spanish and Moroccan, make up 7% of the labour force

Work permits are applied for by employers in Belgium. Some workers, including journalists and sales representatives, do not need work permits but do need residence permits.

Marriage partners and children under 18 accompanying an immigrant do not require residence permits. Foreign nationals can apply for citizenship after 5 years' residence. Children under 18 of new citizens automatically become Belgians. Foreigners married to Belgians can apply for citizenship after 6 months of marriage.

In 1988 Belgium had 858,650 foreign residents, 46% of them women. 62.5% of foreign residents were from EC states, almost half of these from Italy. 18.9% were from African countries, and 11.4% from other non-EC European countries.

EQUAL RIGHTS

The constitution grants all citizens equality in law, and specifically prohibits discrimination on the grounds of sex. Positive action is legal with regard to employment, but it does not apply to social security schemes and superannuation.

The Secretary of State for Social Emancipation in consultation with the Commission on Women's Employment is responsible for equality policy. Government services have had to take steps to promote equal opportunity between men and women from 1 April 1990. All national advisory bodies are required to provide the names of a woman and a man when forwarding candidates for posts.

BIRTH, LIFE AND DEATH

Breakdown of population by sex and age (1000s) (1988)

	all		women		men		% of women in age group
	no	%	no	%	no	%	
0–14	1,802.5	18.3	879.2	17.4	923.3	19.1	48.8
15–24	1,474.7	14.9	722.4	14.3	752.3	15.6	49.0
25–39	2,270.9	23.0	1,113.5	22.0	1,157.4	24.0	49.0
40–59	2,347.1	23.8	1,179.4	23.3	1,167.7	24.2	50.2
60–74	1,341.7	13.6	734.9	14.5	606.8	12.6	54.8
75+	638.8	6.5	424.5	8.4	214.3	4.4	66.5
all	9,875.7	100.0	5,053.9	100.0	4,821.8	100.0	51.2

Source: data from *Demographic Statistics 1990* (Eurostat)

Population increase by region (1987)

region	pop (1000s)	% of total pop	pop density per sq km	natural increase per 1,000	net migration per 1,000	total increase per 1,000
Antwerpen	1,586.3	16.1	553.2	1.8	-0.3	1.5
Brabant	2,220.6	22.5	661.3	0.9	-0.1	0.8
Hainaut	1,272.8	12.9	336.2	-0.5	-2.0	-2.5
Liège	991.6	10.0	256.7	0.5	-0.2	0.3
Limburg	735.7	7.5	303.7	5.2	-1.7	3.5
Luxembourg	226.1	2.3	50.9	2.7	1.0	3.6
Namur	414.5	4.2	113.1	1.4	2.3	3.8
Oost-Vlaanderen	1,328.9	13.5	445.6	0.2	-0.1	0.0
West-Vlaanderen	1,094.0	11.1	349.0	1.6	0.7	2.2
Belgium	**9,870.5**	**100.0**	**323.4**	**1.9**	**0.8**	**2.6**

Source: data from *Demographic Statistics 1990* (Eurostat)

Births, deaths, marriages and divorces (per 1,000 of population)

	1960	1970	1980	1985	1988
birth rate	17.0	14.8	12.6	11.6	12.0
% of births outside of marriage	2.1	2.8	4.1	7.1	7.9*
average age of mother at 1st birth	25.1	24.0	24.6	24.9	–
infant mortality per 1,000 live births	31.2	21.1	12.1	9.8	9.1
fertility rate per woman	2.58	2.20	1.67	1.51	1.54
marriage rate	7.2	7.6	6.7	5.8	6.0
average age at marriage (women)	25.2	23.9	23.9	25.0	26.1
average age at marriage (men)	27.9	26.3	26.5	27.8	28.0
divorce rate	0.5	0.7	1.5	1.9	2.1
life expectancy (women)	73.5	74.2	76.8	–	–
life expectancy (men)	67.7	67.8	70.0	–	–
death rate	12.5	12.3	11.6	11.3	10.5

*1986

Source: data from *Demographic Statistics 1990* (Eurostat)

In 1988, 1-parent households accounted for 6% of households with a child aged 0–4 and 8% of households with a child aged 5–9.

LESBIAN RIGHTS

A common age of consent of 16 for lesbians, gay men and heterosexuals was introduced in 1985 to end discrimination against homosexuals, although the lesbian age of consent was commonly taken to be the same as for heterosexuals. The government is expected to legislate against discrimination and incitement to hatred on the grounds of sexual orientation.

WOMEN AND HEALTH CARE

Women doctors spend an average of 5 minutes longer with patients than men, but their average salary is much lower, a 1989 survey found

Health care is provided from the social security scheme, based on compulsory insurance. The general scheme covers employees and there is a separate scheme for the self-employed. Health care for the unemployed, elderly and needy is subsidised.

Patients pay to see a doctor, and are reimbursed 75% of the fee (100% for the elderly and unemployed). Hospital fees are paid by insurance bodies, though patients pay a contribution towards hospital stays. Prescription drugs are classed into 4 categories for payment, with 'lifesavers' being fully reimbursed.

A 1989 survey by the medical journal *Journal des Médecins* found that 1 in 5 doctors is a woman. In 1988 there was 1 doctor for every 333 people.

Major indicators for women's health (1986)

maternal deaths (all causes) per 100,000 live births	3.42
maternal deaths (abortion) per 100,000 live births	0.85
% of all live births to mothers under 20	3.69
% of all live births to mothers aged 35+	5.79
cancer of the cervix (age 0–64) per 100,000 women	2.26
malignant neoplasm female breast (age 0–64) per 100,000 women	24.94
trachea/bronchus/lung cancer (age 0–64) per 100,000 women	6.25
trachea/bronchus/lung cancer (age 0–64) per 100,000 men	47.51
diseases of the circulatory system (age 0–64) per 100,000 women	40.36
diseases of the circulatory system (age 0–64) per 100,000 men	108.32
suicide and self-inflicted injury per 100,000 women	13.29
suicide and self-inflicted injury per 100,000 men	30.14

Source: data from Health for All 2000 Indicator Presentation System (World Health Organisation Regional Office For Europe)

Abortion and contraception: The 1867 law which banned abortion was overturned on 4 April 1990. Women now have the right to abortion on demand up to 12 weeks if judged by a doctor to be 'in a state of distress'. Before 1990 women who had abortions and doctors who performed them were still prosecuted, and thousands of women travelled abroad for abortions, mainly to the Netherlands.

A 1989 survey found that 68% of women between 15 and 44 used contraception. The pill was the most favoured method (66%).

PARENTAL PAY, LEAVE AND BENEFITS (1989–90)

Maternity leave and pay: Women are entitled to 8 weeks that must be taken after the birth plus 7 weeks that can be taken either before or after. The benefit is equal to 82% of earnings for the first 4 weeks and 75% for the rest. To qualify women must have made 6 months' insurance contributions, and have 120 days of actual or credited employment. An extra week's leave, added in 1991, included the condition that the woman rest for 1 week before delivery.

Birth grants: BFR31,289 for first birth, and BFR21,580 for second and later births. It can be claimed 2 months before the delivery date.

With 14 public holidays a year, Belgians have more than any other EC state. The UK has the lowest with 8

Paternity leave: Increased in February 1991 from 2 to 3 days to be taken within 12 days of the birth. Public sector workers may take 8 days paid leave each year for special reasons (4 days paternity plus 4 days for illness of a family member).

Parental leave: All public sector workers receive 6–12 months' leave for family and personal reasons, which can be taken 5 times before retirement. This is paid at BFR10,504 a month provided the person is replaced by an unemployed person. In the private sector this depends on individual agreements.

If leave is taken in the 12 months after the birth of a child, benefit is paid at BFR12,504. Women aged 25–35 take 86% of family/personal leave. Public sector workers are also entitled to 3 months' unpaid leave in the 12 months after birth; in the private sector this depends on individual agreements.

Other special leave: Public sector workers may take 4 days' paid leave each year in the case of illness of a family member. They may also take 2 months of unpaid leave for family reasons, and may work part time for up to 5 years for family or social reasons. Leave in the private sector depends on individual agreements.

CHILD-CARE PROVISION (1989–90)

In 1990 56% of children from families where both parents worked were looked after by their grandparents, 9.4% were in pre-nursery schools or day-care centres, and 7.6% were in nursery schools.

A 1991 survey found that 22% of Belgian women aged 30 to 40 had experienced physical or sexual violence

Under 3s: 20% are in publicly funded places, half in pre-primary schooling (from 2½ years) while the rest are in nurseries (5% of all 0–3s), at the carer's own home (4%), or in privately-run child care (19%). Budget restrictions have meant very little recent growth in publicly funded child care.

3–5 year olds: 95% are in pre-primary schooling, generally from 8.30 to 15.30 with a 1-hour lunch break and closed on Wednesday afternoons. Provision is generally part of primary schools.

Primary school (6 years up): 8.30 to 15.30 with a 1-hour lunch break and closed on Wednesday afternoons. The school year runs from September to June. In 1988 the ratio of pupils to teachers in primary schools was 15:1.

Outside school hours care: Mainly school based during term time and available from 7.30 to 18.00 and on Wednesday afternoons; provided locally and therefore not universal. There is some provision for school holidays in these centres and also through holiday play schemes, which care for an estimated 11% of children aged 3–14.

Care for sick children: Some projects which provide

work for the unemployed provide care for sick children at home.

Contributions to child-care costs: Parents make a contribution to publicly funded services depending on income. Holiday play schemes are subsidised at BFR25 per child per day. For publicly funded or approved child care up to the age of 3, tax relief is available on 80% of costs up to BFR345 a day (introduced in 1989). The requirement on parents to provide proof of payment for this excludes many who use non-registered child carers. All parents of children under 3 receive a tax reduction of BFR1,000 a year.

STATE BENEFITS (1989–90)

Retirement pension: Normal retirement age is 60 for women and 65 for men, but proposed reforms would enable women and men to retire between 60 and 65 with no loss of pension (currently only men qualify for an early pension). Pensions are earnings related (up to a limit of BFR1,181,242) but minimum annual pensions for full contributions are BFR276,177 for a single pensioner and BFR345,121 for a household. Pensions are automatically adjusted for inflation.

Survivors' pension: Paid at 80% of the retirement pension of the insured person. For those with full contributions, the minimum rate for a dependent marriage partner with no children is BFR271,539 (providing the death was not due to an industrial accident or disease). The survivor must be 45 years old, or an invalid or bringing up a child and not working. Pensions are paid for 12 months when a widow remarries. A 12-month grant can be paid to spouses who do not qualify for survivors' pensions.

Death grant: BFR6,000.

Sickness benefit: 60% of earnings (up to an earnings ceiling of BFR3,156 a day) for up to 12 months. Manual workers are entitled to 14 days (brought up to 30 through collective agreements) on 80% of earnings, and non-manual workers to 30 days on 100% of earnings. Conditions include having paid a minimum number of contributions. There is a waiting period of 1 day unless the person is unemployed, pregnant or has been in contact with an infectious disease.

From February to May 1966 more than 3,000 workers from metal factories in the Liège region took part in one of the most famous strikes for equal pay

Invalidity: Benefits are paid to workers who can only earn one-third of normal earnings in their job category. They must have been insured for 6 months and have worked for 120 days. Benefit is paid until retirement age at 40% of lost earnings or 60% for those with dependants (up to an earnings ceiling of BFR964,759). Minimum for those regularly employed is BFR885 a day (BFR1,106 with dependants). For those who were not in regular employment the minimum is BFR665 a day (BFR887 with dependants).

Family benefits: Monthly payments are BFR2,310 for the first child; BFR4,274 for 2 children; and BFR6,380 for larger families (this is reduced by BFR375 except in cases of low income or if the child is handicapped). In addition, there are age-related payments of BFR803 for children 0–6, and BFR1,187 for ages 6–12. There is an extra payment of BFR1,440 for handicapped children, reduced slightly if child is aged 12–16. An additional allowance of BFR10,390 a month for each handicapped child under 21.

Benefit is normally paid until children are 18, but also up to 25 for children in full-time education and daughters remaining at home, and up to 21 in the case of serious infirmity.

Family benefit rates are higher for those unemployed for 7 months and for pensioners (BFR3,359 for the first child; BFR5,003 for the second and BFR6,508 for larger families). Rates are also higher for invalid workers. Age-related supplements apply in all cases.

Unemployment benefit: Partners with dependants receive 60% of earnings (between a minimum of BFR973 per day and a maximum of BFR1,145). People living together with no dependants receive 55% of earnings (between BFR574 and BFR1,050 a day). Single people receive 60% of earnings (between BFR696 and BFR1,145 per day). Reduced benefits apply after the first year, although workers with at least 20 years of employment receive a supplement. There are proposals to move from a daily control to a fortnightly one.

WOMEN AND EMPLOYMENT

Only 4% of the Belgian police force are women

Statutory rights: The working week is 40 hours and overtime is limited to 65 hours in a 3-month period. However, legislation allows for flexible working time agreements. Paid annual leave is 24 days, and there are 10 statutory public holidays. Minimum wages are set by national collective agreements and are normally paid in full at age 21. Most collective agreements provide that a thirteenth month's wage be paid in December, and for extra pay equal to 3 weeks and 2 days at the summer holiday. Wages cannot be seized in full by creditors and are index-linked by law.

Employment and unemployment (1989)

	% women	% men
economic activity rate	35.7	60.6
employed working part time	24.9	1.7
labour force who are employers or self-employed	10.7	19.2
labour force who are family workers	6.8	0.1
unemployment rate (% of labour force)	13.0	5.3
youth unemployment rate (age 14–24)	20.2	11.4
unemployed who have been unemployed for		
12 months or more	76.9	74.5
all unemployed by sex	60.8	39.2

Source: data from *Labour Force Survey (Results 1989)* (Eurostat)

Part-time workers: In 1989, 89.7% of part-time workers were women, compared with 82% in 1973. The percentage of women workers employed part time has increased from 16.3% in 1981 to 24.9% in 1989. The main reasons given by women for working part time were family commitments (40.3%), not being able to find full-time work (25.9%) and not wanting to work full time (13.8%).

Part-time workers have the same rights as full-time workers except for unemployment benefit, which requires recipients to have worked at least 28 hours a week for a year.

Employment by industrial sector (1000s) (1989)

	women		men		women as % of workforce
	no	%	no	%	
agriculture	32	2.4	88	3.9	26.7
all industry	213	16.2	913	40.3	18.9
energy and water	6	0.5	40	1.8	13.0
mineral extraction and chemicals	26	1.9	158	7.0	14.1
metal manufacturing and engineering	47	3.6	276	12.2	14.6
other manufacturing industry	124	9.4	232	10.3	34.8
building and civil engineering	11	0.8	207	9.2	5.0
all services	1,075	81.4	1,265	55.8	45.9
distributive trades and hotels	290	22.0	349	15.4	45.4
transport and communication	35	2.7	222	9.8	13.6
banking, finance and insurance	112	8.5	176	7.8	38.9
public administration	131	9.9	223	9.8	37.0
other services	506	38.4	294	13.0	63.3
total	**1,320**	**100.0**	**2,266**	**100.0**	**36.8**

Source: data from *Labour Force Survey (Results 1989)* (Eurostat)

Women workers employed part time by industrial sector (%) (1989)

agriculture, hunting and fishing	17.0
energy and water	17.9
mining, quarrying and chemical industry	13.7
metal manufacturing	9.9
other industries	9.9
building and civil engineering	20.5
retail trade, hotels and catering	26.4
transport and communications	13.3
banking, finance and insurance	23.9
other services	30.1
total	**24.9**

Source: data from *Vrouwen in de Belgische Samenleving 1991/Les Femmes Dans La Societé Belge* (Kabinet Van de Staatssecretaris Voor Maatschappelijke Emancipatie/Cabinet Du Secretaire d'Etat à l'Emancipation Sociale)

Women's share of occupational groups (%) (1989)

scientific professions	49.9
company heads, directors and managers	16.1
office workers	51.0
traders, commercial staff and salespeople	48.8
farmers, fisherfolk and forestry workers	24.3
non-agricultural manual workers and labourers	13.2
specialists in services, sports and recreational activities	63.5
armed forces	9.2

Source: data from *Vrouwen in de Belgische Samenleving 1991/Les Femmes Dans La Societé Belge* (Kabinet Van de Staatssecretaris Voor Maatschappelijke Emancipatie/Cabinet Du Secretaire d'Etat à l'Emancipation Sociale)

Women's earnings as a % of men's in industry (October 1987)

	manual hourly earnings	non-manual monthly earnings
energy and water	–	76.3
chemical industry	74.9	65.3
all metal manufacture and engineering	84.9	64.9
mechanical engineering	81.6	61.7
electrical engineering	86.6	66.8
food, drink and tobacco	85.1	66.3
clothing and footwear manufacture	80.2	75.4
printing and publishing	72.8	63.8
all manufacturing industry	74.2	63.6
all industry	75.3	63.8

Source: data from *Earnings in Industry and Services* (Eurostat)

Women's earnings as a % of men's in services (October 1987)

	non-manual monthly earnings
wholesale and retail distribution	63.3
wholesale distribution	65.0
retail distribution	72.8
credit institutions	78.4
insurance (excluding social security)	73.7

Source: data from *Earnings in Industry and Services* (Eurostat)

**Women's average hourly earnings in industry as a %
of men's by total number of employees (1988)**

10–49 employees	76.2
50–99 employees	77.2
100–199 employees	75.5
200–499 employees	78.9
500–999 employees	76.5
1,000–1,999 employees	81.1
2,000+ employees	85.3

Source: data from *Vrouwen in de Belgische Samenleving 1991/Les Femmes Dans La Societé Belge* (Kabinet Van de Staatssecretaris Voor Maatschappelijke Emancipatie/Cabinet Du Secretaire d'Etat à l'Emancipation Sociale)

Women's earnings compared with men's: In 1989 women's average monthly earnings were 62% of men's in industry and 70.8% in services. Women's hourly earnings in industry were 75.3% of men's.

The rate of unemployment for women with children under 10 is the highest in the EC

Working mothers (1988): 54% of women with a child under 10 were employed compared with 92% of men. 68% of women aged 20–39 without children were employed. 12% of women and 5% of men with a child under 10 were unemployed. 30% of employed women with a child under 10 have part-time jobs.

Fewer single mothers with a child 0–4 are working (42%) compared to all mothers (53%). The figure for those with children aged 5–9 is 54% for single mothers and 56% for all mothers.

Unemployment: The proportion of women among all unemployed has risen from 47% in 1973 to 60.8% in 1989. 45.4% of unemployed women are under 30. Unemployment rates are higher for single mothers compared to all mothers: 33% for those with a child aged 0–4 (14% for all mothers) and 22% for those with a child aged 5–9 (11% for all mothers).

WOMEN AND POLITICS

Women won the vote in 1948. After the 13 December 1987 election there were 19 women members in the

House of Representatives (9% of total) and 18 women
(9.8%) in the Senate. The next general election was
held on 24 November 1991, but at the end of
February 1992 a government had still not been formed.

Women in the House of Representatives (as of 8 October 1990)

political party	total no of seats	no of seats held by women	% of seats held by women
Christelijke Volkspartij (CVP)	43	6	14.0
Parti Socialiste (PS)	40	3	7.5
Socialistische Partij (SP)	31	4	12.9
Partij voor Vrijheid en Vooruitgang (PVV)	25	1	4.0
Parti pour les Réformes et la Liberté (PRL)	23	–	–
Parti Social Chrétien (PSC)	18	1	5.6
Volksunie (VU)	16	2	12.5
Anders Gaan Leven (Agalev)	6	1	16.7
Ecologiste	3	–	–
Font Démocratique des Francophones (FDF)	3	1	33.3
Vlaams Blok	2	–	–
Indépendant	2	–	–
total	**212**	**19**	**9.0**

Source: data from *Vrouwen in de Belgische Samenleving 1991/Les Femmes Dans La Société Belge*
(Kabinet Van de Staatssecretaris Voor Maatschappelijke Emancipatie/Cabinet Du Secretaire d'Etat
à l'Emancipation Sociale)

Women in the Senate (as of 30 June 1990)

political party	total no of seats	no of seats held by women	% of seats held by women
CVP	39	5	12.8
PS	36	3	8.3
SP	29	1	3.4
PVV	18	1	5.6
PRL	21	2	9.5
PSC	16	2	12.5
VU	13	–	–
Agalev	5	2	40.0
Ecologiste	3	2	66.7
FDF	2	–	–
Vlaams Blok	1	–	–
total	**183**	**18**	**9.8**

Source: data from *Vrouwen in de Belgische Samenleving 1991/Les Femmes Dans La Société Belge*
(Kabinet Van de Staatssecretaris Voor Maatschappelijke Emancipatie/Cabinet Du Secretaire d'Etat
à l'Emancipation Sociale)

In November
1990, 16.6% of
European MPs
were women

In 1991 Budget Minister Wivina de Meester was the
only woman among 18 members of the national
government, and was the third woman to serve in the
cabinet. Five out of 10 junior ministers were women.

Women in local government (%)

communes (November 1990)

councillors	14.3
deputy mayors	10.4
burgomasters	3.9

provinces (November 1990)

councillors	12.3
permanent deputies	7.4
governors	0.0

regional government (June 1990)

Flemish executive	0.0
Flemish council	9.0
French executive	0.0
French council	6.8
German executive	0.0
German council	4.0

Source: data from *Vrouwen in de Belgische Samenleving 1991/Les
Femmes Dans La Société Belge* (Kabinet Van de Staatssecretaris Voor
Maatschappelijke Emancipatie/Cabinet Du Secretaire d'Etat à
l'Emancipation Sociale)

The number of women magistrates has increased from
1.4% of the total in 1961 to 24.7% in 1990. Three of
Belgium's 95 ambassadors are women.

WOMEN AND EDUCATION

The percentage
of 14–18 year olds
in education is
the highest in the
EC. The lowest is
in Portugal

In 1989 women accounted for only 20% on average
of teaching and support staff in Flemish universities,
and were least represented in the most senior
positions. Women were 34% of temporary scientific
staff, 17% of tenured scientific staff, 8% of lecturers,
6% of professors and 2.9% of tenured professors.

Percentage of female students (1988–89)

	Flemish speaking	French speaking
pre-school education	49.1	48.6
primary education	48.6	48.7
secondary education	48.8	48.4
higher education (excluding university)	52.2	55.0
university education	43.7	42.2
total	**48.7**	**48.5**

Percentage of women students by subject studied (1988–89)

non-university further education (short courses)	Flemish speaking	French speaking
technical subjects	20.9	13.6
economics	57.2	55.8
social studies	71.1	73.9
arts	54.7	55.0
agriculture	20.3	20.3
teacher training	80.4	77.2
total	**61.2**	**63.5**

non-university further education (long courses)	Flemish speaking	French speaking
technical subjects	–	9.4
economics	50.6	55.8
teacher training	–	60.0
technical – agriculture	17.3	–
agriculture	–	18.2
arts	39.4	37.8
total	**32.4**	**34.5**

university		
philosophy and literature	58.5	64.6
law	48.8	49.1
sciences	40.9	40.5
medicine	49.7	45.6
applied sciences	12.9	9.8
social and political sciences	38.7	40.7
total	**43.7**	**42.2**

Source: data from *Vrouwen in de Belgische Samenleving 1991/ Les Femmes Dans La Société Belge* (Kabinet Van de Staatssecretaris Voor Maatschappelijke Emancipatie/Cabinet Du Secretaire d'Etat à l'Emancipation Sociale)

WOMEN AND DETENTION

In September 1988 women made up 5.3% of prisoners; with minors and young adults up to age 25 making up 0.5% and foreigners 31.1%.

% by offence of convicted persons who are women (1987)

forgery	22.3
rape and indecent assault	2.3
murder	11.7
serious bodily injury	5.8
actual bodily harm	13.2
criminal and petty theft	16.2
breach of contract, fraud and deception	25.3
other offences	12.7

Source: data from *Vrouwen in de Belgische Samenleving 1991/ Les Femmes Dans La Société Belge* (Kabinet Van de Staatssecretaris Voor Maatschappelijke Emancipatie/Cabinet Du Secretaire d'Etat à l'Emancipation Sociale)

SOURCES

Abortion Laws in Europe, Planned Parenthood in Europe, Vol 18 No 1, Spring 1989 (Supplement, amended April 1990); *Bargaining Report 101* (Labour Research Department); *Childcare in the European Communities 1985–90 (Women of Europe* Supplement No 51); *Comparative study on rules governing working conditions in the member states* (Commission of the European Communities); *Demographic Statistics 1990* (Eurostat); *Earnings in Industry and Services* (Eurostat); *Employment in Europe 1991* (Commission of the European Communities); *Europa World Year Book 1990* (31st edition); *Health Care Systems and Professional Organisations in the European Community, Information note – Europe* (British Medical Association); Health For All 2000 Indicator Presentation System (World Health Organisation Regional Office for Europe); *Labour Force Survey (Results 1989)* (Eurostat); *Les Actions Positives en Faveur des Femmes en Europe Occidentale* (Institut Syndical Europeen); *Out In Europe* (Peter Tatchell, for Channel 4 Television); *Pocket World in Figures* (The Economist); *Positive action and the constitutional and legislative hindrances to its implementation in the member states of the Council of Europe* (Council of Europe); *Prison Information Bulletin* June 1990 (Council of Europe); *Proposition de Directive Du Conseil concernant la protection au travail de la femme enceinte ou venant d'accoucher* (Commission of the European Communities); *Social Protection in the Member States of the Community* (Commission of the European

Community Directorate General on Employment, Industrial
Relations and Social Affairs); *Third World Guide 91/92*
(Instituto del Tercer Mundo); *Vrouwen in de Belgische
Samenleving 1991 Les Femmes dans la Société Belge* (Kabinet
Van de Staatssecretaris Voor Maatschappelijke
Emancipatie/Cabinet du Secretaire d'Etat à l'Emancipation
sociale); *Women of Europe* (Nos 60, 61, 63, 64, 68, 67, 69)

ADDRESSES

Belgian Embassy, 103–105 Eaton Square, London SW1W 9AB.
Tel: 071 235 5422

Secrétaire d'Etat à l'emancipation sociale, 56 rue de la Loi, 1040
Bruxelles. Tel: (32 2) 219 01 19

Conseil National des Femmes Belges (CNFB), rue de Florence
24, 1050 Bruxelles

Secretariat de la Commission du Travail des Femmes, Ministère
de l'Emploi et du Travail, rue Belliard 51, 1040 Bruxelles

Nationaal Instituut voor Statistiek – NIS, Leuvenseweg 44,
1000 Brussel

Porte Ouverte, Association pour l'émancipation économique de
la travailleuse, Rue Américaine 16, 1050 Bruxelles

Federatie Centra voor Geboortenregeling en Seksuele
Opvoeding (Flemish family planning service), Kon Albertlaan
167, 9000 Gent. Tel: (32 91) 21 07 212

Fédération Belge pour le Planning Familial et l'Education
Sexuelle (French family planning service), 28 rue Lesbroussart,
1050 Bruxelles. Tel: (32 2) 641 93 71

Fédération Générale du Travail de Belgique/Algemeen Belgisch,
Vakverbond, 42 rue Haute, 1000 Bruxelles

FWH (Federatie Werkgroepen Homofile) (lesbian and gay
rights), Dambruggestraat 204, B-2008 Antwerpen.
Tel: (323) 233 2502

Bulgaria

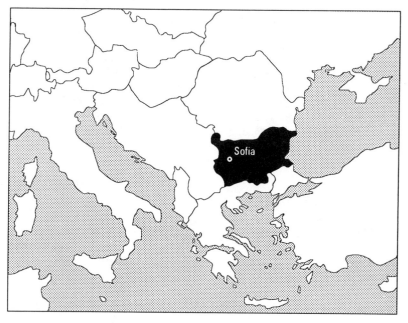

- **Population** 8.99 million
- **Area** 110,994 sq km
- **Population density** 81 people sq km
- **GNP per capita** (1987) £2,573
- **Public spending as % of GNP:** defence 3.6% (1986); education 4.4% (1986); health 3.2% (1987)
- **Currency is the leva** Official exchange rate 1989 £1 = LEV4.5; US$1 = LEV2.8

Price controls were freed in February 1991 and in just over two weeks the prices of some goods had risen by 1,200%

The president is the head of state. The single-chamber Grand National Assembly has 400 members elected every five years (200 directly elected and 200 by proportional representation). Local government is based on 28 districts that are divided into 273 municipalities. All citizens can vote at age 18.

The Turkish minority accounts for almost 10% of the population. In 1985 the government began a programme of forced assimilation, making Turks adopt Slavic names, banning the practice of Islam and the speaking of Turkish. There was a mass exodus of Turks in 1988, but in 1990 the law was changed to allow Turks to use their Islamic names.

BIRTH, LIFE AND DEATH

Population density by region (1988)

region	area sq km	population	pop density per sq km
Sofia (city)	1,310.8	1,209,562	922.8
Burgas	14,656.7	873,905	59.6
Khaskovo	13,891.6	1,047,189	75.4
Lovech	15,150.0	1,068,097	70.5
Mikhailovgrad	10,606.9	666,277	62.8
Plovdiv	13,628.1	1,261,875	92.6
Razgrad	10,842.4	850,862	78.5
Sofia (region)	18,978.5	1,017,214	53.6
Varna	11,928.6	981,274	82.3
total	**110,993.6**	**8,976,255**	**80.9**

Source: *Europa World Year Book 1990* (31st edition)

Births and deaths per 1,000 population (1988)

birth rate (1987)	13.0
death rate	11.9
infant mortality per 1,000 live births	16.0
marriage rate	7.1
life expectancy (women)	75.0
life expectancy (men)	69.2
fertility rate per woman	2.0

Source: data from *Demographic Statistics 1990* (Eurostat)

LESBIAN RIGHTS

Same-sex relationships were illegal until 1968. The age of consent is 21 for lesbians and gay men, compared with 14 for heterosexuals. Public expression of same-sex relationships can be punished under laws which prohibit behaviour that 'causes scandal or entices others to perversity'.

WOMEN AND HEALTH CARE

All medical treatment and services have been free since 1951. Private medical and dental services were legalised in 1989, after a ban introduced in 1972. In 1988 there was 1 doctor for every 323 people.

Major indicators for women's health (1989)

maternal deaths (all causes) per 100,000 live births	18.70
maternal deaths (abortion) per 100,000 live births	5.34
ratio of abortions to 1,000 live births (all ages)	988.90
% of all live births to mothers under 20	20.92
% of all live births to mothers aged 35+	3.44
deaths from cancer of the cervix (age 0–64) per 100,000 women (1988)	4.28
deaths from malignant neoplasm female breast (age 0–64) per 100,000 women	15.08
deaths from trachea/bronchus/lung cancer (age 0–64) per 100,000 women	4.65
deaths from trachea/bronchus/lung cancer (age 0–64) per 100,000 men	38.94
deaths from diseases of the circulatory system (age 0–64) per 100,000 women	91.48
deaths from diseases of the circulatory system (age 0–64) per 100,000 men	217.36
deaths from suicide and self-inflicted injury per 100,000 women	8.39
deaths from suicide and self-inflicted injury per 100,000 men	23.82

Source: data from Health for All 2000 Indicator Presentation System (World Health Organisation Regional Office For Europe)

Abortion and contraception: Since February 1990 abortion has been available on request up to 12 weeks, or 22 weeks where there are medical grounds. There is no time limit if the woman's life is endangered. Abortion is free for women under 18 and, on medical grounds, for women over 35. Doctors have a duty to inform women having abortions about contraception. Previous abortion law, introduced in 1973–4, restricted abortion on request to certain categories of women only, and counselling was compulsory. An estimated 5% of Bulgarians use condoms.

PARENTAL PAY, LEAVE AND BENEFITS

While no official information on this was provided, Christina Staneva and Roumy Slabakova address this in their contributions at the end of this chapter.

CHILD-CARE PROVISION

3–5 year olds: In 1988 79% of all 3–5 year olds were in kindergartens.

Primary school (6 years up): In 1988 the pupil to teacher ratio in primary schools was 18:1.

STATE BENEFITS

Retirement pensions: The retirement age for women varies from 40 to 55 depending on occupation (45 to 60 for men). Pensions are linked to the average monthly pay in 3 of the previous 15 years in employment, plus an allowance of up to 12% based on additional service.

Sickness benefit: Compensation is paid during sick leave.

WOMEN AND EMPLOYMENT

Employment by industrial sector (August 1988)

	women		men		women as % of workforce
	no	%	no	%	
industry	679.0	34.3	732.1	34.6	48.1
construction	65.8	3.3	294.8	13.9	18.2
agriculture	402.7	20.3	476.2	22.5	45.8
forestry	7.4	0.4	9.0	0.4	45.1
transport	49.8	2.5	207.3	9.8	19.4
communications	26.0	1.3	16.6	0.8	61.0

Employment by industrial sector (August 1988) (continued)

	women		men		women as % of workforce
	no	%	no	%	
trade material, technical supply and purchase	225.9	11.4	129.3	6.1	63.6
other branches of material production	17.0	0.9	15.8	0.7	51.8
housing services	35.7	1.8	18.8	0.9	65.5
science and scientific services	42.1	2.1	40.0	1.9	51.3
education	195.7	9.9	68.5	3.2	74.1
culture and art	26.5	1.3	21.0	1.0	55.8
health and social services, sport and tourism	149.1	7.5	52.0	2.5	74.1
finance, banking and insurance	18.9	1.0	3.3	0.2	85.1
government administration	30.2	1.5	24.0	1.1	55.7
other services	7.8	0.4	6.9	0.3	53.1
total	1,979.6	100.0	2,115.6	100.0	48.3

Source: data from *Statistical Reference Book People's Republic of Bulgaria 1989*

WOMEN AND POLITICS

Women have had the right to vote since 1938. The parties, and the number of seats parties hold, in the Grand National Assembly are: Bulgarian Socialist Party (206); Union of Democratic Forces – Coalition of 16 (136); Movement for Freedom and Human Rights (23); Agrarian Party (16); and others (19). In June 1991 8.5% of seats were held by women.

SOURCES

Abortion Laws in Europe, Planned Parenthood in Europe, Vol 18 No 1, Spring 1989 (Supplement, amended April 1990); *Europa World Year Book 1990* (31st edition); Health For All 2000 Indicator Presentation System (World Health Organisation Regional Office for Europe); *Out In Europe* (Peter Tatchell, for Channel 4 Television); *Planned Parenthood in Europe* (Vol 19 No 1) (International Planned Parenthood Federation); *Statistical Reference Book People's Republic of Bulgaria 1989; Third World Guide 91/92* (Instituto del Tercer Mundo)

LETTERS FROM BULGARIA

Christina Staneva, English teacher, Stara Zagora

I vaguely remember some scenes from my childhood during and after the Second World War. I see a dim picture of narrow, muddy streets and the village tavern, where the men, exhausted after the hard work of the fields, had their wine and brandy every night. I can still see the low tile-roofed building with its barred windows and hear the drunken men's voices. I instinctively connected the tavern with the shrill crying of women and children in the awful darkness. Years after, I realised that my instincts had been right – that every night scores, no hundreds, of women had been maltreated by their husbands without any hope, any chance of alternative.

A great many of these women are still alive. They are different people now, grandmothers and great-grandmothers, proud of their families, and people with dignity and self-esteem. What helped them be transformed? What helped the daughters and granddaughters of these semi-illiterate women become doctors, engineers, teachers, vets, agronomists, economists? After the war, there was a change which opened the door of education to all. Women received the right to go to school and university and rushed to go. Women took up all kinds of jobs and were often better at their work. Only the army and navy discriminated against them. Bulgarian women became MPs, in government, in all kinds of Ministries.

The question of the children arose, and maternity leave was given. First only three months were paid, then eight, then one year. Now it is three years and the job is kept for the mother while she is on leave. The time she looks after her children is accepted as years of work and taken into account when she retires.

Of course a coin always has two faces and women had to work twice and thrice more than men: raising children, working and looking after the household. Not all husbands and children are helpful and loving. Some are so selfish that a woman's lot becomes a heavy burden: preparing breakfast, getting the children ready for school, taking the youngest to nursery, waiting for the always late bus, working 8 hours, shopping (often waiting in long queues), cooking, washing up, cleaning, ironing, helping the children do lessons, knitting, sewing, doing extra work to make both ends meet and going to bed in the latest hours of the night. This was and is the life of most women in our country.

Now conditions are getting worse and worse. After more than 30 years, unemployment is hanging like a Damocles sword. Women are the first to be sacked. Some respond by fighting back, some are letting themselves choose the simple role of housewife or mistress, but it is still the old slavery in a refined, modern shape. Our world is still a man's world.

Roumy Slabakova, philologist, Sofia

Life is hard at the moment for both sexes. Women have to queue, yes, but men do too. When you see a queue, it is 85% old women, 5% men and 10% younger women. The families who have an old member, more often an old woman, consider themselves lucky because they are the main suppliers. These old women are very brave and selfless, ready to stand for many hours – up to 8 sometimes. Women have to be very enterprising and inventive with food, to cook with the few available products. There are no easy-to-prepare things as in Western supermarkets.

Socialism wasn't especially bad for women. While it brought low production and a low standard of living, women's rights were not significantly violated. Women got elected, there had to be a certain number of them everywhere, they had (still do) maternity leave and benefits which cannot be compared to any in the capitalist world. There are sufficient kindergartens and nurseries. But that was a facade. For my mother's generation, what socialism did was force them to work. A family couldn't survive without two salaries. Working, a career, was not a matter of choice.

Feminism has never been a major topic of discussion, or even for thought, except when contact with Western thinking provokes it. As an example, we set up a Bulgarian Federation of University Women at Sofia University. Some of my colleagues said they did not 'live' feminism because they felt superior to men. We explained it was about women's studies, but they still answered they did not like to be segregated.

ADDRESSES

Embassy of the Republic of Bulgaria, 186–188 Queen's Gate, London SW7 5HL. Tel: 071 584 9400

Democratic Union of Women of Bulgaria, Bd Patriarche Evtimi 82, Sofia 1463

Central Statistical Office, Council of Ministers, Sofia, Panayot Volov Street 2

Society for Planned Parenthood and Family Development, PO Box No 5, Sofia 1199. Tel: (359 2) 88 31 11

Central Council of Bulgarian Trade Unions, pl D Blagoev 1, Sofia

Czechoslovakia

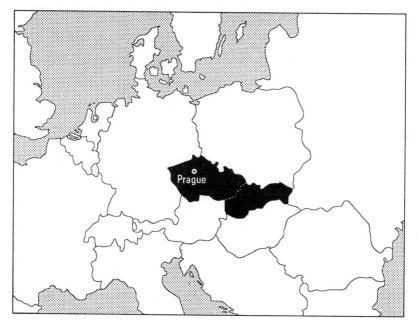

- **Population** 15.6 million, 51.3% female
- **Area** 127,900 sq km
- **Population density** 122.2 people sq km
- **GDP 1988** £27 billion
- **GDP per capita** £1,697
- **Public spending as % of GNP:** defence 4.1% (1986); education 3.6% (1986); health 4.2% (1987)
- **Consumer price index** 1980 = 100; 1989 = 113
- **Currency is the koruna:** official exchange rate 1989 £1 = KCS26.50; US$1 = KCS16.48

Czechoslovakia is a federal state of the Czech republic (in the west) and the Slovak republic, each of which has its own government. The Federal Assembly has two chambers: the House of the People and the House of Nations. The assembly is elected for 5 years, though the June 1990 election was for a transitional period of 2 years. Citizens may vote at age 18. The number of representatives in the House of the People is determined by population. After the June 1990 elections there were 101 deputies for Czechs and 49 for Slovaks. The House of Nations has 150 members, 75 for each republic.

The president is head of state; he or she is elected by the Federal Assembly for 5 years, though in 1990 Vaclav Havel was re-elected for a transitional 2-year period. The president appoints the federal government, which has executive authority, and is led by a prime minister.

The population is 63% Czech and 32% Slovak. In 1987 the rest of the population was made up of Hungarians (3.8%) who live mostly in Slovakia, Germans (0.3%), Poles (0.5%), Ukrainians and Russians (0.3%) and others (0.3%). There is also a Romany community.

Most of the population is Christian: 70% Roman Catholic and 15% Protestant. 80% of people in the Czech republic and 71% in the Slovak republic live in towns.

EQUAL RIGHTS

All citizens are guaranteed equal rights and duties regardless of nationality or race. Women and men are guaranteed equal position in employment, public activities and the family. A new constitution, expected to come into force during 1992, has been drafted and is under negotiation.

The Slovak Governmental Committee for Women and Family was set up in June 1990, but in April 1991 it was reportedly inoperative.

BIRTH, LIFE AND DEATH

Population density by region (1988)

region	area sq km	population	pop density per sq km
Czech republic			
Central Bohemia	10,994	1,122,063	102
Southern Bohemia	11,345	697,721	62
Western Bohemia	10,875	869,393	80
Northern Bohemia	7,819	1,190,584	152
Eastern Bohemia	11,240	1,240,853	110
Southern Moravia	15,028	2,058,386	137
Northern Moravia	11,067	1,969,827	178
Prague (city)	496	1,211,207	2,442
Czech total	78,864	10,360,034	131
Slovak republic			
Western Slovakia	14,492	1,725,825	119
Central Slovakia	17,986	1,608,202	89
Eastern Slovakia	16,191	1,494,483	92
Bratislava (city)	367	435,710	1,187
Slovak total	49,036	5,264,220	107
total	**127,900**	**15,624,254**	**122**

Source: *Europa World Year Book 1990* (31st edition)

Births and deaths per 1,000 population (1988)

birth rate (1987)	13.8
death rate	11.4
infant mortality rate per 1,000 live births	15.0
marriage rate	7.8
life expectancy (women)	74.0
life expectancy (men)	67.5
fertility rate per woman	2.0

Source: data from *Demographic Statistics 1990* (Eurostat)

Birth, death, marriage and divorce rates (per 1,000 of population)

	birth rate	death rate	marriage rate	divorce rate
1970	15.9	11.6	8.8	2.0
1980	16.3	12.2	7.7	2.9
1987	13.8	11.5	7.8	3.2

Source: data from *Statistická rocenka 1988*

LESBIAN RIGHTS

Same-sex relationships were illegal until 1961. The age of consent for lesbians and gay men (previously 18), was brought into line with the age of 15 for heterosexuals in July 1990.

WOMEN AND HEALTH CARE

All health care, including specialised and hospital treatment, rehabilitation, spa treatment and dental care, is free. There is a small fee of KCS1 for a prescription.

In 1988 there was 1 doctor for every 327 people.

Major indicators for women's health (1989)

maternal deaths (all causes) per 100,000 live births	9.59
maternal deaths (abortion) per 100,000 live births	1.92
ratio of abortions to 1,000 live births (all ages)	769.30
% of all live births to mothers under 20	12.95
% of all live births to mothers aged 35+	4.29
deaths from cancer of the cervix (age 0–64) per 100,000 women (1988)	5.91
deaths from malignant neoplasm female breast (age 0–64) per 100,000 women	17.19
deaths from trachea/bronchus/lung cancer (age 0–64) per 100,000 women	6.71
deaths from trachea/bronchus/lung cancer (age 0–64) per 100,000 men	59.75
deaths from diseases of the circulatory system (age 0–64) per 100,000 women	75.71
deaths from diseases of the circulatory system (age 0–64) per 100,000 men	218.47
deaths from suicide and self-inflicted injury per 100,000 women	8.60
deaths from suicide and self-inflicted injury per 100,000 men	29.37

Source: data from Health for All 2000 Indicator Presentation System (World Health Organisation Regional Office For Europe)

Abortion and contraception: Since January 1987 abortion has been available on request up to 12 weeks provided there is a gap of at least 6 months between abortions (unless the woman is over 35, or has given birth twice, or has been raped). Available up to the second trimester in cases where there is a risk to the woman's life and physical health, a risk to foetal health or of foetal handicap, or in cases of rape or other sexual crime. For this, women under 16 must

A 1987 survey of 219 enterprises and plants found that men were twice as likely as women to be in positions of authority: only 6.5% of women managers were directors compared with 20.4% of men

have parental consent. Abortion on medical grounds and up to 8 weeks is free (twice a year); after 8 weeks the charge is KCS500. Abortions must be performed in hospitals and women must apply for abortions in the districts where they live, work or study. An amendment being drafted proposes much greater restrictions on abortion and a new charge of KCS3,000 – almost 1 month's average salary.

The shortage of effective contraceptives and poor sex education have been blamed for the high use of abortion as a method of contraception. In 1991 an estimated 5% of women used oral contraceptives and 15% IUDs. In 1977 a fertility survey found that 30% of women in cities and 45% in rural areas had no knowledge of contraception. Withdrawal was the most common method of birth control, practised by 40% of Czech and 50% of Slovak fertile women. An estimated 1 in 4 women in cities and 1 in 5 in rural areas are pregnant when they marry.

PARENTAL PAY, LEAVE AND BENEFITS

Maternity and paternity leave and pay: 6 months paid at 90% of earnings, but 35 weeks for single mothers and for multiple births. Plus 6 months on benefit with the amount depending on the number of children. From October 1990 fathers have been able to take leave on the same basis as mothers.

Nursing mothers: Mothers with children up to 6 months are entitled to 2 half-hour breaks a day, and to 1 half-hour break for children between 6 and 9 months.

Time off to look after sick children: 60 days on full pay is granted to women, who may also take additional unpaid leave for care of a sick child.

CHILD-CARE PROVISION

3–6 year olds: Almost all children between 3 and 6 are in kindergarten (materská skola).

Primary school (6 years up): Education is compulsory

between the ages of 6 and 16. In 1988 the pupil to teacher ratio in primary schools was 21:1.

STATE BENEFITS

All employees are covered by a single social security system. In April 1990 the law on social security was amended so that all benefits can now be claimed by employees in the private sector.

Retirement pensions: Normal retirement age is 55 for women (60 for men). Pensions in 1990 were KCS1,200 a month for a single pensioner and 2,000 for a couple.

Child allowances: In 1990 child allowance was KCS600–KCS900 a month for each child up to the age of 3, but the mother is not allowed to be employed for more than 2 hours a day.

Sickness benefit: Paid for a maximum of 2 years. Disablement pension can be paid after this period.

WOMEN AND EMPLOYMENT

Total employment by industrial sector (1000s) (1988)

agriculture	839
forestry	94
mining, manufacturing, gas and electricity	2,951
construction	797
trade, restaurants etc	712
other commerce	170
transport	399
communications	106
services	302
education and culture	600
science and research	181
health and social services	397
civil service, jurisdiction	120
others	135
total in employment	7,803
women on maternity leave	358
total labour force	8,161

Source: *Europa World Year Book 1990* (31st edition)

Women's employment by industrial sector (1988)

	Czechoslovakia %	Czech Republic %	Slovak Republic %
agriculture	39.7	40.0	39.5
industry	40.8	40.7	40.9
home trade	75.7	75.2	77.0
international trade	65.4	65.8	63.4
science and research	38.1	36.8	40.9
education	71.6	71.3	72.2
culture	52.1	51.4	53.9
health service	78.8	79.0	78.3
social care	89.0	89.1	88.8
total	**46.0**	**46.3**	**45.5**

Source: *Europa World Year Book 1990* (31st edition)

In 1988 9.7% of women were employed in workplaces where there was a potential risk to their health

Statutory rights: All workers are entitled to annual paid leave of 3–4 weeks depending on their age. The statutory minimum wage is KCS2,000 a month and was to have been raised to KCS3,000 by the end of 1991. Although previously the constitution guaranteed all citizens the right to work, this has been amended to say that the state shares responsibility with employers to help unemployed workers to find jobs or retraining schemes.

Unemployment: This began in the first half of 1990 when the number of people employed fell by 1.3%. Figures for the first half of 1990 show a greater fall in sectors where more women work.

Women's unemployment in the Slovak Republic

	Dec 1990	Feb 1991	% inc.
under 30 years	7,461	12,980	74.0
30–40 years	5,228	9,578	83.2
40–50 years	2,404	4,246	76.6
women without qualifications	4,346	7,702	77.2
women with middle qualifications	8,244	14,853	80.2
women with higher qualifications	2,127	3,149	48.0
gypsy women	2,823	4,669	60.5

Source: *The Influence of Social and Economical Changes in the Czech and Slovak Federal Republic on the Position of Women* (Anna Okruhlicova)

WOMEN AND POLITICS

Women have had the right to vote since 1919. After the elections of 1986 women accounted for 29.4% of the representatives elected to the Federal Assembly. In the Slovak National Council and in local administration 30% of representatives were women. After the 1990 elections 9.4% of those elected to the Federal Assembly and 11% of the Slovak National Council were women. There is 1 woman in the federal government, 1 in the Czech government and none in the Slovak government. The proportion of women in local administration fell to 19% in the 1990 elections.

Women elected to the Federal Assembly in June 1990

political party	total no of seats	no of seats held by women	% of seats held by women
Civic Forum/Public Against Violence	170	14	8.2
Communist Party	45	2	4.4
Christian and Democratic Union/ Christian Democratic Movement	40	4	10.0
Movement for Autonomous Democracy – Society for Moravia and Silesia	16	4	25.0
Slovak National party	15	4	26.7
Coexistence	12	–	0.0
total	**298**	**28**	**9.4**

Source: data from *Statistická rocenka 1988*

WOMEN AND EDUCATION (1989–90)

Women as a percentage of students: gymnasia (60.5%); secondary vocational schools (64.7%); apprentice schools (40.5%); universities (45%).

SOURCES

Abortion Laws in Europe, Planned Parenthood in Europe, Vol 18 No 1, Spring 1989 (Supplement, amended April 1990); *Europa World Year Book 1990* (31st edition); *Doing Business with Eastern Europe – Czechoslovakia* (Business International); *The Influence of Social and Economical Changes in the Czech and Slovak Federal Republic on the Position of Women* (Anna Okruhlicova); Health For All 2000 Indicator Presentation System (World Health Organisation Regional Office for

Europe); *Out In Europe* (Peter Tatchell, for Channel 4
Television); *Planned Parenthood in Europe* (Vol 20, No 2)
(International Planned Parenthood Federation); *Pocket World in
Figures* (The Economist); *Statistická rocenka 1988; Superwomen
and the Double Burden* (ed. Chris Corrin, Scarlet Press); *Third
World Guide 91/92* (Instituto del Tercer Mundo); *Women of
Europe* (No 69); *Women in managerial posts and decision-
making sphere in the Czech and Slovak Federal Republic*
(Miloslava Umlaufová and Anna Okruhlicova); *Women, State
and Party in Eastern Europe* (ed Sharon L Wolchik and Alfred G
Meyer, Duke University Press)

LETTERS FROM CZECHOSLOVAKIA

Anna Okruhlicova of the Educational Research
Institute, Bratislava (edited extracts from her paper
'The Influence of Social and Economical Changes in
the Czech and Slovak Federal Republic on the Position
of Women', delivered to a seminar on reforms and the
status of women, in Vienna, April 1991)

Women represent 46% of all workers but this high
level does not correspond with their representation in
leading or managing posts. Because they must care for
their families as well, women prefer less responsible
and less time-consuming occupations that do not
correspond with their high qualifications.

Due to equal legal working conditions,
Czechoslovakia is a world leader in women's
employment rate, which, in comparison with other
states, is high in all spheres.

But there are lasting differences in the rates of wages
of men and women, which amount to 40%. It is due
to the extent of shortened working hours of women,
but also to the shortcomings in the application of
wage regulations and in the assignment of women to
more demanding labour posts. The problems appear
not only in the actual wage levels, but also in the
dynamics of the growth. With about a third of women,
within a 5-year cycle, the wages were not raised. The
analyses point out that in spite of the legal guarantee,
a woman's wage is still considered to be a supplement
of the family income or a form of 'social help'.

At present women's greatest problems are caused by unemployment, the result of the economic reforms and price liberalisation. Towards the end of February 1991 in the Czech republic there were altogether 74,753 unemployed and 37,978 vacant posts. In the Slovak republic there were 77,570 unemployed and the number of vacant posts was 7,563 but only 29% for women.

Families are mostly dependent on the incomes of both parents. Still, there are a great number of families in which only the woman is the breadwinner. There is still no system to form new employment opportunities. The help of the International Labour Organisation is expected with hope, especially in the sphere of enterprising activities of women.

With the free market, for which the population was practically unprepared, there is a great number of families who gradually approach the limit of minimum living resources. On the other hand, the economical situation of the state imposes limitations on the system of social support.

According to the public opinion survey of March 1991, in 11% of households in Slovakia, the incomes do not cover the needs of the families; 44% live 'from salary to salary', buying only the most important things; 40% live pretty well, though plainly; and 5% of the families need not retrench their needs.

Many people experience the current economical reforms as a shock. From December 1990 up to February 1991 the prices were raised by 31.1%, without any parallel valorisation of wages. Many inhabitants are unable to adjust to the model of life of a democratic society, and what they miss most of all is the systematic juristic education. There is an extraordinary increase in criminality, with the deeds of aggressive character being directed against the weaker – the children, women and old people.

The term 'feminisation of poverty' has appeared, pointing out the negative effects the economical reform has on women. Even though de jure the laws of Czechoslovakia are in accord with the convention their application de facto will be possible only in the improved economical situation and that is still the matter of the far future.

Maria Chaloupkova, psychologist, Stupava

After the 'velvet revolution', marriage and parenthood education was neglected a lot. I think this is because teachers were not sure either of the reaction of parents or of their own position in the public school system. At present, the situation is very unsatisfactory.

In the public, there seem to be two counter streams. There is an increasing puritanism where one does not talk openly with young people about the problems of the sexes' relations (and within this also about sexuality). On the other hand, there is a consumer attitude to sexuality: sex magazines of different levels are available on the street, films, video-programmes, literature about sex, prostitution.

Religiously oriented political parties and movements make efforts for censorship so these kinds of goods would be less available. However, I think it is necessary to engage in more education on this, in the region of emotional relations as well as sexuality, about which one would talk with sensitivity and culture, but most of all truth. As a psychologist, I know that young people's hunger for discussions of this kind is stupendous. Closing our eyes to reality, being silent and avoiding the questions of the young, may lead them to look for answers in improper places.

ADDRESSES

Embassy of the Czech and Slovak Federal Republic,
25 Kensington Palace Gardens, London W8 4QY.
Tel: 071 229 1255

Federace zenskych organizacím hnutí a spolku (Preparatory
Committee of Women's Organisations, Movements and
Associations), Panska 7, 111 53 Prague

Central Council of Trade Unions, Ustrední rada Odboru, nám
Zápotockého 2, 113 59 Prague 3

Lambda Praha (lesbian and gay rights), c/o Jan Lany, PoD
Kotlarkou 14, CS-15000 Praha (Prague) 5 – Smichov.
Tel: (422) 527 388

Denmark

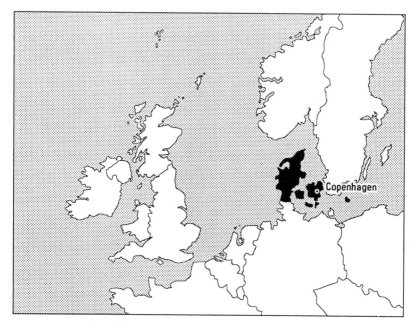

- **Population** 5.1 million, 50.7% female
- **Area** 43,075 sq km
- **Population density** 119 people sq km
- **GDP 1988** Danish krone 724 billion (£67 billion)
- **GDP per capita** £13,013
- **GDP per capita in purchasing power parity** (UK=100) 112
- **Public spending as % of GNP:** defence 2.1% (1986); education 7.5% (1986); health 5.3% (1987)
- **Consumer price index** 1980 = 100; 1989 = 176
- **Currency is the krone** 1989 £1 = DKR10.65; US$1 = DKR6.60

Denmark is a monarchy that includes the outlying territories of Greenland and the Faeroes. Legal power is held jointly by the monarch and parliament (Folketing), which has 179 members. Members are elected for 4 years by proportional representation. In 1978 the age for voting and being able to stand for election was lowered from 20 to 18. While nominally executive power is held by the monarch, in practice it is held by the cabinet, which is led by the prime minister. Local government is based on 14 counties (amtskommuner), one city and one borough. 91% of the population belongs to the Evangelical Lutheran Church and there are small numbers of Protestants and Roman Catholics.

IMMIGRATION AND RESIDENCE RIGHTS

Residence permits are normally granted to all previous Danish citizens and to marriage or long-standing partners, children or others with close ties to Danish residents. Permits are also given to parents over 60 of permanent residents (if residents can support them and there are no children living in a home country to support them). Marriage partners and children under 18 can join those with a residence permit. Children born outside of marriage are Danish only if the mother is a Dane.

Temporary residence permits can be granted to those with specialist skills or with business ties in Denmark.

In 1988 Denmark had 136,177 foreign residents, 45.6% of them women. 47.5% of foreign residents were from countries other than Europe and Africa. 19.7% were from EC states, with the largest groups from the UK and Germany. 29% were from non-EC European countries, and 3.9% were from Africa.

EQUAL RIGHTS

The 1988 Equality Act aims to further the equality of women and men, and special measures to create equal opportunities are allowed. Although positive action is legal, it is treated as a departure from the general principle of equality with regard to employment, and requires prior authorisation.

A 1987–89 survey found that women make up 21.6% of new senior managers, despite accounting for only 16.2% of applicants

The Equal Status Council's duties include allowing exemptions from the act and dealing with equal pay cases. It has 8 members: a chair appointed by the prime minister, 3 members from the National Council of Women, and members representing women's studies, the Danish Women's Society, trade union federations and employers' association.

To achieve a balance between the sexes, public boards must propose equal numbers of women and men for vacant seats.

BIRTH, LIFE AND DEATH

Breakdown of population by sex and age group (1000s) (1988)

	all		women		men		% of women in age group
	no	%	no	%	no	%	
0–14	901.4	17.6	440.7	16.9	460.7	18.2	48.9
15–24	791.0	15.4	384.6	14.8	406.4	16.1	48.6
25–39	1,129.9	22.0	551.8	21.2	578.1	22.9	48.8
40–59	1,260.6	24.6	627.2	24.1	633.4	25.1	49.8
60–74	701.8	13.7	378.6	14.6	323.2	12.8	53.9
75+	344.8	6.7	218.6	8.4	126.2	5.0	63.4
all	5,129.5	100.0	2,601.5	100.0	2,528.0	100.0	50.7

Source: data from *Demographic Statistics 1990* (Eurostat)

Population and population increase by region (1987)

region	pop (1000s)	% of total pop	pop density per sq km	natural increase per 1,000	net migration per 1,000	total increase per 1,000
Hovedstadsregionen	1,715.5	33.5	600.4	-1.7	0.4	-1.3
Øst for Storebælt	586.9	11.5	84.2	-2.2	3.8	1.6
Vest for Storebælt	2,824.8	55.0	84.9	0.8	2.0	2.8
Denmark	5,127.2	100.0	119.0	-0.4	1.6	1.3

Source: data from *Demographic Statistics 1990* (Eurostat)

Births, deaths, marriages and divorces (rates per 1,000 of population)

	1960	1970	1980	1985	1988
birth rate	16.7	14.4	11.2	10.5	11.5
% of births outside marriage	7.8	11.0	33.2	43.0	44.7
average age of mother at 1st birth	23.1	23.7	24.6	25.5	25.9
infant mortality per 1,000 live births	21.5	14.2	8.4	7.9	7.6
fertility rate per woman	2.5	2.0	1.6	1.5	1.6
marriage rate	7.8	7.4	5.2	5.7	6.3
average age at marriage (women)	24.7	24.6	27.9	29.5	30.1
average age at marriage (men)	28.3	27.3	30.8	32.5	32.9
divorce rate	1.5	1.9	2.7	2.8	2.9
life expectancy (women)	74.4[1]	75.9[2]	77.2[3]	–	77.6[4]
life expectancy (men)	70.4[1]	70.7[2]	71.1[3]	–	71.8[4]
death rate	9.6	9.8	10.9	11.4	11.5

[1] 1961–62; [2] 1970–71; [3] 1980–81; [4] 1986–87

Source: data from *Demographic Statistics 1990* (Eurostat)

Figures for 1-parent households suggest the level is similar to that of the UK, which is among the highest in the EC. Official figures suggest that there are 71,319 couples with children who are living together but not married, though this is regarded as an under-estimate.

Family structure (1990)

	no	%
families without children	1,969,361	71.8
single people	1,472,750	53.7
married couples	496,611	18.1
families with children	772,342	28.2
single people	168,256	6.1
married couples	532,767	19.4
unmarried couples	71,319	2.6

Source: data from *Data on Denmark 1990* (Danmarks Statistiks)

LESBIAN RIGHTS

Since 1976 the common age of consent for lesbians, gay men and heterosexuals has been 15. In 1987 a law was introduced making it an offence (punishable by up to 2 years' imprisonment) to incite to hatred on the grounds of sexual orientation (also colour, national or ethnic origin and religion). Also in 1987 a statute was introduced which protects lesbians and gay men from discrimination in the provision of public services and access to public facilities.

Same-sex couples can register their relationship under the Danish Registered Partnership Act 1989, which gives them equal legal status with married couples on inheritance, alimony, taxation and rights of permanent residence in Denmark for foreign partners. However the law does not allow same-sex couples jointly to adopt children.

WOMEN AND HEALTH CARE

Health care is publicly funded, mainly through taxation, and covers everyone in Denmark. Hospital care and primary health care is free; but there are fees towards the cost of prescriptions and dental treatment.

Patients can choose to pay extra to be able to have unlimited choice of a doctor and direct access to specialist care, but only 5% do this. The remaining 95% can choose their GP within a given area and can change doctors once every 12 months, with specialist care available through referral by their GPs. In 1988 there was 1 doctor for every 394 people.

Major indicators for women's health (1988)

maternal deaths (all causes) per 100,000 live births	3.40
maternal deaths (abortion) per 100,000 live births	0.00
ratio of abortions to 1,000 live births (all ages)	360.26
% of all live births to mothers under 20	2.73
% of all live births to mothers aged 35+	8.47
deaths from cancer of the cervix (age 0–64) per 100,000 women	5.43
deaths from malignant neoplasm female breast (age 0–64) per 100,000 women	26.11
deaths from trachea/bronchus/lung cancer (age 0–64) per 100,000 women	20.70
deaths from trachea/bronchus/lung cancer (age 0–64) per 100,000 men	31.23
deaths from diseases of the circulatory system (age 0–64) per 100,000 women	41.97
deaths from diseases of the circulatory system (age 0–64) per 100,000 men	113.10
deaths from suicide and self-inflicted injury per 100,000 women	17.52
deaths from suicide and self-inflicted injury per 100,000 men	32.17

Source: data from Health for All 2000 Indicator Presentation System (World Health Organisation Regional Office For Europe)

Abortion and contraception: Available on request up to 12 weeks, though women under 18 must have parental consent. Abortion is available up to the second trimester, with the permission of a committee, if there is a risk to the woman's life, a risk to foetal health or of foetal handicap or in cases of rape or other sexual crime or if there are social reasons. Women are reimbursed for the costs of abortions. Hospitals must receive all women who want an abortion up to the first trimester. Abortions for non-residents are not allowed.

PARENTAL PAY, LEAVE AND BENEFITS (1989–90)

Maternity leave and pay: 14 weeks, including 4 that must be taken before the birth, plus 10 weeks' parental leave. Benefit is equal to 90% of earnings, up to a monthly maximum of DKR10,000. Most public sector workers receive full pay for 14 weeks. To qualify, women must be covered by national insurance and have worked for 6 months of the previous year, including 40 hours in the 4 weeks before leave.

Paternity leave: 2 weeks (independent of parental leave) paid by benefit equal to 90% of earnings up to a maximum of DKR10,000 a month.

Parental leave: 10 weeks paid at a level equal to 90% of earnings up to DKR10,000 a month.

Time off to look after sick children: All public sector and most private sector workers are entitled to one day on full pay for the first day of a child's illness.

The future: The right to part-time work for parents of young children is likely to be introduced. The private sector trade unions are insisting on equality between women and men, the right to return to full-time work and compensation for loss of earnings for the low paid. The government is proposing benefit payments for a $2^1/_2$ year period of reduced hours.

CHILD-CARE PROVISION (1989–90)

Levels of all child-care services are higher in cities than in rural areas.

Under 3s: 48% are in publicly funded places (highest in the EC). Most of these (60%) were in organised creches, with the rest in nurseries (28%), mixed-age centres (8%) and kindergartens. Denmark is the only EC country where publicly funded services care for more under 3s (48%) than private services (15%) and relatives (8%).

In 1919 Danish women won the legal right to equal pay in the civil service

3–6 year olds: 85% are in publicly funded places. All 6 year olds and some 5 year olds are in pre-primary schooling (3 hours a day). Most non-school provision is in kindergartens (61%), with the rest in mixed-age centres (17%), organised creches (12%) and in out of school hours care (9%).

Primary school (7 years up): There are 9 years of compulsory education from the age of 7. Hours of attendance increase with age from 15–22 hours a week for 7 year olds to 20–27 hours for 10 year olds. Opening hours vary by local authorities, and may start as early as 8.00 and finish as late as 15.00. Hours may also vary on a daily basis. The school year runs from August to June. In 1988 the pupil to teacher ratio in primary schools was 11:1.

Outside school hours care: 44% of 6 year olds and 29% of 7–10 year olds have places in out of school hours care.

Contributions to child-care costs: Parents contribute to public child care (excluding schools) according to income, paying on average one-third of the costs, though some local authorities provide an extra subsidy. The cost of public child-care services has been increasing by more than inflation and wages.

STATE BENEFITS (1989–90)

Retirement pension: Normal retirement age is 67 for women and men. Pensions are paid in 2 elements – a national pension and a supplementary pension. For the former, you must have at least 3 years' residence between the ages of 15 and 67. Basic national pension is DKR44,508 a year (DKR42,408 for a married person) and that is reduced if the person does not have 40 years of residence. Plus DKR11,448 if income is not above a fixed limit. A supplementary pension of DKR7,224 is paid to those who joined the complementary scheme that started on 1 April 1964. People over 50 can qualify for an early pension on grounds of ill health or for social reasons.

Women and men have had equal inheritance rights since 1857

In 1984 65% of women old age pensioners had only the national basic pension to live on, compared with 36% of male pensioners.

Survivors' pensions: 50% of the deceased person's pension is paid to the survivors of those with 10 years of insurance, provided the marriage lasted for at least 10 years and the survivor is 62 years old. There is also a death grant of DKR3,195. Additional assistance can be available in cases of need.

Sickness benefit: Based on the hourly wage (up to DKR65.52 an hour) and number of hours worked, with the first 2 weeks paid by the employer. Paid up to a maximum of 52 weeks in 18 months. Employees must have worked for at least 120 hours in the previous 13 weeks; the self-employed must have worked for 6 months in the previous 12. The self-employed have a waiting period of 3 weeks which can be covered by voluntary insurance. There is no waiting time for employed workers.

Invalidity: Paid to those aged 18 to 67 with at least 3 years' residence whose capacity to work is reduced by at least half because of mental or physical problems. Those aged 50 to 67 can retire with an early pension for health reasons. Benefit is paid until the age of 66. For those incapacitated by 50% the full basic pension of DKR44,508 is paid, while those who are further incapacitated receive that amount plus DKR19,860 invalidity. Those who are totally incapacitated receive the full basic pension, plus invalidity, plus DKR28,728 for unemployment. Rates may be less if both marriage partners apply. In addition, there are supplements for pensioners and early retirers and benefits for outside assistance and constant attendance.

Family benefits: Parents receive DKR550 a month for a child aged 0–3 and DKR466 a month for a child aged 4–18. Single parents receive an extra DKR337 for every child (reduced if income is over a DKR180,000 a year) and a monthly payment of DKR257 per household. Benefits are paid until children are 18. In cases of multiple births, payment of DKR5,000 is paid once a year for 4 years. There are also extra payments if 1 or both parents are pensioners and a one-off allowance of DKR15,000 for an adoption.

Unemployment benefit: Paid at 90% of earnings up to a maximum of DKR2,454 a week, for not more than $2^{1}/_{2}$ years. The maximum benefit for young people who have completed their education and are without work is DKR1,962 a week.

WOMEN AND EMPLOYMENT

Statutory rights: Paid annual leave is 30 days. There is no legislation governing the length of the working week, overtime or statutory public holidays. Minimum pay is set by collective agreements at industry level and applies only to engineering workers and some white collar workers.

Employment and unemployment (1989)

	% women	% men
economic activity rate	59.9	74.0
employed working part time	40.1	9.4
labour force who are employers or self-employed	3.0	14.4
labour force who are family workers	3.9	–
unemployment rate (% of labour force)	8.9	7.5
youth unemployment rate (age 14–24)	12.4	10.7
unemployed who have been unemployed for 12 months or more	27.7	21.4
all unemployed by sex	50.2	49.8

Source: data from *Labour Force Survey (Results 1989)* (Eurostat)

Part-time workers: In 1989 78.1% of part-time
workers were women. Everyone working more than
15 hours a week has the same right to social security
benefits.

Employment by industrial sector (1000s) (1989)

	women		men		women as % of workforce
	no	%	no	%	
agriculture	35	2.9	115	8.0	23.3
all industry	188	15.8	527	37.0	26.3
energy and water	–	–	22	1.5	21.4
mineral extraction and chemicals	17	1.4	35	2.5	32.7
metal manufacturing and engineering	42	3.5	147	10.3	22.2
other manufacturing industry	108	9.1	157	11.0	40.8
building and civil engineering	19	1.6	167	11.7	10.2
all services	963	81.3	784	55.0	55.1
distributive trades and hotels	183	15.4	222	15.5	45.2
transport and communication	52	4.4	143	10.0	26.7
banking, finance and insurance	118	9.9	138	9.7	46.1
public administration	94	7.9	92	6.5	50.5
other services	517	43.6	189	13.3	73.2
total*	1,196	100.0	1,434	100.0	45.5

* includes 11,000 women and 8,000 men whose industrial sector was not stated.

Source: data from *Labour Force Survey (Results 1989)* (Eurostat)

Women employees of WS Shamban Europe SA were awarded DKR 1 million when they won their equal pay for work of equal value case brought by the women's labour union Kvindeligt Arbejderforbund

Women's earnings compared with men's: On average
women earn 72% as much as men, though the
proportion is higher for non-qualified women
compared with non-qualified men (89%). Average
hourly earnings for unskilled women increased from
79.7% of men's in 1970 to 88.7% in 1987. Average
monthly pay for non-manual women workers
increased from 63.5% in 1970 to 71.9% in 1987.

A bill proposed in March 1991 by the Social
Democratic Party to amend the laws on equal pay for
work of equal value would shift the burden of proof
to employers, who would have to show that the jobs
being compared were not of equal value.

**Women's earnings as a % of men's in industry
(April 1988)**

	non-manual monthly earnings
chemical industry	89.6
all metal manufacture and engineering	85.9
mechanical engineering	85.8
electrical engineering	85.8
food, drink and tobacco	86.8
clothing and footwear manufacture	96.1
printing and publishing	72.4
all manufacturing industry	84.2
all industry	84.2

Source: data from *Earnings in Industry and Services* (Eurostat)

Denmark has the highest level of births outside marriage in the EC with 44.7% of all births. Lowest levels were in Greece (2.1%) and Italy (5.8%), Eurostat figures show

Working mothers (1988): 79% of women with a child under 10 were employed (the highest level in the EC and the same employment rate as for women aged 20–39 without children) compared with 95% of men. 40% of employed women with a child under 10 have part-time jobs. 8% of women and 3% of men with a child under 10 were unemployed.

Fewer single mothers work than all mothers: 69% for lone mothers with a child aged 0–4 (76% for all) and 74% for lone mothers with a child aged 5–9 (80%).

Unemployment rates are higher (11%) for lone mothers with a child aged 0–4 (9% for all mothers) but the same (8%) for those with a child aged 5–9.

WOMEN IN TRADE UNIONS

The Danish Women Workers' Union is for unskilled and semi-skilled women. The fifth largest union in Denmark, it organises women in industrial and service jobs in public and private sectors. One of its main aims is to organise training for members.

WOMEN AND POLITICS

The right to vote in municipal elections was won in 1908, and in parliamentary elections in 1915.

Members of the Folketing are elected by a complicated mathematical system of proportional representation. A former politician has estimated that there are only 40 people in Denmark who actually understand the electoral method. Another has said there are only 1 or 2 members of the Folketing itself with a clear grasp of the Danish electoral system.

Women elected to parliament (the Folketing) in December 1990

political party	total no of seats	no of seats held by women	% of seats held by women
Social Democratic Party	69	24	34.8
Conservative Party	30	7	23.3
Liberal Party	29	9	31.0
Socialist People's Party	15	6	40.0
Progress Party	12	4	33.3
Centre Democratic Party	9	5	55.6
Radical Liberal Party	7	3	42.9
Christian People's Party	4	1	25.0
Greenland and Faroes (2 seats each)	4	–	–
total	179	59	33.0

Source: data from *DKN Information, Newsletter special issue September 1991* (National Council of Women in Denmark)

In 1990 24.4% of Denmark's ordained ministers were women, but there were no women bishops and only three women deacons

The number of women MPs increased after the December 1990 election to 59 (33% of the total). There are 4 women ministers out of 19: Anne Birgitte Lundholt (industry and energy), Ester Larsen (health), Else Winther Andersen (social affairs) and Grete Fogh Rostbøll (cultural affairs). In the 1989 European Parliament elections, 6 of the 16 members elected were women (37.5%).

In the most recent municipal elections of 1989, women won 26.4% of municipal seats and 29% of county seats. 26.2% of city council representatives are women, and women are represented on every town council in Denmark. Women make up 29.4% of representatives on departmental councils; strongest proportions are People's Socialist Party (36.6%), Radical Left (33%) and Social Democrats (28.8%). One in 3 candidates in the 1989 municipal elections was a woman.

Three of Denmark's 70 ambassadors are women.

WOMEN AND EDUCATION

Percentage of women students by level of education and subject studied (1989)

basic vocational education

service-related	95.0
trade and office work	64.0
technical trades	32.0
iron and metal industries	7.0
total	**50.2**

upper secondary education

language studies	78.0
mathematics	46.0
total	**58.1**

higher education

shorter courses	83.0
medium courses	46.0
longer courses	45.0

Source: data from *Statistisk Årbog 1990*

A booklet called 'Girls and boys are of equal value' for children aged 4 to 10 was launched in 1985

About 80% of scientific teachers at universities are men, and only 5% of professors are women.

Courses in women's studies are available at all universities including Aalborg, Aarhus, Copenhagen, the Technical University of Denmark, Odense, and the Feminist Research Centre at Roskilde.

WOMEN AND DETENTION

Women as a % of those convicted of criminal offences involving sentences more serious than fines (1988)

all convictions	10.3
sex offences	2.4
all crimes of violence:	3.5
offences against public authorities	3.5
murder	0.0
attempted murder	33.3
assaulting an inoffensive person	2.3
other crimes of violence	4.4
all offences against property:	11.2
forgery	27.1
arson	14.4
housebreaking	3.4
theft	10.6
fraud	22.5
embezzlement	23.6
receiving stolen goods	13.7
robbery	5.2
malicious damage	2.0
other crimes against property	7.5
all other crimes:	17.0
narcotics	15.6

Source: data from *Statistisk Årbog 1990*

People convicted in 1988 by sex and age group

	% of women convicted	% of men convicted convicted	% of women in age group convicted
15–19	11.4	17.0	7.1
20–24	27.3	31.8	8.9
25–29	20.7	19.6	10.8
30–39	26.3	21.3	12.3
40–49	11.8	7.8	14.7
50+	2.5	2.4	10.4
all ages	100.0	100.0	10.3

Source: data from *Statistisk Årbog 1990*

SOURCES

Abortion Laws in Europe, Planned Parenthood in Europe, Vol 18
No 1, Spring 1989 (Supplement, amended April 1990); *Childcare
in the European Communities 1985–90* (Women of Europe
Supplement No 51); *Comparative Study on rules governing
working conditions in the member states* (Commission of the
European Communities); *Danish Equal Status Council Annual
Report 1990; Data on Denmark 1990* (Danmarks Statistik);
Demographic Statistics 1990 (Eurostat); *DKN Information,
Newsletter special issue,* September 1991 (National Council of
Women in Denmark); *Earnings in Industry and Services*
(Eurostat); *Factsheet Denmark, Electing the Folketing* (Royal
Danish Ministry of Foreign Affairs); *Employment in Europe
1991* (Commission of the European Communities); *Europa
World Year Book 1990* (31st edition); *Health Care Systems and
Professional Organisations in the European Community,
Information note – Europe* (British Medical Association); Health
For All 2000 Indicator Presentation System (World Health
Organisation Regional Office for Europe); *Kvinnor och män i
Norden 1988; Labour Force Survey (Results 1989)* (Eurostat);
*Les Actions Positives en Faveur des Femmes en Europe
Occidentale* (Institut Syndical Europeen); *Out In Europe* (Peter
Tatchell, for Channel 4 Television); *Pocket World in Figures* (The
Economist); *Positive action and the constitutional and legislative
hindrances to its implementation in the member states of the
Council of Europe* (Council of Europe); *Proposition de Directive
Du Conseil concernant la protection au travail de la femme
enceinte ou venant d'accoucher* (Commission of the European
Communities); Royal Danish Embassy; *Social Protection in the
Member States of the Community* (Commission of the European
Community Directorate General on Employment, Industrial
Relations and Social Affairs); *Statistisk Årbog 1990; Third World
Guide 91/92* (Instituto del Tercer Mundo); *Women of Europe*
(Nos 61, 63, 67, 68, 69); *Women and Men in the Nordic
Countries* (Christina Österberg and Birgitta Hedman, Nordic
Council of Ministers); *Women's Studies and Research on Women
in the Nordic Countries* (ed Mie Berg Simonson and Mona
Eliasson for Nordic Forum)

LETTERS FROM DENMARK

Jette Donvang of the Danish Women's Society, Bagsvaerd

In terms of equal rights, Danish women are probably
far better off than most other countries. We feel,
however, that there is still a lot to fight for. We have
not got equal pay for equal work, despite a law about
it. Far from it. Somehow it seems to be getting worse.

We want more representation in politics, boards, councils and committees. Children, housekeeping etc is still too much women's responsibility. Until this has changed, we can't expect equality.

Tine Lise Jacobsen, aged 25, and Ruth Pedersen, aged 50, from Copenhagen

There is a tendency for women to wait to have children until after their education and they are economically stable – usually in their late 20s or early 30s. Of about 60,000 births yearly, 44,000 are to working women and of these there are an estimated 2,000 women who are fired due to their six-month maternity leave (even though they are protected by law). Women get a subsidy, whether previously employed or not. Fathers are entitled to 14 days, but the higher his position the less likely he is to take the full 14 days for fear of being fired. As far as child care goes, in the Copenhagen commune, it takes from 12 to 17 months before there is an opening. Other, 'richer' communes, have less of a waiting list.

ADDRESSES

Royal Danish Embassy, 55 Sloane Street, London SW1X 9SR.
Tel: 071 235 1225

The Council for Equal Treatment, Ligestillingsraadet,
Frederiksgade 21,1, 1265 København K. Tel: (45 1) 33 92 33 11

Danmarks Statistik, Sejrøgade 11, 2100 København Ø.
Tel: (45 1) 31 29 82 22

Kvindeligt Arbejderforbund i Danmark (Women Workers'
Union of Denmark), Ewaldsgade 3, 2200 København N.
Tel: (45 1) 31 39 31 15

Dansk Kvinders Nationalråd (Danish Women's Society),
Niels Hemmingsensgade 10, 1153 København K.
Tel: (45 1) 33 12 80 87

Foreningen for Familieplanlægning (family planning service),
Aurehøjvej 2, 2900 Hellerup. Tel: (45 31) 62 56 88

LBL (Landsforeningen for Bøsser og Lesbiske) (lesbian
and gay rights), PO Box 1023, DK-1007 København K.
Tel: (45 1) 13 19 48

Finland

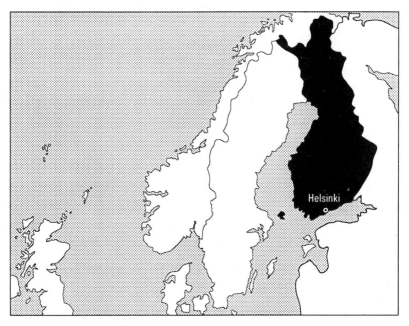

- **Population** 5.1 million, 52% female
- **Area** 338,144 sq km
- **Population density** 15.1 people sq km
- **GDP 1988** Finnish markka 438 billion (£65.1 billion)
- **GDP per capita** £13,117
- **GDP per capita in purchasing power parity** (UK=100) 106
- **Public spending as % of GNP:** defence 1.7% (1986); education 5.9% (1986); health 6.0% (1987)
- **Consumer price index** 1980 = 100; 1989 = 185
- **Currency is the markka** 1989 £1 = FIM6.55; US$1 = FIM4.06

The Republic of Finland's single-chamber parliament is the Eduskunta, which has 200 members elected by proportional representation for 4 years. The president, who has supreme executive power, is directly elected for 6 years. The president appoints the cabinet, which is headed by the prime minister.

Finland has 12 provinces administered by an appointed governor. The mainly Swedish-speaking residents of the Åland Islands also elect a local parliament (Landsting), which has power over internal affairs. Local government is based on 461 municipalities.

Just over 6% of the population is Swedish, which is the second official language after Finnish. There are an estimated 10,000 Sami people in Lapland (0.2% of the population).

One quarter of Finland lies north of the Arctic Circle. As a legacy of the Ice Age Finland is still emerging from the sea and grows by 7 sq km each year. It has more lakes, in relation to its size, than any other country in the world – a total of 187,888. 65% of Finland is forest, and only 8% is cultivated.

IMMIGRATION AND RESIDENCE RIGHTS

Foreigners who want to work in Finland should obtain a work permit before arriving. Citizens of the other Nordic countries and foreigners permanently living in Finland do not require work permits.

Residence permits are required for stays of over 3 months. They are granted to spouses of Finns or those who have a child with a Finnish citizen or have lived with a Finn for a year elsewhere. If a relationship or marriage lasts less than 2 years, the residence permit is not continued unless the foreigner has a child in Finland, is pregnant, has not completed a course of study, or is a victim of domestic violence. Foreigners do not have the same rights as Finns to own land or houses.

Foreigners can apply for citizenship if they have lived permanently in Finland for 5 years and know Finnish

or Swedish. Spouses of Finns and former citizens
of Finland or other Nordic countries can apply for
citizenship more quickly.

Children become citizens at birth if the mother is
Finnish, if the father is Finnish and married to the
mother, if born in Finland and not a citizen of another
country. Children with Finnish fathers and foreign
mothers who are not married can apply for citizenship
through their guardians. Children normally also have
the citizenship of the foreign parent.

EQUAL RIGHTS

The Equality Act of 1987 aims to prevent sex
discrimination and to promote equality between
women and men. The Equality Ombudsperson
supervises compliance with the Act and publishes
information on equality legislation. The Equality
Board deals with cases of non-compliance and advises
courts on compensation. It also has powers to prohibit
discriminatory practice under penalty of fine. The
services of the ombudsperson and the board are free.
The law also forbids discrimination on the grounds
of race, nationality, ethnic origin and religion.

BIRTH, LIFE AND DEATH

Breakdown of population by sex and age group (1000s) (1987)

	all		women		men		% of women in age group
	no	%	no	%	no	%	
0–14	952.2	18.6	465.7	17.5	486.5	19.8	48.9
15–24	688.8	13.5	337.4	12.7	351.4	14.3	49.0
25–39	1,201.9	23.5	585.8	22.1	616.1	25.1	48.7
40–59	1,209.2	23.7	606.4	22.8	602.8	24.6	50.2
60–74	621.0	12.2	367.0	13.8	254.0	10.5	59.1
75+	436.1	8.5	292.7	11.0	143.4	5.8	67.1
all	5,109.2	100.0	2,655.0	100.0	2454.2	100.0	52.0

Source: data from *Finnish Report on the United Nations Convention on the Elimination of all Forms
of Discrimination Against Women to the CEDAW Committee, Vienna 28.2 – 2.3.1989* (Ministry of
Social Affairs and Health, Finland)

60% of families live in towns, 40% in the countryside. A quarter of Finns live in very sparsely populated areas (centres of less than 200 people).

Population density by region (1988)

region	area sq km*	population	pop density per sq km*
Uudenmaan	9,898	1,226,344	123.9
Turun-Porin	22,170	715,608	32.3
Ahvenanmaan	1,527	24,045	15.7
Hämeen	17,010	684,431	40.2
Kymen	10,783	335,922	31.2
Mikkelin	16,342	207,675	12.7
Kuopion	16,511	255,893	15.5
Pohjois-Karjalan	17,782	176,189	9.9
Vaasan	26,447	444,060	16.8
Keski-Suomen	16,230	249,504	15.4
Oulun	56,866	434,847	7.7
Lapin	93,057	199,841	2.1
total	304,623	4,954,359	16.3

* excludes inland water which totals 33,522 sq km

Source: *Europa World Year Book 1990* (31st edition)

Births and deaths per 1,000 population (1988)

birth rate	12.7
death rate	9.9
infant mortality rate per 1,000 live births	6.0
marriage rate	5.3
life expectancy (women)	78.8
life expectancy (men)	71.0
fertility rate per woman	1.7

Source: data from *Demographic Statistics 1990* (Eurostat)

Marriage and divorce	1900	1950	1980	1987
% unmarried women	58.9	50.8	41.6	41.1
% unmarried men	63.0	55.6	48.9	49.1
% married women	33.2	38.0	42.7	41.5
% married men	34.0	41.2	45.5	44.1
% widowed and divorced women	7.9	11.2	15.7	17.0
% widowed and divorced men	3.0	3.2	5.6	6.8

Source: data from *Finnish Report on the United Nations Convention on the Elimination of all Forms of Discrimination Against Women to the CEDAW Committee, Vienna 28.2 – 2.3.1989* (Ministry of Social Affairs and Health, Finland)

Under marriage law both partners own the property they had before marriage and all other property acquired in their own name(s). Exceptions are the family home, furniture and belongings of their children. However, couples planning to marry can draw up marriage agreements covering property ownership which will be applied in law.

Divorce is granted after a court hearing followed by a 6-month reconciliation period, even if one partner does not want a divorce. Shared property is divided equally unless specified differently in a marriage agreement or in cases where the marriage has lasted less than 5 years in which case the court can decide the division.

Corporal punishment of children is banned Women have had equal rights to inheritance since 1878. If a child is born to a married woman, her husband is legally assumed to be the father. If she is unmarried the local authority welfare board has a responsibility to establish paternity, but in practice will not do so if the mother opposes this. Only when paternity is established do children born outside marriage have equal rights to those born in marriage. Children have the right to receive maintenance from their parents until their eighteenth birthdays.

LESBIAN RIGHTS

Same-sex relationships were illegal until 1971. The age of consent for same-sex relationships is 18, compared with 16 for heterosexuals. The promotion of same-sex relationships is illegal under Section 20:9.2 of the penal code, which forbids 'public encouragement of fornication between members of the same sex'.

WOMEN AND HEALTH CARE

The national health insurance scheme covers all residents. The services of public doctors and other medical personnel, including physiotherapists, are free; however patients pay a small part of the costs of hospital treatment and some prescribed drugs. Drugs for chronic illnesses are free.

Patients first contact their local health centres or private practitioners, who will refer them to a specialist or hospital if necessary. Dental care is free up until the age of 17. In 1988 there was 1 doctor for every 428 people.

Circulating information on contraception became a punishable act in 1889

Child health clinic services, available since 1925, are used by 80% of Finns. They provide free services from the start of pregnancy until the child starts school. They arrange maternity and paternity training courses, emphasising that child-care responsibilities are equal for men and women. Almost 80% of fathers attend the delivery of the first child. There are school nurses, doctors and dentists. Sex education is part of the school curriculum.

Major indicators for women's health (1988)

maternal deaths (all causes) per 100,000 live births	11.06
maternal deaths (abortion) per 100,000 live births	3.16
ratio of abortions to 1,000 live births (all ages) (1987)	217.20
% of all live births to mothers under 20 (1987)	4.37
% of all live births to mothers aged 35+ (1987)	8.82
deaths from cancer of the cervix (age 0–64) per 100,000 women (1987)	0.94
deaths from malignant neoplasm female breast (age 0–64) per 100,000 women	16.65
deaths from trachea/bronchus/lung cancer (age 0–64) per 100,000 women	4.02
deaths from trachea/bronchus/lung cancer (age 0–64) per 100,000 men	27.64
deaths from diseases of the circulatory system (age 0–64) per 100,000 women	44.85
deaths from diseases of the circulatory system (age 0–64) per 100,000 men	170.64
deaths from suicide and self-inflicted injury per 100,000 women	11.30
deaths from suicide and self-inflicted injury per 100,000 men	44.95

Source: data from Health for All 2000 Indicator Presentation System (World Health Organisation Regional Office For Europe)

Abortion and contraception: Legal on medical, ethical and eugenic grounds since 1950, and on social grounds since 1970. Available up to 12 weeks if there is a risk to the woman's mental health, in cases of rape or other sexual crimes, or on social grounds with the approval of two doctors and the State Medical Board. Available up to 20 weeks if there is a risk to the woman's health or of foetal handicap. Abortion is always available to women under 17 or over 40. It is free under national health insurance though women pay hospital fees of FIM60 a day. Finland has the lowest abortion rate in the Nordic countries (10 per 1,000 fertile women). There are reportedly very few illegal abortions.

Family planning advice is free from health-care centres. Condoms are on sale, but a doctor's appointment is necessary for a prescription for the pill or for an IUD to be inserted.

PARENTAL PAY, LEAVE AND BENEFITS (1989)

Maternity and parental leave and pay: 105 days' maternity leave plus 170 days' parental leave which can be taken by either parent, making a total of 263 days (plus 60 for multiple births).

Women must take 30 days before the due date. Leave is usually paid at 80% of earned income and the minimum (covered by health insurance) was FIM1,157 a month after tax in 1989. Parental pay is granted to adoptive parents for a total of 234 days.

Paternity leave: Fathers increasingly are taking one to two weeks' leave after the birth.

Maternity benefit: Granted to all women who have been pregnant for 180 days. 80% choose to receive this benefit as a 'maternity pack' (including baby clothes and equipment, and contraceptives) as its value is double the financial alternative (FIM640 in 1989). Granted to Finnish mothers living abroad and foreign women residents.

Right of return to work: Mothers have the right to look after their children for 3 years and return to their former job, or a job of the same quality and level.

Time off to care for sick children: Four days' leave allowed to arrange for child care or to take care of a sick child under 10.

CHILD-CARE PROVISION (1989–90)

0–6 year olds: Since 1990, families with children under 3 have been guaranteed a municipal day-care place or a home-care allowance of FIM1,500 a month. Parents can also cut their daily hours and claim a partial home-care allowance to compensate for loss of earnings. Municipal day-care covers childminding and kindergartens. 5% of kindergarten places are private. Just over 40% of children from 1 to 6 years have places in municipal day care.

The 1987 Toy Agreement expresses a wish to refrain from manufacturing, importing and selling war toys

Primary school (7 years up): Education is compulsory between the ages of 7 and 15. For the first 2 years, hours are 21 a week, then 25 for years 3 and 4. The school year is 190 days, and there is a break from the beginning of June to mid August. Pupils in grades 1 to 9 in comprehensive schools get free cooked school lunches and some authorities also provide free meals for older children. Native language instruction is offered in some schools. Classes are taught in Finnish and Swedish. In 1988 the pupil to teacher ratio in primary schools was 14:1.

Contributions to child-care costs: There is an income related charge for day care; the poorest families receive free child care. See 0–6 year olds for details of home-care allowances.

STATE BENEFITS (1989–90)

Retirement pensions: Retirement age is 65 in the private sector and 63 in the public sector. Pensions are made up of a basic flat-rate payment plus an earnings related pension, up to a maximum of 60% of pay after 40 years' service. The minimum pension was FIM2,069 a month in 1989. Pensions of more than the flat-rate minimum are taxable.

The Equality Act is being amended so women can either continue to take early retirement or are guaranteed work until age 63 or 65. In 1984 41% of all female pensioners had only their basic state pensions to live on compared with 14% of male pensioners.

Early retirement pensions: Paid at age 60–64 to those who stop working. This enables spouses to retire at the same time if one is a few years older. Since 1986, a special invalidity pension has been paid at 55 to those with a reduced capacity to work, for example because of poor health, ageing, or work-related stress. More women than men apply for these pensions. Early retirement is common – in 1989 the average age of pension entitlement was 59.

Part-time pension: Introduced in the private sector in 1987 and paid to employees aged 60–64 who transfer to part-time work as compensation for loss of income.

Survivors' pensions: Currently being reformed to grant equal rights to widowers (widows had been in a better position, with the exception of state employees and seafarers).

A 1917 decree gave women the right to 4 weeks' maternity leave and women in late pregnancy the right not to do dangerous work

Disability benefit: Paid at the same rate as the basic flat-rate retirement pension. Additional payments can be made depending on income from other pensions and there is also a discretionary housing allowance.

Sickness benefits: A daily allowance of 80% of earnings, covered by sickness insurance. Paid as a minimum allowance of FIM1,157 for those with no income from work. Accident insurance also provides 80% of pay plus the costs of treatment in cases of industrial accidents, occupational diseases and accidents travelling to and from work.

Unemployment: Provided by trade union unemployment funds and providing average unemployment benefit of 60% of earnings paid as a daily allowance for 2 years. After that the unemployed can claim a flat-rate daily allowance (FIM56 after tax in 1989) from public funds. The flat-rate allowance is also paid to those who are not trade union members and is paid without time limit. The long-term unemployed over 60 can also receive an unemployment pension.

Child benefit: Monthly payments average FIM300 for each child, though the benefit amount is larger for larger families. Child benefit is not means-tested and is paid up until the age of 17. Lone parents can get an additional child maintenance allowance.

Living allowance: Those whose income from pay or benefits falls below a certain level qualify for a basic living allowance of FIM1,138 and up a month.

WOMEN AND EMPLOYMENT

Statutory rights: Normal working hours should not exceed 8 hours in any 24 hours or 40 hours a week. Overtime is regulated and may not exceed 20 hours in a 2-week period if done in addition to normal day work, or 16 hours in a 2-week period if done on rest days. Overtime is paid at 150% of basic rates and 200% on Sundays.

Prostitution is not a crime, though pimping is

Employees are entitled to 2 days' annual leave for every month of employment, and 25 days' leave after 12 months of employment. Annual leave must be on full pay, though many collective agreements entitle employees to an additional holiday payment. Employers must provide references.

Women are banned by law from underground manual work in mining. The 1946 Hours of Work Act, banning women in industry from nightwork, was repealed early in 1989.

There is no minimum wage but in most sectors minimum rates of pay are set through collective agreements. People under 20 unemployed for 5 months must be given 6 months' employment by their municipalities.

Women in employment (1990)

	women		men	
	no (1000s)	%	no (1000s)	%
labour force participation	1,213	72.5	1,343	78.9
employed	1,179	47.8	1,289	52.2
employees who are part time	133	11.3	61	4.7
unemployed	34	2.8	54	4.0
% of total unemployed	–	38.6	–	61.4

Source: data from Central Statistical Office, Finland

Part-time work: In 1989 68.4% of part-time workers were women. They are entitled to the same rights to paid leave as full-time workers if they work 35 hours a month for a year and the same pension rights if they work 20 hours a week or earn over a certain amount.

Employment by industrial sector (1988)

	women		men	
	no (1000s)	%	no (1000s)	%
agriculture and forestry	74	35.7	133	64.3
manufacturing	186	33.5	369	66.4
construction	19	9.2	187	90.8
trade	221	56.1	173	43.9
transport and communications	50	27.9	129	72.1
finance	135	56.5	104	43.5
services	492	71.7	194	28.3

Source: data from Central Statistical Office, Finland

Work hours: Average weekly hours worked are 35.9 in female-dominated areas and 40.9 in male-dominated. Women are more likely to work irregular hours, including shiftwork and periodical work.

Where women work (1987): 10% were employed by the state, 33% by local authorities and 57% by private employers. 8% of women worked in technology, science and humanities; 25% in administrative, office and accounting work; 22% in services; 12% in industry; 9% in commercial work; 3% in transport and communications and 1% in agriculture and forestry. Of rural women, 46% worked in the service sector, 39% in agriculture and 14% in industry. More than one in five farmers' wives (21%) worked outside the farm.

Most common occupations by sex, showing percentage share (1989)

women	% share of group	men	% share of group
secretaries, typists and general office workers	91.2	building workers	97.4
shop assistants, supervisors	70.5	technicians	93.3
cleaners, hospital assistants	95.3	plumbers, platers and welders	92.5
nurses, laboratory and dental assistants	94.8	drivers of motor vehicles	96.6
chefs, cooks, kitchen staff and restaurant workers	89.8	toolmakers, fitters and machine repairers	98.2
teachers	61.8	electricity, electronic and telephone assemblers	83.6
bank and insurance workers	85.5	business executives	78.4
social welfare and day-care workers	93.9	shop assistants and supervisors	29.5
local authority home assistants and private day-care workers	99.6	sales reps and office sales staff	63.5
financial planners and accountancy staff	84.2	agriculture and forestry workers	79.5

Source: data from *Women and Men in Finland* (Central Statistical Office)

Sexual harassment: This is a matter of occupational health and safety by law. A 1987 survey showed that 34% of women had experienced sexual harassment at work in the previous two years. Occupational groups where highest levels of harassment of women were reported were police officers (70%), construction workers (60%) and journalists (44%).

Women's earnings compared to men's: Equal pay cases are dealt with under the Equality Act which states that equal pay must be given for work of equal value as well as for the same work. The International Labour Organisation Convention on Equal Pay was ratified in 1960. Employers were obliged to treat their workers equally from 1970 when the ILO Discrimination Convention was ratified and the Labour Protection Act amended. An additional legal responsibility on officials and employers to promote equality came into effect in 1987.

The earnings of full-time women workers are on average 78% of men's full-time earnings. Pay differences increase between the ages of 20 and 40, showing how the position of women is weakened by career breaks for family responsibilities.

In industry women's earnings range from 62% of men's in metal mining and extraction plants, and 74% in chemical manufacture to 85% in printing and binding, 89% in manufacturing of wood veneers and wooden houses, and 90% in carpentry and manufacture of furniture.

Among state employees women earn 71% as much as men in real estate, 75% in restaurants and hotels and 87% in agriculture, forestry and fishing. In the municipal sector the gap is widest at 67% in utilities, but narrows to 90% in recreational and cultural services and 96% in welfare institutions.

Equality bonus: Paid since 1988 according to the numbers of women employed. In some sectors this is given to the lowest paid workers, mainly benefiting women, though in others it is given to all employees.

Labour force participation of women aged 15–64 by number of children (1989)

	women in population (1000s)	women in labour force (1000s)	labour force participation rate
with no children under 18	988	624	63.1
with children under 18	670	572	85.3
1 child	307	266	86.6
2 children	261	228	87.5
3+ children	102	77	75.9
with children under 7	327	256	78.1
1 child	225	185	82.3
2+ children	102	71	69.0
total	**1,658**	**1,196**	**72.1**

Source: *Women and Men in Finland* (Central Statistical Office)

Taxation: Married couples have paid income tax separately since the mid 1970s. An overall tax reform is being carried out, which proposes that parents should choose which one benefits from child-care deductions. This is instead of expenses being deducted from the spouse with the largest income, usually the husband, as at present. The minister responsible for taxation is a woman.

WOMEN IN TRADE UNIONS

Wages and conditions are determined by free collective bargaining. Studies show better pay is considered to be a more important goal for women than men, but women consider job content and job satisfaction to be the most important feature of their work, compared to men who quote level of wages. Women form a slight majority of unionised wage earners.

Women's participation at assembly meetings, councils and boards of the four main trade union organisations

	SAK (1991)	TVK (1988)	AKAVA (1988)	STTK (1989)
% of women at assembly meetings	37.0	65.2	34.9	13.5
% of women on councils	39.8	67.7	–	13.7
% of women on boards	22.2	57.1	19.1	3.7

SAK = Central Union of Finnish Trade Organisations
TVK = Confederation of Salaried Employees
AKAVA = Confederation of Unions for Academic Professionals
STTK = Confederation of Technical Employee Organisations
Source: data from *Women and Men in Finland* (Central Statistical Office)

WOMEN AND POLITICS

In 1906 Finland became the first country in Europe where women won the vote, and the second in the world after New Zealand. The right to vote in parliamentary elections was followed in 1918 by the right to vote in local elections.

In 1907 Finland became the first country in the world to elect women to parliament when 19 women won seats. The first woman cabinet member was appointed in 1926.

In 1908, the first year women could vote, 60% of women compared with 69% of men cast their votes. Voting levels peaked between 1962 and 1966 at 84% for women and 86% for men. In the 1991 election 73.2% of women and 71.0% of men cast their votes.

In June 1991 Minister for Health and Social Affairs Eeva Kuuskoski became the first minister to give birth while in office

In the spring 1991 election, 77 of the 200 MPs elected were women, a record 38.5%. However, none of the 13 heads of government ministries is a woman. Within the ministries' 60 departments only one director general is a woman. Two of the 23 members of the supreme court are women (8.7%). Three (5.5%) of Finland's 55 ambassadors are women.

An amendment to the Equality Act sets out a goal that the number of either sex on government committees and municipal bodies should not be under 40%.

The first election after this goal was defined was the municipal local elections of 1989, with 27% of the councillors elected being women (31.5% in towns and 25% in rural areas). The number of women elected to local councils has increased from 7.6% in 1960 to 27.2% in 1988; in the same period the number of women candidates increased from 11.1% to 32.4%.

WOMEN AND EDUCATION

Pupils and students by school type and sex (1989)

	female %	male %
comprehensive schools	49	51
upper secondary schools	58	42
vocational schools and colleges	55	45
universities	54	46
total	51	49

Source: data from *Women and Men in Finland* (Central Statistical Office)

Percentage of women students by subject studied (1989)

vocational education institutions

humanities and aesthetics	70.6
teacher training	83.0
commerce and clerical	68.9
technology and natural science	15.4
transport and communication	13.6
medical and health	92.0
agriculture and forestry	32.3

universities

arts	75.8
education (class teaching)	82.2
education (kindergarten class teaching)	92.2
economics and business administration	45.4
technology and natural science	27.5
medicine	61.2
agriculture and forestry	42.5

Source: data from *Women and Men in Finland* (Central Statistical Office)

Women have outnumbered men in higher education since 1981. In 1985 13% of women and 11% of men (aged 22 years) received university-level education. 41% of post-graduate students were women. The most female-dominated field was home economics (93%) and the most male-dominated was engineering (86%). Courses in women's studies are available at the universities of Helsinki and Tampere, and are being introduced in Turku and Jyväskylä.

Financial support for students is made up of a study loan and a study benefit (non-repayable). The state pays interest repayments on study loans for former students who are pregnant or receiving parental leave or family allowance. Extra support for married students with young children is paid as benefit.

A quota system for entrance to teacher-training colleges which aimed to increase the numbers of male teachers and favoured men over women with better qualifications was abandoned in 1987 as it contravened the Equality Act. 90% of university teachers are men.

WOMEN AND DETENTION

The percentage of women among prisoners in 1988
was 3.2%. There were 5.9% of minors (age 21) and
young adults detained and 0.3% of foreigners.
Providing it is to the advantage of the child, mothers
can live with their babies in prison. In practice an
upper age limit for children of 2 years applies.

SOURCES

Abortion Laws in Europe, Planned Parenthood in Europe, Vol 18
No 1, Spring 1989 (Supplement, amended April 1990)
(International Planned Parenthood Federation, Europe Region);
Central Statistical Office of Finland; *Childhood in Finland*
(Central Union for Child Welfare in Finland); *Europa World
Year Book 1990* (31st edition); *Facts about Finland* (Ottava
Publishing); *Finnfacts 7–8/1988;* The Finnish Embassy; *Finnish
Report on the UN Convention on the Elimination of all Forms of
Discrimination Against Women to the CEDAW Committee,
Vienna 28.2 – 2.3.89* (Ministry of Social Affairs and Health,
Finland); *The Foreign Woman in Finland* (Ministry of Social
Affairs and Health); Health For All 2000 Indicator Presentation
System (World Health Organisation Regional Office For
Europe); *Initial Report of Finland on the Implementation of the
Convention on the Elimination of all Forms of Discrimination
Against Women* (1988); *Kvinnor och män i Norden 1988; Les
Actions Positives en Faveur des Femmes en Europe Occidentale*
(Institut Syndical Europeen); *Out In Europe* (Peter Tatchell, for
Channel 4 Television); *Pocket World in Figures* (The
Economist); *Prison Information Bulletin* June 1990 (Council of
Europe); *Social Security and Health Care in Finland* (Ministry of
Social Affairs and Health); *The Spirit of Finland – women in
Finland special issue* (Number 3, 1991); *Third World Guide
91/92* (Instituto del Tercer Mundo); *Women and Men in Finland*
(Central Statistical Office); *Women and Men in the Nordic
Countries* (Christina Österberg and Birgitta Hedman, Nordic
Council of Ministers); *Women of Europe* (No 69); *Women's
Studies and Research on Women in the Nordic Countries* (ed.
Mie Berg Simonson and Mona Eliasson for Nordic Forum);
Working in Finland (Työsuojeluhallitus, Työministeriö)

ADDRESSES

Embassy of Finland, 32 Grosvenor Gardens,
London SW1W 0DH. Tel: 071 235 9531

Council for Equality Between Men and Women, Ministry of
Social Affairs and Health, PO Box 267, 00171 Helsinki.
Tel: (358 0) 1601

Väestöliitto (family planning service), Kalevankatu 16, 00100
Helsinki 10. Tel: (358 0) 640 235

Central Statistical Office of Finland, Tilastokeskus,
Henkilötilastot, Annankatu 44, 00100 Helsinki

Central Organisation of Finnish Trade Unions, Suomen
Ammattiliittojen, Keskusjärjestö, Siltasaarenkatu 3a,
00530 Helsinki. Tel: (358 0) 77 211

SETA (Seksuaalinen Tasavertaisuus), (lesbian and gay rights),
PO Box 55, SF – 00531 Helsinki. Tel: (010 358 0) 76 9641

France

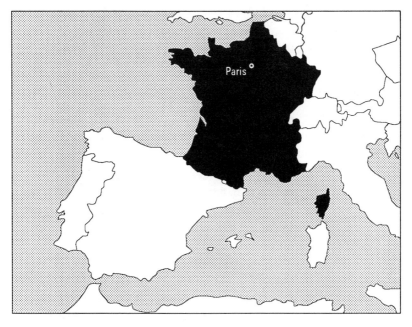

- **Population** 55.6 million, 51.3% female
- **Area** 543,965 sq km
- **Population density** 102.3 people sq km
- **GDP 1988** French francs 5,159 billion (£589 billion)
- **GDP per capita** £10,542
- **GDP per capita in purchasing power parity** (UK=100) 103
- **Public spending as % of GNP:** defence 3.9% (1986); education 5.9% (1986); health 6.6% (1987)
- **Consumer price index** 1980 = 100; 1989 = 180
- **Currency is the franc** 1989 £1 = FF9.3; US$1 = FF5.78

France has a 2-chamber parliament made up of the
312-member Senate and the 577-member National
Assembly. The Senate, elected for 9 years by an
electoral college, has 321 members representing
metropolitan France (which includes Corsica), overseas
territories and French nationals abroad. Members of
the National Assembly, including the 22 from overseas
territories, were elected by proportional representation
until 1988 when the government reintroduced direct
election for single-member constituencies, with the
victor needing an absolute majority to avoid a second
ballot. The National Assembly is elected for 5 years.

Executive power is held by the president who is
directly elected for 7 years. He or she appoints the
council of ministers, which is led by the prime minister.

Local government in metropolitan France is based on
21 administrative regions containing 96 departments.
Administrative and federal power is held by
departmental general council and regional assemblies.
Corsica has its own directly elected legislative assembly.

French is the main language and there are Breton and
Basque speaking minorities. 80% of the population is
Roman Catholic.

French overseas territories include the overseas
'départements' of French Guiana, Guadeloupe,
Martinique and Réunion (administered by elected
councils); the 'collectivités territoriales' of Mayotte
and St Pierre et Miquelon (administered by appointed
commissioners); and the territories of French
Polynesia, French Southern and Antarctic Territories,
New Caledonia and the Wallis and Futuna Islands
(administered by appointed high commissioners).

IMMIGRATION AND RESIDENCE RIGHTS

In 1982 France had 3,680,100 foreign residents,
42.8% of them women. 42.9% of foreign residents
were from other EC states, 8.1% from non-EC
European countries, 42.8% from African countries
and 8.6% from other countries.

EQUAL RIGHTS

The principle of equal rights for women and men was introduced into the preamble of the consitution in 1946. Positive action is recognised in law as a means of achieving equality and is specifically allowed with regard to employment. By law all private-sector employers must submit a report on the position of their women workers and it must include an equality action plan to enable women to catch up.

In 13th-century Beauvaisis a husband was permitted to beat his wife 'reasonably'

Responsibility for equality programmes rests with the Supreme Council on Equality at Work in conjunction with the Special Unit for Equality at Work. The Ministry for Women's Rights was created in 1981 and the Secretary of State for Women's Rights was established in 1988.

BIRTH, LIFE AND DEATH

Births, deaths, marriages and divorces (per 1,000 of population)

	1960	1970	1980	1985	1988
birth rate	18.0	16.8	14.9	14.0	13.8
% of births outside marriage	6.1	6.8	11.4	19.6	26.3
average age of mother at 1st birth	24.3[1]	23.8	24.9	25.9	26.6
infant mortality per 1,000 live births	27.4	18.2	10.0	8.3	7.8
fertility rate per woman	2.7	2.5	2.0	1.8	1.8
marriage rate	7.0	7.8	6.2	4.9	4.9
average age at marriage (women)	25.2	23.8	24.6	26.2	27.3
average age at marriage (men)	28.0	26.0	27.1	28.7	29.8
divorce rate	0.7	0.8	1.5	1.9	1.9
life expectancy (women)	73.6	75.9	78.4	80.0[2]	–
life expectancy (men)	66.9	68.4	70.2	71.8[2]	–
death rate	11.5	10.7	10.2	10.0	9.4

[1] 1965; [2] 1985–88

Source: data from *Demographic Statistics 1990* (Eurostat)

Breakdown of population by sex and age group (1000s) (1988)

	all no	all %	women no	women %	men nos	men %	% of women in age group
0–14	11,425.0	20.5	5,568.3	19.5	5,856.7	21.6	48.7
15–24	8,588.5	15.4	4,226.5	14.8	4,362.0	16.1	49.2
25–39	12,783.6	22.9	6,375.2	22.3	6,408.4	23.6	49.9
40–59	12,513.2	22.4	6,258.9	21.9	6,254.3	23.0	50.0
60–74	6,757.0	12.1	3,726.3	13.0	3,030.7	11.2	55.1
75+	3,683.1	6.6	2,433.0	8.5	1,250.1	4.6	66.1
all	55,750.4	100.0	28,588.2	100.0	27,162.2	100.0	51.3

Source: data from *Demographic Statistics 1990* (Eurostat)

Population, population density and population increase by region (1987)

region	pop (1000s)	% of total pop	pop density per sq km	natural increase per 1,000	net migration per 1,000	total increase per 1,000
Ile de France	10,289.6	18.5	856.6	8.1	-2.4	5.7
Champagne-Ardenne	1,359.0	2.4	53.1	5.1	-4.4	0.7
Picardie	1,779.9	3.2	91.8	5.6	-2.4	3.2
Haute-Normandie	1,705.1	3.1	138.4	6.5	-1.1	5.3
Centre du Bassin Parisien	2,340.7	4.2	59.8	3.0	2.2	5.2
Basse-Normandie	1,382.4	2.5	78.6	4.9	-2.2	2.7
Bourgogne	1,612.3	2.9	51.1	1.5	0.6	2.0
Pas de Calais	3,928.3	7.1	16.4	6.7	-7.0	-0.3
Lorraine	2,323.8	4.2	98.7	-5.2	7.5	2.3
Alsace	1,609.6	2.9	94.4	4.8	0.4	5.2
Franche-Comté	1,088.1	2.0	67.2	-4.6	4.8	0.2
Pays de la Loire	3,048.5	5.5	95.0	4.8	0.9	5.6
Bretagne	2,768.0	5.0	101.7	2.4	1.1	3.5
Poitou-Charentes	1,595.6	2.9	61.8	1.2	2.8	3.9
Aquitaine	2,730.4	4.9	66.1	0.6	3.7	4.3
Midi-Pyrénées	2,373.4	4.3	52.3	0.3	2.5	2.7
Limousin	733.3	1.3	43.3	-3.7	0.7	-3.0
Rhône-Alpes	5,189.9	9.3	118.8	5.4	0.8	6.1
Auvergne	1,328.8	2.4	51.1	-0.5	-0.7	-1.3
Languedoc-Roussillon	2,066.7	3.7	75.5	1.0	11.6	12.6
Provence-Alpes-Côte d'Azur	4,130.4	7.4	131.5	2.5	5.9	8.4
Corse	246.7	0.4	28.4	0.8	3.2	4.1
France	55,630.5	100.0	102.3	4.3	-0.1	4.2

Source: data from *Demographic Statistics 1990* (Eurostat)

One-parent households in 1988 accounted for 7% of households with a child aged 0–4 and 11% of households with a child aged 5–9.

LESBIAN RIGHTS

In 1982 a common age of consent of 15 was introduced (previously there had been higher ages for homosexual relationships introduced by the pro-Nazi government in 1942). Same-sex relationships are no longer mentioned in the penal code. Anti-discrimination laws were introduced in 1985 to protect lesbians and gay men in areas of employment and access to goods and services.

WOMEN AND HEALTH CARE

Health care is funded by insurance contributions and is part of the social security system. The 3 main funds cover salaried employees, farmers and agricultural workers, and the self-employed. A number of other special funds cover the rest of the population.

World champion Catherine Marsal of France won the EC's first women's cycling race in September 1990

Patients can choose their doctor and can consult a specialist without being referred by a GP. Most doctors charge fees agreed by their professional organisations and the insurance bodies, in return for contributions to their own sickness and pension funds. Doctors can, however, choose to set their own fees and forfeit these benefits.

Patients are reimbursed for 70%–75% of the costs of consultations and medicines, though some people with chronic ailments are exempt. It is possible to take out insurance cover against these costs. Hospital-stay costs are paid direct by social security, though patients must contribute except in cases of pregnancy or industrial injury.

There are 4 compulsory ante-natal check-ups but the government wants to increase this to 7. In 1988 there was 1 doctor for every 433 people.

Major indicators for women's health (1988)

maternal deaths (all causes) per 100,000 live births	9.34
maternal deaths (abortion) per 100,000 live births	0.39
ratio of abortions to 1,000 live births (all ages) (1987)	210.00
% of all live births to mothers under 20	2.59
% of all live births to mothers aged 35+	11.03
deaths from cancer of the cervix (age 0–64) per 100,000 women	1.79
deaths from malignant neoplasm female breast (age 0–64) per 100,000 women	17.80
deaths from trachea/bronchus/lung cancer (age 0–64) per 100,000 women	3.73
deaths from trachea/bronchus/lung cancer (age 0–64) per 100,000 men	35.69
deaths from diseases of the circulatory system (age 0–64) per 100,000 women	21.74
deaths from diseases of the circulatory system (age 0–64) per 100,000 men	70.16
deaths from suicide and self-inflicted injury per 100,000 women	10.99
deaths from suicide and self-inflicted injury per 100,000 men	29.91

Source: data from Health for All 2000 Indicator Presentation System (World Health Organisation Regional Office For Europe)

Abortion and contraception: Abortion is available on request up to 10 weeks after consulting a doctor and a 1-week wait. Girls under 18 must have parental consent. It is available up to the second trimester with a certificate from 2 doctors where there is a risk to a woman's life or physical health or a risk to foetal health or of foetal handicap. Women are reimbursed 80% of abortion costs. Medical staff may refuse to perform abortions on conscientious grounds. In December 1990 the state council decided that the abortion law was not contrary to the European Convention on Human Rights. The number of abortions carried out fell between 1981 and 1986 and has been stable since 1986.

From January 1991 advertising for contraceptives came under the same conditions as for medicines. Previously advertising was allowed only for condoms as a way of preventing sexually transmitted diseases.

Since February 1990 medical treatment for infertility has come under the social security system, a move that has limited the sometimes very high fees.

PARENTAL PAY, LEAVE AND BENEFITS (1989–90)

Maternity leave and pay: 16 weeks, including 6 that must be taken before the birth, paid at 84% of earnings. For third and subsequent children, women get an extra 2 weeks before and 8 weeks after the birth. Two extra weeks are given for multiple births, with an additional 10 weeks for any subsequent multiple births.

Birth grants: An allowance of FF813 a month is paid from the fourth month of pregnancy to the third month after the birth, for each child. The allowance continues as a means-tested benefit until the child is 3.

Nursing mothers: Women are entitled to 1 hour a day off work to breastfeed their child up to the age of 12 months.

Maternity leave was introduced in 1909, giving women 8 weeks' leave

Parental and paternity leave: Leave is available until a child is 3 and can be taken full time or part time (parents can share leave, both working part time). Leave is unpaid, unless 1 parent is unemployed and there are 3 or more children, when a flat-rate benefit, worth FF2,578 a month in 1989, is paid.

Time off to care for sick children: No statutory right, but the public sector allows 12 days leave to all women and men who are widowed or divorced. In the private sector many collective agreements provide for this leave (44% in 1984).

CHILD-CARE PROVISION (1989–90)

Under 3s: 20% are in publicly funded places, with just over half of these in pre-primary schooling and the rest in nurseries, kindergartens or creches. Apart from pre-primary schooling most places are provided by local authorities. Best provision of pre-primary schooling is in large towns. Most child care (40-45%) for children under 3 with employed parents is private. There are an estimated 1.2 million children under 3 with working parents.

3–5 year olds: 95% are in pre-primary schooling (8.30 to 16.30 with a 2-hour lunch break, open Saturdays and closed Wednesdays).

Primary school (6 years up): 8.30 to 16.30, with a 2-hour lunch break. Most schools provide supervised meals during the break. Schools are open Saturdays and closed Wednesdays. The school year runs from September to June. In 1988 the pupil to teacher ratio in primary schools was 19:1.

On 5 September 1990 the Cour de Cassation ruled for the first time that a husband was guilty of raping his wife

Outside school hours care: When available, this is from 7.30 to 18.30 including Wednesdays and holidays in recreation centres normally attached to schools. Used by 10%–15% of 3–5 year olds.

Contributions to child-care costs: Parents pay a proportion of the costs of care for children under 3, according to income and family size (14% for 1 child, but at a lower rate for more children). Subsidies are paid to employed parents paying for care for a child under 3 in their own home (FF2,200 a month) and to parents paying for private care for a child under 6 (FF450 a month, though take-up of the benefit is low). Parents of at least 3 children who 'interrupt activities' – i.e. interrupt their working lives or further education – to educate a child under 3 receive a monthly allowance of FF2,524 full time and FF1,262 half time. Parents can claim a tax reduction on child-care costs for children under 6 of 25% (up to FF3,750 for each child).

There is a means-tested allowance of FF354 paid at the start of the school year for school-age children.

STATE BENEFITS (1989–90)

Retirement pension: Normal retirement age is 60 for women and men. Full pensions of 50% of earnings (up to an annual earnings ceiling of FF129,600) are paid after $37^1/_2$ years of contributions, and the minimum full pension is FF33,261 a year. There is a means-tested supplement of FF4,000 if the pensioner's marriage partner is aged 65, and an additional 10% for pensioners who brought up 3 or more children.

A poll in France in January 1990 found that 52% thought women held too little political power with 79% wanting more women candidates

Mothers are credited with 2 years of insurance for each child. Pensions are adjusted each January and July by law. Normally earnings are forbidden.

Survivors' pensions: The spouse must have been insured for 3 months for the surviving marriage partner to receive these pensions.

Reversion pensions are paid to surviving marriage partners of old age pensioners who have insufficient means, are aged 55 or over, and whose marriage lasted for at least 2 years. Invalid survivors' pensions are paid to surviving marriage partners of old age pensioners who are disabled and aged 55 or over. Old age survivors' pensions are paid to surviving marriage partners aged 55 or over.

All of these are paid at 52% of the pension of the person who died (minimum is FF14,800 a year). There is a 10% supplement for those who have brought up 3 children, and survivors who care for a child receive FF424 a month for each one. The invalid survivor's pension is the only one discontinued on remarriage. A means-tested pension is available to those who are under 55 if they brought up at least 1 child.

When the supply of labour fell during the Black Death, women grape pickers in Languedoc received 80% of men's wages, instead of their customary 50%

Death grant: Worth a minimum of 1% of annual earnings for insured people who die and have worked or been on benefit for 120 hours in the previous month.

Sickness benefit: To qualify, workers must have a certain number of contributions or work hours. People out of hospital receive 50% of earnings (66% from day 31 with 3 children). If in hospital, benefit is 20% with no dependants and 50% with 2 children. Benefit, which is pegged to wage rises, is paid for up to 360 days in a 3-year period but this is extended for 'protracted sickness'. In addition, there is a means-tested allowance for handicapped adults of FF2,762 a month.

Invalidity: Paid to workers with 12 months of contributions and 800 hours of work who cannot earn more than one-third of normal earnings for their jobs and region. Benefit is paid until the age of 60 when an old age pension is paid.

Those who are still able to work receive 30% of their average earnings, while those unable to work receive 50%. There is a supplement of 40% for those who require the help of another person (subject to a minimum of FF51,561 a year).

Family benefits: A means-tested benefit (family complement) of FF737 a month is paid to families with 1 child under 3 and to families with at least 3 children. In addition, there is a family allowance of FF566 for the second child and FF725 for later children. There are also supplements of FF159 for second and later children over the age of 10, and of FF283 for those over 15.

Tax records from Paris in 1300 show that of 200 crafts listed, between 80 and 90 had women and men members, and 12 were all-female

Single parents receive an allowance to bring their income up to a guaranteed minimum of FF2,655.27 a month, plus FF885 for each child.

Supplement for handicapped children is FF566 each, and the severely handicapped qualify for a constant care allowance of FF1,274 a month and a daily help allowance of FF424 a month.

Benefit is paid until the age of 17, or 20 for those in training or education, girls at home and in cases of serious infirmity. (For school and child-care benefits see Child-care Provision section.)

Unemployment: Those with 3 to 6 months of contributions receive 30% of daily wages (minimum of FF89 a day). Workers with at least 6 months of contributions receive 40.4% of daily wages (minimum is FF119). Benefit runs from 3 months to 60 months, depending on contributions, and there is a reduced allowance at the end of the entitlement. The long-term unemployed can claim a daily allowance of FF68 (more for young people, those over 57½ and single women).

WOMEN AND EMPLOYMENT

Statutory rights: The working week is limited to 39 hours, though this can be extended to 44 hours by collective agreement. Overtime is restricted to 9 hours a week, or 130 hours a year, unless higher levels are authorised. Paid annual leave is 30 days and there are 11 statutory public holidays.

In 1991 the national minimum wage at age 18 was FF32.60 an hour (90% at 17 and 80% at 16). This is indexed to prices. An estimated third of workers receive a thirteenth month bonus at Christmas. Wages cannot be seized in full by creditors.

Employment and unemployment (1989)

	% women	% men
economic activity rate	46.0	65.4
employed working part time	23.6	3.5
labour force who are employers or self-employed	7.1	16.4
labour force who are family workers	5.8	0.9
unemployment rate	12.6	7.3
youth unemployment rate (age 14–24)	23.1	16.2
unemployed who have been unemployed for 12 months or more	49.8	45.9
all unemployed by sex	57.3	42.7

Source: data from *Labour Force Survey (Results 1989)* (Eurostat)

Employment by industrial sector (1000s) (1989)

	women		men		women as % of workforce
	no	%	no	%	
agriculture	525	5.7	978	7.8	34.9
all industry	1,595	17.4	4,957	39.8	24.3
energy and water	54	0.6	226	1.8	19.3
mineral extraction and chemicals	167	1.8	513	4.1	24.6
metal manufacturing and engineering	437	4.8	1,558	12.5	27.3
other manufacturing industry	801	8.7	1,159	9.3	40.9
building and civil engineering	135	1.5	1,502	12.0	8.2
all services	7,039	76.9	6,535	52.4	51.9
distributive trades and hotels	1,673	18.3	1,998	16.0	45.6
transport and communication	338	3.7	963	7.7	26.0
banking, finance and insurance	929	10.1	980	7.9	48.7
public administration	937	10.2	1,089	8.7	46.2
other services	3,162	34.5	1,505	12.1	67.8
total*	9,205	100.0	12,542	100.0	42.3

* includes 45,000 women and 71,000 men whose industrial sector was not stated.

Source: data from *Labour Force Survey (Results 1989)* (Eurostat)

Part-time workers: In 1989 83.3% of part-time workers were women. Part-time workers have the same rights as full-time workers.

Women's earnings as a % of men's in industry (October 1987)

	manual hourly earnings	non-manual monthly earnings
chemical industry	77.9	66.0
all metal manufacture and engineering	83.8	65.9
mechanical engineering	81.9	63.8
electrical engineering	86.0	65.8
food, drink and tobacco	80.6	61.0
clothing and footwear manufacture	85.4	65.5
printing and publishing	74.1	62.8
all manufacturing industry	79.5	65.1
all industry	80.8	65.1

Women's earnings as a % of men's in services (October 1987)

	non-manual monthly earnings
wholesale and retail distribution	63.6
wholesale distribution	65.8
retail distribution	68.9
credit institutions	75.4
insurance (excluding social security)	70.2

Source: data from *Earnings in Industry and Services* (Eurostat)

Marie-Ange Parère became France's first woman fire chief in 1990 in Béziers

Working mothers (1988): 56% of women with a child under 10 were employed compared with 93% of similar men. 75% of women aged 20–39 without children were employed. 10% of women and 5% of men with a child under 10 were unemployed. 27% of employed women with a child under 10 had part-time jobs.

Employment rates are higher for lone mothers than all mothers: 54% for lone mothers with a child aged 0–4 (53% for all mothers) and 66% for lone mothers with a child aged 5–9 (44% for all).

Unemployment rates are also higher for lone mothers: 23% for those with a child aged 0–4 (10% for all mothers) and 18% for those with a child aged 5–9 (8% for all mothers).

WOMEN AND POLITICS

Women won the vote in 1907. Of the 51 Elysée staff in 1991, 24 were women, including Anne Lauvergeon, deputy secretary-general to the president, Beatrice Marre, first private secretary to the president, and Caroline de Margerie, responsible for European affairs.

Elected women (%) (June 1990)

National Assembly	5.0
Senate	3.0
European Parliament (French MEPs)	21.0
Regional councils	10.0
General councils (departments)	4.0

Source: data from *Les Femmes en France* (Secrétariat d'Etat Chargé des Droits des Femmes)

5% of the members of town and city councils were women in 1991. Only 1 of France's ambassadors overseas is a woman.

WOMEN AND EDUCATION

62% of staff employed in national education are women. 75% of secondary teachers are women.

WOMEN AND DETENTION

In September 1988 women made up 4.5% of all prisoners; minors (age 21) and young adults made up 12.2%, and foreigners 25.8%.

SOURCES

Abortion Laws in Europe, Planned Parenthood in Europe, Vol 18 No 1, Spring 1989 (Supplement, amended April 1990); *Bargaining Report 101* (Labour Research Department); *Childcare in the European Communities 1985–90* (Women of Europe Supplement No 51); *Comparative Study on rules*

governing working conditions in the member states (Commission
of the European Communities); *Demographic Statistics 1990*
(Eurostat); *Earnings in Industry and Services* (Eurostat);
Employment in Europe 1991 (Commission of the European
Communities); *Europa World Year Book 1990* (31st edition);
*Health Care Systems and Professional Organisations in the
European Community, Information note – Europe* (British
Medical Association); Health For All 2000 Indicator
Presentation System (World Health Organisation Regional
Office for Europe); *A History of Their Own – Women in Europe
from Prehistory to the Present, Volumes I and II,* (Bonnie
Anderson and Judith Zinsser, Penguin); *Labour Force Survey
(Results 1989)* (Eurostat); *Labour Research* September 1991
(Labour Research Department); *Les Actions Positives en Faveur
des Femmes en Europe Occidentale* (Institut Syndical Europeen);
Les Femmes en France (Secrétariat d'Etat Chargé des Droits des
Femmes); *Out In Europe* (Peter Tatchell, for Channel 4
Television); *Pocket World in Figures* (The Economist); *Positive
action and the constitutional and legislative hindrances to its
implementation in the member states of the Council of Europe*
(Council of Europe); *Proposition de Directive Du Conseil
concernant la protection au travail de la femme enceinte ou
venant d'accoucher* (Commission of the European
Communities); *Prison Information Bulletin* June 1990 (Council
of Europe); *Social Protection in the Member States of the
Community* (Commission of the European Community
Directorate General on Employment, Industrial Relations and
Social Affairs); *Third World Guide 91/92* (Instituto del Tercer
Mundo); *Women of Europe* (Nos 64, 67, 68, 69)

LETTERS FROM FRANCE

Beatrice Roca, filmmaker, Paris

From my point of view, the main difficulty today for
women who don't want to be alone at home is their
lack of self-confidence. This inhibition is a
psychological heritage, passed on from mother to
daughter over many generations. In my family, a
Catholic and aristocratic one, my grandmother wanted
to study law, but it was not 'fit' for a woman in the
bourgeoisie. She tried to study secretly to be a shorthand
typist, but her father stopped her. However, after she
was married, her *leit motiv* was 'You are on the earth
to enjoy and serve your husband and your children'.

My mother grew up in the strict laws of her mother.
She obtained her chemistry PhD the year of my birth

and, at the same time, gave up the idea of working to follow my father abroad and to start a family. She brought up her 5 children with authority, but continually expressed feelings of personal frustration. Her daughters were trained to be perfect hosts, her sons exempted from housework. As soon as her children were independent, she became responsible for an association, SOS Mamans, which keeps children who cannot be admitted in a nursery so their mothers can work.

My mother gave me her own mother's first name. I've always thought that it would be impossible for me to have a professional activity and to have children, without losing my psychological equilibrium. Now I am a film director and am writing a screenplay precisely about these stakes: how to get rid of the psychological heritages.

Ann Barlow, Cheshire, who lived in Ferney Voltaire

There is very good pre-school provision in France. State-run nurseries (écoles maternelles) cater for 2 to 6 year olds. A child starts by attending for only a few half days a week and building up to a full day by the age of 4 to 5. This sounds ideal, but there are drawbacks. Only in larger schools is there any kind of lunch-time provision. In Ferney Voltaire, school closed at 11.30am and reopened at 1.30pm. Of the 5 schools in Ferney Voltaire, only 1 ran a canteen. Lunch-time recreation schools ran on 1 or 2 days a week. Added to that Wednesday was a half-day holiday, in some schools a full day's holiday. Friends who had worked from 9am to 4pm in England found they had to think about getting a childminder for the lunch-break.

Wherever I have lived (France, Britain and Germany), mothers have to juggle their lives, around children's school hours. Childminders and reciprocal arrangements with friends seem to be part and parcel of life for any mother who wants to develop her own life; whether it be at work, further study or recreation.

Cecile Signoret, trainer for women returning to work, St Mathieu de Tréviers

In France, several bodies exist for women's employment training, for the most part private ones, but connected with the National Employment Agency, which allow women who have never worked or have lost their job to improve their qualifications or to be retrained.

So, for example, a mother who has never been in the work-force, but who wants to find a job as a secretary can, if she has been on unemployment benefit for more than a year, take advantage of an intensive course with a view to obtaining a qualification.

Organisations put typewriters, computers and a whole range of facilities at the disposal of applicants so that self-training, without any age limit, can be started or brought up to date in all the modern techniques of office practice.

Moreover, mothers can benefit from a training allowance approaching the total allowance of the SMIG (Interprofessional Guaranteed Minimum Salary) of about FF4,000 a month.

ADDRESSES

French Embassy, 58 Knightsbridge, London SW1X 7JT. Tel: 071 235 8080

Secretariat d'Etat Chargé des Droits des Femmes, rue Le Peletier 31, 75009 Paris. Tel: (33 1) 42 46 99 69

Centre National d'information et de Documentation des Femmes et des Familles, Maison de l'Information, 7 rue du Jura, 75013 Paris

Union Féminine Civique et Sociale, 6 rue Béranger, 75003 Paris. Tel: (33 1) 42 72 19 18

Mouvement Français pour le Planning Familial (family planning service), 4 Square St Irenée, 75011 Paris. Tel: (33 1) 48 07 29 10

Confédération Général du Travail, Complexe Immobilier, Intersyndical CGT, 263 rue de Paris, 93516 Montreuil Cedex

GPL (Gais pour les Liberties) (lesbian and gay rights), BP 451, 75830 Paris Cedex 17. Tel: (33 1) 45 75 23 55

Germany

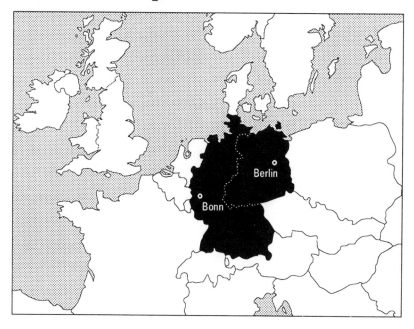

- **Population** 78.2 million, 52% female (west); 52.1% (east)
- **Area** 356,910 sq km
- **Population density** 219.1 people sq km
- **GDP 1988 (former east)** £55.6 billion
- **GDP per capita (former east)** £3,426
- **GDP 1988 (former west)** Deutschmarks 2,122 billion (£749 billion)
- **GDP per capita (former west)** £12,241
- **GDP per capita in purchasing power parity (former west)** (UK=100) 112
- **Public spending as % of GNP (east):** defence 4.9% (1986); education 3.8% (1986); health 2.6% (1987)
- **Public spending as % of GNP (west):** defence 3.1% (1986); education 4.5% (1986); health 6.3% (1987)
- **Currency is the Deutschmark** 1989 £1 = DM2.74; US$1 = DM1.70
  Official exchange rate for the East German mark for 1989 was £1 = EM2.71; US$1 = EM1.68

The Federal Republic of Germany was established in October 1990 with the unification of the former Federal Republic of Germany (West Germany) and the German Democratic Republic (East Germany).

Germany is made up of 16 Länder, each with its own constitution, legislature and government.

Dr Rita Süssmuth was elected by an overwhelming majority as the first President of the reunified German Parliament

The country has a 2-chamber parliament. The Bundesrat or upper house has 68 seats, with each Länder having between 3 to 6 seats, depending on population. The lower house is the Bundestag (federal assembly), which has 662 deputies elected for 4 years by a mixture of proportional representation and direct election. Executive authority rests with the federal government led by the chancellor, who is elected by the Bundestag and appoints ministers. The president, elected by a special federal convention, is the constitutional head of state but exercises little influence.

The flow of people to western Germany, particularly since the Berlin wall began to crumble and finally came down in 1989, will lead to major population changes by the year 2000. In 1989, 343,800 people left East Germany – which has lost a total of 733,000 since 1970 – and there were only 960 immigrants. 76.6% of those who left in 1989 were under 40.

There is a Serbian-speaking minority of about 100,000 in former East Germany.

Almost everyone in western Germany is Christian – half Roman Catholics and half Protestants. 35% of eastern Germans are Protestants (mainly of the Evangelical Church) and 7% are Catholic.

IMMIGRATION AND RESIDENCE RIGHTS

EC nationals do not need work permits, nor do their marriage partners and children under 21, whatever their nationalities. However, they are required to obtain a residence permit as soon as they start work, which must be no later than 3 months after arrival (otherwise a permit is not granted). EC nationals not intending to work in Germany should obtain a

Between 1984–88
West Germany
had the most
asylum seekers in
Europe, with 47%
of the EC total of
789,500. Lowest
were in Belgium
and Norway
(both 2%) and
the UK (3%)

residence permit before arrival (proof of financial means and health insurance are required).

Citizens of Austria, Finland, Iceland, Norway, Sweden and Switzerland can apply for residence and work permits after arrival. Citizens of other countries who want to work or to stay in Germany for longer than 3 months should have a visa before they arrive.

In 1988 West Germany had 4,489,105 foreign residents, 28.4% from other EC states. 57.3% were from non-EC European countries, 3.0% from African countries and 11.3% from other countries.

EQUAL RIGHTS

The principle of equality between women and men was introduced into the Basic Law of West Germany in 1949. In 1986 the Ministry for Youth, Family Affairs, Women and Health was set up and, in 1991, this was divided into 3 different ministries: women and youth, the family and the elderly, and health. All 3 are headed by women. Many Länder (regions) have equal rights offices.

BIRTH, LIFE AND DEATH

**Breakdown of population by sex and age group (1000s) (1988)
(former West Germany)**

	all		women		men		% of women in age group
	no	%	no	%	no	%	
0–14	8,940.8	14.6	4,353.0	13.7	4,387.8	15.0	48.7
15–24	9,547.4	15.6	4,652.5	14.6	4,894.9	16.8	48.7
25–39	13,629.0	22.3	6,679.0	21.0	6,950.0	23.8	49.0
40–59	16,380.9	26.7	8,039.4	25.3	8,341.5	28.5	49.1
60–74	8,287.1	13.5	5,021.2	15.8	3,265.9	11.2	60.6
75+	4,452.6	7.3	3,073.5	9.7	1,379.1	4.7	69.0
all	61,237.8	100.0	31,818.6	100.0	29,219.2	100.0	52.0

Source: data from *Demographic Statistics 1990* (Eurostat)

Breakdown of population by sex (former East Germany without West Berlin) (1000s)

	women	men	total	pop index 1950 = 50	av age
1980	8,883	7,857	16,740	91.04	37.16
1985	8,766	7,889	16,655	90.58	37.17
1988	8,702	7,973	16,675	90.68	37.25
1989	8,560	7,873	16,433	89.37	37.52

Source: *Doing Business with Eastern Europe: East Germany* (Business International)

Breakdown of population by age group (former East Germany without West Berlin)

	children (%)	working age population (%)	retirement age (%)
1980	18.89	63.21	17.9
1985	18.61	64.84	16.55
1988	19.00	64.96	16.04
1989	19.05	64.80	37.64

Source: *Doing Business with Eastern Europe: East Germany* (Business International)

Population and population increase by region (1987) (former West Germany)

region	pop (1000s)	% of total pop	pop density per sq km	natural increase per 1,000	net migration per 1,000	total increase per 1,000
Schleswig-Holstein	2,554.2	4.2	162.4	-1.9	-21.2	-23.1
Hamburg	1,592.8	2.6	2,110.5	-4.6	15.3	10.8
Niedersachsen	7,162.1	11.7	151.0	-1.4	-3.3	-4.7
Bremen	660.1	1.1	1,632.9	-4.1	8.9	4.8
Nordrhein-Westfalen	16,711.8	27.4	490.5	-0.5	3.0	2.4
Hessen	5,507.8	9.0	260.9	-1.2	-3.6	-4.9
Rheinland-Pfalz	3,630.8	5.9	182.9	-1.2	6.3	5.2
Baden-Württemberg	9,286.4	15.2	259.7	1.3	-2.4	-1.1
Bayern	10,902.6	17.9	154.5	0.0	-8.7	-8.7
Saarland	1,055.7	1.7	410.9	-1.7	12.9	11.2
West Berlin	2,012.7	3.3	191.9	-5.5	76.6	71.1
West Germany	61,077.0	100.0	245.6	-0.7	0.9	0.2

Source: data from *Demographic Statistics 1990* (Eurostat)

Population and population density by region (December 1989)
(former East Germany)

region	area sq km	women (1000s)	total pop (1000s)	pop density per sq km
Berlin city	403	670.3	1,279.2	3,174
Cottbus	8,262	449.5	875.6	106
Dresden	6,738	901.1	1,713.1	254
Erfurt	7,349	636.4	1,222.9	166
Frankfurt (Oder)	7,186	361.2	706.1	98
Gera	4,004	380.1	728.1	182
Halle (Saale)	8,771	911.5	1,748.0	199
Karl-Marx-Stadt (Chemnitz)	6,009	964.0	1,817.5	302
Leipzig	4,966	702.1	1,333.1	268
Magdeburg	11,526	643.4	1,237.9	107
Neubrandenburg	10,948	314.6	615.8	56
Potsdam	12,568	573.9	1,111.2	88
Rostock	7,075	465.1	909.8	129
Schwerin	8,672	304.4	590.2	68
Suhl	3,856	283.0	545.3	141
total	108,333	8560.6	16,433.8	152

Source: *Europa World Year Book 1990* (31st edition)

Births, deaths, marriages and divorces per 1,000 population
(former West Germany)

	1960	1970	1980	1985	1988
birth rate	17.6	13.3	10.1	9.6	11.1
% of births outside marriage	6.3	5.5	7.6	9.4	10.0
average age of mother at 1st birth	24.9	24.3	25.2	26.2	26.7
infant mortality per 1,000 live births	33.8	23.6	12.6	8.9	7.5
fertility rate per woman	2.4	2.0	1.5	1.3	1.4
marriage rate	9.4	7.3	5.9	6.0	6.5
average age at marriage (women)	25.2	24.9	25.8	27.4	27.9
average age at marriage (men)	28.5	28.3	29.0	30.3	31.0
divorce rate	0.9	1.3	1.6	2.1	2.1
life expectancy (women)	72.4[1]	73.8[2]	76.9[3]	78.4[4]	–
life expectancy (men)	66.9[1]	67.4[2]	70.2[3]	71.8[4]	–
death rate	11.7	12.0	11.6	11.5	11.2

[1] 1960–62; [2] 1970–72; [3] 1980–82; [4] 1985–87

Source: data from *Demographic Statistics 1990* (Eurostat)

Births and deaths per 1,000 population (1988)
(former East Germany)

birth rate	13.0
death rate	12.8
infant mortality per 1,000 live births	9.0
marriage rate	8.5
life expectancy (women)	76.2
life expectancy (men)	70.4
fertility rate per woman	1.7

Source: data from *Demographic Statistics 1990* (Eurostat)

Births (including stillbirths) 1955–84
(former East Germany)

	total	% of births outside marriage
1955	298,782	13.1
1965	284,723	9.8
1970	239,431	13.3
1974	180,588	16.3
1980	246,778	22.9
1981	239,194	25.6
1982	241,515	29.3
1983	225,073	33.5
1984	229,371	33.6

Source: *East Germany to the 1990s – Can it Resist Glasnost?*
(Economist Intelligence Unit)

Under federal divorce law, the partner who is less well off has the right to alimony if she or he cannot work because of child-care responsibilities. A new change in the law means that pension rights are divided on divorce for partners who have none, a provision that benefits mainly women.

In East Germany, custody was normally awarded to the woman after a divorce, which partly accounts for the higher number of female single parents. In 1989 1 in 3 children were born outside of marriage in East Germany compared with 1 in 10 in West Germany.

In East Germany, before reunification, 88% of

women were employed and therefore ineligible for a 'living allowance' or alimony on divorce. Since unification they are covered by the federal divorce law. There were 100,000 divorces a year in East Germany, where 2.2 million children were being raised by single parents.

The proportion of 1-parent households in West Germany was one of the highest in the EC in 1989; 9% of households with a child aged 0–4 and 11% with a child aged 5–9.

LESBIAN RIGHTS

In 1982 lesbian activist Uschi Sillge addressed East Germany's first public conference on homosexuality since the Second World War

The law on homosexual age of consent is due to be rationalised by 1995. In the former East Germany, same-sex relationships were illegal until 1968. A common age of consent of 14 was introduced in 1989, now the second lowest in Europe. Before then the age of consent was higher for gay men (18 from 1968). In the former West Germany, the age of consent for lesbians and heterosexuals is 14, compared with 18 for gay men. Asylum has been granted to homosexuals at risk of persecution on the grounds of their sexual orientation.

WOMEN AND HEALTH CARE

Health care is funded by health insurance, which is compulsory for those earning below a certain level, the unemployed, students and the disabled. Others, including the self-employed, can opt in to the scheme. Contributions are based on earnings and are shared between employer and employee. Limited contributions for pensioners are being introduced. There are also private insurance schemes.

Patients pay a fixed contribution towards prescriptions and hospital treatment. Patients can register with a doctor for a 3-month period. Referral from a GP is not necessary for specialist treatment.

In East Germany, primary health care was provided through a system of polyclinics – community-based centres providing a range of medical services – unlike the system of independent doctors' practices that operates in western Germany and is now being imposed throughout the country. The polyclinics are being allowed to operate until 1995. The compulsory insurance scheme has been introduced in the east.

In 1988 there was 1 doctor for every 424 people in East Germany and 1 doctor for every 369 people in West Germany.

Major indicators for women's health in East Germany (1989)

maternal deaths (all causes) per 100,000 live births	11.56
maternal deaths (abortion) per 100,000 live births	0.00
% of all live births to mothers under 20 (1986)	10.67
% of all live births to mothers aged 35+ (1986)	2.59
deaths from cancer of the cervix (age 0–64) per 100,000 women (1988)	5.44
deaths from malignant neoplasm female breast (age 0–64) per 100,000 women	16.29
deaths from trachea/bronchus/lung cancer (age 0–64) per 100,000 women	4.30
deaths from trachea/bronchus/lung cancer (age 0–64) per 100,000 men	35.66
deaths from diseases of the circulatory system (age 0–64) per 100,000 women	55.45
deaths from diseases of the circulatory system (age 0–64) per 100,000 men	143.45
deaths from suicide and self-inflicted injury per 100,000 women	13.29
deaths from suicide and self-inflicted injury per 100,000 men	37.74

Source: data from Health for All 2000 Indicator Presentation System (World Health Organisation Regional Office For Europe)

Major indicators for women's health in West Germany (1989)

maternal deaths (all causes) per 100,000 live births	5.28
maternal deaths (abortion) per 100,000 live births	0.44
ratio of abortions to 1,000 live births (all ages) (1986)	134.63
% of all live births to mothers under 20 (1985)	3.52
% of all live births to mothers aged 35+ (1985)	8.61
deaths from cancer of the cervix (age 0–64) per 100,000 women (1988)	2.88
deaths from malignant neoplasm female breast (age 0–64) per 100,000 women	20.76
deaths from trachea/bronchus/lung cancer (age 0–64) per 100,000 women	5.87
deaths from trachea/bronchus/lung cancer (age 0–64) per 100,000 men	31.75
deaths from diseases of the circulatory system (age 0–64) per 100,000 women	35.17
deaths from diseases of the circulatory system (age 0–64) per 100,000 men	106.39
deaths from suicide and self-inflicted injury per 100,000 women	8.19
deaths from suicide and self-inflicted injury per 100,000 men	21.97

Source: data from Health for All 2000 Indicator Presentation System (World Health Organisation Regional Office For Europe)

The European Parliament has condemned medical examinations forced on women suspected of travelling to the Netherlands to have abortions. In March 1991 the magazine *Der Spiegel* reported 10 cases of women forced to have gynaecological tests at the border

Abortion and contraception: On unification it was agreed that the former East Germany would continue to have different laws on abortion, though the treaty says the law should be revised by the end of 1992. In the meantime, women from western Germany will not be prosecuted for having abortions in the east. The issue has been fiercely debated within women's organisations, political parties and parliament. Here is the current law:

In western Germany, abortion is available up to 12 weeks in cases of rape or other sexual crimes, or on social or psychological grounds with the permission of 2 doctors, including the one who does the abortion. Available up to 22 weeks on eugenic grounds with a 3-day waiting period after counselling. Available without time limit on medical or social-psychiatric grounds with forced counselling. Abortions on social-psychiatric grounds are rejected by some hospitals, and there are big regional differences in availability of services. The International Planned Parenthood Federation estimates that West German women have 10,000 abortions every year in other countries, most of which are illegal.

In eastern Germany, abortion is available on demand up to 12 weeks, though women under 18 must have parental consent. Available up to the second trimester on medical/psychological or eugenic grounds with the consent of a medical committee. If the woman has had an abortion in the last 6 months approval is only granted by a specialist commission of doctors. Abortion is free of charge, and there are very few illegal abortions.

PARENTAL PAY, LEAVE AND BENEFITS

West Germany (1989–90)

Maternity leave and pay: 6 weeks before the birth plus 8 weeks afterwards on full pay, plus 4 weeks for premature and multiple births. Pay is made up of a basic maternity benefit with the balance paid by employers. To qualify, women must have either worked or been on unemployment benefit for 9 of the previous 12 months.

Nursing mothers: Women are entitled to time off work to breastfeed.

Parental leave and benefit and paternity leave:
18 months available to either parent paid at DM600 monthly (parents may work up to 18 hours a week and still claim benefit) for the first 6 months, then payment is reduced according to household income (though 40% of families still qualify for full benefit). There are plans to extend this leave to up to 3 years. 98% of mothers claimed the right to this leave with about 47% returning to work at the end of the 18 months. This compares with 0.6% of fathers who took parental leave.

Time off for sick children: Either parent is entitled to 5 days' paid leave to care for a sick child under 8.

East Germany (1988–89)

Maternity leave: Was 26 weeks on full pay, including 6 which had to be taken before the birth, plus an additional 2 weeks for multiple births, or if there were complications.

Parental leave: Total shared leave was 5 months at full earnings plus 7 months at 80% of earnings. Available to both parents but almost always taken by women.

CHILD-CARE PROVISION

West Germany (1988–89)

Under 3s: 3% have publicly funded places in nurseries or centres for children of mixed ages.

3–school age (6/7): 68% have kindergarten places (both public and private) though only 12% of places are full-time. 6% of 5–6 year olds attend pre-primary schooling (available only in some areas).

Primary schools (from ages 6/7): 4–5 hours in the mornings with hours often varying day to day. Very few primary schools (accounting for 4% of primary children) are open all day. No meals are provided. The school year runs from August to July. In 1988 the pupil to teacher ratio in primary schools was 17:1 in East and West Germany.

A 1990 survey by the Federal Education Ministry found that 40% of parents wanted their children to attend school all day. Only 11% of high school students attend schools that are open all day.

Outside school hours care: Available to 4% of 6–10 year olds, mainly through local authority places.

Contributions to child-care costs: Parents make a contribution based on income (excluding schools). Tax relief is available up to DM12,000 on the costs of a full-time domestic worker.

East Germany (1988–89)

Under 3s: Previously 81% of 1–2 year olds had free publicly funded places. The objective was to provide a place for every child.

3–school age: 94% had free kindergarten places, though many child-care facilities for this age group and under 3s are now reported as closing.

STATE BENEFITS

The following information is for West Germany in July 1990. Proposed provisions for social security would take into account insurance periods spent in either part of Germany, and allow for East German pensions to be 'exported'.

Retirement pension: In principle legal retirement age is 65 for everyone, though women can retire at 60 if insured for the previous 20 years. Early pensions are also available to the unemployed and at age 63 after 35 years' service. To qualify for a pension, a person must have 60 months of insurance contributions. Payments are earnings related (up to a limit of DM75,600) and also depend on the number of contributions. Pensions are increased each year.

> 'To me it is often a source of great pleasure and wonderment to see that the entire female body was created for the purpose of nurturing children.'
> Martin Luther

Survivors' pensions: Paid to spouses of people who had 60 months of insurance, provided they were married at the time of death or financially dependent. Spouses receive six-tenths of the occupational invalidity pension. Children who have lost 1 parent receive one-tenth while children who have lost both receive one-fifth; all children also receive an extra payment based on basic salary. Full pension is paid for 3 months after the death; it is then reduced if a surviving spouse earns more than DM1,050. Pension is discontinued on remarriage with a grant of 2 years' survivors' pension.

Women are to be allowed to do voluntary military service on the basis of equal treatment

Sickness benefit: Paid at 80% of normal salary with the employer paying for 6 weeks. Benefit for the same illness is limited to 78 weeks in a 3-year period. Waiting time is 1 day. This benefit can be claimed for 5 days a year for the care of a sick child under age 8.

Invalidity: Paid to those who cannot earn more than half their normal earnings or who cannot work regularly and earn only a minimum income, in both cases because of sickness or infirmity. Benefit is based on the number of years of insurance contributions and earnings. To qualify, workers must have 60 months of contributions including 36 immediately before the complaint. Handicapped people must have paid 240 months of insurance. Benefit is paid until the age of 65 when the old age pension is paid.

Family benefits: DM50 a month for 1 child; DM130 for 2; DM220 for 3 and DM240 for larger families. Benefits are paid until children are 16, or 27 for vocational training and further education and girls remaining at home, and without limit in cases of serious infirmity. Benefits are reduced from the second child if the family income is more than DM26,600 (plus DM9,200 per child). There is also an education allowance of DM600 a month for the first 18 months (this is income related after the seventh month).

Unemployment benefit: Between 58% and 68% of earnings for claimants with dependants and 56% to 63% for claimants without children. Benefit can be claimed for 12 months to 64 months depending on age and length of period in work.

WOMEN AND EMPLOYMENT

In 1500 Drutgin van Caster, a woman goldsmith, was appointed as artisan to Emperor Maximilian

Statutory rights: The working week is limited to 48 hours, with overtime restricted to 2 hours a day for up to 30 days a year. However, legislation allows for flexible working time agreements to spread hours over longer periods. Paid annual leave is 18 days, and there are 10 to 14 statutory public holidays.

Minimum wages are set by collective agreements and must be observed. Almost all employees receive an annual bonus worth an average of 92% of monthly salary paid at Christmas or in the summer. Wages cannot be seized in full by creditors.

Employment and unemployment (1989) (former West Germany)

	% women	% men
economic activity rate	42.1	70.3
employed working part time	30.7	2.3
labour force who are employers or self-employed	5.6	11.4
labour force who are family workers	4.6	0.4
unemployment rate	7.5	4.5
youth unemployment rate (age 14–24)	5.9	5.2
unemployed who have been unemployed for		
12 months or more	46.0	52.3
all unemployed by sex	52.1	47.9

Source: data from *Labour Force Survey (Results 1989)* (Eurostat)

Part-time work: In 1989 89.6% of part-time workers were women. To qualify for social security benefits, part-time workers must work for at least 19 hours a week, or earn at least DM410 (1989).

Employment by industrial sector (1000s) (1989) (former West Germany)

	women no	women %	men no	men %	women as % of workforce
agriculture	473	4.4	583	3.5	44.8
all industry	2,660	24.8	8,346	50.0	24.2
energy and water	54	0.5	452	2.7	10.7
mineral extraction and chemicals	355	3.3	1,135	6.8	23.8
metal manufacturing and engineering	991	9.3	3,443	20.6	22.4
other manufacturing industry	1,060	9.9	1,629	9.8	39.4
building and civil engineering	199	1.9	1,689	10.1	10.5
all services	7,570	70.7	7,774	46.5	49.3
distributive trades and hotels	2,384	22.3	2,172	13.0	52.3
transport and communication	396	3.7	1,181	7.1	25.1
banking, finance and insurance	1,018	9.5	1,198	7.2	45.9
public administration	860	8.0	1,651	9.9	34.2
other services	2,912	27.2	1,573	9.4	64.9
total	**10,702**	**100.0**	**16,703**	**100.0**	**39.1**

Source: data from *Labour Force Survey (Results 1989)* (Eurostat)

Employment by industrial sector (1000s) (former East Germany)

	1987	1988	1989
industry	3,479.4	3,482.5	3,186.9
agriculture and forestry	928.5	928.2	923.5
construction	568.9	566.6	559.9
commerce	881.0	883.2	876.8
transport and communications	632.7	636.0	639.1
other	2,080.2	2,097.9	2,094.6
women	4,200.3	4,203.9	4,177.7
men	4,370.3	4,390.5	4,369.7
total	**8,570.7**	**8,594.4**	**8,547.3***

* includes apprentices   Source: *Europa World Year Book 1990* (31st edition)

Where women work: In 1989 women in East
Germany accounted for 48.9% of workers in
agriculture and forestry and 37.4% in industry. 72%
of retail trade staff, 77% of teachers, 83% of health

service employees and 99% of commercial cleaners. Within industry, women were most prominant in light industry (57.7%), textiles (66.9%) and food processing (47.1%).

Women's earnings as a percentage of men's: In East Germany in 1990, women were earning between 76% and 91% of men's earnings in industry.

Women's earnings as a % of men's in industry (April 1988, West Germany)

	manual hourly earnings	non-manual monthly earnings
energy and water	77.5	69.3
chemical industry	74.5	72.0
all metal manufacture and engineering	76.5	65.6
mechanical engineering	77.2	64.5
electrical engineering	78.0	66.8
food, drink and tobacco	70.9	69.5
clothing and footwear manufacture	79.0	70.0
printing and publishing	73.4	65.5
all manufacturing industry	73.1	66.5
all industry	**73.4**	**66.5**

Source: data from *Earnings in Industry and Services* (Eurostat)

Women's earnings as a % of men's in services (April 1988, West Germany)

	non-manual monthly earnings
wholesale and retail distribution	64.6
wholesale distribution	68.4
retail distribution	67.1
credit institutions	77.2
insurance (excluding social security)	77.6

Source: data from *Earnings in Industry and Services* (Eurostat)

Average net monthly income of households

	West			East		
	1970 (DM)	1983 (DM)	% increase	1970 (EM)	1983 (EM)	% increase
households with 1 or more wage earners	1,606	3,556	121	1,031	1,653	60
pensioner household	994	2,323	133	315	560	78

Source: *East Germany to the 1990s – Can it Resist Glasnost?* (Economist Intelligence Unit)

EM = East German Marks

A survey of 2,000 women found that 72% had experienced sexual harassment at work

Working mothers: In 1989 in East Germany 90% of women with children were employed, one of the highest rates in the world.

In West Germany in 1988, 38% of women with a child under 10 were employed compared with 94% of men. 76% of women aged 20–39 without children were employed. 5% of women and 3% of men with a child under 10 were unemployed. Employment rates were much higher for lone mothers than all mothers; 41% for lone mothers with a child aged 0–4 (34% for all mothers) and 52% for lone mothers with a child aged 5–9 (39%).

WOMEN AND POLITICS

Women won the right to vote in Germany in 1919.

In the December 1990 election, which inaugurated a united Germany, women won 20.5% of the seats in the Bundestag. The next federal election is due in December 1994. Women make up 4 of the 20 cabinet members and 8 of the 53 ministers. Women's representation in local government is about 17%.

One of Germany's 135 ambassadors is a woman. There are also 3 women general consuls.

Women in the Bundestag after the election of December 1990

political party	total no of seats	no of seats held by women	% of seats held by women
CDU/CSU	319	44	13.8
FDP	79	16	20.3
SPD	239	65	27.2
PDS/LL	17	8	47.1
Bündnis '90/Greens	8	3	37.5
total	662	136	20.5

SPD – Social Democratic Party
CDU – Christian Democratic Union
CSU – Christian Social Union
FDP – Free Democratic Party
PDS/LL – Party of Democratic Socialism

Source: data from Embassy of the Federal Republic of Germany, London

WOMEN AND EDUCATION

% of women in higher education by subject (West Germany) (1988)

linguistics and cultural studies	61
sports	61
art and fine arts	58
veterinary medicine	58
agriculture, forestry and food science	47
law, economics and social sciences	31
human medicine	47
engineering sciences	12
mathematics and natural sciences	31

Source: data from *Women in Society* (Press and Information Office, Federal Government, Bonn)

% of women students in higher education (East Germany) (1989)

all university and polytechnic students	48.6
teacher training	73.0
economics	66.7
medicine	55.2
mathematics and science	46.0
technical colleges	
nursing and health care	95.9
teacher training	88.6

Source: data from *Superwomen and the Double Burden* (ed Chris Corrin, Scarlet Press)

Women as a % of school leavers entering occupational training (East Germany)

	1980	1985	1989
secretary	99.8	99.7	99.8
clothes factory worker	99.9	99.5	99.4
textiles worker	96.6	94.7	95.3
salesperson	98.2	97.1	95.6
data processor	82.8	77.8	70.0
electronics worker	49.8	33.0	19.5
machine builder	8.3	5.8	5.8
toolmaker	11.9	9.0	5.2

Source: data from *Superwomen and the Double Burden* (ed Chris Corrin, Scarlet Press)

WOMEN AND DETENTION

In September 1988 in West Germany women made up
4.1% of all prisoners, and foreigners made up 14.5%.

SOURCES

Abortion Laws in Europe, Planned Parenthood in Europe, Vol 18
No 1, Spring 1989 (Supplement, amended April 1990);
Bargaining Report 101 (Labour Research Department);
Childcare in the European Communities 1985–90 (Women of
Europe Supplement No 51); *Comparative Study on rules
governing working conditions in the member states* (Commission
of the European Communities); *Demographic Statistics 1990*
(Eurostat); *Doing Business with Eastern Europe: East Germany*
(Business International); *Earnings in Industry and Services*
(Eurostat); *East Germany to the 1990s – Can it Resist Glasnost?*
(Economist Intelligence Unit); Embassy of the Federal Republic
of Germany; *Employment in Europe 1991* (Commission of the
European Communities); *Europa World Year Book 1990* (31st
edition); *Health Care Systems and Professional Organisations in
the European Community, Information note – Europe* (British
Medical Association); Health For All 2000 Indicator
Presentation System (World Health Organisation Regional
Office for Europe); *A History of Their Own – Women in Europe
from Prehistory to the Present, Volumes I and II* (Bonnie
Anderson and Judith Zinsser, Penguin); *Labour Force Survey
(Results 1989)* (Eurostat); *Les Actions Positives en Faveur des
Femmes en Europe Occidentale* (Institut Syndical Europeen);
Out In Europe (Peter Tatchell, for Channel 4 Television); *Pocket
World in Figures* (The Economist); *Positive action and the
constitutional and legislative hindrances to its implementation in
the member states of the Council of Europe* (Council of Europe);
*Proposition de Directive Du Conseil concernant la protection au
travail de la femme enceinte ou venant d'accoucher* (Commission
of the European Communities); *Prison Information Bulletin*
June 1990 (Council of Europe); *Social Protection in the Member
States of the Community* (Commission of the European
Community Directorate General on Employment, Industrial
Relations and Social Affairs); *Superwomen and the Double
Burden* (ed Chris Corrin, Scarlet Press);*Third World Guide 91/92*
(Instituto del Tercer Mundo); *Women in Society* (Press and
Information Office, Federal Government, Bonn); *Women of
Europe* (Nos 66, 67, 68, 69); *Women, State and Party in Eastern
Europe* (ed Sharon L Wolchik and Alfred G Meyer, Duke
University Press)

LETTER FROM GERMANY

Dr Florence Hervé, Dusseldorf, editor of
Frauenzimmer im Haus Europa (Cologne 1991)

In recent years there has been a growing campaign to
improve education and employment for women, with
schemes to improve the status of women and adoption
of job quota systems. Above all, there has been an
enormous change in women's own political attitudes.

With the move to a single European market and
German reunification, achievements have been put in
jeopardy and rights taken away. Women in the former
DDR are the worst affected . . . Women in the east
enjoyed rights grounded in both the constitution and
in everyday life, such as their sisters in the west could
only dream about. Under the law, men and women
had 'equal rights in all areas of social, national and
personal life'. With reunification a number of
regulations ensuring social and employment rights
have been abolished.

● Mothers were previously allowed 4 weeks leave
per year to look after a sick child. Since 1991 the old
West German rules apply: 5 days annually to care for
a child up to the age of 8!

● East German women had the right to a day off for
housework once a month (as, incidentally, did single
men). This arrangement ceases in 1992.

● Maternity leave for women in the east used to be
26 weeks. Since the beginning of 1991, this has been
reduced to 14.

● One of the most significant rulings, still under
debate, affects a woman's right to have an abortion.
In the east, conditions involved 'time limits'; in the
west, 'sufficient grounds'.

● Women in the east had the right to child-care
facilities. From the early 1980s, parents could send
children to kindergarten, for those between age 3 and
school age, or to a day-care centre. Over a period of 9
months, 172,000 child-care places have been abolished.

It seems the future will depend on the strength of the extraparliamentary campaign for women's rights. Over the past 25 years, the feminist movement has gained ground, with women's refuges, peace groups and university courses in women's studies. The new feminism has brought about positive changes in the political landscape. Women are playing an increasingly important role in business, the church and politics. There are more than 500 equal opportunities organisations at local authority level . . .

At the same time, women have fallen prey to the new self-centred individualism that has become rife in Germany . . . The three new Ks – Karriere, Konkurrenz, Konsum (career, competition, consumerism) – appear to have replaced the Kinder, Kuchen, Kirche of the era of National Socialism.

Many committed women continue to strive for equal treatment in all social spheres. It is now a matter of breaking away from male-dominated structures and bringing about social reforms that will lead to long-term prospects of liberation.

ADDRESSES

German Embassy, 25 Belgrave Square, Chesham Place, London SW1X 8PZ. Tel: 071 235 5033

Bundesministerium für Frauen und Jugend, Kennedy-Allee 105-107, D-5300 Bonn 2

Deutscher Juristinnenbund (vereinigung der Juristinnen, Volkswirtinnen und Betriebswirtinnen), Straßchensweg 28, W-5300 Bonn 1. Tel: (49 228) 238613

Pro Familia (family planning service), Cronstettenstrasse 30, 6000 Frankfurt am Main 1. Tel: (49 69) 55 09 01

Deutscher Gewerkschaftsbund, 4000 Düsseldorf 30, Hans-Böckler Str 39, Postfach 2601

Schulenverband der DDR (lesbian and gay rights – former East) c/o Sonntagsclub, PSF 229, DDR – 1030 Berlin

Bundesverband Homosexualitat (lesbian and gay rights), Beet-hovenstrasse 1, D-500 Köln (Cologne) 1. Tel: (49 221) 237 871

Greece

- **Population** 10 million, 50.8% female
- **Area** 131,990 sq km
- **Population density** 75.7 people sq km
- **GDP 1988** drachmas 7,446 billion (£32.24 billion)
- **GDP per capita** £3,251
- **GDP per capita in purchasing power parity** (UK=100) 55
- **Public spending as % of GNP:** debts 8.2% (1987); defence 5.7% (1986); education 2.5% (1986); health 3.5% (1987)
- **Consumer price index** 1980 = 100; 1989 = 515
- **Currency is the drachma** 1989 £1 = DR254.5; US$1 = DR157.8

Greece has a single-chamber parliament with 300 members directly elected for four years. Voting is compulsory over the age of 18. The president is the head of state, elected by parliament for 5 years. The president appoints the prime minister and they jointly appoint the cabinet.

There are 2 forms of the official language: the formal language is Katharevoussa, whereas Demotiki is spoken and taught in schools. 97% of the people belong to the Greek Orthodox Church.

EQUAL RIGHTS

The constitution established the general principle of sexual equality as well as the right of all working people to equal pay for work of equal value. Positive action is legal as a means of achieving equality between women and men and is specifically allowed with regard to employment. The General Secretariat for Equality was set up in 1985, within the ministry to the president's office, with responsibility for promoting equality. The Council for Equality between Men and Women, set up in 1983, acts as an advisory body.

BIRTH, LIFE AND DEATH

Breakdown of population by sex and age group (1000s) (1988)

	all		women		men		% of women in age group
	no	%	no	%	no	%	
0–14	1,994.2	20.0	962.9	19.0	1,031.3	21.0	48.3
15–24	1,495.1	15.0	722.6	14.2	772.5	15.7	48.3
25–39	2,043.2	20.5	1,015.5	20.0	1,027.7	20.9	49.7
40–59	2,567.1	25.7	1,330.8	26.2	1,236.3	25.2	51.8
60–74	1,296.1	13.0	699.5	13.8	596.6	12.1	54.0
75+	593.2	5.9	343.6	6.8	249.6	5.1	57.9
all	9,988.9	100.0	5074.9	100.0	4,914.0	100.0	50.8

Source: data from *Demographic Statistics 1990* (Eurostat)

Natural increase per 1,000 population is 1.1. Net migration per 1,000 people is 1.3, giving a total increase per 1,000 population of 2.4.

Population in principal towns (1981)

Athinai	885,737
Thessaloniki	406,413
Piraeus	196,389
Patras	142,163
Larissa	102,426
Iraklion	102,398
Volos	71,378
Kavala	56,705
Canea	47,451
Serres	46,317

Source: *Europa World Year Book 1990* (31st edition)

Births, deaths, marriages and divorces for every 1,000 population

	1960	1970	1980	1985	1988
birth rate	18.9	16.5	15.5	11.7	10.8
% of births outside marriage	1.2	1.1	1.5	1.8	2.6
average age of mother at 1st birth	25.6	24.0	23.3	23.7	24.2
infant mortality per 1,000 live births	40.1	29.6	17.9	14.1	11.0
fertility rate per woman	2.3	2.3	2.2	1.7	1.5
marriage rate	7.0	7.7	6.5	6.4	4.8
average age at marriage (women)	24.6	23.1	22.5	23.1	23.8
average age at marriage (men)	28.8	28.4	27.6	27.9	28.4
divorce rate	0.3	0.4	0.7	0.8	0.9
life expectancy (women)	70.4	73.6	76.6	77.6	–
life expectancy (men)	67.3	70.1	72.2	72.6	–
death rate	7.3	8.4	9.1	9.4	9.3

Source: data from *Demographic Statistics 1990* (Eurostat)

Civil marriages became legal in March 1982, when partners could for the first time choose not to get married in church. One-parent households in 1988 accounted for 2% of households with a child aged 0–4 and 4% of households with a child aged 5–9, one of the lowest levels in the EC.

LESBIAN RIGHTS

In 1987 a common age of consent of 15 was introduced. Before then the age of consent was higher for gay men (17 compared with 16). A law introduced in 1981 on public health allows forced testing of gay men for sexually transmitted diseases. It has been used by police to harass lesbians and gay men.

WOMEN AND HEALTH CARE

A national health system was introduced in 1983. Previously health care was provided by many separate social insurance funds which led to inequalities in care. All hospitals are now state controlled. Employees pay insurance contributions which are shared by employers. Health care for insured patients is free, though dependants may pay up to 20%. Insurance bodies reimburse 15%–20% of the costs of hospital treatment, with the balance paid by the state.

Women over 20 are encouraged to have annual gynaecological check-ups, but in 1990 less than 10% actually had them. Teenage pregnancies are rising. In 1985 they accounted for 5.4% of all pregnancies but this had doubled by 1989. In 1988 there was 1 doctor for every 344 people.

Major indicators for women's health (1988)

maternal deaths (all causes) per 100,000 live births	5.58
maternal deaths (abortion) per 100,000 live births	0.93
ratio of abortions to 1,000 live births (all ages)	95.82
% of all live births to mothers under 20	8.57
% of all live births to mothers aged 35+	7.34
deaths from cancer of the cervix (age 0–64) per 100,000 women (1987)	1.10
deaths from malignant neoplasm female breast (age 0–64) per 100,000 women	14.72
deaths from trachea/bronchus/lung cancer (age 0–64) per 100,000 women	4.95
deaths from trachea/bronchus/lung cancer (age 0–64) per 100,000 men	32.79
deaths from diseases of the circulatory system (age 0–64) per 100,000 women	36.80
deaths from diseases of the circulatory system (age 0–64) per 100,000 men	99.60
deaths from suicide and self-inflicted injury per 100,000 women	2.02
deaths from suicide and self-inflicted injury per 100,000 men	5.67

Source: data from Health for All 2000 Indicator Presentation System (World Health Organisation Regional Office For Europe)

Abortion and contraception: Abortion is available on request up to 12 weeks, though women under 18 must have parental consent. It is available up to 20 weeks on medical/psychological grounds or in cases of rape or other sexual crimes; and up to 24 weeks on eugenic grounds. Abortions are free in public hospitals, though most are performed in private clinics at a charge of between DR25,000 and DR35,000.

The pill has been available without a prescription since 1963, but abortion is still a common method of birth control. In 1985 28.6% of abortions were carried out on women under 18. A 1985 survey found that 61% of women relied on withdrawal as their only contraceptive method; 6.5% used the pill, and 15% the IUD (the nature of the sample means this may be higher than average).

PARENTAL PAY, LEAVE AND BENEFITS (1989–90)

Maternity leave and pay: 15 weeks, including 6 that must be taken before the birth, paid by benefit equivalent to 100% of earnings. To qualify, women must have paid 200 days of national insurance contributions in the previous 2 years. Public sector workers have the right to 4 months on full pay (2 months before and 2 months after the birth).

Nursing mothers: Women are entitled to take time off work to breastfeed.

Parental leave: 3 months' unpaid leave for each parent, though this can be refused by an employer if more than 6% of the workforce claims leave during 1 year. Leave is extended to 6 months for lone parents.

Reduced hours: Women can reduce working hours by 2 a day without loss of pay until the child is 2, and by 1 hour until the child is 4.

Leave to care for sick children: Unpaid leave according to the number of children under 16 (or over 16 for children with disabilities) – 6 days for 1 child, 8 days for 2 children and 10 days for 3 or more. Parents of a child with a disability employed by organisations with over 50 workers may reduce their day by 1 hour unpaid.

Other special leave: Parents employed by larger private organisations can take up to 4 days' unpaid leave to visit their children's schools, though this must be agreed with the employer and is shared if both parents are employed.

CHILD-CARE PROVISION (1989–90)

Under 3s: 4%–5% are in publicly funded places, which are free and mostly in kindergartens. 2% of pre-school children (8 months to $5^1/_2$ years) use private services, some of which also receive some public funding.

80% of Greek women believe it is essential to have a family

$3–5^1/_2$: 65%–70% are in publicly funded places, either in pre-primary schooling ($3^1/_2$ hours a day) or in kindergartens. Seasonal kindergartens in some rural areas provide services during busy agricultural periods. All publicly funded child-care services are free. 2% of pre-school children (8 months to $5^1/_2$ years) use private services, some of which also receive some public funds.

Primary school ($5^1/_2$ years and up): 20 hours a week in the first 3 years, increasing to 24–26 hours. Many schools operate a shift system with some children attending in the mornings and others in the afternoons. The school year runs from September to June. In 1988 the pupil to teacher ratio in primary schools was 23:1.

STATE BENEFITS (1989–90)

Retirement pensions: Normal retirement age is 60 for women and 65 for men. To qualify you must have paid contributions for 4,050 working days. Basic pension is 70%–30% of earnings, and allocated in inverse proportion to the amount of earnings. Minimum pension is DR58,220 a month. Plus DR4,367 a day for a dependent spouse and 20% of pension for a first child, 15% for a second and 10% for a third, up to a maximum of DR47,000 for all children.

Pensions are index linked and increase 3 times a year. Monthly earnings are limited to DR101,885.

Early retirement with full pension is available from 57 (62 for men) with 10,000 days of insurance or from 58 (women and men) with 10,500 days. Early retirement with full pension is also possible at 55 for women employed in arduous or unhealthy work (60 for men) and at 57 in construction work (62 for men). The right of women in the civil service to retire after 15 years of employment was abolished in 1990.

The 1990 prize for the most Euro-minded woman went to environmental campaigner Niki Goulandris, co-founder of the Goulandris Natural History Museum

Survivors' pensions: Paid to widows or disabled widowers without means whose marriage lasted for at least 6 months (2 years if the widow of a pensioner). Pension is 70% of the old age pension, subject to a minimum of DR52,400 a month. Pension payments stop on remarriage. 20% of the old age pension is paid to surviving children until they are 18 or for students until they are 25, or without time limit if they are disabled. Children who have lost both parents are paid 60% to 80% of the old age pension.

Sickness benefit: Waiting time is 3 days. For those with 100 days of work (subject to contributions) during the previous year, benefit is paid for up to 182 days at 50% of average earnings, plus 10% for each dependant (up to 4). Maximum benefit is DR3,529 a day. The minimum for those without dependants is DR642 a day. After 182 days the insured person may qualify for invalidity pension.

For those with 300 days of work (subject to contributions) in the previous 2 years, benefit is paid for up to 360 days at 25% of average earnings up to a maximum of DR321 a day for those without dependants (DR1,891 with dependants). For those with 1,500 days of insurance in the 5 years preceding the illness, benefit is paid for up to 720 days.

Invalidity: Full benefit is paid to those who cannot earn more than one-third of normal earnings for the job. Those who can no longer earn more than half normal earnings are paid 75% of benefit, and those who cannot earn more than two-thirds are paid 50%

of benefit if they are over 55. Benefit is paid from the day invalidity exists without time limit, unless the person becomes eligible for an old age pension.

To qualify for invalidity benefit, workers must have paid a certain number of contributions depending on their age (1,500 days for those under 33; 400 for under 22s and 300 for under 21s). Those aged 33 and up must have worked for 4,050 days in total or 1,500 days in the previous 12 years, although there are exceptions.

Totally blind people receive a pension of at least DR58,220 a month if they have 4,050 days of contributions. There are also special benefits for quadriplegia and paraplegia.

'The most important point concerning the evolution of women's rights is the internationalisation of the problem.'
Professor Alice Marangopoulous

Family benefits: DR920 a month for the first child; DR3,170 for two children; DR6,920 for three; and DR8,000 for four. For each additional child DR1,500 is paid. In addition, for third children born in or after 1982, there is an extra DR1,000, and there are special allowances of DR500 a month for the third child; DR750 for the fourth; and DR1,000 for the fifth child. Plus DR1,250 for a handicapped child.

Benefits are reduced if the family income is more than DR1,400,001 a year.

After the birth of a third child, there is a monthly benefit of DR34,000 for three years. A smaller 'lifelong' benefit will then follow.

Benefit is normally paid until children are 18, but until 22 if in further education and without limit in cases of serious infirmity. Parents who are widowed, invalids or soldiers can receive an extra DR1,250.

Unemployment benefit: Basic rates are 40% of daily earnings for manual workers and 50% for non-manual, subject to a minimum of two-thirds the daily minimum wage (DR2,911). The maximum, including allowances for dependants, is 70% of earnings. Benefit can be claimed for 12 months for at least 250 days of work.

WOMEN AND EMPLOYMENT

Statutory rights: The working week is limited to 5 days, and in the private sector to 40 hours. Overtime is restricted to 3 hours a day, 18 hours a week, and 150 hours a year. Paid annual leave is 24 days and there are 13 statutory public holidays.

In 1991 the national minimum wage was DR73,490 a month. All wages, including the national minimum, were index linked and increased every 4 months until 1990, when the new government refused to implement the increases. Wages cannot be seized in full by creditors. Normal wage bonuses include a thirteenth month's pay at Christmas and half a month's pay at Easter and at the start of annual leave.

Employment and unemployment (1989)

	% women	% men
economic activity rate	35.1	65.6
employed working part-time	8.0	2.4
labour force who are employers or self-employed	18.5	42.8
labour force who are family workers	31.4	5.1
unemployment rate	12.4	4.6
youth unemployment rate (age 14–24)	33.9	16.9
unemployed who have been unemployed for		
12 months or more	58.7	42.2
all unemployed by sex	61.3	38.7

Source: data from *Labour Force Survey (Results 1989)* (Eurostat)

Part-time workers: In 1989 64% of part-time workers were women. Part-time workers have the same rights as full-time workers. Recent changes have included a special protection scheme for part-time workers.

Employment by industrial sector (1000s) (1989)

	women		men		women as % of workforce
	no	%	no	%	
agriculture	415	32.3	515	21.6	44.6
all industry	222	17.3	723	30.3	23.5
energy and water	6	0.5	42	1.7	12.5
mineral extraction and chemicals	15	1.1	73	3.1	17.0
metal manufacturing and engineering	12	1.0	105	4.4	10.3
other manufacturing industry	188	14.6	266	11.1	41.1
building and civil engineering	–	–	237	9.9	–
all services	648	50.4	1,147	48.1	36.1
distributive trades and hotels	237	18.4	454	19.0	34.3
transport and communication	27	2.1	214	9.0	11.2
banking, finance and insurance	66	5.2	103	4.3	39.1
public administration	76	5.9	170	7.1	30.9
other services	242	18.8	207	8.7	53.9
total	**1,285**	**100.0**	**2,386**	**100.0**	**35.0**

Source: data from *Labour Force Survey (Results 1989)* (Eurostat)

Women's earnings as a % of men's in industry (October 1987)

	manual hourly earnings	non-manual monthly earnings
chemical industry	78.1	61.9
mechanical engineering	82.3	61.1
electrical engineering	94.2	69.6
food, drink and tobacco	84.9	70.4
clothing and footwear manufacture	80.7	73.3
printing and publishing	75.8	70.1
all manufacturing industry	78.7	65.1

Source: data from *Earnings in Industry and Services* (Eurostat)

Women's earnings as a % of men's in services (October 1987)

	non-manual monthly earnings
retail distribution	76.0
credit institutions	79.2
insurance (excluding social security)	77.3

Source: *Earnings in Industry and Services* (Eurostat)

It takes an average wait of 10 years to have a phone installed in Greece. The waiting list is estimated to be 1.5 million

Working mothers: In 1988 41% of women with a child under 10 were employed compared with 95% of similar men. 52% of women aged 20–39 without children were employed, one of the lowest levels in the EC. 12% of employed women with a child under 10 had part-time jobs. Greece has more employed women classified as 'family workers' (people who are not formally employed but work for a family member or business) than any other EC country – 24% compared with 6% overall.

Employment rates are higher for lone mothers than all mothers, because of greater levels of full-time employment; in 1988 figures were 47% for lone mothers with a child aged 0–4 (40% for all mothers) and 58% for lone mothers with a child aged 5–9 (41%).

Unemployment rates were twice as high for lone mothers: 14% for those with a child aged 0–4 (6% for all mothers) and 12% for those with a child aged 5–9 (6% for all mothers).

WOMEN IN TRADE UNIONS

Greek General Confederation of Labour, made up of 169 trade union bodies, has 25% women members, but a move to introduce a quota of 25% in ruling bodies was rejected during 1991. The proportion of women representatives on its administrative bodies has dropped from 7% to 2%. At its last congress, only 3.5% of delegates were women.

A survey by the Women's Secretariat found that only 4.49% of elected members of boards of directors of federations and regional labour centres were women. Within the confederation itself, there are no women on the 15-strong executive.

WOMEN AND POLITICS

Women hold 14 seats in the parliament, which accounts for only 4.7%. On the following page there is a breakdown, by party and gender, of the April 1990 general election.

Women in parliament (April 1990)

political party	total no of seats	no of seats held by women	% of seats held by women
New Democracy	152	8	5.3
Panhellenic Socialist Movement	124	6	4.8
Communist Party	7	0	0.0
Coalition of the Left	14	1	7.1
Greens	1	1	100.0
Independents	2	0	0.0
total	300	16	5.3

Source: data from Embassy of Greece, London

44% of women over 60 believe a wife should vote for the same party as her husband

In 1991 there were 8 women mayors out of a total of 352 (2.3%). 3% of local councillors were women and 46 out of a total of 5,563 presidents of community councils were women (0.8%).

One of Greece's 117 ambassadors was a woman, but the percentage of women was much higher among other diplomatic ranks: counsellors (5.3%), first secretaries (15%), second secretaries (30%), third secretaries (26%) and embassy attachés (36%).

WOMEN AND DETENTION

In 1988, 4.4% of prisioners were women; 6% were minors (below age 21) and young adults; 22.9% were foreigners.

SOURCES

Abortion Laws in Europe, Planned Parenthood in Europe, Vol 18 No 1, Spring 1989 (Supplement, amended April 1990) (published by International Planned Parenthood Federation, Europe Region); *Bargaining Report* 101 (Labour Research Department); *Childcare in the European Communities 1985–90* (*Women of Europe* Supplement No 51); *Comparative Study on Rules Governing Working Conditions in the Member States* (Commission of the European Communities); *Demographic Statistics 1990* (Eurostat); *Earnings in Industry and Services* (Eurostat); Embassy of Greece; *Europa World Year Book 1990* (31st edition); *Health Care Systems and Professional Organisations in the European Community, Information note –*

Europe (British Medical Association); Health For All 2000 Indicator Presentation System (World Health Organisation Regional Office for Europe); *Labour Force Survey (Results 1989)* (Eurostat); *Labour Research* September 1991 (Labour Research Department); *Les Actions Positives en Faveur des Femmes en Europe Occidentale* (Institut Syndical Europeen); *Out In Europe* (Peter Tatchell, for Channel 4 Television); *Planned Parenthood in Europe* (Vol 20, No 2) (International Planned Parenthood Federation, Europe Region); *Pocket World in Figures* (The Economist); *Positive action and the constitutional and legislative hindrances to its implementation in the member states of the Council of Europe* (Council of Europe); *Proposition de Directive Du Conseil concernant la protection au travail de la femme enceinte ou venant d'accoucher* (Commission of the European Communities); *Prison Information Bulletin* June 1990 (Council of Europe); *Social Protection in the Member States of the Community* (Commission of the European Community Directorate General on Employment, Industrial Relations and Social Affairs); *Third World Guide 91/92* (Instituto del Tercer Mundo); *Women of Europe* (Nos 64, 66, 68, 69); *Women of Europe* correspondent Poly Miliori; *Women's Struggle* (A Journal of the League for Women's Rights Nos 13, 37)

LETTER FROM GREECE

Poly Miliori, novelist, Athens, extracted from a speech given in Madrid in June 1990

You must not forget that Greece was occupied by the Turks for four centuries. During those centuries women were outcast from public life, in order to be protected against the Turks. They were worshipped as bearers of Greek children, as teachers of the Greek language and of Christian religion. Our history is the main reason for the conservative character of morals in Greece. The EC legislation became the alibi of many changes in Greek legislation. It helped a lot and will continue to help. In our present time:

- The woman keeps her surname on marriage.

- She has equal rights with her husband over the children.

- Her children out of wedlock are legally recognised.

- She has conquered the right to abortion.

Family and civil law changes preceded by far changes in accepted ethical and moral standards. They legalised claims of the women's movement, but the old mentality still exists.

Working women in Greece have the same problems as many other women in Europe: how to manage their private and social lives. The number of nurseries is inadequate and the primary schools function at most inconvenient hours for the parents – children are sent home early and many of the schools, due to shortages of classrooms, work in morning and afternoon shifts on a rotation basis.

Although creches and nurseries will be a very great help, I believe they will not solve the problem. Until the time comes when both parents face the raising of children in the same way – I mean with responsibility but also with joy – women's situation will not change.

ADDRESSES

Embassy of Greece, 1A Holland Park, London W11 3TP. Tel: 071 727 8040

General Secretariat for Equality, Ministry to the Presidency, 2 Mousseou Str, Plaka, 105 55 Athens. Tel: (301) 321 20 94

League for Women's Rights, 41 Solonos Street, Athens 10672. Tel: (30 1) 361 62 36

A Panagopoulou, General Secretary, Women's Union of Greece, 8 Enianos Street, Athens

Family Planning Association of Greece, 121 Solonos Street, Athens 106 78. Tel: (30 1) 36 06 390

Greek General Confederation of Labour, Odos Patission 69, Athens

EOK (lesbian and gay rights), PO Box 26077, 10022 Athens. Tel: (30 1) 52 3 9017

Hungary

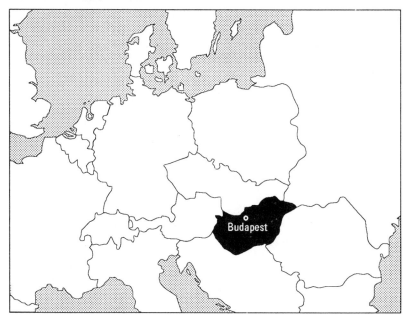

- **Population** 10.5 million, 51.9% female
- **Area** 93,030 sq km
- **Population density** 112 people sq km
- **GDP 1988** forints 1,411 billion (£17.4 billion)
- **GDP per capita** £1,628
- **GDP per capita in purchasing power parity** (UK=100) 47
- **Public spending as % of GNP:** defence 2.4% (1986); education 3.8% (1986); health 3.2% (1987)
- **Consumer price index** 1980 = 100; 1989 = 224
- **Currency is the forint** Official exchange rate 1989 £1 = FT100; US$1 = FT62.14

A 1990 Gallup
poll found
Hungary to be
the most
pessimistic nation
in Europe: 84%
expected 1991 to
be worse than
1990, compared
with 78% of
Czechoslovaks
and 49% of
Bulgarians

The republic of Hungary has a single-chamber parliament, the National Assembly, which has 386 members elected for 4 years by a mixture of proportional representation and direct election. The head of state is the president, elected by the National Assembly for 4 years. Local government is based on 19 counties plus the capital city. Voting is from the age of 18.

While 96% of the people are classed as ethnic Hungarian, this includes the gypsy population, estimated at almost 1 million (roughly 9.6% of total) in 1990. Minority groups include Germans (1.9%), Slovaks (1%), Croats (0.8%), Romanians (0.3%), Serbs and Slovenes (both .05%).

Most people are Christian, with the Roman Catholic Church the largest with 6 million members. An estimated 2 million belong to the Hungarian Reformed Church.

Almost 1 in 5 Hungarians (19.1% in 1990) live in Budapest, only a slight increase since 1960 (18.1%). However from 1960 to 1990 there was a big population drop in villages (60.3% to 38%) and an increase in towns (21.6% in 1960 to 42.9% in 1990).

BIRTH, LIFE AND DEATH

Breakdown of population by sex and age group (1000s) (1990 projection)

	all		women		men		% of women in age group
	no	%	no	%	no	%	
0–14	2,121.4	20.3	1,036.6	19.1	1,080.0	21.5	48.9
15–24	1,452.6	13.9	705.5	13.0	743.4	14.8	48.6
25–29	637.5	6.1	309.3	5.7	326.5	6.5	48.5
30–49	3,061.9	29.3	1,535.8	28.3	1,527.0	30.4	50.2
50–59	1,201.8	11.5	651.3	12.0	557.6	11.1	54.2
60–69	1,118.2	10.7	640.4	11.8	477.2	9.5	57.3
70+	856.9	8.2	548.1	10.1	311.4	6.2	64.0
total	10,450.3	100.0	5,427.0	100.0	5,023.1	100.0	51.9

Source: data from *Statistical Pocket Book of Hungary 1989* (Statistical Publishing House, Budapest)

Population density by region (1990)

region	area sq km	population (1000s)	pop density per sq km
Baranya	4,487	419	93
Bács-Kiskun	8,362	545	65
Békés	5,632	412	73
Borsod-Abaúj-Zemplén	7,247	762	105
Csongrád	4,263	439	103
Fejér	4,373	421	96
Györ-Moson-Sopron	4,012	425	106
Hajdú-Bihar	6,211	549	88
Heves	3,637	335	92
Jász-Nagykun-Szolnok	5,607	426	76
Komárom-Esztergom	2,251	315	140
Nógrád	2,544	227	89
Pest	6,394	950	149
(including Budapest)	525	2,016	3,840
Somogy	6,036	345	57
Szabolcs-Szatmár	5,938	572	96
Tolna	3,704	254	69
Vas	3,337	276	83
Veszprém	4,689	382	81
Zala	3,784	307	81
total	93,033	10,377	112

Source: *Europa World Year Book 1990* (31st edition)

Births, deaths, marriages and divorces for every 1,000 of population

	1930	1960	1970	1980	1989
birth rate	25.4	14.7	14.7	13.9	11.4
fertility rate per woman	–	–	2.01	1.89	1.88
infant mortality rate per 1,000 live births	152.5	47.6	35.9	23.2	15.8
life expectancy (women)	51.8	70.1	72.1	72.7	74.0[1]
life expectancy (men)	48.7	65.9	66.3	65.5	66.2[1]
death rate	15.5	10.2	11.6	13.6	13.3
marriage rate	9.0	8.9	9.3	7.5	6.2
divorce rate	0.6	1.7	2.2	2.6	2.3

[1] 1988

Source: data from *Statistical Pocket Book of Hungary 1989* (Statistical Publishing House, Budapest)

Population aged over 15 by marital status (1990)

	% all	% women	% men
single	20.3	15.8	25.3
married	61.5	58.5	64.8
widowed	11.2	17.8	3.9
divorced	7.0	7.9	6.0

Source: *Women of Hungary* (Eva Eberhardt, *Women of Europe* supplement number 32)

LESBIAN RIGHTS

Same-sex relationships were illegal until 1961 when the lesbian and gay age of consent was fixed at 20. It was lowered to 18 in 1978. The heterosexual age of consent is 14. Section 199 of the penal code refers to homosexuality as 'illicit sexual practices'.

WOMEN AND HEALTH CARE

Infant mortality decreased from 23 in 1980 to 17 in 1987 per 1,000 live births. More than 99% of babies are born in hospital. In 1988 there was 1 doctor for every 304 people.

Major indicators for women's health (1989)

maternal deaths (all causes) per 100,000 live births	15.41
maternal deaths (abortion) per 100,000 live births	2.43
ratio of abortions to 1,000 live births (all ages)	734.00
% of all live births to mothers under 20	12.25
% of all live births to mothers aged 35+	6.17
deaths from cancer of the cervix (age 0–64) per 100,000 women (1988)	6.35
deaths from malignant neoplasm female breast (age 0–64) per 100,000 women	20.86
deaths from trachea/bronchus/lung cancer (age 0–64) per 100,000 women	12.02
deaths from trachea/bronchus/lung cancer (age 0–64) per 100,000 men	61.80
deaths from diseases of the circulatory system (age 0–64) per 100,000 women	98.29
deaths from diseases of the circulatory system (age 0–64) per 100,000 men	255.92
deaths from suicide and self-inflicted injury per 100,000 women	20.40
deaths from suicide and self-inflicted injury per 100,000 men	62.67

Source: data from Health for All 2000 Indicator Presentation System (World Health Organisation Regional Office For Europe)

A 1990 poll for the National Institute of Health Care found 33% of people believe abortion is a fundamental human right, 17% want to retain the current law, 30% agree with abortion only if the life of the woman or child is in danger, and 2% are against it

Abortion and contraception: Abortion is available on request up to 12 weeks (18 weeks for minors) if the woman is single, over 35, inadequately housed, already has 2 children, or is suffering from ill health or bad social conditions. Available up to 20 weeks on health grounds. Abortions in 1990 cost FT2,000 each (estimated as 30% of a monthly income).

Since the April 1990 elections right-wing and religious groups have argued that abortion should be made illegal or more severely restricted. A petition in support of women's right to legal abortion was launched in July 1990 by the Feminist Network, with the support of the Green Party.

In 1986 54% of women were using oral contraceptives and 26% the IUD. Only 11% practised withdrawal, until the 1960s the most commonly used method of contraception.

PARENTAL PAY, LEAVE AND BENEFITS (1990)

Maternity leave and pay: 24 weeks on full pay including 4 that must be taken before the delivery date, provided national insurance contributions have been paid for 2 years before. There is also a flat-rate payment equal to two-thirds of average monthly income provided the mother has attended 4 required medical checks.

In a 1986 survey, 12% of working women said that, apart from sleeping, they had no free time

Child-care allowance and grant: Available for 2 years after maternity leave to mothers previously employed, and equal to 75% of previous salary. In the third year women are entitled to child-care grant equivalent to 40% of the average female wage. Fathers are entitled to child-care allowance from the second year but rarely claim it. In 1986 89% of eligible women were claiming either child-care allowance or grant. The numbers of women opting to care for their children until the third birthday has increased from 44% of manual and 23% of non-manual workers in the early 1970s to 60% of manual and 43% of non-manual workers in 1986.

Right of return to work: Legal changes in 1991 mean women who take the full 3 years of maternity leave have lost the right to have their jobs kept open.

CHILD-CARE PROVISION (1990)

Under 4s: 62.2% are looked after by mothers on maternity leave or on child-care allowance/grant, and 24.9% are in state funded places. Creches are available for all children under 3, though the long periods of leave available to mothers mean that most children in creches are 18 months to 3 years. Creches are open until 6pm.

64% of women between the ages of 15 and 55 registered as 'housewives' in the 1949 census, compared with 15% in the micro census of 1984

4–6 year olds: 77.9% are in nurseries, which are 30% workplace based and 70% run by the state. Nurseries are open until 6pm. 17.4% in this age group are cared for by their mothers – 8% while on child-care leave, 5.6% who are housewives; 2.9% who work at home and 0.9% who combine child-care with employment.

Primary school (6 years up): In 1988 the pupil to teacher ratio in primary schools was 14:1.

Outside school hours care: 65.7% of 7–10 year olds and 38.1% of 11–14 year olds have publicly funded places in after-school facilities, where children can do homework with supervision until 4pm or longer at the parents' request.

Care for sick children: Leave of 60 days on full pay plus 30 days on sick pay is available to women (and men who are lone parents) who have paid the necessary social security contributions, until the child is 3. If the illness lasts for longer, the mother qualifies for a caring benefit, and an allowance is also paid for each sick child.

Contributions to child-care costs: Child care is heavily subsidised by the state.

STATE BENEFITS (1990)

The constitution guarantees the right of all citizens to social security benefits.

Child benefit: Previously available only to employed parents, with the father claiming, this was made a universal benefit in March 1990. It is a flat-rate payment equal to one-third of average monthly income, for households with 2 or more children up to 16 (or 19 if still at school). It is also paid to families with 1 child up to the age of 6.

It takes between 10 and 15 years for a couple to buy a home. Construction by the State has fallen sharply, and the cost of building privately rose by 238% between 1980 and 1988

Retirement pensions: Retirement age is 55 (60 for men). Average pensions are 65% of average monthly income, but only 45%–50% for pensioners over 70. In 1987 26% of pensioners had incomes below subsistence level. 60% of pensioners are women.

Unemployment benefit: Paid at 70% of pay (to those who have been working for 12 months) for 1 year, up to a maximum of 3 times the average minimum income; then at 50% for a further year, with no benefit after that. In April 1991 the average monthly unemployment benefit paid to women was FT5,512 (77.6% of the average of FT7,102 paid to men).

WOMEN AND EMPLOYMENT

Equality: The 1967 Labour Code prohibits the 'disadvantageous differentiation' among workers on the grounds of sex (also race, nationality, origin and age). However the code also bans women and minors from 'work which would have disadvantageous consequences for their physical health and future development'. Jobs deemed to be dangerous include mining, piloting aeroplanes and driving tractors. The ban on women bus drivers was lifted in the 1980s during a shortage of male drivers.

Employers can specify the gender of applicants for job vacancies. At the end of 1989, registers of jobs available showed that 68% were reserved for men.

Statutory rights: The minimum monthly wage in April 1991 was FT7,000.

Second economy: A major factor affecting working women is the high level of paid work undertaken in addition to existing jobs. Eva Eberhardt's report

Ilona Hardy, director of Hungary's stock market which opened in summer of 1990, is the first woman ever to head a stock market

Women of Hungary estimates that 75% of families take part in the 'second economy', with working days totalling 11–12 hours, little leisure time at weekends and virtually no holidays.

A 1986 survey of married working couples on how much domestic work was carried out by the woman alone was highest for ironing (83.2%), washing (79.2%) and cooking (78%). Highest rates of shared domestic chores were finance and bills (47.4%), cleaning (20.2%) and daily shopping (20%). For activities carried out by the man alone, home repairs came first (74.1%) followed by weekend shopping in only 6.5% of families.

Economic activity (1989)

	% women	% men
economic activity rates	41.7	54.2
labour market participation rates	73.9	80.5

Where people work by industrial sector

no (millions)	agriculture	industry	other	total
1960	1.83	1.35	1.56	4.74
1970	1.25	1.79	1.94	4.98
1980	1.04	1.70	2.33	5.07
1987	0.94	1.53	2.41	4.88
%	agriculture	industry	other	total
1960	38.6	28.5	32.9	100.0
1970	25.1	35.9	39.0	100.0
1980	20.5	33.5	46.0	100.0
1987	19.3	31.2	49.5	100.0

Source: *Doing Business with Eastern Europe – Hungary* (Business International)

Breakdown of economic activity of women of working age (%) (1988)

active wage earners	74.0
on child-care leave	8.0
pensioners (widowed and disabled)	3.9
students	7.3
dependants	6.8

Source: data from *Women of Hungary* (Eva Eberhardt, *Women of Europe* supplement number 32)

Unemployment: While the figure is low – 1.5% at the beginning of 1990 – this is a 50% increase from 1989. In 1989 women made up 40% of registered unemployed. In April 1991 unemployment was rising by 17% a month.

Part-time workers: The vast majority of women workers are employed full time. Only 3% of women work part time, and 6% are self-employed, either. Part-time workers have the same employment rights as full-time workers and are entitled to the same benefits in proportion to their hours of work.

Analysis of active wage earners in the socialist sector (%)

	1985		1988	
	women	men	women	men
manual workers	59.5	78.5	58.3	78.2
skilled	12.1	45.4	14.4	46.0
semi-skilled	30.0	23.4	29.8	23.1
unskilled	15.9	9.7	14.1	9.1
non-manual workers	40.5	21.5	41.7	21.8
in engineering	3.5	9.7	3.5	9.7
in administrative office work	10.5	7.0	11.4	7.0
health and culture	12.4	3.5	11.8	3.5
bookkeeping and accountancy	14.1	1.3	15.0	1.6

Source: *Superwomen and the Double Burden* (ed Chris Corrin, Scarlet Press)

Women's average pay as a percentage of men's by sector (1987)

	%
industry	73
construction industry	69
agriculture and forestry	70
transport	71
commerce	80
water works	66

Source: data from *Women of Hungary* (Eva Eberhardt, *Women of Europe* supplement number 32)

Women's average pay as a percentage of men's by occupations (1987)

	%
mechanical instrument makers	85
weavers	90
textile workers	75
postal workers	93
food shop assistants	88
hairdressers	89
office workers	90
managers	86

Source: data from *Women of Hungary* (Eva Eberhardt, *Women of Europe* supplement number 32)

Comparative earnings: Equal pay was guaranteed in law when the constitution was amended in 1972. As a result the earnings differential is greater for older women than for younger. The concentration of women in the lowest paid jobs is the main reason for women's lower earnings.

WOMEN IN TRADE UNIONS

The Women's Steering Committee of Trade Unions reports that among their main areas of work is the new draft Labour Code, which excludes rights commonly granted by Western countries, such as the general principle of banning women from nightwork. An estimated 100,000 women were working night-shift in April 1991.

WOMEN AND POLITICS

Women won the right to vote in 1945. After the spring 1990 election, 7.3% of MPs are women. Under the previous government a quota system applied and 21% of MPs were women. The Hungarian Social Democratic Party is the only political party with a policy for women as part of its programme.

Women elected to the Hungarian parliament 1990

political party	total no of seats	no of seats held by women	% of seats held by women
Hungarian Democratic Forum	164	8	4.9
Alliance of Free Democrats	94	8	8.5
Independent Smallholders' Party	44	5	11.4
Hungarian Socialist Party	33	3	9.1
Federation of Young Democrats	22	2	9.1
Christian Democratic People's Party	21	1	4.8
independents	8	1	12.5
total	**386**	**28**	**7.3**

Sources: *Women of Hungary* (Eva Eberhardt, *Women of Europe* supplement number 32); *The Parliament of the Republic of Hungary (Fact Sheets on Hungary 1990 No 2)* (Ministry of Foreign Affairs, Budapest)

WOMEN AND EDUCATION

Choice of further education at the age of 14 (%)

	1980		1987	
	women	men	women	men
skill/training school	36.1	57.8	36.7	57.2
technical college	26.7	24.3	27.7	25.9
gymnasium	27.7	13.8	28.1	14.1
total	**90.5**	**95.9**	**92.5**	**97.2**

Source: *Superwomen and the Double Burden* (ed Chris Corrin, Scarlet Press)

% of full-time students who are women in higher education (1987)

teacher training	51.7
medicine	54.4
health work	96.3
economics	64.6
law and public administration	57.3
engineering	15.3
agriculture	31.2
veterinary medicine	19.5
total	**51.7**

Source: *Women of Hungary* (Eva Eberhardt, *Women of Europe* supplement number 32)

In 1987 34.2% of vocational training students were female, with high concentrations in the garment

(98.2%), textile (98.1%) and leather (79.6%) industries. Teaching is heavily dominated by women, particularly in pre-school and primary education. 1987 figures show that 100% of kindergarten and pre-school teachers were women, 94% of teachers of the handicapped and 88% of primary teachers were women. 72% of teacher trainers were also women.

SOURCES

Abortion Laws in Europe, Planned Parenthood in Europe, Vol 18 No 1, Spring 1989 (Supplement, amended April 1990); *Doing Business with Eastern Europe – Hungary* (Business International); *Europa World Year Book 1990* (31st edition); *Fact Sheets on Hungary 1990. No 1: The Republic of Hungary. No 2: The Parliament of the Republic of Hungary* (Ministry of Foreign Affairs, Budapest); Health For All 2000 Indicator Presentation System (World Health Organisation Regional Office for Europe); *Hungarian Observer* (Vol 3 No 8, Vol 4 No 4); *Out In Europe* (Peter Tatchell, for Channel 4 Television); *Planned Parenthood in Europe* (Vol 19 No 2) (International Planned Parenthood Federation); *Pocket World in Figures* (The Economist); *Statistical Pocket Book of Hungary 1989* (Statistical Publishing House, Budapest); *Superwomen and the Double Burden* (ed. Chris Corrin, Scarlet Press); *Third World Guide 91/92* (Instituto del Tercer Mundo); *Women of Europe* (No 68); *Women of Hungary* (Eva Eberhardt, *Women of Europe* supplement No 32); *Women in Hungary* (Central Statistical Office, Budapest 1980); Women's Steering Committee of Trade Unions

ADDRESSES

Embassy of the Republic of Hungary, 35 Eaton Place, London SW1 8BY. Tel: 071 235 7191/4048

Hungarian Book Agency, 87 Sewardstone Road, London E2 9HN. Tel: 071 980 9096

Pro Familia Hungarian Scientific Society (family planning service), Buday László u 1-3,1024 Budapest. Tel: (36 1) 35 85 30

Women's Steering Committee of Trade Unions, Magyar Szakszervezetek, Országos Szövetsége, 1415 Budapest VI, Dózsa György út 84/b

Homeros Lambda (lesbian and gay rights), c/o Peter Ambrus, Menesi UT 17/B/1/7, 1118 Budapest XI. Tel: (361) 377 173/414 315

Iceland

- **Population** 253,785, 49.8% female
- **Area** 103,000 sq km
- **Population density** 2.5 people sq km
- **GDP per capita** £10,292
- **Public spending as % of GNP:** defence 3.5% (1986); education 3.7% (1986); health 6.9% (1987)
- **Consumer price index** 1980 = 100; 1989 = 1,711
- **Currency is the króna** 1989 £1 = ISK88.9; US$1 = ISK55.1

The president is head of state and is elected for 4 years. While the president holds executive power and appoints the prime minister and other ministers, in practice she (or he) has only nominal powers.

Legislative power is held jointly by the president and the parliament (Althing), whose 63 members are elected for 4 years by proportional representation. The Althing chooses 21 members to form the upper house; the remaining 42 form the lower house. Local government is based on provinces, districts and municipalities. The age for voting was lowered from 20 to 18 in 1987.

Iceland is Europe's second largest island, after Britain. 82,000 sq km of its area is unproductive including 12,000 sq km of glaciers. 1,100 sq km is cultivated with 20,000 sq km devoted to rough grazing. More than half the population lives in or around the capital Reykjavik. 93% of people belong to the state church, the Evangelical Lutheran Church.

IMMIGRATION AND RESIDENCE RIGHTS

Unless citizens of another Nordic country, foreigners who want to work for 3 or more months must have work permits before starting. Work permits, issued by the Ministry of Social Affairs after consultation with trade unions, are not generally issued unless there is a shortage of domestic labour. Most foreign workers in Iceland are in the seasonal fish processing industry or have jobs in hospitals. During their first 2 years foreign workers can transfer up to 40% of their earnings into foreign currency. Marriage partners of Icelandic nationals who have lived in Iceland for at least 2 years do not need residence permits, which all other foreigners who are staying longer than 3 months must have.

Equal rights legislation was passed in 1976 within a year of a 1-day strike by women

Individuals can apply for Icelandic citizenship after 10 years of residence (5 if citizens of another Nordic country). Foreign partners of Icelandic nationals can apply for citizenship after 3 years of marriage or 5 years of cohabitation.

EQUAL RIGHTS

The 1985 Law on the Equal Status and Equal Rights of Women and Men establishes equal rights and status 'of women and men in every sphere'. Although it prohibits any form of sex discrimination, it specifies that special allowances for women on account of pregnancy and childbirth is not discrimination.

The Equal Status Council implements the law. It consists of 7 members taken from the supreme court, the Ministry of Social Affairs, employers' and employees' groups, plus women's groups. The council, funded by the state treasury, carries out research and formulates policy and can bring legal proceedings to enforce compliance. Fines can be imposed on law-breakers.

BIRTH, LIFE AND DEATH

Breakdown of population by sex and age group (1989)

	all		women		men		% of women in age group
	no	%	no	%	no	%	
0–14	63,446	25.0	31,024	24.6	32,422	25.4	48.9
15–24	42,418	16.7	20,809	16.6	21,609	17.0	49.1
25–39	61,457	24.2	30,043	23.8	31,414	24.7	48.9
40–59	49,685	19.6	24,593	19.5	25,092	19.7	49.5
60–74	25,353	10.0	13,131	10.4	12,224	9.6	51.8
75+	11,426	4.5	6,755	5.4	4,671	3.7	59.1
all	253,785	100.0	126,353	100.0	127,432	100.0	49.8

Source: data from *Tölfraeðihandbók* (Hagstofa Islands)

Births and deaths per 1,000 population (1988)

birth rate	16.1
death rate	8.0
infant mortality rate per 1,000 live births	5.0
marriage rate	4.0
life expectancy (women)	80.4
life expectancy (men)	74.8
fertility rate per woman	2.05

Source: data from *Demographic Statistics 1990* (Eurostat)

According to the 1984 census, 21% of families with children were supported by a lone parent, an increase of 20% since 1974.

Parents who live together share custody of children until the age of 16, at which point children are judged as able to handle their own affairs. Children become financially independent in law at the age of 18. Unmarried women with children have sole custody unless living with the fathers. Women and men have had equal status in marriage since 1923.

LESBIAN RIGHTS

The age of consent for lesbians and heterosexuals is 16 (18 for gay men). Unlike heterosexual prostitution, homosexual prostitution is illegal. Distinctions between heterosexuality and homosexuality are expected to be removed from the penal code. The lesbian and gay movement receives a small amount of funding from the government.

WOMEN AND HEALTH CARE

Health insurance covers medical treatment, hospital and maternity expenses.

General practitioners are employed by health-care centres, which provide free services and consultations including maternity care, infant and child care, cancer screening and family and parental counselling. Fees are charged for specialist services at a fixed rate for each consultation: in 1990 this was ISK300 for pensioners and the disabled and ISK900 for others. In 1990 prescription charges were ISK500–750 (ISK170–230 for pensioners and the disabled). Ambulance service charges were ISK1,700 for each trip in 1990. In 1988 there was 1 doctor for every 425 people.

Dental care is free for children aged 6–16, with 75% of charges being refunded for children under 6. Social security rules apply to dental treatment of pensioners.

Major indicators for women's health (1989)

maternal deaths (all causes) per 100,000 live births	0.00
maternal deaths (abortion) per 100,000 live births	0.00
ratio of abortions to 1,000 live births (all ages)	146.93
% of all live births to mothers under 20	6.60
% of all live births to mothers aged 35+	10.77
deaths from cancer of the cervix (age 0–64) per 100,000 women (1988)	2.72
deaths from malignant neoplasm female breast (age 0–64) per 100,000 women	20.27
deaths from trachea/bronchus/lung cancer (age 0–64) per 100,000 women	19.39
deaths from trachea/bronchus/lung cancer (age 0–64) per 100,000 men	15.41
deaths from diseases of the circulatory system (age 0–64) per 100,000 women	30.25
deaths from diseases of the circulatory system (age 0–64) per 100,000 men	76.60
deaths from suicide and self-inflicted injury per 100,000 women	5.15
deaths from suicide and self-inflicted injury per 100,000 men	13.06

Source: data from Health for All 2000 Indicator Presentation System (World Health Organisation Regional Office For Europe)

Abortion: Available up to 12 weeks because of social circumstances, on medical grounds or if a women has been raped. Generally abortions are not permitted after 16 weeks unless there are serious medical grounds.

PARENTAL PAY, LEAVE AND BENEFITS (1990)

Maternity and paternity leave and pay: 6 months' leave can be shared by both parents. Adoptive and foster parents can share combined leave of up to 5 months. During leave all mothers receive a maternity subsidy and (if previously employed) both parents qualify for a proportion of their pay, the size of which depends on their trade union agreements with employers. Government employees receive their full average earnings over the previous 12 months for the first 3 months, and their full basic salary for the second 3 months. Central and local government women employees can also extend maternity leave to 12 months with a proportionate loss of earnings.

Motherhood allowance: This is paid to widowed, unmarried and divorced mothers responsible for their children's upkeep until they are 18. The allowance may also be paid to fathers in similar circumstances.

Time off to look after sick children: There is no legislation for this, but government employees and private sector workers with union agreements can take up to 7 days a year to take care of children under 13.

CHILD-CARE PROVISION (1990)

0–5 year olds: 8.9% of children aged 6 months to 5 years have full-time child-care places, almost all of which are reserved for the children of lone parents and students. 35% of all children aged 2–5 have half-day places in playschools. Most day-care centres are publicly funded, though there are long waiting lists for municipal care centres.

Primary school (6 years up): Primary education is compulsory from age 6 to 16. The school year is from September to May. Tuition and textbooks are free. In 1985 two-thirds of schoolchildren had discontinuous school hours.

Outside school hours care: Places are reserved for the 6 to 10 year old children of lone parents.

Contributions to child-care costs: In 1973 the first ever child-care law established a joint responsibility of the state and municipal authorities to provide child-care services.

STATE BENEFITS (1990)

Pensions: Normal retirement age is 65 (public sector) or 70 (private sector) for women and men. The law requires individuals to make contributions to a pension fund for old age pensions and disability benefits. Employers are legally responsible for making pension fund payments. Employers contribute 6%, and employees 4% of earnings.

Survivors' benefits: A surviving spouse under 67 is entitled to 6 months' benefits after the death, plus an additional 12 months if supporting a child under 18. Only women are entitled to a widow's pension after this period, provided they are over 50 when their husbands die or are under 50 and have children. Women without children who are under 50 at the time of death can qualify when they reach 50, as long as the marraige lasted at least 20 years. The widow's pension is paid until the age of 67, when the normal retirement pension is paid.

Child benefit: Paid for each child under 16 who is a dependant of a taxpayer. There is a special child benefit paid to low-income families. Parents with official child maintenance awards receive payments from the Social Security Institute.

Children's allowance: Paid for children under 18 years if 1 parent is dead or receiving disability allowance, provided the child or either parent has been living in Iceland for at least 3 years.

Sickness and accident benefit: Paid to all citizens over 17 if they are not entitled to other benefits, with the amount paid depending on how much work is missed. People whose occupation is housework are also entitled to sickness benefit. All paid employees are insured against accident, and those in housework can pay for accident insurance as part of their tax returns.

Benefit levels vary with length of employment and whether the illness or accident is work related. Minimum rights during an employee's first 12 months are 2 days' full pay for each month of service.

Health insurance: see Women and Health Care section.

Unemployment benefit: To qualify you must be a trade union member and have worked a minimum of 425 hours in the previous 12 months. Benefit is paid as a flat-rate daily allowance ranging from (June 1991) ISK2,105 (for those who have worked for 1,700 hours in the previous 12 months) to ISK526 (for 425 hours). For each child under 18 an additional benefit of ISK84.20 a day is paid. Benefit is paid for 5 days a week up to a maximum of 260 days in a period of 12 months.

WOMEN AND EMPLOYMENT

The number of women working outside the home rose from 20% in 1960 to 84% in 1986. The same year 90% of women between 16 and 74 had their own incomes. The highest proportion of working mothers is 95% for those with one child; the proportion decreases with the number of children.

Women in employment (1991)

	women		men	
	no (1000s)	%	no (1000s)	%
employed	93.2	71.9	113.2	84.7
apprenticeship	.3	0.2	0.9	0.7
unemployed	1.2	0.9	1.7	1.3
working at home	15.3	11.8	0.3	0.2
retired/disabled	6.1	4.7	3.7	2.8
ill/temporarily disabled	0.6	0.5	0.9	0.7
students	12.4	9.6	12.6	9.4
others	0.4	0.3	0.1	0.1
total	129.6	100.0	133.7	100.0

Source: data from *Hagtíðindi – Monthly Statistics, No 6 1991* (Hagstofa Islands)

Full-time/part-time employment by sex (1991)

	women		men	
	no	%	no	%
full-time workers	45,200	49.3	99,600	88.2
part-time workers	40,000	43.6	7,600	6.7
workers with no formal hours	2,000	2.2	3,300	2.9
occasional workers	4,500	4.9	2,500	2.2
total	91,700	100.0	112,900	100.0

Source: data from *Hagtíðindi – Monthly Statistics, No 6 1991* (Hagstofa Islands)

The first Icelandic feature film to be made by a woman was Sóley, produced in 1982 by the director Róska

The average working week in 1986 for women was 36.7 total hours of work, compared with 52.2 for men. This breaks down into 35 hours normal working week plus 1.7 hours in a second job, compared with 50 hours normal working plus 2 hours in a second job for men.

Statutory rights : All paid workers have the right to a paid holiday. The minimum is 24 days (4 weeks plus

4 days) for those with the same employer for 12
months, though this is extended to 6 weeks for some.
Others are entitled to 2 days' paid holiday for each
month worked the previous year. The holiday year
runs from 1 May until 30 April, with holidays being
given in one block between 2 May and 15 September.
A holiday bonus of at least 10.17% of wages is paid,
based on the minimum vacation period.

Employment by industrial sector (1991)

	women		men	
	no	**%**	**no**	**%**
agriculture	4,000	4.3	7,700	6.8
fishing	700	0.8	9,300	8.2
manufacturing (incl. fish processing)	15,800	16.9	19,800	17.5
electricity and water supply	300	0.3	2,300	2.0
construction	800	0.9	15,400	13.6
wholesale and retail trade	13,100	14.1	18,100	16.0
hotels and restaurants	3,800	4.1	2,600	2.3
transport and communications	4,200	4.5	9,200	8.1
finance	5,400	5.8	2,200	1.9
business services	3,500	3.8	6,200	5.5
government services	4,100	4.4	8,200	7.2
education	6,500	7.0	2,900	2.6
health and social services	23,900	25.6	4,300	3.8
other services	6,900	7.4	5,000	4.4
household services	200	0.2	–	–
total	**93,200**	**100.0**	**113,200**	**100.0**

Source: data from *Hagtíðindi – Monthly Statistics, No 6 1991* (Hagstofa Islands)

Average earnings: Despite the fact that Iceland was
the first Nordic country to ratify the International
Labour Organisation Convention on equal pay in
1958 and the Equal Pay Act of 1961, women's
average income was still only 61% of men's in 1986
and has not improved significantly since then.

Taxation: Tax is deducted at source, at a single rate
and with a single personal allowance. In 1990 the rate
was 39.79% and the personal allowance was
ISK257,784.

WOMEN IN TRADE UNIONS

Women make up 46% of the Icelandic Federation of Labour, and have one-third of the seats on its central committee. The proportion of women in the federation of public sector workers is 64%, with women in 53% of the seats on its central committee.

WOMEN AND POLITICS

Women won the right to vote in local elections in 1909, and in parliamentary elections in 1915. The first woman was elected to the Althing, the Icelandic parliament, in 1922 but it was 1970 before a woman was appointed to the cabinet. Iceland has had a woman president, Vigdis Finnbogadóttir, since 1980.

Women elected to parliament (the Althing) after the 20 April 1991 general election

political party	total no of seats	no of seats held by women	% of seats held by women
Independence Party	26	4	15.4
Progressive Party	13	2	15.4
People's Alliance	9	2	22.2
Social Democrats	10	2	20.0
Women's List	5	5	100.0
total	63	15	23.8

Source: data from Embassy of Iceland, London

One of the 10 ministers appointed after the 1991 election is a woman.

Vigdis Finnbogadóttir became the first woman in the world elected president when she became President of Iceland in 1980

The Women's Alliance emerged out of a tradition in Iceland of all-women election lists that began in 1908 when women in Reykjavik put forward a special list of women candidates for the local elections which won 21% of the vote. The 4 women elected (out of 15 council members) were the first women to win seats on municipal councils in Iceland. In 1922 women again put forward their own list – this time for the parliamentary election – and Ingibjörg Björnsson became the first woman MP.

After the 1986 elections, 19% of municipal councillors and 32% of city and town councillors were women. There are 7 women on the 15-strong Reykjavik city council, by far the largest council in Iceland.

One of Iceland's 12 ambassadors is a woman.

WOMEN AND EDUCATION

Women and men have had equal rights to education since 1911, when Iceland became the first country in the world to grant women the same statutory rights as men.

Between 1975 and 1985, 98% of the students of the Nursing School of Iceland were women; 12 men obtained a diploma in this period

Eleven colleges in Iceland offer university level courses. The largest, with 5,000 students, is the University of Iceland. Foreign students there are offered a 2-year course in Icelandic. Most university level education is run by the state and there are no fees. Students, including foreigners who have worked in Iceland for 3 years, can apply to the Icelandic Student Loan Fund for loans to fund their studies.

Projects in women's studies are co-ordinated by the Forum for Icelandic Women's Studies in Reykjavik.

% of women students in further education (1986)

teaching	83
other education	83
social science/behavioural science	71
medicine/pharmacy	71
arts subjects	67
law	46
commerce/economics	40
natural sciences	40
religion	38
mathematics/data technology	23
technical subjects	15

Source: data from *Kvinnor och män i Norden – Fakta om jämställdheten 1988* (Nordic Council of Ministers)

WOMEN AND DETENTION

In 1988 the proportion of women among prisoners was 3.4%. Minors (age 22) and young adults detained accounted for 12.4%, and foreigners for 1.1%.

SOURCES

An Outline of History 1975–1985 Jónína Margrét Gudnadóttir; Embassy of Iceland; *Demographic Statistics 1990* (Eurostat); *Employment in Iceland – Practical Information for Foreign Nationals* (Ministry of Social Affairs); *Europa World Year Book 1990* (31st edition); *Hagtídindi – Monthly Statistics* No 6, 1991 (Hagstofa Islands); Health for All 2000 Indicator Presentation System (World Health Organisation Regional Office For Europe); *Icelandic Law and Icelandic Society* (Ministry of Social Affairs 1990); *Kvinnor och män i Norden – Fakta om jämstäldheten 1988* (Nordic Council of Ministers); *Les Actions Positives en Faveur des Femmes en Europe Occidentale* (Institut Syndical Europeen); *Out In Europe* (Peter Tatchell, for Channel 4 Television); *Prison Information Bulletin* June 1990 (Council of Europe); *Third World Guide 91/92* (Instituto del Tercer Mundo); *Tölfrædihandbók 1990* (Hogstofa Islands); *Women and Equality in Iceland* (Jafnréttisrád); *Women and Men in the Nordic Countries* (Christina Österberg and Birgitta Hedman, Nordic Council of Ministers); *Women's Status on the Labour Market in Iceland Today;* Speech by Lára V Júliusdóttir, Icelandic Federation of Labour, 1990; *Women's Studies and Research on Women in the Nordic Countries* (ed. Mie Berg Simonson and Mona Eliasson for Nordic Forum)

LETTER FROM ICELAND

Lára V Júliusdóttir of the Icelandic Federation of Labour, 1990.

Women's role as mother is the main reason women do not have equality in the labour market. The more children women have, the less work they can do outside their home. Taking care of the children depends mostly on the mother, in spite of all the discussion on equality in my country.

Better education does not seem to have a great effect on this – women seem to choose this model themselves. If women really want equality in the labour market they must share the responsibility of the home with their husbands.

The income of women is lower than men's for day rates and overtime. This is the issue over which women have fought the hardest for the past years. Also the difference in working time in Iceland is considerably more than in the other Nordic countries – for men 52 hours and for women 42 hours a week. While this can explain the biggest part of the income difference, there is still an unexplained difference of about 10%.

With equality legislation, and through general agreements, attempts have been made to improve the status of women workers. From 1980 we have had maternity leave law, and today it is 6 months long. Parents are allowed 7 absence days per year on full pay if children get sick and the labour movement has pressed hard to get more day-care centres built.

In spite of all this women are being discriminated against in their work. Pregnant women are fired, new mothers are being put in different jobs when they come back from maternity leave, middle-aged women are sent home and younger women hired instead, for a company's 'facelift', and women tolerate sexual harassment in the workplace. These matters are often very delicate and hard to deal with. The equal status council deals with a lot of them and people from the unions sit on the council.

Of course, we hope for the best in the future. Women in Iceland are very much aware of their position and try hard through the unions, in politics and in the workplace to improve things. One woman said to me once, 'My grandmother told my mother that the key to equality was the right to vote. My mother told me that the key to equality was education, and the situation is still what it is. What shall I tell my daughter?'

ADDRESSES

Embassy of Iceland,1 Eaton Terrace, London SW1W 8EY.
Tel: 071 730 5131/2

The Equal Status Council, Laugavegi 13, 101 Reykjavik

Kvenfelagasamband Islands, Federation of Icelandic Women's
Societies, Tungata 14, 101 Reykjavik

Kvennalistinn, The Women's List, Laugavegur 17,
101 Reykjavik. Tel: (354 1) 13725

Hagstofa Islands, Statistical Bureau of Iceland, Skuggasund 3,
150 Reykjavik. Tel: (354 1) 609800

Icelandic Federation of Labour, Grensásvegur 16A,
108 Reykjavik. Tel: (354 1) 83044

Samtokin '78, (lesbian and gay rights), PO Box 4166,
124 Reykjavik. Tel: (354 1) 28 539

Ahugahopur Um Islemskar Kvennarannsoknir (Forum for
Icelandic Women's Studies), Háskóli Islands, 101 Reykjavik.
Tel: (354 1) 91 69 44 48/91 2 62 69

Kvennasögusafen Islands (Iceland's Library for Women's
History), Hjardarhaga 26, 107 Reykjavik.
Tel: (354 1) 91 1 22 04

Ireland

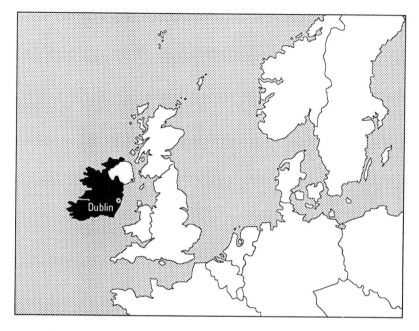

- **Population** 3.5 million, 50% female
- **Area** 70,282 sq km
- **Population density** 50.4 people sq km
- **GDP 1988** Irish £21 billion (£20.5 billion)
- **GDP per capita** £5,692
- **GDP per capita in purchasing power parity** (UK=100) 62
- **Public spending as % of GNP:** defence 1.9% (1986); education 6.9% (1986); health 7.8% (1987)
- **Consumer price index** 1980 = 100; 1989 = 206
- **Currency is the punt** 1989 £1 = IR£1.03; US$1 = IR£0.64

When Mary Robinson started her campaign for the presidency in May 1990, bookmakers put her chances at 100 to 1. Six months later she was elected with 52% of the vote

Ireland has a 2-chamber parliament – the Senate (Seanad Éireann), which has restricted powers, and the House of Representatives (Dáil Éireann). The Senate has 60 members, 11 nominated by the prime minister and 49 directly elected for 5 years. The House has 166 members elected for 5 years by single transferable vote, a form of proportional representation. The head of state is the president, who is directly elected for 7 years. Executive power is held by the prime minister (Taoiseach) appointed by the president on nomination by the Dáil. Other ministers are nominated by the prime minister and approved by the Dáil.

Irish is the official first language, but its vernacular use is restricted to certain areas. English is universally spoken. 95% of the population is Roman Catholic and 5% Protestant.

IMMIGRATION AND RESIDENCE RIGHTS

Citizens of other EC states and those who can show that 1 parent or grandparent was born in Ireland can live there without restriction. EC citizens do not require work permits. Citizens of other countries cannot work unless their prospective employer has obtained a work permit from the Ministry of Labour.

Anyone born outside Ireland whose mother or father is Irish and born in Ireland has automatic rights to citizenship. If the mother or father is Irish but born outside the country, a child can become a citizen by registering at the Department of Foreign Affairs, or an Irish embassy. After 3 years of marriage partners of Irish citizens can apply for citizenship.

In 1988 Ireland had 83,500 foreign residents, 52.2% of them women. 79.5% of foreign residents were from other EC states.

EQUAL RIGHTS

The constitution states that 'all citizens shall, as human persons, be held equal before the law.'

However, the Council for the Status of Women is campaigning for an Equal Status Act. In Ireland it is legal to limit women's access to financial services and sports, entertainment or refreshment facilities, and to refuse to rent accommodation to women.

BIRTH, LIFE AND DEATH

In 1987 the natural increase for every 1,000 of the population was 7.8, but because of the number of people leaving the country – there was a net migration rate of minus 7.1 – the total increase for every 1,000 population was just 0.7.

Breakdown of population by sex and age group (1000s) (1988)

	all		women		men		% of women in age group
	no	%	no	%	no	%	
0–14	1,001.7	28.3	487.5	27.5	514.2	29.1	48.7
15–24	611.3	17.3	298.8	16.9	312.5	17.7	48.9
25–39	730.6	20.6	364.2	20.6	366.4	20.7	49.8
40–59	668.8	18.9	329.3	18.6	339.5	19.2	49.2
60–74	376.5	10.6	200.1	11.3	176.4	10.0	53.1
75+	150.4	4.2	91.1	5.1	59.3	3.4	60.6
all	3,539.3	100.0	1,771.0	100.0	1,768.3	100.0	50.0

Source: data from *Demographic Statistics 1990* (Eurostat)

Population density by province (1986)

region	area sq km	population	pop density per sq km
Connaught	17,122	431,409	25.2
Leinster	19,633	1,852,649	94.4
Munster	24,127	1,020,577	42.3
Ulster (part)	8,012	236,008	29.5
total	68,894	3,540,643	51.4

Source: *Europa World Year Book 1990* (31st edition)

Births, deaths, marriages and divorces for every 1,000 of population

	1960	1970	1980	1985	1988
birth rate	21.4	21.9	21.8	17.6	15.3
% of births outside marriage	1.2	2.7	5.0	8.6	11.7
average age of mother at 1st birth	27.2	25.3	24.9	26.0	26.0
infant mortality per 1,000 live births	29.3	19.5	11.1	8.8	9.2
fertility rate per woman	3.8	3.9	3.2	2.5	2.2
marriage rate	5.5	7.0	6.4	5.3	5.1
average age at marriage (women)	27.2	25.1	24.4	25.3	25.8[1]
average age at marriage (men)	30.9	27.7	26.6	27.4	27.9[1]
life expectancy (women)	71.9[2]	73.5[3]	75.6[4]	–	76.7[5]
life expectancy (men)	68.1[2]	68.8[3]	70.1[4]	–	71.0[5]
death rate	11.5	11.4	9.9	9.4	8.9

[1] 1987; [2] 1960–62; [3] 1970–72; [4] 1980–82; [5] 1985–87

Source: data from *Demographic Statistics 1990* (Eurostat)

One-parent households accounted for 6% of households with a child aged 0–9 in 1988.

LESBIAN RIGHTS

The 1989 Prohibition of Incitement to Hatred Act makes it illegal to incite hatred on the grounds of sexual orientation (also race, colour, religion, membership of a travelling community and ethnic or national background).

WOMEN AND HEALTH CARE

Public health care is funded by the Department of Health, and private care is also available. Charges for public medical care are means tested according to income (for those on low income, the number of dependants and household expenditure are also taken into account). Patients on low incomes receive free health care, and 'middle-income' patients are entitled to free or subsidised GP services, dental and opthalmic services. Patients on high incomes have to pay for most health care, apart from free or subsidised in-patient hospital care and treatment for some chronic illnesses. There is a state-run voluntary health insurance scheme which is eligible for tax relief. In 1988 there was 1 doctor for every 689 people.

Major indicators for women's health (1988)

maternal deaths (all causes) per 100,000 live births	1.83
maternal deaths (abortion) per 100,000 live births	0.00
% of all live births to mothers under 20 (1987)	4.35
% of all live births to mothers aged 35+ (1987)	16.68
deaths from cancer of the cervix (age 0–64) per 100,000 women (1987)	3.15
deaths from malignant neoplasm female breast (age 0–64) per 100,000 women	26.70
deaths from trachea/bronchus/lung cancer (age 0–64) per 100,000 women	13.59
deaths from trachea/bronchus/lung cancer (age 0–64) per 100,000 men	30.07
deaths from diseases of the circulatory system (age 0–64) per 100,000 women	51.97
deaths from diseases of the circulatory system (age 0–64) per 100,000 men	148.70
deaths from suicide and self-inflicted injury per 100,000 women	4.84
deaths from suicide and self-inflicted injury per 100,000 men	12.06

Source: data from Health for All 2000 Indicator Presentation System (World Health Organisation Regional Office For Europe)

Ireland is the only EC member state where all abortions are illegal

Abortion and contraception: Abortion is illegal under the constitution (since 1983 following a referendum) and also under the Offences Against the Person Act (1861). In June 1991 the European Court upheld Ireland's ban on abortion information, saying it relates to 'a policy choice of a moral and philosophical nature' which is up to individual states to decide. However the EC position is likely to change as a result of the 1992 case of a 14-year-old rape victim who was prevented by Irish law from having an abortion in England where she had already travelled to have her pregnancy terminated. Within weeks the Irish supreme court ruled she should be allowed to have an abortion because the pregnancy posed a special threat to her life. She had threatened suicide. An estimated 8,000 Irish women travel to have abortions each year, mainly in England.

Irish law prohibits the sale of contraceptives except from chemists and clinics. In May 1990 the Irish Family Planning Association was convicted by

Ireland's District Court for unlawful sale of a contraceptive. Detective Sergeant John McKeown told the court he had bought a packet of condoms from an IFPA counter in Dublin's largest Virgin record store. The IFPA was fined IR£400.

PARENTAL PAY, LEAVE AND BENEFITS (1989–90)

Maternity leave and pay: 14 weeks, including 4 that must be taken before the birth, paid by welfare benefit worth up to 70% of gross earnings. However, because this payment is tax free, it can work out to be roughly equal to net income. An additional 4 consecutive weeks may be taken, though this is unpaid.

Paternity leave: No statutory leave, though many employers grant 2 days' discretionary leave.

CHILD-CARE PROVISION (1989–90)

All services are heavily concentrated in the Dublin area.

Under 3s: Less than 2% are in publicly funded places, which are provided by private organisations. Places are generally not available for children of employed parents, but are provided only for disadvantaged children or those deemed to be 'at risk'.

3–5 year olds: An estimated 55% are in publicly funded places. Almost all 5 year olds and 55% of 4 year olds attend primary school. In addition, 2% to 3% of 3–5 year olds attend centres providing care for children of mixed ages. An estimated 12% attend playgroups for an average of 5–6 hours a week.

Primary school (6 years up): Up to the age of 7 the school day is normally from 9.00 to 13.30. After that, the school day normally ends between 15.00 and 15.30. Lunchtime breaks are supervised. The school year runs from September to August. In 1988 the pupil to teacher ratio in primary schools was 27:1.

Outside school hours care: A small number of projects providing work for young unemployed people offer

after school care, covering less than 0.1% of 6–10
year olds.

STATE BENEFITS (1989–90)

From April 1990 employees earning less than IR£60
a week did not have to pay national insurance
contributions.

Retirement and old age pensions: Retirement pensions
are paid at 65 and old age pensions at 66 for women
and men. To qualify for a retirement pension you
must have become insured before the age of 55
(56 for old age), have paid at least 156 weeks of
contributions and averaged 24 weeks a year (20 for
old age). The maximum for each is IR£61 a week
(IR£65 if living alone and IR£65 if over 80).

**'One woman in
the house be
always working.'
Irish proverb**

Additional payments include IR£39 for a dependent
spouse (IR£45.70 if spouse is over 66), IR£12.80 for
first and second child, and IR£11 for later children.
Pensions are increased yearly. Earnings are allowed
for old age pensions but not for retirement pensions.

Pre-retirement allowance: Introduced in March 1990
to replace long-term unemployment benefit for those
over the age of 60, which means they no longer have
to register regularly.

Survivors' pensions: To qualify, the deceased or
the survivor must have paid at least 156 weeks of
contributions and contributed regularly in the
previous 5 years. A survivor's pension is paid to a
widow who is not living with a man as his wife, and
to a man whose wife was receiving old age or
retirement pension, including an allowance for him as
a dependant. The pension is IR£56 a week (IR£60 if
age 80 or over) plus IR£4 for those aged 66 and over
living alone. The pension stops on remarriage.
Widows also receive IR£15 for each child under 18
(21 in full-time education).

Children who have lost both parents receive an
allowance until age 18 (21 if in full-time education) if
26 weeks of contributions were paid by a parent or

step-parent. The allowance of IR£35 a week is paid to their guardians.

A death grant of between IR£20 and IR£100 is paid if certain contributions requirements are fulfilled.

In a 1986 referendum on whether to allow divorce, 36.5% voted in favour, 63.5% voted against

Sickness benefit: There are 2 types of benefit: flat rate and pay-related. To qualify for the former, workers must have paid 39 weekly contributions and, for the latter, they must also have been earning at least IR£72 a week. Full flat-rate benefit (paid for those with 48 contributions) is IR£48 a week plus IR£31 for one dependent adult, and about IR£11 per child, for up to 180 days. Pay-related benefit is 12% of earnings (between IR£72 and IR£220) for up to 375 days. Flat-rate benefit and pay-related benefit cannot exceed 75% of normal weekly earnings. Waiting time for flat rate is 3 days, and for pay-related benefit is 18 days.

Invalidity: Paid to those incapable of working for 12 months who are unlikely to be able to work for another 12 months. At least 260 weekly contributions must have been paid, including 48 in the year before the claim is made. Benefit is paid from the day invalidity exists (normally after a sickness benefit period of at least 12 months) with no time limit. Weekly payments are IR£54, plus IR£36 for a dependent marriage partner, IR£12 for first and second children and IR£11 for other children. Invalidity pensions cannot be paid on top of any other pensions.

At the end of 1987, 30,945 women or 45.2% of the total were receiving invalidity benefit. 67.7% of women on invalidity benefit had been receiving it for over a year, compared with 53% of men.

Family benefits: IR£15.80 a month each for the first to fourth child and IR£22.90 for later children. Allowances are doubled for triplets and quadruplets. Single parents whose income is no more than IR£6 a week qualify for an allowance of IR£66.50 a week plus IR£13.50 a week for second and later children. There is also IR£83 a month for handicapped children living at home. Benefits are paid until the age of 16 (18 if in further education or seriously infirm).

Birth grants of IR£300 are paid for triplets and IR£400 for quadruplets.

Unemployment benefit: A flat-rate benefit of IR£48 a week plus 12% of weekly earnings between IR£72 and IR£220. The flat-rate benefit is paid for up to 390 days and the earnings-related supplement up to 375 days. Those who do not qualify for benefit receive unemployment assistance up to IR£52.

WOMEN AND EMPLOYMENT

Statutory rights: The working week is limited to 48 hours, with overtime restricted to 2 hours a day, 12 hours a week and 240 hours a year. Paid annual leave is 3 weeks, and there are 8 statutory public holidays. Minimum wages for certain industrial sectors are set by joint labour committees and cover an estimated 35,000 workers. Adult rates are paid at age 20.

In 1987 46.5% of women working part-time said they would accept a full-time job

Equality: The Employment Equality Act outlaws discrimination against an employee or prospective employee on the grounds of sex or marital status. However it is not unlawful to give women special treatment connected to pregnancy or childbirth. It is also permissible to provide vocational training for women or men for work previously done only or mainly by the opposite sex.

Employment and unemployment (1989)

	% women	% men
economic activity rate	33.7	69.2
employed working part time	16.7	3.1
labour force who are employers or self-employed	7.5	29.4
labour force who are family workers	3.6	2.2
unemployment rate	16.5	15.9
youth unemployment rate (age 14–24)	19.6	23.7
unemployed who have been unemployed for 12 months or more	57.4	71.5
all unemployed by sex	33.8	66.2

Source: data from *Labour Force Survey (Results 1989)* (Eurostat)

Unemployment: Both Irish men and women have
been hit very hard by long-term unemployment. In
1987 over a third (33.5%) of unemployed women
were not claiming unemployment benefit or
assistance, compared with 12.9% of unemployed men.
In April–May 1987 women accounted for 20.8% of
unemployed receiving either benefit or assistance.
31.5% of unemployed women claimed unemployment
benefit, compared with 27.7% of unemployed men.
30.2% of unemployed women claimed unemployment
assistance, compared with 58.4% of unemployed men.

Employment by industrial sector (1000s) (1989)

	women		men		women as % of workforce
	no	%	no	%	
agriculture	16	4.6	153	20.8	9.5
all industry	70	19.6	244	33.3	22.3
energy and water	–	–	13	1.7	–
mineral extraction and chemicals	6	1.6	29	4.0	17.1
metal manufacturing and engineering	22	6.1	51	6.9	30.1
other manufacturing industry	38	10.6	78	10.7	32.8
building and civil engineering	3	0.7	73	9.9	3.9
all services	273	75.9	336	45.9	44.8
distributive trades and hotels	84	23.4	121	16.6	41.0
transport and communication	12	3.3	48	6.6	20.0
banking, finance and insurance	39	10.9	50	6.8	43.8
public administration	17	4.8	44	6.0	27.9
other services	120	33.4	73	10.0	62.2
total	360	100.0	735	100.0	32.9

Source: data from *Labour Force Survey (Results 1989)* (Eurostat)

Women's work: Women account for 74.1% of health-
service workers but are concentrated in the lesser paid
occupations. In 1988 87.3% of nursing and allied
workers were women, compared with 29.9% of
medical and dental staff.

Women as a % of the workforce by occupational groups (1987)

farmers	4.3
other agricultural workers and workers in forestry and fishing	14.2
electrical and electronic workers	18.9
engineering and related trades	7.4
wood workers	1.7
leather, textile and clothing	63.8
food, drink and tobacco	22.0
paper and printing	20.5
other production workers, including mining, quarrying and turf	21.5
building and construction	0.9
supervisors of manual workers	11.8
labourers and unskilled workers	1.2
transport and communications workers	8.3
warehouse and stores, workers, packers and bottlers	25.9
clerical workers	74.1
proprietors and managers	21.1
shop assistants and bar staff	54.0
other commercial workers	9.7
professional and technical workers	50.3
service workers	54.2
administrative, executive and managerial workers	17.4
others	9.2
total	**32.4**

Source: data from *Women in the Labour Force* (John Blackwell, Employment Equality Agency)

Women part-time workers by occupational group (%) (1988)

service workers	27.6
commercial sector	19.1
professional and technical	18.5
clerical workers	17.0
agricultural workers	10.5
production workers	4.3
others	3.0

Source: *Who Needs Flexibility, Part-time working ... The Irish Experience* (Eileen Drew, Employment Equality Agency)

Part-time workers: In 1989 73.2% of part-time workers were women. In April 1991, under the Worker Protection Act, part-time workers were given the same statutory rights as full-time employees, if they worked at least 8 hours a week and had worked for the same employer for 13 weeks.

In 1988 51.2% of single women said they worked part time because they could not find full-time work. The reasons were: 22.4% were in training or education; 10.9% because of illness or disability; 3.1% because of family responsibilities; and only 12.4% because they did not want to work full time.

For married women, the main reason given for working part time was family responsibilities (49.4%). Other reasons were: because they did not want to (28.7%); they could not find full-time work (15%); illness or disability (6.4%); training or education (0.4%).

55% of women full-time workers had no dependent children, compared with 28% of part-time workers.

Women's average hourly earnings as a % of men's in industry by sector (adult rates, 1988)

non-metallic mineral products	70
chemicals etc	62
metals and engineering	77
food	78
drink and tobacco	64
textiles	66
clothing, footwear and leather	73
timber and wooden furniture	81
paper and printing	62
other manufacturing	68
all manufacturing industries	68
mining, quarrying and turf	62
transportable goods industries	68
electricity, gas and water	67
all industries	67

Source: *Who Needs Flexibility, Part-time working ... The Irish Experience* (Eileen Drew, Employment Equality Agency)

Temporary workers: Figures from 1986 show that 49.5% of temporary workers were women, half of whom were employed in public sector services and 23.7% in distribution, hotels and catering. Most male temporary workers worked in construction and public sector services (both 20.3%), distribution, hotels and catering (15.6%), and banking and business (12.2%).

'There are not many lady bankers or MPs or whatever who want to give their time to help others, as they already have their own families to look after.' The UK Rotary Club President, commenting on the votes by some Irish Rotary Clubs to keep women out

Second jobs: Official 1986 figures show 3,600 women had second jobs (20.6% of all workers with second jobs). Almost half (44.4%) of them had second jobs in public-sector services; 22.2% in hotels and catering and distribution, and 8.3% in agriculture and forestry.

Working mothers (1988): 23% of women with a child under 10 are employed compared with 79% of men, the lowest level for both in the EC. 67% of women aged 20–39 without children are employed.

8% of women and 17% of men with a child under 10 are unemployed. The unemployment rate for women with a child under 10 is the highest in the EC. 30% of employed women with a child under 10 have part-time jobs.

Employment rates are lower (17%) for lone mothers with a child aged 0–4 (25% for all mothers) and higher (23%) for lone mothers with a child aged 5–9 (19%).

Unemployment rates are higher for lone mothers: 14% for those with a child aged 0–4 (8% for all mothers) and 12% for those with a child aged 5–9 (7% for all mothers).

Labour force participation rates for women by age and number of dependent children (1987)

	age 20–24	age 25–34	age 35–44	age 45–49
childless	79.0	81.8	49.6	31.1
1	38.8	47.6	31.4	21.9
2	19.4	28.5	25.5	20.6
3+	5.3	13.2	16.9	18.7
total	45.5	35.9	22.6	21.8

Source: data from *Women in the Labour Force* (John Blackwell, Employment Equality Agency)

WOMEN IN TRADE UNIONS

Women's participation in the 5 unions with most women members (1989)

union	no of women members	% of women members	% of women executive committee	% of women on delegates to conf.	% of women full-time officials
ITGWU	50,000	33	11	10	5
INTO	18,256	75	13	40	40
NIPSA	18,198	51	25	33	21
ATGWU	17,500	25	4	–	3
FWUI	15,645	29	19	24	12

ITGWU – Irish Transport and General Workers' Union
INTO – Irish National Teachers' Organisation
NIPSA – Northern Ireland Public Service Alliance
ATGWU – Amalgamated Transport and General Workers' Union
FWUI – Federated Workers' Union of Ireland

Source: data from *Progress Report – Implementation of Equality Report Programme for Progress* (Irish Congress of Trade Unions)

WOMEN AND POLITICS

Women won the vote in 1935. In the June 1989 general election, women were elected to 12 seats in the Dáil, representing 8.7% of the seats. President Mary Robinson was elected in 1990.

Women elected to parliament (the Dáil Eireann) in June 1989

political party	total no of seats	no of seats held by women	% of seats held by women
Fianna Fáil	77	4	5.2
Progressive Democrats	6	2	33.3
Fine Gael	55	6	10.9
total	**138**	**12**	**8.7**

Source: data from the Irish Embassy, London

WOMEN AND DETENTION

In September 1988, 2.6% of all prisoners were women, 29.3% were minors (age 21) and young adults and 0.9% were foreigners.

SOURCES

Abortion Laws in Europe, Planned Parenthood in Europe, Vol 18 No 1, Spring 1989 (Supplement, amended April 1990); *Childcare in the European Communities 1985–90 (Women of Europe* Supplement No 51); *Childcare in Ireland: Challenge and Opportunity* (Employment Equality Agency); *Comparative Study on rules governing working conditions in the member states* (Commission of the European Communities); *Demographic Statistics 1990* (Eurostat); *Discrimination Irish-style: Why we need an Equal Status Act* (Council for the Status of Women); *Employment Equality Act 1977* (Employment Equality Agency); *Europa World Year Book 1990* (31st edition); *Health Care Systems and Professional Organisations in the European Community, Information note – Europe* (British Medical Association); Health For All 2000 Indicator Presentation System (World Health Organisation Regional Office for Europe); *A History of Their Own – Women in Europe from Prehistory to the Present, Volumes I and II,* (Bonnie Anderson and Judith Zinsser, Penguin); *Labour Force Survey (Results 1989)* (Eurostat); *Les Actions Positives en Faveur des Femmes en Europe Occidentale* (Institut Syndical Europeen); *Out In Europe* (Peter Tatchell, for Channel 4 Television); *Planned Parenthood in Europe* (Vol 20, No 2) (International Planned Parenthood Federation); *Pocket World in Figures* (The Economist); *Positive action and the constitutional and legislative hindrances to its implementation in the member states of the Council of Europe* (Council of Europe); *Proposition de Directive Du Conseil concernant la protection au travail de la femme enceinte ou venant d'accoucher* (Commission of the European Communities); *Prison Information Bulletin* June 1990 (Council of Europe); *Social Protection in the Member States of the Community* (Commission of the European Community Directorate General on Employment, Industrial Relations and Social Affairs); *Progress Report – Implementation of Equality Report Programme for Progress* (Irish Congress of Trade Unions); *Third World Guide 91/92* (Instituto del Tercer Mundo); *Who Makes The Decisions?* (Council for the Status of Women); *Who Needs Flexibility, Part-time working . . . The Irish Experience* (Eileen Drew, Employment Equality Agency); *Women In The Labour Force* (John Blackwell, Employment Equality Agency); *Women of Europe* (Nos 64, 69)

ADDRESSES

Irish Embassy, 17 Grosvenor Place, London SW1X 7HR.

Council for the Status of Women in Ireland, 62 Lower Mount Street, Dublin 2

Employment Equality Agency, 36 Upper Mount Street, Dublin

Irish Family Planning Association, Halfpenny Court, 36-37 Lower Ormond Quay, Dublin 1. Tel: (353 1)73 08 77

Central Statistical Office, St Stephens Green House, Earlsfort Terrace, Dublin 2

Irish Congress of Trade Unions, 19 Raglan Street, Dublin 4

The Training and Employment Agency, 27-33 Upper Baggot Street, Dublin 4. Tel: (353 1) 685777

Trade Union Women's Forum, c/o Margaret de Courcy, SIPTU, Liberty Hall, Dublin 1

GLEN (Gay and Lesbian Equality Network), NGF (National Gay Federation), 10 Fownes Street Upper, Dublin 2. Tel: (353 1) 710 939

Italy

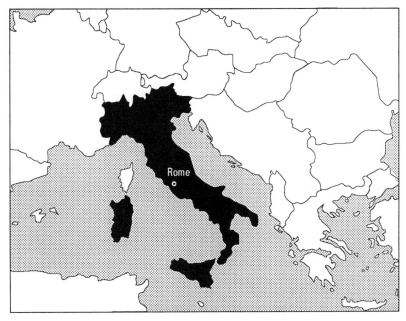

- **Population** 57.4 million, 51.4% female
- **Area** 301,270 sq km
- **Population density** 190.5 people sq km
- **GDP 1988** Lire 1,079,000 billion (£514 billion)
- **GDP per capita** £8,948
- **GDP per capita in purchasing power parity** (UK=100) 100
- **Public spending as % of GNP:** defence 2.3% (1986); education 4% (1986); health 4.5% (1987)
- **Consumer price index** 1980 = 100; 1989 = 242
- **Currency is the lira** 1989 £1 = LIT2,050; US$1 = LIT1,271

The republic of Italy has a 2-chamber parliament elected for 5 years by proportional representation. The Senate has 315 elected members from regional seats and 7 life members. The Chamber of Deputies has 630 members. Minimum age for voting is 25 for the Senate and 18 for the Chamber. The president is head of state and is elected for 7 years.

There are 20 regions, with 5 having special status: Sicilia, Sardegna, Trentino-Alto Adige, Friuli-Venezia Giulia and Valle d'Aosta. The main language is Italian but German and Latin are spoken in Alto Adige near the Austrian border and French in Valle d'Aosta. 90% of the population is Roman Catholic.

EQUAL RIGHTS

Ancient Roman law allowed a husband to kill his wife without punishment for adultery or drinking wine

The constitution establishes equality in law irrespective of sex, the moral and legal equality of women and men in marriage (within the limits of the law ensuring family unity) and for equality between women and men in employment. The National Committee for Equality was set up in 1983. A bill is under discussion to provide a legal framework for positive action and to create a national commission for equality.

BIRTH, LIFE AND DEATH

Breakdown of population by sex and age group (1000s) (1988)

	all		women		men		% of women in age group
	no	%	no	%	no	%	
0–14	10,218.6	17.8	4,973.2	16.9	5,245.4	18.8	48.7
15–24	9,437.2	16.4	4,630.5	15.7	4,806.7	17.2	49.1
25–39	12,228.4	21.3	6,091.5	20.6	6,136.9	22.0	49.8
40–59	14,357.7	25.0	7,338.8	24.9	7,018.9	25.2	51.1
60–74	7,775.2	13.5	4,315.4	14.6	3,459.8	12.4	55.5
75+	3,381.0	5.9	2,159.7	7.3	1,221.3	4.4	63.9
all	57,398.1	100.0	29,509.1	100.0	27,889.0	100.0	51.4

Source: data from *Demographic Statistics 1990* (Eurostat)

Population, population density and population increase by region (1987)

region	pop (1000s)	% of total pop	pop density per km	natural increase per 1,000	net migration per 1,000	total increase per 1,000
Piemonte	4,383.3	7.6	172.6	-3.8	1.8	-1.9
Valle d'Aosta	114.1	0.2	35.0	-2.6	5.3	2.7
Liguria	1,754.3	3.1	323.9	-6.7	0.5	-6.2
Lombardia	8,881.6	15.5	372.3	-1.0	1.2	0.3
Trentino-Alto Adige	881.1	1.5	64.7	1.1	0.8	1.9
Veneto	4,373.9	7.6	238.2	-0.9	1.4	0.5
Friuli-Venezia Giulia	1,212.4	2.1	154.5	-5.5	1.7	-3.8
Emilia-Romagna	3,927.6	6.8	177.5	-4.4	2.5	-1.9
Toscana	3,569.9	6.2	155.3	-3.9	2.8	-1.1
Umbria	818.0	1.4	96.7	-2.5	3.3	0.8
Marche	1,427.8	2.5	147.3	-1.4	2.4	1.0
Lazio	5,126.7	8.9	298.0	1.1	2.3	3.5
Campania	5,710.9	10.0	420.1	6.7	0.3	7.0
Abruzzi	1,256.1	2.2	116.4	0.3	2.8	3.2
Molise	334.4	0.6	75.4	0.6	1.1	1.8
Puglia	4,034.6	7.0	208.5	5.5	-0.8	4.7
Basilicata	620.9	1.1	62.1	3.8	-1.5	2.3
Calabria	2,143.0	3.7	142.1	5.1	-1.5	3.6
Sicilia	5,126.7	8.9	199.4	4.3	1.2	5.6
Sardegna	1,647.5	2.9	68.4	3.0	1.0	4.0
Italy	**57,344.8**	**100.0**	**190.3**	**0.4**	**1.3**	**1.7**

Source: *Demographic Statistics 1990* (Eurostat)

Births, deaths, marriages and divorces for every 1,000 of population

	1960	1970	1980	1985	1988
birth rate	18.2	16.9	11.4	10.1	9.9
% of births outside marriage	2.4	2.2	4.3	5.4	5.8
average age of mother at 1st birth	26.0	25.0	24.4	25.1	25.5[1]
infant mortality per 1,000 live births	43.9	29.6	14.6	10.5	9.5
fertility rate per woman	2.4	2.4	1.7	1.4	1.3
marriage rate	7.7	7.3	5.7	5.2	5.5
av age at marriage (women)	25.1	24.3	24.5	24.9	25.4[1]
av age at marriage (men)	29.2	28.1	28.2	28.3	28.7[1]
divorce rate	–	0.2[2]	0.2	0.3	0.5
life expectancy (women)	72.3	74.9	77.4	–	79.1[3]
life expectancy (men)	67.2	69.0	70.6	–	72.6[3]
death rate	9.6	9.7	9.8	9.6	9.4

[1] 1987; [2] 1975; [3] 1985–87   Source: data from *Demographic Statistics 1990* (Eurostat)

Between 1971 and 1990 the number of legal separations increased by 314%. In 1988, 1-parent households accounted for 4% of households with a child aged 0–4 and 5% of households with a child aged 5–9.

LESBIAN RIGHTS

A common age of consent of 14 for lesbians, gay men and heterosexuals was introduced in 1889, the second lowest common age of consent in Europe. (However, amendments to the law in that year stated that sex with a 14–16 year old is a punishable offence if the young person complains to the authorities and is 'sexually innocent and morally pure'.)

Before 1889 relationships between gay men were illegal, though in some Italian principalities they were legalised in 1792.

Regulations covering municipal registration and record offices introduced in 1989 do not distinguish between same-sex and heterosexual relationships, defining a family as 'a group of cohabiting persons tied by bonds of affection'.

WOMEN AND HEALTH CARE

A universal national health service was set up in 1978, funded by direct contributions from both employees and employers. The self-employed pay a 'health tax'. Consultations are free but patients are expected to make a small payment for hospital stays, and there are fixed charges for prescriptions, though there are many exemptions for named drugs and medical conditions.

In 1988 there was 1 doctor for every 706 people.

Major indicators for women's health (1988)

maternal deaths (all causes) per 100,000 live births	7.63
maternal deaths (abortion) per 100,000 live births	1.04
ratio of abortions to 1,000 live births (all ages) (1986)	351.75
% of all live births to mothers under 20 (1981)	6.01
% of all live births to mothers aged 35+ (1981)	9.05
deaths from cancer of the cervix (age 0–64) per 100,000 women (1987)	0.89
deaths from malignant neoplasm female breast (age 0–64) per 100,000 women	19.25
deaths from trachea/bronchus/lung cancer (age 0–64) per 100,000 women	5.07
deaths from trachea/bronchus/lung cancer (age 0–64) per 100,000 men	42.26
deaths from diseases of the circulatory system (age 0–64) per 100,000 women	30.73
deaths from diseases of the circulatory system (age 0–64) per 100,000 men	84.48
deaths from suicide and self-inflicted injury per 100,000 women	3.81
deaths from suicide and self-inflicted injury per 100,000 men	10.87

Source: data from Health for All 2000 Indicator Presentation System (World Health Organisation Regional Office For Europe)

Abortion: Available on social grounds up to 90 days after a wait of one week, and with a doctor's certificate. Available after 90 days with forced counselling, on medical and eugenic grounds or if the pregnancy is a result of rape or other sexual crimes. Under these circumstances women under 18 must have the consent of their parents or a judge. Abortion is free of charge. There is widespread refusal by medical staff to perform abortions on conscientious grounds. The International Planned Parenthood Federation estimated that in 1983 there were 100,000 illegal abortions.

PARENTAL PAY, LEAVE AND BENEFITS (1989–90)

Maternity leave and pay: 20 weeks, including 8 before the birth, is paid at 80% of earnings. In the public sector women can have an extra 4 weeks at 100% of earnings and a further 16 weeks at 30% after the birth. In the private sector they can have an extra 4 weeks at 80%. To qualify, women have to be working and covered by national insurance at the start of their pregnancy.

Reduction in hours: Employed mothers with children

under 1 can cut their hours by 2 hours a day without loss of pay.

In a court case in 1987 fathers won the right to maternity leave and the mother's daily rest periods at work if the mother dies or is severely disabled

Parental and paternity leave: Parental leave is 6 months on benefits equivalent to 30% of earnings which must be taken before the child is 12 months. While leave is granted only to the mother, who may transfer it to the father, legislation is likely to extend the right to this leave to fathers.

Time off to care for sick children: Unpaid leave available to mothers (but not fathers) of children under 3.

CHILD-CARE PROVISION (1989–90)

Under 3s: 5% are in publicly funded nursery places, with a small number in private nurseries.

3–5 year olds: 87% are in pre-primary schooling. This is provided by central government (49% of all pre-primary schooling), local authorities (15%) or private organisations with state funding (37%). State-run schools must open for 8 hours a day, some may open for longer. Just under 70% of children in pre-primary schooling attend for 7 hours a day.

'If the father is dead, the family suffers. If the mother dies, the family cannot exist.' Sicilian proverb

Primary school (6 years up): Most open from 8.30 to 12.30 for 6 days a week, though just under 20% of children go to full-time (8 hours) primary schools. The school year runs from September to June. In 1988 the teacher/pupil ratio in primary schools was 14:1. A bill before parliament addresses the need for longer primary school hours. However, because teachers' hours have been cut there is a need for more staff, at a time of reduced public spending.

Outside school hours care: Provided by local authorities and available in some schools, but not widespread.

Contributions to child-care costs including tax relief: Parents pay a proportion of the costs of care for children under 3, according to income. Government guidelines say this contribution should be 36% of the cost, but that can be reduced by local authority contributions.

Regional trends: Children in the north are more likely to have access to public nursery places, pre-primary schooling, and full-time primary schooling than those in the south. Regional differences are widening because the fixed contribution (0.1% of payroll) that employers pay to the government to fund nurseries can now be spent freely by the regions.

STATE BENEFITS (1989–90)

Retirement pension: Since 1991 women and men have been able to retire at 62. Normal retirement age in the public sector is 65 for both women and men; in the private sector 55 for women and 60 for men. Private sector pensions are paid to those with 15 years of contributions. Full pensions are paid after 40 years of contributions. Those over 65 without an income are entitled to a minimum social pension of LIT3,764,150 plus a supplement of LIT390,000 (age 60 to 65) or LIT650,000 (aged 65 plus). Otherwise pensions are based on years of contributions and average earnings during the previous 5 years up to an annual ceiling of LIT44,848,000. Minimum pensions are increased 4 times a year to take account of the cost of living, and annually by the average increase in earnings.

Only 3.3% of managers are women, an Italian Confederation of Executives survey found

Survivors' pension: Paid to survivors of insured people with 5 years of contributions, including 3 in the previous 5 years. Pension is 60% of the invalidity or old age pension of the person who has died. The pension stops on remarriage, with a grant equal to 2 years' pension. Surviving children are paid 20% each up to 3 children, when 40% is divided by the number of children. If there is no surviving marriage partner, children are paid 40% each, up to 3 children when the full pension is divided by the number of children. If no other survivors, the parents, sisters and brothers of the insured person are entitled to 15%.

Death grant is LIT20,000. Special allowances are paid to the survivors of an insured person who had not yet qualified for a pension. These are 45 times the total contributions paid (between a minimum of LIT43,200 and a maximum of LIT129,600), and are given in priority to marriage partners, followed by children, then parents.

Sickness benefit: 50% of earnings, then 66.6% from day 21 if the claimant is not in hospital, for up to 180 days a year. Waiting time is 3 days. Those with TB receive a range of allowances, including a Christmas grant. Non-industrial workers do not receive cash benefits but employers must pay their salaries for at least 3 months.

Invalidity: Invalidity allowance is paid to workers whose capacity to work is reduced to less than one-third by sickness or infirmity. Paid until retirement age, it is based on the number of years of insurance contributions and average earnings for the previous 5 years but is made up to the minimum guaranteed pension.

Those permanently incapable of any work receive an incapacity pension, which is based on the amount of contributions, average earnings and the number of years between invalidity and retirement age. A monthly allowance is paid to those who need daily care.

Family benefits: Benefit is calculated according to family income and number of children. A family of four with an income of LIT21–24 million would qualify for a monthly benefit of LIT110,000; the same family with an income of LIT30–33 million would receive LIT20,000. Benefit is not paid to a family earning more than LIT33 million. Benefit is paid until the age of 18, though there is no time limit in cases of serious infirmity.

Unemployment benefit: 20% of average daily wages over the previous 3 months for up to 180 days a year, unless unemployment is due to redundancy or closure, in which case a special allowance of two-thirds of wages is paid for 180 days.

WOMEN AND EMPLOYMENT

Statutory rights: The working week is limited to 48 hours. There is no legislation governing levels of overtime, though the law allows for flexible working time agreements to restrict hours. There is a statutory right to paid annual leave, but the number of days is not specified. There are 4 national and 11 other statutory public holidays.

Paola Bazzola became Italy's first woman football referee in January 1991

The constitution entitles an employee to a wage 'proportionate to the quality and quantity of his [sic] work and in any case sufficient to guarantee a free and decent life to him and his family'. In law this has meant the right to a minimum wage determined by the courts, normally equal to the levels set by collective agreements.

A new system of index linking was being negotiated for 1992; until then part of wages was fully linked with the remainder partially linked. Many employees receive a thirteenth month bonus at Christmas, and some a fourteenth month at the start of annual leave. Wages cannot be seized in full by creditors.

Equal pay: During 1991 parliament reversed the burden of proof in discrimination cases, so the employer must prove there is no discrimination rather than the woman having to prove it does exist. A national committee for equal pay and equal treatment for female and male workers was created in 1991.

Employment and unemployment (1989)

	% women	% men
economic activity rate	34.6	64.7
employed working part time	10.9	3.1
labour force who are employers or self-employed	16.8	28.6
labour force who are family workers	8.2	2.4
unemployment rate	17.4	7.4
youth unemployment rate (age 14-24)	38.7	26.0
unemployed who have been unemployed for 12 months or more	71.7	68.1
all unemployed by sex	57.6	42.4

Source: data from *Labour Force Survey (Results 1989)* (Eurostat)

Part-time workers: In 1989 64.7% of part-time
workers were women. The amount of pension paid is
calculated pro rata according to the number of hours
worked. Maximum child benefit is paid to those
working more than 24 hours a week; those working
less hours receive proportionately reduced payments.

Employment by industrial sector (1000s) (1989)

	women		men		women as % of workforce
	no	%	no	%	
agriculture	655	9.2	1,257	9.2	34.3
all industry	1,646	23.2	5,013	36.5	24.7
energy and water	20	0.3	194	1.4	9.3
mineral extraction and chemicals	139	2.0	574	4.2	19.5
metal manufacturing and engineering	255	3.6	1,192	8.7	17.6
other manufacturing industry	1,142	16.1	1,393	10.2	45.0
building and civil engineering	91	1.3	1,660	12.1	5.2
all services	4,786	67.5	7,452	54.3	39.1
distributive trades and hotels	1,613	22.8	2,824	20.6	36.4
transport and communication	162	2.3	994	7.2	14.0
banking, finance and insurance	324	4.6	531	3.9	18.9
public administration	494	7.0	1,189	8.7	29.4
other services	2,195	31.0	1,913	13.9	53.4
total	7,087	100.0	13,722	100.0	34.1

Source: data from *Labour Force Survey (Results 1989)* (Eurostat)

Women's earnings as a % of men's in industry (October 1985)

	manual hourly earnings	non-manual monthly earnings
chemical industry	86.5	70.6
mechanical engineering	89.5	67.2
electrical engineering	92.8	69.3
food, drink and tobacco	89.8	68.0
clothing and footwear manufacture	94.0	68.4
printing and publishing	81.0	66.9
all manufacturing industry	84.4	68.6
all industry	82.7	69.2

Source: data from *Earnings in Industry and Services* (Eurostat)

In 14th century Florence, women were paid 7 soldi, compared with 15 for men, for a day's work

Working mothers: In 1988 42% of women with children under 10 were employed compared with 95% of similar men. 55% of women aged 20–39 without children were employed, one of the lowest levels in the EC. 8% of women and 3% of men with a child under 10 were unemployed. 11% of employed women with a child under 10 had part-time jobs.

Employment rates are higher for lone mothers than all mothers, because of greater levels of full-time employment; figures for 1988 were 58% for lone mothers with a child aged 0–4 (40% for all mothers) and 64% for lone mothers with a child aged 5–9 (41%). Unemployment rates were also higher for lone mothers: 11% for those with a child aged 0–4 (10% for all mothers) and 13% for those with a child aged 5–9 (7% for all mothers).

WOMEN AND POLITICS

In June 1987, women were elected to 80 seats in the Chamber of Deputies (12.7%) and 21 seats in the Senate (6.5%).

Women elected to the Chamber of Deputies in June 1987

political party	total no of seats	no of seats held by women	% of seats held by women
Democrazia Cristiana	234	10	4.3
Partito Comunista	157	45	28.7
(now Partito Democratico della Sinistra)			
Partito Socialista	94	5	5.3
Movimento Sociale	35	1	2.9
Partito Repubblicano	21	0	0.0
Sinistra Indipendente	20	8	40.0
Partito Socialista Democratico	17	0	0.0
Verde	13	6	46.2
Federalista Europeo	12	3	25.0
Partito Liberale	11	0	0.0
Democrazia Proletaria	8	2	25.0
others	8	0	0.0
total	630	80	12.7

Source: data from the Italian Embassy, London

Women elected to the Senate in June 1987

political party	total no of seats	no of seats held by women	% of seats held by women
Democrazia Cristiana	127	4	3.2
Partito Comunista	85	11	12.9
(now Partito Democratico della Sinistra)			
Partito Socialista	45	2	4.4
Sinistra Indipendente	17	1	5.9
Movimento Sociale	16	1	6.3
others	12	0	0.0
Partito Repubblicano	9	1	11.1
Federalista Europeo	6	0	0.0
Sociale Democratico	7	1	14.3
total	324	21	6.5

Source: data from the Italian Embassy

Women won the right to vote in 1945

For the first time in an Italian government there were two women among the 32 cabinet ministers: Margherita Boniver, Minister of Immigration, and Rosa Russo Iervolino, Social Affairs Minister. A new Parliament was due to be elected in April 1992.

Three of Italy's 110 ambassadors are women.

WOMEN AND DETENTION

In 1988 women made up 5% of prisoners, with minors (age 18) and young adults making up 1.4% and foreigners 8.9%.

SOURCES

Abortion Laws in Europe, Planned Parenthood in Europe, Vol 18 No 1, Spring 1989 (Supplement, amended April 1990) (published by International Planned Parenthood Federation, Europe Region); *Bargaining Report* 101 (Labour Research Department); *Childcare in the European Communities 1985–90* (Women of Europe Supplement No 51); *Comparative Study on Rules Governing Working Conditions in the Member States* (Commission of the European Communities); *Demographic Statistics 1990* (Eurostat); *Earnings in Industry and Services* (Eurostat); *Europa World Year Book 1990* (31st edition); *Health Care Systems and Professional Organisations in the European*

Community, Information note – Europe (British Medical
Association); Health For All 2000 Indicator Presentation System
(World Health Organisation Regional Office for Europe); *A
History of Their Own – Women in Europe from Prehistory to the
Present, Volumes I and II,* (Bonnie Anderson and Judith Zinsser,
Penguin); Italian Embassy, London; *Labour Force Survey
(Results 1989)* (Eurostat); *Les Actions Positives en Faveur des
Femmes en Europe Occidentale* (Institut Syndical Europeen);
Out In Europe (Peter Tatchell, for Channel 4 Television); *Pagine
Rosa – guida ai diritti delle donne* (Commissione Nazionale per
la Realizzazione della Parità tra donna e uomo); *Pocket World in
Figures* (The Economist); *Positive Action and the Constitutional
and Legislative Hindrances to its Implementation in the Member
States of the Council of Europe* (Council of Europe); *Proposition
de Directive Du Conseil concernant la protection au travail de la
femme enceinte ou venant d'accoucher* (Commission of the
European Communities); *Prison Information Bulletin* June 1990
(Council of Europe); *Social Protection in the Member States of
the Community* (Commission of the European Community
Directorate General on Employment, Industrial Relations and
Social Affairs); *Third World Guide 91/92* (Instituto del Tercer
Mundo); *Women of Europe* (Nos 68, 69)

ADDRESSES

Italian Embassy, 14 Three Kings Yard, Davies Street,
London W1Y 2EH. Tel: 071 629 8200

Commissione Nazionale per la Realizzazione della Parità tra
Donna e Uomo, Presidenza del Consiglio dei Ministri,
Via Buoncompagni 15, 00187 Roma

Unione Italiana Centri Educazione Matrimoniale e
Prematrimoniale (family planning service), Via Eugenia Chiesa
1, 20122 Milano. Tel: (39 2) 78 39 15

Confederazione Generale Italiana del Lavoro, Corso d'Italia 25,
00198 Roma

Confederazione Italiana dei Sindacati Lavoratori, Via Po 21,
00198 Roma

Unione Italiana del Lavoro, Via Lucullo 6, 00187 Roma

Arci Gay Nazionale (lesbian and gay rights), PO Box 691, 40100
Bologna. Tel: (39 51) 436 700/433 395

Luxembourg

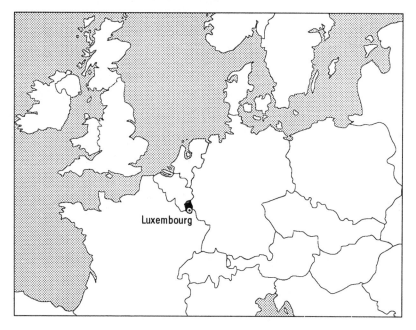

- **Population** 0.4 million, 51.3% female
- **Area** 2,586 sq km
- **Population density** 143.7 people sq km
- **GNP per capita** 1987 £11,501
- **Public spending as % of GNP:** defence 12% (1986); education 2.6% (1987)
- **Consumer price index** 1980 = 100; 1989 = 149
- **Currency is the Luxembourg franc** 1989 £1 = LFR63.5; US$1 = LFR39.4

In 1989 Erna Hennicot-Schoepgas became the first woman president of the Chamber of Deputies

Luxembourg, which borders on Belgium, France and Germany, is a monarchy with executive power held by the Grand Duke, though this is normally exercised by the council of ministers. Legislative power is held by the parliament, the Chamber of Deputies, which has 60 members who are elected by proportional representation. There is also an advisory council of state, which has 21 members appointed by the Grand Duke, but their decisions can be over-ruled by the chamber. The country is divided into 12 cantons.

The official language is Letzeburgish (a German-Moselle-Frankish dialect), but French is used mostly for administration while German is the main written language of business and the media.

94% of the population is Roman Catholic and 1% Protestant. More than 26% of the population are citizens of other countries, the highest proportion of any EC country. Foreigners make up 52% of workers in industry, and 83% in construction. 13% of the labour force are citizens of France, Belgium or Germany. Overall, 33% of the labour force work in industry, 4% in agriculture and 63% in the services sector.

IMMIGRATION AND RESIDENCE RIGHTS

Individuals with relatives who are citizens can apply for citizenship by registering with the authorities. Those with no links can apply for citizenship if they are over 18 and have lived there for 10 years (5 of which must be continuous). This qualifying period may be reduced in special cases, including children born in Luxembourg to foreigners, children who have completed compulsory schooling there, and foreign marriage partners of Luxembourg citizens.

EQUAL RIGHTS

The constitution guarantees equality for all citizens before the law. Although this does not specifically refer to sexual equality, the Constituent Assembly has adopted a text stating that the constitution recognises no distinction between female and male citizens and asking the government 'to ensure that genuine sexual equality pertains in all situations to which the law applies'. The law allows for 'measures to promote equal opportunity for men and women, in particular by removing existing inequalities which affect women's opportunities', and specifically allows for positive action in the workplace.

In 1989 the Department on the Status of Women was created as part of the Ministry of the Family.

BIRTH, LIFE AND DEATH

Breakdown of population by sex and age group (1000s) (1988)

	all no	all %	women no	women %	men no	men %	% of women in age group
0–14	63.0	16.9	30.8	16.1	32.2	17.8	48.9
15–24	53.4	14.4	26.2	13.7	27.2	15.0	49.1
25–39	91.4	24.6	45.3	23.7	46.1	25.5	49.6
40–59	94.8	25.5	46.7	24.5	48.1	26.6	49.3
60–74	47.3	12.7	27.3	14.3	20.0	11.1	57.7
75+	21.8	5.9	14.5	7.6	7.3	4.0	66.5
all	371.7	100.0	190.8	100.0	180.9	100.0	51.3

Source: data from *Demographic Statistics 1990* (Eurostat)

Births, deaths, marriages and divorces per 1,000 population

	1960	1970	1980	1985	1988
birth rate	16.0	13.0	11.5	11.2	12.4
% of births outside marriage	3.2	4.0	6.0	10.2	12.1
infant mortality per 1,000 live births	31.5	24.9	11.5	9.0	8.7
fertility rate per woman	2.2	2.0	1.5	1.4	1.5
marriage rate	7.1	6.3	5.9	5.3	5.5
average age at marriage (women)	–	23.2	24.5	25.5	26.3
average age at marriage (men)	–	26.3	27.6	28.7	29.2
divorce rate	0.5	0.6	1.6	1.8	2.1
death rate	11.9	12.3	11.3	11.0	10.3

Source: data from *Demographic Statistics 1990* (Eurostat)

In 1987, the natural increase per 1,000 population
was 0.6 and the net migration – the number of
newcomers – was 6.4, making the total increase
7 per 1,000.

Life expectancy

	1961–63	1970–72	1978–80	1985–88
life expectancy (women)	72.2	73.4	75.9	77.9
life expectancy (men)	66.5	67.1	69.1	70.6

Source: data from *Demographic Statistics 1990* (Eurostat)

One-parent households in 1988 accounted for 5% of
households with a child aged 0–4 and 7% of
households with a child aged 5–9.

LESBIAN RIGHTS

It was illegal for gay men to have sex until 1792.
A common age of consent of 14 for heterosexuals,
lesbians and gay men was introduced in 1854.
In 1971 this was raised to 18 for gay men,
though the government is considering abolishing
this discrimination.

WOMEN AND HEALTH CARE

Health care is funded through insurance and the
government. Employees must join one of 12 health
insurance funds, which share contributions between
employees and employers. The self-employed pay the
full cost of contributions.

The state pays for health care for those who cannot be
insured, including students and the unemployed, as
well as for maternity services, and care needed as a
result of road accidents or school sports. Grants are
available for the disabled who need constant care.

Patients pay about 20% of the costs of consultations
and medicines, and a daily charge for hospital stays.
Patients see a specialist without being referred. In
1988 there was 1 doctor for every 554 people.

Major indicators for women's health (1989)

maternal deaths (all causes) per 100,000 live births	0.00
maternal deaths (abortion) per 100,000 live births	0.00
% of all live births to mothers under 20	2.62
% of all live births to mothers aged 35+	8.57
deaths from cancer of the cervix (age 0–64) per 100,000 women (1988)	1.89
deaths from malignant neoplasm female breast (age 0–64) per 100,000 women	22.21
deaths from trachea/bronchus/lung cancer (age 0–64) per 100,000 women	6.85
deaths from trachea/bronchus/lung cancer (age 0–64) per 100,000 men	41.06
deaths from diseases of the circulatory system (age 0–64) per 100,000 women	40.00
deaths from diseases of the circulatory system (age 0–64) per 100,000 men	99.54
deaths from suicide and self-inflicted injury per 100,000 women	9.20
deaths from suicide and self-inflicted injury per 100,000 men	28.03

Source: data from Health for All 2000 Indicator Presentation System (World Health Organisation Regional Office For Europe)

Abortion and contraception: Available on social and medical grounds up to 12 weeks, with a doctor's certificate and after a wait of 7 days. Available up to the second trimester if there is a risk to a woman's physical or mental health, to foetal health or of foetal handicap, or in cases of rape or other sexual crimes. Women are reimbursed for the costs of abortion. Most doctors refuse to perform abortions on conscientious grounds, and many women travel to have abortions, mainly to the Netherlands.

PARENTAL PAY, LEAVE AND BENEFITS (1989–90)

Maternity leave and pay: 16 weeks, including 8 that must be taken before the birth, paid by benefit equal to 100% of earnings. There is an extra 4 weeks if breastfeeding or for premature and multiple births. To qualify, women must have had national insurance cover for 6 months out of the previous year. This benefit has now been extended to homemakers and self-employed women.

Prenatal allowance: LFR16,583 is paid to mothers who have had the required medical check-ups, and have lived legally in Luxembourg for a year before the birth.

Birth grant: An additional LFR16,583 is paid, provided one of the mother's parents was legally resident in Luxembourg for the previous year, and that the mother has had the required medical check-ups. Plus LFR16,583 paid as a postnatal allowance if the child has had required check-ups.

Paternity leave: 2 days' paid leave.

Parental leave: Public sector workers can take 1 year's unpaid leave, or work part-time until a child is 4. Proposed legislation would provide 2 years' unpaid leave to private-sector workers.

CHILD-CARE PROVISION (1989–90)

Public funding for child care increased by 235% between 1985 and 1990. Services are concentrated in and around Luxembourg city (75% of places), with only 8% of places in the rural east and north.

Under 3s: 1%–2% are in centres caring for children of mixed ages, either run by local authorities or run privately with a state grant.

3–4 years olds: 55%–60% are in publicly funded places. Almost all 4 year olds are in the first year of pre-primary schooling (voluntary) from 8.00 to 11.30 or 8.00 to 12.00 for six days, and for 3 days also from 14.00 to 16.30.

5 year olds: Compulsory schooling starts with a second year of pre-primary (hours as before), usually provided in primary schools. There are a few places for children during the lunch break in mixed-age centres, and some schools now provide supervised meals.

Primary school (6 years up): From 8.00 to 11.30 or 12.00 for 6 days, and for 3 days also from 14.00 to 16.30. The school year runs from September to July.

Outside school hours care: 1%–2% are covered by centres for children over 4 (with a varying upper age limit), or by local authority provision. Some authorities run holiday playschemes.

Care for sick children: In 1988 a service was established to provide care for sick children at home. It has since been extended with government support.

Contributions to child-care costs: Parents contribute to public services (excluding schools) according to income and family size. A tax reduction of LFR18,000 is available for child care (up to age 14).

An allowance of LFR9,232 is paid to parents for educating a child under the age of 2, if they have no income or their joint income is not more than LFR94,168 if educating 1 child; LFR125,558 for 2 children, or LFR156,947 for 3 children. See the Family benefits section under State Benefits for details of the allowance for schoolchildren.

STATE BENEFITS (1989–90)

There are proposals to reform pensions, taxation and health insurance laws.

Retirement pension: Normal retirement age is 65 for women and men, and to qualify they must have paid 120 months of insurance. Pensions are paid as a lump sum plus proportional supplements of 1.6% of earnings (up to an annual limit of LFR1,506,696) which are linked to wage increases. For 40 years of contributions, the minimum lump sum is LFR329,892 a year (those with fewer years of contributions receive proportionally less).

The state pays contributions for up to 3 years for leave after the birth of a child (this has been extended from 1 year). Workers with 480 months of insurance can retire with an early pension at 60.

Survivors' pensions: To qualify, the deceased must have been insured for 12 of the previous 36 months. Couples must have been married for at least a year before the death, unless there is a child.

The pension for partners is the full lump sum to which the deceased was entitled, plus two-thirds of the proportional supplements. The pension stops on remarriage with a grant of 60 months' payments if under 50, and 36 months' payments if 50 or over.

Children are entitled to one-third of the flat-rate supplements and 20% of the proportional supplements of the person who has died. This is doubled for children who have lost both parents.

Death grant: LFR32,313 (paid at 50% if a child under 6 dies and at 20% for stillborns).

Sickness benefit: Full salary is paid for a maximum of 52 weeks.

Invalidity: Paid to those who cannot carry on their previous employment or other work, because of sickness or infirmity. Twelve months of insurance contributions must have been paid in the previous 36 months (unless invalidity is from an industrial injury or disease). Benefit is paid immediately to those with permanent incapacity, and paid after sickness benefit runs out for those with temporary incapacity. At 65, an old age pension is paid instead. Minimum invalidity pension, paid as a lump sum with earnings-related supplements, is LFR329,892 a year after 40 years' contributions (reduced proportionally for fewer years). Pensions are reduced if earnings are above a certain level.

Family benefits: LFR1,893 a month for the first child; LFR5,770 for 2, LFR12,694 for 3, plus LFR5,678 for fourth and later children. For handicapped children, there is an extra LFR1,893. Benefit is normally paid until the age of 18, or 25 if in vocational training or further education. There is no limit in cases of serious infirmity.

In addition, an allowance is paid for schoolchildren at the start of the school year, in 2 levels: those over 6 years old and those over 12. The benefit is LFR1,846 for 1 younger child or LFR2,770 for an older child; LFR3,693 for 2 younger children or LFR4,616 for 2 older; and LFR6,001 for 3 younger children or LFR7,386 for 3 older. For other allowances, see Child-care Provision.

Pia Meyer, age 23, became the first Luxembourg woman airline pilot in 1990

Unemployment benefit: 80% of earnings (up to $2\frac{1}{2}$ times the minimum wage) for 182 days over 12 months, then at $1\frac{1}{2}$ times for the remaining 183 days. Benefit is reduced to 60% of earnings if the joint income is above this. People who are 'difficult to place' can receive benefit for an additional 182 days, and there are also special allowances for those unemployed over 50.

Geriatric-care benefit: About LFR10,000 for families with dependent senior citizens who cannot live alone. It can take months to be given a place in retirement or nursing homes.

Child-rearing benefit: Now granted to homemakers and women with low incomes for 2 years. Also, see Maternity leave and pay under Parental Benefits.

WOMEN AND EMPLOYMENT

Statutory rights: The working week is limited to 40 hours (though this can be overruled by the Minister for Employment) and overtime is restricted to 2 hours a day. Paid annual leave is 25 days and there are 10 statutory public holidays.

The national minimum wage was LFR35,933 a month in April 1991, though lower rates apply in agriculture and domestic work. The full rate is paid at age 18. Wages are index linked. Wages cannot be seized in full by creditors. Two-thirds of working women earn the minimum wage.

Employment and unemployment (1989)

	% women	% men
economic activity rate	34.1	67.8
employed working part time	17.0	2.0
labour force who are employers or self-employed	5.7	11.0
unemployment rate	2.3	1.1

Source: data from *Labour Force Survey (Results 1989)* (Eurostat)

Part-time work: In 1989 81.8% of part-time workers were women. Part timers must work at least 20 hours a week to qualify for unemployment benefit and domestic workers must work at least 17 hours a week to qualify for social security.

A survey of why women were interested in part-time work found that 25% quoted financial reasons, with 25% saying they were isolated in the home.

Employment by industrial sector (1000s) (1989)

	women no	women %	men no	men %	women as % of workforce
agriculture	2	3.4	4	4.0	33.3
all industry	5	8.6	40	40.1	11.1
energy and water	–	–	2	1.6	–
mineral extraction and chemicals	1	1.5	13	13.0	7.1
metal manufacturing and engineering	1	1.0	5	4.5	16.7
other manufacturing industry	2	3.7	9	8.9	18.2
building and civil engineering	1	1.5	12	12.1	7.7
all services	47	88.0	56	55.9	45.6
distributive trades and hotels	15	27.9	16	16.0	48.4
transport and communication	2	3.5	8	8.4	20
banking, finance and insurance	9	16.5	10	10.3	47.4
public administration	4	6.8	9	8.9	30.8
other services	18	33.2	12	12.3	60.0
total	53	100.0	100	100.0	34.6

Source: data from *Labour Force Survey (Results 1989)* (Eurostat)

Women's earnings as a % of men's in services (April 1987)

	non-manual monthly earnings
wholesale and retail distribution	57.4
wholesale distribution	63.7
retail distribution	60.3
credit institutions	68.7
insurance (excluding social security)	64.1

Source: data from *Earnings in Industry and Services* (Eurostat)

Women's earnings as a % of men's in industry (April 1987)

	manual hourly earnings	non-manual monthly earnings
energy and water	93.0	77.0
chemical industry	56.6	53.8
all metal manufacture and engineering	67.0	56.8
mechanical engineering	70.3	57.7
food, drink and tobacco	66.5	54.3
clothing and footwear manufacture	40.5	48.5
printing and publishing	–	59.8
all manufacturing industry	60.9	54.5
all industry	65.3	55.4

Source: data from *Earnings in Industry and Services* (Eurostat)

Working mothers (1988): 38% of women with a child under 10 were employed compared with 98% of similar men. 69% of women aged 20–39 without children were employed. 2% of women and 1% of men with a child under 10 were unemployed. The unemployment rates for women and men with a child under 10 were the lowest in the EC. 26% of employed women with a child under 10 had part-time jobs.

Employment rates are much higher for lone mothers than all mothers: in 1988 it was 75% for lone mothers with a child aged 0–4 (36% for all mothers) and 63% for lone mothers with a child aged 5–9 (36%). Unemployment rates were as low for single mothers as for all mothers (less than 3%).

WOMEN AND POLITICS

Women won the vote in 1919. Of the 60 seats in the Chamber of Deputies, 8 or 13.3% are held by women. Voting is compulsory. The number of women in the 60-member Chamber by political party in 1991 was: Parti Chrétian, 4 women out of 22 members; Parti Ouvrier Socialiste, 3 out of 18; Parti Démocratique, 1 out of 11.

WOMEN AND DETENTION

Women made up 5% of all prisoners in September 1988. Minors (age 21) and young adults made up 5.3% and foreigners 41.3%.

SOURCES

Abortion Laws in Europe, Planned Parenthood in Europe, Vol 18 No 1, Spring 1989 (Supplement, amended April 1990); *Childcare in the European Communities 1985–90* (Women of Europe Supplement No 51); *Comparative Study on rules governing working conditions in the member states* (Commission of the European Communities); *Demographic Statistics 1990* (Eurostat); *Earnings in Industry and Services* (Eurostat); Embassy of the Grand Duchy of Luxembourg, London; *Europa World Year Book 1990* (31st edition); *Health Care Systems and Professional Organisations in the European Community, Information note – Europe* (British Medical Association); Health For All 2000 Indicator Presentation System (World Health Organisation Regional Office for Europe); *Labour Force Survey (Results 1989)* (Eurostat); *Les Actions Positives en Faveur des Femmes en Europe Occidentale* (Institut Syndical Europeen); *Luxembourg in figures 1990* (STATEC); *Out In Europe* (Peter Tatchell, for Channel 4 Television); *Positive action and the constitutional and legislative hindrances to its implementation in the member states of the Council of Europe* (Council of Europe); *Prison Information Bulletin* June 1990 (Council of Europe); *Proposition de Directive Du Conseil concernant la protection au travail de la femme enceinte ou venant d'accoucher* (Commission of the European Communities); *Social Protection in the Member States of the Community* (Commission of the European Community Directorate General on Employment, Industrial Relations and Social Affairs); *Women of Europe* (Nos 62, 63, 67, 69)

ADDRESSES

Embassy of Luxembourg, 27 Wilton Crescent, London SW1X 8SD. Tel: 071 235 6961

Service Centrale de la Statistique et des Etudes Economiques, Ministère de l'Economie, 19-21 Boulevard Royal, 2449 Luxembourg. Tel: (35 2) 478 611

Fédération National des Femmes Luxembourgeoises, 1 rue de la Forge, L 1535 Luxembourg

Confédération Générale du Travail du Luxembourg, 60 Blvd JF Kennedy, BP 149, 4002 Esch-sur-Alzette

Malta

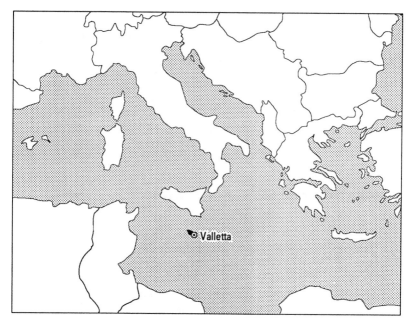

- **Population** 0.36 million, 50.7% female
- **Area** 316 sq km
- **Population density** 1,115.2 people sq km
- **GDP 1988** LM670.1 million (£1,241 million)
- **GDP per capita** £3,447
- **Public spending as % of GNP:** education 3.6% (1987)
- **Consumer price index** 1980 = 100; 1989 = 103
- **Currency is the lira** 1989 £1 = LM0.54; US$1 = LM0.33

The single-chamber parliament is the House of Representatives, which is elected for 5 years by proportional representation. A party with over 50% of the vote automatically has a majority in the house. The president is elected for 5 years by the house.

Official languages are English and Maltese, but Italian is also widely spoken. Major industries are ship repairing and building, wholesale and retail trade, and tourism.

Until 1964, Malta was a British colony. In 1989, 399 people left Malta (about half for Australia) and 722 returned to settle. Over 85% of the population are practising Roman Catholics.

IMMIGRATION AND RESIDENCE RIGHTS

The conditions for citizenship by naturalisation in the Maltese Citizenship Act refer only to the male gender. They are that an alien or stateless person must have lived in Malta for 12 months before applying; that he must have lived in Malta for 4 of the 6 previous years; know Maltese or English; and be of good character. Naturalisation without this required residence period may be granted if an individual has a Maltese father (or mother if born after 1 August 1989), or is a former citizen of Malta.

Maltese women who marry foreign citizens have the right to dual nationality. Foreign citizens marrying Maltese women are entitled to the same rights as Maltese citizens.

EQUAL RIGHTS

The government's 5-year work programme for 1987–92 committed it to removing 'discrimination between men and women so as to bring about complete equality of the sexes'. In July 1991 the constitution was amended to recognise equality between women and men as a fundamental human right and to provide for a legal remedy in cases of sex discrimination. The Commission for the Advancement of Women was set up in 1989 to formulate new

In December 1978 a law banning women from filling jobs previously held by men was amended family law, mainly to eliminate discrimination between the sexes in marriage. In October 1991 a White Paper proposed amendments to the civil code towards accomplishing this. The Secretariat for the Equal Status of Women and the Commission for the Advancement of Women campaigns for legal reform of the civil code on marriage, children and property; conditions of employment; social security laws; income tax laws; and broadcasting and advertising standards.

BIRTH, LIFE AND DEATH

Breakdown of population by sex and age group (1000s) (1989)

	all		women		men		% of women in age group
	no	%	no	%	no	%	
0–14	83.2	23.5	40.4	22.6	42.6	24.5	48.8
15–24	49.7	14.1	24.1	13.5	25.4	14.6	48.5
25–39	83.9	23.8	41.2	23.1	42.8	24.6	49.1
40–59	84.2	23.9	44.1	24.7	40.3	23.2	52.4
60–74	37.7	10.7	20.5	11.5	17.0	9.8	54.4
75+	13.7	3.9	8.2	4.6	5.7	3.3	59.9
all	352.4	100.0	178.5	100.0	173.9	100.0	50.7

Source: Central Office of Statistics, Malta

Births, deaths, and marriages per 1,000 people

	1980	1985	1988	1990
birth rate	17.2	15.9	15.8	15.1
death rate	9.9	8.3	7.8	7.6
infant mortality per 1,000 live births	15.2	13.6	7.9	9.0
marriage rate	17.5*	15.0	14.5	–

* 1981

Source: *Demographic Review of the Maltese Islands 1990* (Central Office of Statistics, Malta)

In 1988 life expectancy was 77.6 for women and 72.8 for men.

Draft amendments to the civil code proposed in October 1991 would mean the husband was no longer the head of the family and responsible for his wife's maintenance. Both marriage partners would have equal rights and responsibilities in marriage and joint responsibility for their children. The amendments would also replace paternal responsibility with parental responsibility, give women the right to keep their own name on marriage, though children would have to take their father's name with the right to add on their mother's. However the amendments do not remove the dowry, which has been retained as a contractual obligation.

Divorce does not exist in Maltese law, though since 1975 foreign divorces have been recognised. Personal separation 'from bed and board' can be granted on the grounds of cruelty, adultery, threats or serious injury, desertion for 2 years, or irretrievable breakdown of the marriage provided it is at least 4 years old. Marriages can also be annulled on the grounds of sterility and impotence.

LESBIAN RIGHTS

Homosexual relationships were illegal until 1973. Although there is no legal age of consent, in practice 18 is the common age of consent for lesbians, gay men and heterosexuals.

WOMEN AND HEALTH CARE

All primary health care and hospital services are free. Those on low incomes and those who suffer from certain chronic diseases qualify for free drugs and medicines. A programme of community health care provides immunisation, child clinics and school medical services. Seven health centres provide a 24-hour general practice service which includes ante-natal, gynaecology, post-natal and family welfare services.

In 1988 there was 1 doctor for every 829 people.

Major indicators for women's health (1989)

maternal deaths (all causes) per 100,000 live births	0.00
maternal deaths (abortion) per 100,000 live births	0.00
% of all live births to mothers under 20	2.65
% of all live births to mothers aged 35+	13.77
deaths from cancer of the cervix (age 0–64) per 100,000 women (1988)	1.50
deaths from malignant neoplasm female breast (age 0–64) per 100,000 women	23.71
deaths from trachea/bronchus/lung cancer (age 0–64) per 100,000 women	4.21
deaths from trachea/bronchus/lung cancer (age 0–64) per 100,000 men	31.09
deaths from diseases of the circulatory system (age 0–64) per 100,000 women	52.18
deaths from diseases of the circulatory system (age 0–64) per 100,000 men	108.32
deaths from suicide and self-inflicted injury per 100,000 women	2.74
deaths from suicide and self-inflicted injury per 100,000 men	10.26

Source: data from Health for All 2000 Indicator Presentation System (World Health Organisation Regional Office For Europe)

Abortion and contraception: Abortion is illegal. Contraception is provided free by the family welfare clinics. The Cana Movement, a Catholic organisation which offers marriage counselling services, advises the use of the rhythm method.

PARENTAL PAY, LEAVE AND BENEFITS (1988–89)

Women have been allowed to serve on juries since July 1972

Maternity leave and pay: 13 weeks on full pay, including 5 after the birth, plus special unpaid leave for medical complications. Adoptive mothers are entitled to 5 weeks on full pay. In the public sector women have the right to an additional 12 months' unpaid leave, provided they work for at least 6 months afterwards (otherwise they must refund their 13 weeks' pay for maternity leave). Women not entitled to paid maternity leave qualify for a maternity benefit for up to and including 3 children. Benefit is LM5.50 a week for 8 weeks from when the woman submits a medical certificate saying she has entered the eighth month of pregnancy, then for a further 5 weeks on production of a birth certificate.

Parental allowance: A social security benefit of LM2.0 a week is paid to unemployed mothers who decide to stay at home to care for children under the age of 11, provided the joint gross income of the woman and her partner does not exceed LM2,400 a year. If a woman dies or no longer has care of the child following separation, the allowance can be transferred to any other unemployed person in the household who cares for the child.

CHILD-CARE PROVISION

Under 3s: The first government-sponsored day-care centre for children under 3 of working parents was opened in 1991 in partnership with the Malta Development Corporation. There are also private and religious child-care facilities that are normally fee paying, though lower income parents may qualify for economic assistance.

3–5 year olds: Free state kindergartens are available in all towns and villages. There are also a number of private and religious child-care facilities which are normally fee-paying.

Primary school (5 years up): Education is compulsory between 5 and 16. State-provided education is free from kindergarten to university.

STATE BENEFITS (1988–89)

Social assistance benefits are funded through insurance contributions, paid by employees, employers and from a consolidated fund. Anyone receiving a pension or social assistance is entitled to a bonus, paid in instalments in June and December. In October 1991 the Social Security Act was amended to remove discrimination against married women who were required to start paying their contributions afresh after they married. They now retain their entitlement to sickness and unemployment benefits.

Retirement pension: Normal pensionable age is 61 for both women and men. For those who continue working, retirement begins when they end employment or age 65, whichever comes first.

Widows' pension: Widows who are self-employed retain their right to pensions, but are classed as self-employed.

Family allowance: Paid to single parents with custody of a child. Benefits paid to single-parent families are means tested.

Marriage grant: Paid as a lump sum provided the person marrying has been employed or self-employed for the previous 6 months.

Prostitution is illegal, with soliciting carrying a 3-month prison sentence

Child allowance: Paid to the head of household for all children up to age 16 provided they live in the household, at the weekly rate of LM3.50 for the first child, LM2.70 for the second, LM1.70 for the third and LM1.00 for subsequent children. There is an extra LM3.00 a week for children with disabilities. A weekly allowance is paid for children of 16 or over if they are in full-time education (LM1.00), or unemployed (LM0.40). All those who receive child allowances qualify for a family bonus worth LM1.00 a week.

Milk grant: Heads of household on social assistance are entitled to a milk grant if they have care or custody of a child under 40 weeks who cannot be breastfed, until the child is 40 weeks old.

Invalidity pension: Paid to those who cannot work because of serious disease or disability. Length of payment is assessed for each case.

Care allowance: Single and widowed women looking after an elderly or disabled relative full time qualify for social assistance. This may soon be extended to unemployed housewives.

Emergency assistance: A woman 'rendered destitute by the head of household to the extent that she becomes an inmate of any institute for the care and welfare of such persons' is entitled to emergency assistance of up to LM10.00 for 7 consecutive days up to a maximum of LM100 in any year, for any period when she does not qualify for other benefits.

WOMEN AND EMPLOYMENT

Equal rights: Article 14 of the Maltese Constitution says the state will aim to ensure that women workers enjoy the same rights, and the same wages for the same work as men. In 1967 it was decided the wages of women government workers should be raised by stages to reach parity with men doing the same work by 1971. Wage parity for the same work in the private sector was achieved in 1976.

Statutory rights: The working week is regulated to 40 hours in the public sector, and is normally 40 hours in the private sector. There is a national minimum wage. All employees are entitled to a bonus paid twice a year.

Employment and unemployment (1990)

	% women	% men
economic activity	18.7	56.1
% in employment	18.3	53.7
employed who are self-employed	7.4	14.5
unemployment rate	2.3	4.4
all unemployed by sex	15.0	85.0

Source: data from Secretariat for the Equal Status of Women, Ministry for Social Policy

Employment by industrial sector (1988)

	women		men		women as % of workforce
	no	%	no	%	
government employees	8,074	25.6	28,135	30.1	22.3
agriculture and fishing	428	1.4	2,740	2.9	13.5
oil	30	0.1	531	0.6	5.4
quarrying and clay pits	4	0.0	310	0.3	1.3
manufacturing	11,312	35.9	24,418	26.1	31.7
construction	101	0.3	5,761	6.2	1.7
electricity and gas	102	0.3	1,758	1.9	5.5
wholesale and trade	3,264	10.4	8,934	9.6	26.8
transport and communications	1,073	3.4	8,156	8.7	11.6
finance and insurance	1,533	4.9	2,539	2.7	37.7
business, community, leisure and personal services	5,577	17.7	10,193	10.9	35.4
total	31,498	100.0	93,475	100.0	25.2

Source: data from Department of Labour and Emigration

Wage earners by sex and occupation (1990)

	% of women earners	% of men earners	% women in occupational group
administrative and clerical	16.0	10.2	39.9
messenger	3.6	1.4	49.9
professional	1.8	2.6	20.1
technical and supervisory	1.1	4.8	7.6
dept grades	36.0	30.6	30.5
industrial	11.4	39.3	9.7
apprentices and trainees	5.1	5.7	24.8
worker students	1.4	0.6	44.1
pupil workers	11.0	4.4	48.2
casual and part-time workers	12.7	0.5	90.2
total	100.0	100.0	

Source: data from Department of Labour and Emigration

Margaret Mortimer was the first woman to head a government department when she became Director of Education in 1970

Taxation: Major tax reform in 1990 reduced the top rate of income tax from 65% to 35% and increased the tax-free threshold from LM495 to LM1,526 for single taxpayers and from LM450 to LM2,180 for married taxpayers. The system of grossing the income of a married couple has been abolished, which has reduced the rate of tax. An estimated 5,489 households will be an average of LM6.30 a week better off because a wife and husband's incomes are each taxed at the single rate.

WOMEN AND POLITICS

Women won the right to vote and to stand for election in 1947. Of the 69 seats in the House of Representatives, only 2 (2.9%) are held by women. The last elections were held in May 1987: 65 of the 69 seats are directly elected, with 4 nominated by the majority party. Malta's only woman minister was Agatha Barbara who was head of state (president). There are no women magistrates or judges.

WOMEN AND EDUCATION

State-provided education is free from kindergarten to university. Most students over 16 receive education grants. The government also subsidises private schools, which are mainly religious, so that all secondary private education is also free. Between the end of primary school and 16, education is provided in single-sex schools. Primary, post-16 and tertiary schooling is co-educational. Subjects on offer in secondary and trade schools are heavily gender-biased.

In 1988–89, 1 of the 14 professors at the University of Malta was a woman; 4.8% of all university academics and 36.4% (1987–88) of university students were women.

WOMEN AND DETENTION

In September 1988 women made up 0.5% of prisoners. Minors (age 18) and young adults made up 2.7% of prisoners, and foreigners 20.4%.

SOURCES

Abstract 1988 No 42 (Central Office of Statistics); Central Office of Statistics, Malta; Department of Labour and Emigration; *Demographic Review of the Maltese Islands 1990* (Central Office of Statistics, Malta); *Economic Trends December 1990* (Central Office of Statistics); *Economic Survey January–September 1990* (Economic Planning Division, Ministry for Economic Affairs); *Equal partners in marriage – updating of the family law* (Ministry for Social Policy); *Europa World Year Book 1990* (31st edition); Health For All 2000 Indicator Presentation System (World Health Organisation Regional Office for Europe); *Les Actions Positives en Faveur des Femmes en Europe Occidentale* (Institut Syndical Europeen); Ministry for Social Policy; *OPM Circular 102/87* (Office of the Prime Minister); *Out In Europe* (Peter Tatchell, for Channel 4 Television); *Prison Information Bulletin June 1990* (Council of Europe); Secretariat for the Equal Status of Women, Ministry for Social Policy; *Social Security Act 1987* (as amended); *The National Council of Women of Malta Silver Jubilee Supplement; Third World Guide 91/92* (Instituto del Tercer Mundo)

ADDRESSES

Malta High Commission, 16 Kensington Square, London W8.

Secretariat for the Equal Status of Women, Ministry for Social Policy, Palazzo Ferreria, Valletta. Tel: (356) 60 31 66

National Council of Women, 23 St Andrew Street, Valletta.

The Netherlands

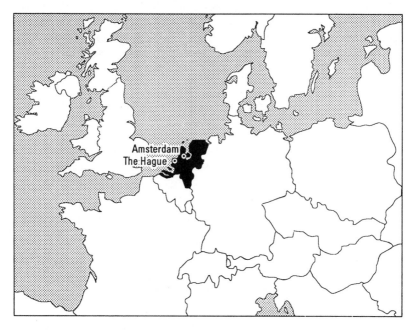

- **Population** 14.7 million, 50.6% female
- **Area** 41,864 sq km
- **Population density** 350.3 people sq km
- **GDP 1988** guilders 451 billion (£141.4 billion)
- **GDP per capita** £9,561
- **GDP per capita in purchasing power parity** (UK=100) 103
- **Public spending as % of GNP:** defence 3.1% (1986); education 6.6% (1986); health 7.5% (1987)
- **Consumer price index** 1980 = 100; 1989 = 125
- **Currency is the guilder** 1989 £1 = HFL3.1; US$1 = HFL1.92

Women and girls who have been attacked can ask for related court proceedings to be conducted by a woman judge

The kingdom of the Netherlands has Amsterdam as its capital but the seat of government is The Hague. Legislative power is held by the 2-chamber parliament: the first chamber, whose 75 members are elected for 6 years by the 12 provincial councils, and the 150-member second chamber, elected for 4 years by proportional representation. Voting is from the age of 18.

More than half the country lies below sea level – dykes and pumping stations are needed to keep the land dry. 20% of the land is used for arable farming, 36% for dairy farming, 13% is wooded and 28% is taken up with towns, roads and areas of water. 5% of the workforce is in agriculture and fishing, 28% in industry and 67% in services.

32% of the population do not practise religion, 36% are Roman Catholic, and 20% belong to the Dutch Reformed Church.

IMMIGRATION AND RESIDENCE RIGHTS

In 1988 the Netherlands had 591,847 foreign residents, 44% of them women. 26.5% of foreign residents were from other EC states, 32.5% from non-EC European countries, 25.2% from African countries and 15.7% from other countries.

EQUAL RIGHTS

The constitution grants all citizens equality in law, and specifically prohibits discrimination on the grounds of sex. The law allows for employers to give preferential treatment to one sex in order to remove inequalities.

Between 1978 and 1988, government grants for equal rights activities increased by 1,888%

The post of State Secretary for Equal Opportunity Policy, established in 1971, was abolished in 1986, when responsibility for equal rights was given to the Minister of Employment and Social Security. Ministers must consult the Equal Opportunity Council when considering related issues. The 13-member council is appointed by the government.

BIRTH, LIFE AND DEATH

Breakdown of population by sex and age group (1000s) (1988)

	all		women		men		% of women in age group
	no	%	no	%	no	%	
0–14	2,718.7	18.5	1,328.8	17.9	1,389.9	19.1	48.9
15–24	2,473.8	16.8	1,211.0	16.3	1,262.8	17.4	49.0
25–39	3,592.2	24.4	1,757.1	23.6	1,835.1	25.2	48.9
40–59	3,418.5	23.2	1,684.8	22.6	1,733.7	23.8	49.3
60–74	1,737.1	11.8	953.1	12.8	784.0	10.8	54.9
75+	774.6	5.3	506.5	6.8	268.1	3.7	65.4
all	14,714.9	100.0	7,441.3	100.0	7,273.6	100.0	50.6

Source: data from *Demographic Statistics 1990* (Eurostat)

Population, population density and population increase by region (1987)

region	pop (1000s)	% of total pop	pop density per sq km	natural increase per 1,000	net migration per 1,000	total increase per 1,000
Groningen	557.6	3.8	187.8	2.1	-5.0	-2.9
Friesland	599.1	4.1	112.2	3.8	-2.9	0.9
Drenthe	435.3	3.0	162.4	3.7	1.6	5.3
Overijssel	1,007.0	6.9	294.6	5.1	–	–
Gelderland	1,777.8	12.1	345.6	4.5	–	–
Flevoland	189.6	1.3	89.5	13.9	–	–
Utrecht	959.6	6.5	684.5	5.2	5.7	10.9
Noord-Holland	2,343.5	16.0	641.0	3.4	3.1	6.4
Zuid-Holland	3,197.3	21.8	951.9	4.3	2.5	6.8
Zeeland	355.5	2.4	116.9	2.8	-3.2	-0.4
Noord-Brabant	2,148.0	14.6	422.6	5.5	1.8	7.4
Limburg	1,093.5	7.5	495.1	3.7	-0.5	3.2
Netherlands	**14,663.8**	**100.0**	**350.3**	**4.4**	**1.8**	**6.2**

Source: data from *Demographic Statistics 1990* (Eurostat)

Births, deaths, marriages and divorces per 1,000 population

	1960	1970	1980	1985	1988
birth rate	21.0	18.4	12.9	12.3	12.7
% of births outside marriage	1.4	2.1	4.1	8.8	10.2
average age of mother at 1st birth	25.6	24.3	25.6	26.5	27.2
infant mortality per 1,000 live births	17.9	12.7	8.6	8.0	6.8
fertility rate per woman	3.1	2.6	1.6	1.5	1.6
marriage rate	7.8	9.5	6.4	5.7	6.0
average age at marriage (women)	25.4	23.7	24.5	26.3	27.3
average age at marriage (men)	28.3	26.2	27.4	29.1	30.1
divorce rate	0.5	0.8	1.8	2.3	1.9
life expectancy (women)	75.3	76.5	79.3	–	78.9*
life expectancy (men)	71.5	70.7	72.7	–	72.2*
death rate	7.7	8.5	8.1	8.5	8.4

* 1983–88

Source: data from *Demographic Statistics 1990* (Eurostat)

One-parent household accounted in 1988 for 9% of households with a child aged 0–4 and 10% of households with a child aged 5–9.

Alimony is paid until death or age 65, when the beneficiary becomes eligible for a pension and part of their spouse's pension (depending on years of marriage). A proposed bill would limit alimony to 12 years after divorce, with the right to appeal for an extension of 12 more years. For childless couples married less than 5 years, alimony would be paid for the amount of time married.

LESBIAN RIGHTS

Since 1971, 16 has been the common age of consent. Previously, from 1911 when ages of consent were re-introduced after a 100-year gap, it had been 18 for lesbians and heterosexuals, compared with 21 for gay men. Section 1 of the constitution prohibits discrimination 'on any grounds whatsoever'. However, legislation specifically banning discrimination against lesbians and gay men is expected. There have been cases where the foreign partners of lesbians and gay men have been allowed to immigrate and take up residence. Asylum has also been granted to homosexuals at risk of persecution on the grounds of their sexual orientation.

Lesbian and gay couples can draw up contracts giving them the same rights as married couples to property, taxation, and hospital and prison visits – though not in adoption and social security. The main political parties have accepted the principle that laws should be introduced that recognise lesbian and gay relationships.

WOMEN AND HEALTH CARE

Health care is being reorganised from a system of separate insurance schemes to 1 universal national health insurance scheme which will fund 85% of medical-care costs. Contributions will depend on income. State funding is available for municipal health services, preventive medicine including children's vaccination programmes and the school dentistry service. In 1988 there was 1 doctor for every 428 people.

Major indicators for women's health (1988)

maternal deaths (all causes) per 100,000 live births	9.64
maternal deaths (abortion) per 100,000 live births	1.07
ratio of abortions to 1,000 live births (all ages)	96.40
% of all live births to mothers under 20	2.24
% of all live births to mothers aged 35+	8.68
deaths from cancer of the cervix (age 0–64) per 100,000 women	2.33
deaths from malignant neoplasm female breast (age 0–64) per 100,000 women	23.71
deaths from trachea/bronchus/lung cancer (age 0–64) per 100,000 women	8.87
deaths from trachea/bronchus/lung cancer (age 0–64) per 100,000 men	39.13
deaths from diseases of the circulatory system (age 0–64) per 100,000 women	31.14
deaths from diseases of the circulatory system (age 0–64) per 100,000 men	99.74
deaths from suicide and self-inflicted injury per 100,000 women	7.28
deaths from suicide and self-inflicted injury per 100,000 men	13.29

Source: data from Health for All 2000 Indicator Presentation System (World Health Organisation Regional Office For Europe)

Abortion and contraception: Available up to 24 weeks, if the woman is in an 'intolerable situation' jointly defined by her and her doctor, and after a waiting period of 5 days. Women under 18 need parental consent and a doctor must conclude that the woman decided to have an abortion of her own free will. The law is liberally interpreted and there are very few illegal abortions. Most abortions take place in private non-profit clinics. Almost half of all abortions are carried out on German, Belgian and Spanish women.

PARENTAL PAY, LEAVE AND BENEFITS (1989–90)

Maternity leave and pay: 16 weeks, including 4–6 that must be taken before the birth, paid by state benefit equal to 100% of earnings (up to a maximum). To qualify, women must have worked for at least 6 months, though in practice this is often waived.

Parental and paternity leave: A scheme before parliament would grant each parent 6 months' unpaid part-time leave (weekly working hours reduced to 20) that could be claimed until the child is 4, but not transferred from 1 parent to the other.

CHILD-CARE PROVISION (1989–90)

There have been major changes in how child-care services are funded, with more money committed from the government. (See Child-care costs at end of section for details). The result is that the number of publicly funded nurseries doubled during 1990. By 1993 public funding for child-care services (excluding schools) will have increased by 583% since 1989. In addition to extra funds for local authorities, each new full-time place is subsidised by a government payment of 15,000 guilders. 95% of local authorities have applied for additional funds for child-care services.

Under 3s: 1.5% are in publicly funded places but since many of these are used part time the actual percentage is estimated at 2%–3%. 10% go to playgroups, but most for very short hours. An estimated 1%–2% of under 4s are in private or workplace nurseries.

3–5 year olds: 50% start primary school early (compulsory schooling begins at 5, but almost all children start school a year early). An additional 1.5% are in publicly funded places. 25% go to playgroups, again mostly for very short hours.

Primary school (5 years up): 9.00 to 16.00 with a 2-hour lunch break, though more schools are moving to a shorter day with a shorter break. All Amsterdam schools, for example, run from 8.30 to 15.00 with a 1-hour break. Lunch supervision must be provided if parents request it and will pay for it. Roughly 66% of schools provide lunch supervision and about 30% of 4–12 year olds use it. 1% of children go to special lunchtime centres, some of which also provide out of school care. The school year runs from August to July. In 1988 the pupil to teacher ratio in primary schools was 17:1.

Outside school hours care: Provided not by schools but in separate centres, attended by an estimated 1% of 5–10 year olds. In 1990, HFL73 million was set aside to provide out of school hours care for the children of working parents, with provision for this sum to increase each year.

Contributions to child-care costs: Parents pay for child-care services, apart from schools, according to their incomes. Some of the money used to fund the government's new commitment to child-care was created in 1989 by abolishing the tax relief on child-care costs introduced in 1984.

> **Government workers with young children can work reduced hours with a payment of 75% for hours not worked**

> **In 1956 the law was changed so that married women no longer needed their husband's permission to enter into a legal transaction**

STATE BENEFITS (1989–90)

State benefits have been index linked since January 1990.

Retirement pensions: Normal retirement age is 65 for women and men. Full pensions are paid after 50 years of insurance, otherwise pensions are reduced.

The single person's pension is HFL1,317 a month. Pensioners with partners, including same-sex partners, are each paid HFL918 if both are over 65, and if one is under 65 the pension is HFL1,317 (if this partner is on a low income, there is an additional payment). Single-parent pensioners receive HFL1,652. Holiday allowances are HFL79 a month for single pensioners, HFL56 for each pensioner partner in a couple and HFL102 for single parents. Pensions are adjusted in line with the minimum wage.

Survivors' pensions: This system is to undergo a fundamental review so that it covers widowers as well as widows. Now pensions are paid to the widows who have dependent children, are disabled or are at least 40. The husband must have been insured at the time of his death. Survivors' pension is replaced with old age pension at 65.

Widow's pension is HFL1,580 a month (HFL2,262 for women with dependent children), plus a holiday allowance of at least HFL99 a month. Widows with no pension rights are entitled to HFL1,580 plus holiday allowance a month for between 6 and 19 months. Women who remarry receive a grant of 1 year's pension before it stops.

Orphans are entitled to between HFL505 and HFL1,011 a month plus a holiday allowance. The same pensions are paid to children whose father has died and whose mother is not their guardian.

Death grant: Calculated by taking the daily wage and multiplying it by the number of days between the death and the last day of the second month after death (plus a supplement if 70% of the daily wage is less than the social minimum).

Sickness benefit: Paid at 70% of the daily wage (up to a maximum daily wage of HFL270.60) for up to 52 weeks. Waiting time is 2 days.

Invalidity: Paid to those partially or completely incapable of working because of sickness or infirmity. All workers under 65 are covered by a scheme which pays benefit for 15% incapacity to work, from when sickness benefit ends until the age of 65. Depending on the degree of incapacity, allowances range from 14% of daily earnings to 70% (from HFL19 for 25% incapacity to HFL64.54 for 80% incapacity). Plus a holiday allowance of 8% paid in May.

In a 1985 report, 60% of the Dutch population said domestic chores should be shared equally between women and men. Yet that year women spent an average of 34 hours a week on domestic duties, compared with a man's 9.9 hours

Family benefits: Based on the number of children aged 6–17 in the family. Benefit is HFL112 a month for 1 child; 141 each for 2 children; HFL150 each for 3; HFL163 for 4; HFL171 for 5; HFL180 for 6; HFL186 for 7 and HFL193 each for 8. Children under 6 qualify for 70% of the basic amount; children aged 12–17 for 130%, and children aged 18–24 for 100%. A special quarterly allowance of HFL17 is paid to families with 1 child, and of HFL35 to families with more than 1 child.

Benefits are doubled for invalid children under 16 not living at home, or under 17 and not living at home or in another adult household. Benefits are also doubled for those aged 18–24 who are students, in occupational training or who carry out household tasks and are mainly supported by the applicant. Benefits are trebled if the 18–24 year olds are studying or in occupational training and not living in the household but supported by the applicant.

Unemployment benefit: 70% of earnings for 6 months to 5 years depending on contributions, then 70% of the statutory minimum wage for 1 year. A supplement can be claimed if benefits are less than the social minimum. Benefits are paid at lower rates for single people under the age of 23.

WOMEN AND EMPLOYMENT

Statutory rights: The working week is restricted to 48 hours, with overtime limited to between a half-hour and $3\frac{1}{2}$ hours a day. However longer working days are allowed if they are the exception. Paid annual leave is 4 weeks. There are 6 public holidays (plus 1 additional public holiday every 5 years).

In 1991 the national minimum wage was HFL2,041 a month. Full rates are paid at age 23. Workers are legally entitled to a holiday bonus worth 8% of annual salary. Wages have not been index linked since the mid 1980s. Wages cannot be seized in full by creditors.

Employment and unemployment (1989)

	% women	% men
economic activity rate	41.7	69.4
employed working part time	59.9	15.0
labour force who are employers or self-employed	7.4	11.5
labour force who are family workers	4.8	0.3
unemployment rate	11.9	6.8
youth unemployment rate (age 14-24)	14.1	12.7
unemployed who have been unemployed for		
12 months or more	43.5	55.1
all unemployed by sex	52.0	48.0

Source: data from *Labour Force Survey (Results 1989)* (Eurostat)

Employment by industrial sector (1000s) (1989)

	women no	women %	men no	men %	women as % of workforce
agriculture	70	3.1	216	5.7	24.5
all industry	250	11.2	1,353	35.8	15.6
energy and water	8	0.4	56	1.5	12.5
mineral extraction and chemicals	25	1.1	155	4.1	13.9
metal manufacturing and engineering	48	2.1	355	9.4	11.9
other manufacturing industry	137	6.2	399	10.5	25.6
building and civil engineering	33	1.5	388	10.3	7.8
all services	1,906	85.6	2,210	58.5	46.3
distributive trades and hotels	472	21.2	634	16.8	42.7
transport and communication	71	3.2	293	7.8	19.5
banking, finance, insurance	230	10.3	413	10.9	35.8
public administration	113	5.1	280	7.4	28.8
other services	1,021	45.9	589	15.6	63.4
total	2,234	100.0	3,796	100.0	37.0

* includes 8,000 women and 17,000 men whose industrial sector was not stated.

Source: data from *Labour Force Survey (Results 1989)* (Eurostat)

Part time: In 1989 70.2% of part-time workers were women. Minimum wage legislation only applies to those who normally work more than $33\frac{1}{3}$ hours a week. Full pension rights depend on working at least 20 hours a week, and domestic workers must do 16 hours a week to qualify for social security.

Women's earnings as a % of men's in industry (October 1986)

	manual hourly earnings	non-manual monthly earnings
all metal manufacture and engineering	82.0	63.1
electrical engineering	86.6	–
food, drink and tobacco	74.9	59.4
printing and publishing	–	66.2
all manufacturing industry	74.9	62.3
all industry	74.2	62.7

Source: data from *Earnings in Industry and Services* (Eurostat)

Women's earnings as a % of men's in services (October 1986)

	non-manual monthly earnings
wholesale and retail distribution	58.4
wholesale distribution	62.5
retail distribution	64.3
credit institutions	59.9
insurance (excluding social security)	66.7

Source: data from *Earnings in Industry and Services* (Eurostat)

36% of women police officers leave their jobs early, mainly because of lack of career advancement

Working mothers (1988): 32% of women with a child under 10 were employed compared with 91% of similar men. 68% of women aged 20–39 without children were employed. 8% of women and 5% of men with a child under 10 were unemployed.

Part-time employment among mothers is very high – 84% of employed women with a child under 10 work part time. The growth in part-time working among mothers was responsible for an 8% increase in the employment rate for mothers with a child under 10 between 1985 and 1988. 9% of employed fathers work part time, the highest level in the EC. 15% of employed mothers are in temporary jobs, compared with 10% overall in the EC, mostly because they cannot find permanent work.

77.3% of women graduates would like to continue their education but half lack the opportunity, says the Association of Women Graduates

Employment rates are lower for lone mothers than all mothers. 18% for lone mothers with a child aged 0–4 (29% for all mothers) and 19% for lone mothers with a child aged 5–9 (33% for all). This difference is largely explained by the much lower level of part-time employment of lone mothers compared with all mothers.

However unemployment rates are higher for lone mothers: 12% for those with a child aged 0–4 (6% for all mothers) and 17% for those with a child aged 5–9 (9% for all mothers).

WOMEN IN TRADE UNIONS

Roughly 40% of workers are members of trade unions. The Federatie Nederlandse Vakbeweging (FNV) is the largest trade union confederation. One of its 17 affiliates is the Vrouwenbond (the women's union) which has more than 9,000 members, who in some cases are also members of other FNV unions.

At the end of 1990 21% of FNV members were women, compared with 12% in 1980. Women account for 20% of the members of FNV policy-making bodies and 33% of salaried officials.

Four of the 17 affiliated unions have a woman president and 11 of the 17 have special structures for women. The affiliate with the largest number of women members is AbvaKabo, the public services union – whose members account for 45% of all women members.

WOMEN AND POLITICS

Women won the vote in 1919. After the 1989 election, 41 MPs were women, representing 27% of all MPs. There are 6 women in the 25-strong cabinet, and 3 of 14 ministers are women. In municipal councils women hold 22% of the 11,000-plus seats. 13% of aldermen and 8.3% of mayors are women.

One of the Netherlands' 94 ambassadors is a woman.

Women elected to parliament (the Tweede Kamer) after the September 1989 general election

political party	total no of seats	no of seats held by women	% of seats held by women
Christian Democratic Alliance	54	10	18.5
Labour Party	49	16	32.7
People's Party for Freedom and Democracy	22	8	36.4
Democrats '66	12	4	33.3
Green Left	6	3	50.0
Calvinist Political Party	3	0	0.0
Reformational Political Federation	1	0	0.0
Calvinist Political Union	2	0	0.0
Centre Democrats	1	0	0.0
total	**150**	**41**	**27.3**

Source: data from Ministerie van Binnenlandse Zaken

WOMEN AND EDUCATION

More than 1 in 4 (26.8%) of the Dutch population is in full-time education

The proportion of women among first-year matriculation students increased from 21.7% in 1970 to 45.9% in 1990.

80% of women students at the 9 trade union vocational training colleges have found employment after their courses.

% of women students at university by subject studied (1987–88)

all arts and humanities:	60.6
theology	42.8
arts	63.5
philosophy	33.7
medical sciences:	47.6
medicine	45.8
dentistry	30.2
veterinary science	46.4
other medical fields	70.5
pure sciences:	19.1
mathematics and natural sciences	26.3
engineering	10.2
agriculture	37.6
social sciences:	41.0
law	44.7
economics	17.7
sociology and political sciences	47.5
psychology	62.9
pedagogic and andragogic sciences	77.5
other social sciences	57.9
geography and prehistory	34.5
physical training	46.4
business administration	22.2
others	41.6
theological universities	37.4
Netherlands University of Business	29.0

Source: *Statistical Yearbook of the Netherlands 1990* (Netherlands Central Bureau of Statistics)

Teaching staff by sex (1987–88)

	women	men	women as % of teaching staff
basic education	53,208	30,798	63.3
special education	7,358	7,401	49.9
secondary education	27,384	69,681	28.2
vocational colleges	4,289	10,983	28.1

Source: *Statistical Yearbook of the Netherlands 1990* (Netherlands Central Bureau of Statistics)

**Women's participation in adult education
(% of all students) (1987)**

senior secondary education	65.6
junior secondary education	75.7
junior vocational training	28.1
short courses in vocational training	15.0
senior vocational training	34.1
vocational colleges	47.9
university education	41.6
correspondence courses	33.9
non-formal oral education	52.0
health-care training	80.1
retail and trade education	36.9
Open University	37.7
local government training institutes	29.1
residential adult education	54.0

Source: *Statistical Yearbook of the Netherlands 1990* (Netherlands Central Bureau of Statistics)

WOMEN AND DETENTION

In September 1988, women made up 3.6% of prisoners. Minors (age 23) and young adults accounted for 15.3%, and foreigners for 21.2%.

SOURCES

Abortion Laws in Europe, Planned Parenthood in Europe, Vol 18 No 1, Spring 1989 (Supplement, amended April 1990); *Bargaining Report 101* (Labour Research Department); *Childcare in the European Communities 1985–90* (Women of Europe Supplement No 51); *Comparative Study on rules governing working conditions in the member states* (Commission of the European Communities); *Demographic Statistics 1990* (Eurostat); *Earnings in Industry and Services* (Eurostat); *Employment in Europe 1991* (Commission of the European Communities); *Europa World Year Book 1990* (31st edition); *Health Care Systems and Professional Organisations in the European Community, Information note – Europe* (British Medical Association); Health For All 2000 Indicator Presentation System (World Health Organisation Regional Office for Europe); *The Kingdom of The Netherlands* (Foreign Information Service, Ministry of Foreign Affairs); *Labour Force Survey (Results 1989)* (Eurostat); *Labour Research* September 1991 (Labour Research Department); *Les Actions Positives en*

Faveur des Femmes en Europe Occidentale (Institut Syndical Europeen); Ministerie van Binnenlandse Zaken; *The Netherlands in brief* (Foreign Information Service, Ministry of Foreign Affairs); *Out In Europe* (Peter Tatchell, for Channel 4 Television); *Pocket World in Figures* (The Economist); *Prison Information Bulletin June 1990* (Council of Europe); *Positive action and the constitutional and legislative hindrances to its implementation in the member states of the Council of Europe* (Council of Europe); *Proposition de Directive Du Conseil concernant la protection au travail de la femme enceinte ou venant d'accoucher* (Commission of the European Communities); *Social Protection in the Member States of the Community* (Commission of the European Community Directorate General on Employment, Industrial Relations and Social Affairs); *Statistical Yearbook of the Netherlands 1990* (Netherlands Central Bureau of Statistics); *Third World Guide 91/92* (Instituto del Tercer Mundo); *Women of Europe* (Nos 63, 66, 67, 68, 69)

ADDRESSES

Royal Netherlands Embassy, 38 Hyde Park Gate, London SW7 5DP. Tel: 071 584 5040

Emancipatieraad, Anna van Hannoverstraat 4–6, Postbus 90806, 2509 LV Den Haag. Tel: (31 70) 333 47 82

Ministerie van Sociale Zaken en Werkgelegenheid, Directie Coördinatie Emancipatiebeleid, Postbus 90801, 2509 LV Den Haag. Tel: (31 70) 333 44 44

Nederlandse vrouwen Raad, Groot Hertoginnelaan 41, 2517 EC Den Haag

Netherlands Central Bureau of Statistics, Prinses Beatrixlaan 428, POB 959, 2270 AZ Voorburg. Tel: (31 70) 337 38 00

Rutgers Stichting, Postbus 17430, Groot Hertoginnelaan 201, 2502 CK Den Haag. Tel: (31 70) 363 17 50

Women's Secretariat, Netherlands Trade Union Confederation, PO Box 8456, 1005 AL Amsterdam

NVIH-COC (lesbian and gay rights), Rozenstraat 8, 1016 NX Amsterdam. Tel: (31 20) 23 1192/23 4596

Norway

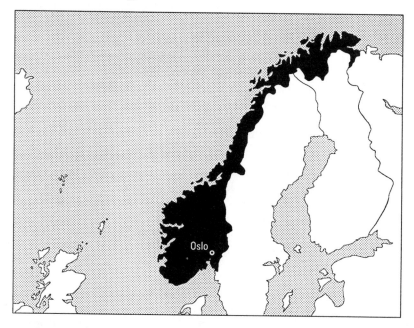

- **Population** 4.23 million, 50.6% female
- **Area** 323,895 sq km
- **Population density** 13.1 people sq km
- **GDP 1988** krone 594 billion (£56.4 billion)
- **GDP per capita** £13,469
- **GDP per capita in purchasing power parity** (UK=100) 127
- **Public spending as % of GNP:** defence 3.2% (1986); education 6.8% (1986); health 5.5% (1987)
- **Consumer price index** 1980 = 100; 1989 = 203
- **Currency is the krone** 1989 £1 = NKR10.7; US$1 = NKR6.62

Norway is a hereditary monarchy which in May 1990 changed the law of succession to allow the eldest child of the monarch, whether female or male, to ascend to the throne.

Legislative power is held by the parliament, the Storting, which has 165 members elected for 4 years by proportional representation. The Storting divides itself into 2 chambers – the Lagting (the upper house) and the Odelsting (the lower house). Executive power is held by the monarch but in practice is exercised by the council of ministers. Voting is from the age of 18.

Two forms of the Norwegian language are officially recognised as equal. Bokmål is the older version which is used by about 80% of children in schools. Only 20% use Nynorsk (new Norwegian). Lappish is spoken by the Sami community in the north. 92% of the population are members of the Evangelical Lutheran Church.

IMMIGRATION AND RESIDENCE RIGHTS

Foreign residents not in employment, except citizens of other Nordic countries, must apply for residence permits to stay for more than 3 months and must have work permits. Trial periods of employment may not legally last more than 6 months.

Residence and work permits are not normally issued unless individuals have a Norwegian parent or are covered by special exclusions, which include au pairs, academics, entertainers and missionaries.

Residence permits are also normally granted to spouses, heterosexual (but not lesbian or gay) partners and dependent children, including foster and adopted children, of foreign nationals who hold residence or work permits. The parents of foreign nationals under 18 with residence or work permits may also be granted residence permits. Settlement permits are granted to foreign nationals who have been residents for 3 years continuously.

Citizenship is normally granted to those over 18 who have been residents for 7 years who can support themselves and do not have a criminal record. Nordic citizens can apply for citizenship after 2 years, and those married to Norwegian citizens after 4 years. Since 1979 all children of Norwegian women have had the right to citizenship. However, children of Norwegian fathers only have citizenship rights if their parents are married.

EQUAL RIGHTS

The Equal Status Act of 1979 seeks to ensure equal treatment in all areas related to employment, politics education and family life, with religion the only area exempted. Article 21 of the Act requires all government and municipal appointed committees to have at least 40% representation of either sex. In the area of family life, however, the Act has had little impact, as political and educational measures are thought more likely to achieve a more equal share of family responsibilities than legal sanctions.

'Women perform two-thirds of the world's work hours for 10% of the wages and 1% of the world's wealth,' said Inger Prebensen, first woman director of Postspare-banken, Norway's largest customer bank

As well as promoting equal status, the Act 'is aimed particularly at improving the position of women'. Positive discrimination such as quota systems in favour of recruiting women to the civil service comply with the Act, and complaints by men that they are being discriminated against will normally be rejected by the Equal Status Ombud, who enforces it.

The king appoints both the ombud and the Equal Status Appeals Board, whose seven members include representatives from employers and employees. The Equal Status Council is an independent consultative body. Individuals can lodge complaints with the ombud, who can also initiate complaints. If a voluntary settlement is not reached, the ombud takes the complaint to the board. Violations of the Act are punishable by fines and/or imprisonment.

BIRTH, LIFE AND DEATH

Breakdown of population by age and sex (1990)

	all		women		men		% of women in age group
	no	%	no	%	no	%	
0–16	861,509	20.4	420,374	19.6	441,135	21.1	48.8
16–66	2,766,034	65.3	1,361,180	63.6	1,404,854	67.1	49.2
67+	605,573	14.3	358,282	16.7	247,291	11.8	59.2
total	4,233,116	100.0	2,139,836	100.0	2,093,280	100.0	50.6

Source: *Minifacts on Equal Rights 1991* (Likestillings Rådet)

Population and population density by region (1987)

region	area sq km	population	population density per sq km
Østfold	237,242	3,890.6	61.0
Akershus	406,859	4,587.1	88.7
Oslo	450,808	426.6	1,056.7
Hedmark	186,664	26,120.2	7.2
Oppland	182,531	24,073.1	7.6
Buskerud	223,136	13,850.5	16.1
Vestfold	194,619	2,139.7	91.0
Telemark	163,347	14,186.2	11.5
Aust-Agder	96,041	8,484.7	11.3
Vest-Agder	142,181	6,816.5	20.9
Rogaland	329,630	8,553.1	38.5
Hordaland	405,130	14,961.5	27.2
Sogn og Fjordane	106,192	17,924.5	5.9
Møre og Romsdal	237,873	14,596.3	16.3
Sør-Trøndelag	248,181	17,839.1	13.9
Nord-Trøndelag	126,874	21,056.2	6.0
Nordland	240,450	36,301.9	6.6
Troms	146,608	25,121.1	5.8
Finnmark	74,271	45,878.6	1.6
mainland Norway	**4,198,637**	**306,807.5**	**13.7**

Source: data from *Statistisk Årbok 1988* (Statistisk Sentralbyrå)

One in three young marriages ends in divorce, 1988 figures suggest

Births and deaths per 1,000 population

birth rate (1988)	13.6
death rate (1988)	10.7
infant mortality per 1,000 live births (1988)	8.0
marriage rate (1989)	5.0
life expectancy (women) (1990)	79.9
life expectancy (men) (1990)	73.3
fertility rate per woman (1990)	1.9
% of births outside marriage (1990)	36.0

Source: data from *Demographic Statistics 1990* (Eurostat)

Women and men have had equal inheritance rights since 1854. Before then daughters inherited only half as much as sons. The 1927 Marriage Act created the principle of equal economic and legal status for wives and husbands. The 1913 Castberg Act gives all children equal rights, regardless of whether their parents are married.

The woman's vow of obedience to her husband was removed from the marriage service in 1920

Married women without incomes have the right to part of their husbands' incomes to cover children and home and personal expenses. If a woman does not receive enough money she can apply to the authorities, which will fix an amount for her to be paid monthly and arrange for it to be deducted from her husband's wages. Unmarried women living with partners have no right to maintenance allowances.

Upon marriage women and men retain separate ownership of their own property, which is not divided on divorce. Unless they draw up a separate agreement, joint ownership applies to all joint property, which is divided equally on divorce. Where both partners agree to divorce there is a 1-year separation period; if one partner objects, the period is 2 years. For serious offences, such as infidelity, rape and violence, divorce can be granted in a court of law without any period of separation. Children of 12 and over are consulted on custody and their wishes are taken into account. Single mothers automatically have sole responsibility for their children, though they can inform the population register if joint responsibility applies.

Composition of family units (1989)

	%
single mothers	6.3
single fathers	0.8
childless married couples	23.8
married couple, 1 child	8.2
married couple, 2 children	9.8
married couple, 3 or more children	4.0
single people	47.0

Source: data from *Minifacts on Equal Rights 1991* (Likestillings Rådet)

In 1989 the average size of family was 2.18 people.

LESBIAN RIGHTS

A common age of consent of 16 was introduced in 1972 (before then all male homosexual acts were illegal). Laws prohibiting discrimination on the grounds of sexual orientation were introduced in 1981.

Foreign partners of lesbians and gay men can be granted residence rights on proof of a long-term relationship. Asylum has also been granted on the grounds of sexual orientation to homosexuals at risk of persecution. The government is considering giving legal recognition to lesbian and gay relationships. In 1990 the lesbian and gay movement was given a government grant of £100,000.

WOMEN AND HEALTH CARE

Health centres provide free examinations and vaccinations, run courses for pregnant women and provide prenatal care. Patients pay a contribution towards doctors' fees, with the remainder paid by national insurance. Hospital treatment is free. All schools have nurses and many employers provide health services at work. In Oslo there is a special health-care service for immigrants in Arendalsgate 3.

In 1924 the first health centre for mothers was opened in Oslo

Dental treatment is expensive with patients paying their own costs, except for extractions, braces and operations, when national insurance pays part of the cost. Children receive free dental treatment at school.

In 1988 there was 1 doctor for every 448 people.

Major indicators for women's health (1988)

maternal deaths (all causes) per 100,000 live births	3.48
maternal deaths (abortion) per 100,000 live births	0.00
ratio of abortions to 1,000 live births (all ages)	275.56
% of all live births to mothers under 20 (1985)	5.69
% of all live births to mothers aged 35+ (1985)	7.82
deaths from cancer of the cervix (age 0–64) per 100,000 women (1987)	4.29
deaths from malignant neoplasm female breast (age 0–64) per 100,000 women	17.59
deaths from trachea/bronchus/lung cancer (age 0–64) per 100,000 women	9.55
deaths from trachea/bronchus/lung cancer (age 0–64) per 100,000 men	20.95
deaths from diseases of the circulatory system (age 0–64) per 100,000 women	32.02
deaths from diseases of the circulatory system (age 0–64) per 100,000 men	121.48
deaths from suicide and self-inflicted injury per 100,000 women	9.22
deaths from suicide and self-inflicted injury per 100,000 men	24.31

Source: data from Health for All 2000 Indicator Presentation System (World Health Organisation Regional Office For Europe)

In 1913 Katti Anker Møller began the fight for abortion rights by proposing that the law threatening a woman with 3 years in prison if she 'kills her unborn child' be repealed

Abortion and contraception: Available on request up to 12 weeks, and up to the second trimester on medical or eugenic grounds, or in cases of rape or other sexual crime, and if the woman has gone to a board of two doctors. Medical staff may refuse to perform terminations on conscientious grounds but may not refuse to give pre-operative or post-operative care. Abortion is free.

Everyone, including under 16s, has the right to free guidance and counselling on contraception, but contraceptives must be paid for. Help is available from doctors and health clinics and, in some areas, from special contraceptive and sexual health clinics.

PARENTAL PAY, LEAVE AND BENEFITS (1990–91)

Maternity and parental leave and pay: 28 weeks on full pay, including 6 weeks which must be taken before the birth and 6 after the birth. The remaining

16 weeks can be shared with the father or, if the mother is not living with the father, any other person who helps with child care. Parents can take additional leave without pay to bring their total leave to 1 year.

Maternity grant: Women not in paid employment are entitled to a maternity grant paid as a fixed non-taxable sum for each child.

Nursing mothers: Mothers who work full time have the right to 2 half-hour breaks a day to breastfeed. Alternatively, they can have a shorter working day.

Paternity leave: Fathers have the right to 2 weeks' leave of absence connected with the birth of a child, normally without pay, if they live with the mother.

Time off to look after sick children: A total of 10 days a year, on sickness allowance, is allotted for the care of children under 10 who are ill, or in cases where the person (this includes a spouse) who normally cares for a child is ill. Single parents are entitled to 20 days.

CHILD-CARE PROVISION (1989)

0–7 years: 34% of children were in child-care centres: 6% of under 2s; 28% of 2–4 year olds; 54% of 4–6 year olds; and 70% of 6 year olds. Full-time day-care centres are open from 7.30am to 5pm, part-time centres for 5 or 6 hours a day. In 1989 47% of children in child-care centres were there for 41 hours or more each week; 9% for between 31 and 40 hours; 25% for between 16 and 30 hours; and 19% for between 6 and 15 hours. In day-care centres with 4 or more immigrant children the local authority can apply for funding for a 'mother tongue assistant'.

Primary school (7 years up): Compulsory schooling is 9 years. Hours range from 16 to 30 a week and the school year runs from August to June. Local authorities are obliged to provide instruction in Norwegian for immigrant pupils. Some mother tongue instruction is available. In 1988 the pupil to teacher ratio in primary schools was 16:1.

STATE BENEFITS (1989–90)

All benefits are index linked to inflation and, apart from family allowance, are taxable. Normal qualifying period of residence for some cash benefits is 3 years, but this can be waived. Citizens of Denmark, Sweden, Finland, Iceland, the UK, France, Netherlands, Italy, Yugoslavia and the USA qualify for some benefits without being insured.

Retirement pension: Normal retirement age is 67 for both women and men. Pensions are made up of a basic pension, paid to everyone who has been insured for 3 years, a supplementary pension and a compensation supplement. For married pensioners, the size of pension for both is calculated on the insurance period of the person who has been insured longest. Pensioners supporting a spouse or children receive supplementary payments. In 1984 82% of women pensioners had only a basic state pension compared with 40% of men.

Norway's maternity leave dates back to 1936 when the Worker Protection Act gave mothers 12 weeks leave of absence with the right to return to their old jobs

Sickness allowance: Paid at full wages – for the first 14 days by the employer, and then by the national insurance scheme. A medical certificate is required for sick leave of more than 3 days. Sick leave of up to 3 days without a medical certificate can be taken 4 times a year.

Disability pension: This earnings-related benefit is paid to those between the ages of 16 and 67 whose working capacity has been reduced by 50% to 100%. Housewives also qualify for disability pension, though stricter criteria are applied than for women in paid employment. For those previously on no income or low income, the payment is equal to the minimum retirement pension. Child supplements are paid on top of the disability pension.

Single mothers and separated/divorced women: May be eligible for temporary benefits until their youngest child finishes third grade. They can also receive a transitional allowance to pay for essentials. Maintenance payments from fathers are deducted from benefit. The amount of benefit also depends on the woman's income, with payments stopping if she returns to her husband or remarries.

Survivors' benefits: Funeral grants are paid to those whose spouses were insured when they died. A monthly survivor's pension is paid depending on level of income. Transitional allowance – paid at the same rate as a pension – is also available for spouses who are unable to support themselves or who have applied for a pension. There is an educational allowance for a spouse who aims to become able to support herself fully or partially, and women working outside the home or studying can also apply for an allowance towards child care, as well as a supplement or loan for housing or removal costs.

Carers who have been looking after a family member for at least 5 years, and who are under the age of 67, have the same rights as widows if the person for whom they have been caring dies. If unable to work, they are entitled to a pension.

Both natural and adopted children under 18 are entitled to their parents' pensions if one or both of them dies, whether or not the parents were married. The children must be resident in Norway and one of the parents must have been insured for 3 years. If a child is born after the father dies, the mother gets a maternity grant.

Family allowance: Paid for all children from 30 days after birth to 31 December in the year the child becomes 16. Single parents receive family allowance for one more child than they actually have.

Special welfare assistance: Not a national insurance benefit, but available from local authority welfare offices for those temporarily unable to support themselves.

WOMEN AND EMPLOYMENT

In 1989 women accounted for 45% of people in employment. 48% of women were working part time, compared with 8% of men. The average working

Half of Norway's beat police officers are women

week was 29 hours for women and 39 for men. In 1989, women accounted for 37.8% of the registered unemployed, 42.5% of job applicants, and 98% of those doing unpaid domestic work at home.

Statutory rights: Employment law limits working time to 9 hours a day or 40 hours a week (38 if this includes weekends); overtime rates of basic pay plus 40% must be paid beyond these hours. Employees have a legal right to rest breaks if they work more than 5.5 hours a day. They must have 1 weekly break of 36 consecutive hours.

All employees have the right to 5 weeks' paid holiday (6 weeks if they are over 60) except part-time employees of less than 3 months. A holiday allowance of not less than 10.2% of the previous year's earnings must be paid in addition to normal pay. Employees who do not belong to the Norwegian State Church are entitled to 2 days a year for religious holidays. Employers must provide references.

Employment by industrial sector (1989)

industrial sector	% of employed women	% of employed men	% of women in workforce
agriculture, forestry and fisheries	4	8	28
mining, oil, power, construction	3	15	12
industry	9	21	26
wholesale and retail trade, hotels and restaurants	21	15	53
transport, storage, post and telecommunications	5	10	29
banking, insurance, finance, commercial service and property management	8	7	47
public, social and private services	50	23	64
total	**100**	**100**	**45**

Source: data from *Minifacts on Equal Rights 1991* (Likestillings Rådet)

Proportion of women at various levels of office work (1989)

	%
simple routine work	88
work requiring qualifications	93
work involving individual responsibility	24
senior posts	7
managing directors and general managers	4
total % of women in office work	**48**

Source: data from *Minifacts on Equal Rights 1991* (Likestillings Rådet)

Women's participation in the major occupations (1986)

	%
retail sales	75
office staff	92
cleaners	97
company managers	6
teachers	64
nursing auxiliaries	96
engineers	8
construction workers	0
truck and van drivers	2
nurses	20
repair mechanics (machines, and motor vehicles)	0
secretaries (office)	96
electricians	0
warehouse workers	12
farm labourers	64
relief housewives	100
workshop mechanics	3
sales staff	20
lecturers, high school teachers	52

Source: *Kvinnor och män i Norden – Fakta om jämställdheten 1988* (Nordic Council of Ministers)

Women's average hourly wage as a % of men's (1989)

in industry	86
in office work	
simple routine work	93
work requiring qualifications	93
work involving individual responsibility	92
senior posts	93
in shops	
senior posts	88
work involving individual responsibility	86
other posts	90

Source: data from *Statistisk Årbok 1988* (Statistisk Sentralbyrå)

Working mothers

% of women employed by age of youngest child (1989)

0–2 years	68
3–6 years	75
7–10 years	82
11–15 years	83

% of women employed by number of children (1989)

1 child	81
2 children	75
3 children	67
4+ children	58

Source: data from *Minifacts on Equal Rights 1991* (Likestillings Rådet)

Taxation: Couples who are married or living together and have children can choose whether to be taxed jointly or separately. Most national insurance benefits are taxable. People receiving retirement or disability pensions are taxed at a lower rate.

WOMEN AND POLITICS

Women won the vote in local elections in 1910, and in parliamentary elections in 1913. The first woman MP was elected in 1922 and the first woman in the cabinet was appointed in 1945.

The campaign 'Women on Municipal Councils', launched by the Oslo Women's Rights Union, led to a 50% increase in women's representation in both 1967 and 1971. In May 1987 a record was set when women took 40.5% of the seats on Norway's 19 county councils.

Gro Harlem Brundtland became Norway's first woman prime minister in 1981. Her term ended later that year when the Conservatives won the election, but she returned after the Labour victory in 1986. (The next parliamentary election is due in September 1993.) There are 9 women among her 19 cabinet ministers – in line with the 40% representation required under the Equal Status Act.

By the end of 1989, 40.6% of county councillors, 33% of national board and committee members, and 36% of municipal board and committee members were women. The Labour Party, Left Socialist Party and the Progress Party apply a 40% women quota system.

Two of Norway's 55 ambassadors are women.

Women elected to parliament (the Storting) after the September 1989 general election

political party	total no of seats	no of seats held by women	% of seats held by women
Labour Party	63	32	50.8
Conservative Party	37	11	29.7
Left Socialist	17	7	41.2
Progress Party	22	1	4.5
Christian Democrats	14	5	35.7
Centre Party	11	3	27.3
Freedom for Finnmark	1	0	0
total	165	59	36.0

Source: data from Royal Norwegian Embassy, London

WOMEN AND EDUCATION

Upper secondary school follows on from compulsory schooling. In some areas this is open to adults with a choice of class hours so education can be combined with employment. Folk high schools (folkehøgskoler) provide an alternative to further education for pupils who have finished secondary school. These are normally boarding schools offering 1 or 2 years of instruction in a range of subjects. Students can apply for non-repayable grants as well as loans.

In 1839 'feeble women over the age of 40, who were otherwise unable to make a living' were permitted to become master craftsmen

The percentage of women students is greater or equal to men at all levels of education. Figures for 1988 were: 51% in upper secondary schools; 57% in colleges, and 50% in universities. However, women accounted for 61% of students completing lower degrees but 39% of those completing higher degrees.

The choice of subjects in upper secondary school in 1988 still reflected traditional roles with girls making up 98% of health and social work classes, 84% in handicrafts and applied arts, and 82% in domestic science, but only 13% in maritime and fisheries, 18% in manual and industrial classes, and 40% in sports.

Percentage of women students in higher education by college (1989)

Agricultural University of Norway	48
College of Economics and Business Administration	35
Advanced College of Technology	24
colleges of education	78
colleges of engineering	22
colleges of social work	82
colleges of health education	90

Percentage of women students in universities by subject (1989)

languages	71
psychology	71
economics	39
mathematics	29
physics and chemistry	39
law	52
medicine	51
dentistry	56
total in all colleges and universities	**54**

Source: *Minifacts on Equal Rights 1991* (Likestillings Rådet)

Courses in women's studies are available at the
Universities of Oslo and Bergen and are being
introduced at the University of Trondheim.

WOMEN AND DETENTION

Minors (below age 21) and young adults detained
accounted for 6.5% and foreigners for 11% in 1988.
In 1986, women accounted for 3.8% of prisoners.

**% of women in penal institutions by type of institution
and sanction (1986)**

all types of penal institution	3.8
central prisons	10.5
local prisons	2.3
all types of sanctions	3.8
serving sentence in default of paying a fine	6.3
prison or military arrest	3.5
security detention	6.5
custody	4.6

Source: data from *Statistisk Årbok 1988* (Statistisk Sentralbyrå)

SOURCES

Abortion Laws in Europe, Planned Parenthood in Europe, Vol 18
No 1, Spring 1989 (Supplement, amended April 1990)
(International Planned Parenthood Federation, Europe Region);
Demographic Statistics 1990 (Eurostat); *Effective
Implementation of Equality Measures in Compliance with
National Legislation and International Agreements Report* by
Ingse Stabel, Equal Status Ombud; *Europa World Year Book
1990* (31st edition); Health for All 2000 Indicator Presentation
System (World Health Organisation Regional Office For
Europe); *Immigrant Women's Rights in Norway* (Foreign
Women's Group, Ministry of Local Government and Labour);
*Immigration Act 1988; Kvinnor och män i Norden – Fakta om
jämställdheten 1988* (Nordic Council of Ministers); *Les Actions
Positives en Faveur des Femmes en Europe Occidentale* (Institut
Syndical Europeen); *Minifacts on Equal Rights* (Likestillings
Rådet); *Milestones in 150 Years History of Norwegian Women*
(Likestillings Rådet); *The Norwegian Equal Status Act; Out In
Europe* (Peter Tatchell, for Channel 4 Television); *Pocket World
in Figures* (The Economist); *Prison Information Bulletin* June
1990 (Council of Europe); The Royal Norwegian Embassy;
Statistik Årbok 1988 (Statistisk Sentralbyrå); *Third World Guide*

91/92 (Instituto del Tercer Mundo); *Women and Men in the Nordic Countries* (Christina Österberg and Birgitta Hedman, Nordic Council of Ministers); *Women in Norwegian Politics* (Royal Ministry of Foreign Affairs); *Women's Studies and Research on Women in the Nordic Countries* (ed. Mie Berg Simonson and Mona Eliasson for Nordic Forum); *The Working Environment Act and The Annual Holidays Act* (Arbeidstilsynet – The Labour Inspection)

LETTERS FROM NORWAY

Kari Dæhlin, editor for Norwegian Broadcast Corporation, Oslo

My student loan was not that big, but it's very hard for most people. It takes 20 years of your life to pay for your education. When the government introduced student loans it was a positive step because it widened access for those who could not afford higher education otherwise. But a 4-year education cost NKR21,000 then and it's NKR589,000 today. The interest accumulates when you graduate.

Now my career is the major issue for me. I work for the Norwegian Broadcast Corporation as an editor. It's a very male-dominated business but as an editor I find most people feel it's easier to communicate with a woman than a man.

As far as roles go, in Oslo it's very hard to get child care if you are a couple with two incomes. Sharing child care is possible because you can choose which parent looks after the child. But it's almost always the woman because the man earns more and you can't afford to lose the income. That's the drawback. The roles are forced on us by circumstances; roles we didn't want 10 years ago, but we've still got them today.

Siri Mjaaland, teacher, Oslo

As a 'double working mother', I have an almost full-time job (92%) teaching in grammar school plus 2 children. There's never enough time for everything, but what I do take very seriously, as I think most

Norwegian women do, is giving priority to my children. Nearly all my spare time is spent with them (but sometimes I still have a guilty conscience).

Public kindergartens are a privilege for the few in this country and school doesn't start until children are 7 and lasts for only 3 hours a day the first year, then maybe 3 to 4 the next, and so on. I have been lucky to get my kids into the public kindergartens (the first time because I was a single parent; the second because they had just changed the rules for intake). They are now drawing lots, though they still give priority to some. These kindergartens are very good, usually situated in the neighbourhood – but expensive (about £225 a month). There are private kindergartens about the same price (subsidised by the state), but far too few, and then we have thousands of 'day mothers'.

In Oslo, the kindergarten situation is so bad that many women don't dare to have more children, being well aware of the great trouble and uncertainty in getting a good place for your kids to stay. And most women my age (30 to 45) work outside the home.

ADDRESSES

Royal Norwegian Embassy, 39 Eccleston Street, London SW1W 9NT. Tel: 071 235 7151

Utlendingsdirektoratet (Directorate of Immigration), Postboks 8108 Dep 0032 Oslo 1. Tel: (47 2) 530 890

Likestillings Rådet (The Equal Status Council), Postboks 8004 Dep, 0030 Oslo 1

Statistik Sentralbyrå (Central Bureau of Statistics), Skippergate 15, POB 8131 Dep, 0033 Oslo 1. Tel: (47 2) 86 49 73

Norsk Forening for Familieplanlegging (family planning), Grakam Veien 18a, 0389 Oslo 3. Tel: (47 2) 14 49 27

Landsorganisasjonen i Norge (Norwegian Confederation of Trade Unions), Folkets Hus, Youngs gate 11, 0181 Oslo 1. Tel: (47 2) 40 10 50

Norske Kvinners Nasjonalrad (Norwegian Women's National Council), Fr Nansenspl. 6, 0160 Oslo 1

DNF-48 (lesbian and gay rights), Postboks 1305, Vika, 0112 Oslo 1. Tel: (010 47 2) 429 854

Poland

- **Population** 37.9 million, 51.2% female
- **Area** 312,683 sq km
- **Population density** 121.1 people sq km
- **GDP 1988** Estimate £40.3 billion
- **GDP per capita** £1,066
- **GDP per capita in purchasing power parity** (UK=100) 38
- **Public spending as % of GNP:** defence 3.3% (1986); education 4.5% (1986); health 4.0% (1987)
- **Consumer price index** 1980 = 100; 1989 = 2,756
- **Currency is the zloty:** official exchange rate 1989 £1 = ZL10,465; US$1 = ZL6,500

'Polish women are responsible. They do not want to run politics; they want to raise their children.' President Lech Walesa, answering a question on the lack of women in his government in April 1991

Legislative power is held by the 2-chamber National Assembly, which is elected for 4 years. The assembly is made up of the Senate with 100 members and the Sejm with 460 members. Executive power is held by the president, who is directly elected for 5 years. Poland is divided into 49 voivodships, or provinces, which are administered by appointed governors, and there are also 2,348 local councils. Voting age is 18; candidates must be 21.

While agriculture continues to be an important economic sector, 70% of workers are now employed in industry or elsewhere. In 1989 state industry accounted for 95.2% of all industrial sales, but the private sector is growing rapidly. From 1980 to 1989 private employment was up by 10%, while all employment fell by 1.2%.

98% of the population is Polish, with Germans, Ukrainians, Byelorussians and Slovaks the main minority groups. 95% of the population is Roman Catholic.

EQUAL RIGHTS

The first constitution of the Polish People's Republic stated in 1952 that 'women . . . enjoy the same rights as men in all spheres of life: state, political, economic and cultural'. The role of the government's Plenipotentiary for Women's Affairs has altered with recent political change in Poland. A government report cites one of his or her basic goals as 'to ensure that the new legal acts do not infringe equal rights of women in all spheres of life'.

BIRTH, LIFE AND DEATH

Women make up 51.2% of the population, with significantly more women living in urban areas (108.3 females for every 100 males) than in the countryside (100.8 females for every 100 males). Almost two-thirds of families were living in urban areas at the end of 1988.

Population density by region* (1988)

region	area sq km	population (1000s)	pop density per sq km
Warszawskie	3,788	2,412.9	637.0
Bialskopodlaskie	5,348	303.0	56.7
Bialostockie	10,055	684.5	68.1
Bielskie	3,704	889.9	240.3
Bydgoskie	10,349	1,098.4	106.1
Chelmskie	3,866	244.3	63.2
Ciechanowskie	6,362	424.1	66.7
Czestochowskie	6,182	772.6	125.0
Elblaskie	6,103	473.9	77.7
Gdanskie	7,394	1,410.9	190.8
Gorzowskie	8,484	494.0	58.2
Jeleniogórskie	4,378	514.5	117.5
Kaliskie	6,512	703.7	108.1
Katowickie	6,650	3,931.5	591.2
Kieleckie	9,211	1,122.5	121.9
Koninskie	5,139	464.6	90.4
Koszalinskie	8,470	499.0	58.9
Krakowskie	3,254	1,219.6	374.8
Krosnienskie	5,702	487.6	85.5
Legnickie	4,307	505.3	125.2
Leszczynskie	4,154	381.2	91.8
Lubelskie	6,792	1,006.2	148.1
Lomzynskie	6,684	343.5	51.2
Lódzkie	1,523	1,141.1	749.2
Nowosadeckie	5,576	685.4	122.9
Olsztynskie	12,327	741.3	60.1
Opolskie	8,535	1,008.0	118.1
Ostroleckie	6,498	391.6	60.3
Pilskie	8,205	472.9	57.6
Piotrkowskie	6,266	637.5	101.7
Plockie	5,117	512.1	100.1
Poznanskie	8,151	1,316.8	161.6
Przemyskie	4,437	402.4	90.7
Radomskie	7,294	742.7	101.8
Rzeszowskie	4,397	710.6	161.6
Siedleckie	8,499	646.0	76.0
Sieradzkie	4,869	406.8	83.5
Skierniewickie	3,960	415.2	104.8
Slupskie	7,453	406.5	54.7

Population density by region* (1988) (continued)

region	area sq km	population (1000s)	pop density per sq km
Suwalskie	10,490	463.2	44.2
Szczecinskie	9,981	958.0	96.0
Tarnobrzeskie	6,283	591.0	94.1
Tarnowskie	4,151	660.8	159.2
Torunskie	5,348	653.2	122.1
Walbrzyskie	4,168	738.0	177.1
Wloclawskie	4,402	427.0	97.0
Wroclawskie	6,287	1,119.2	178.0
Zamojskie	6,980	488.5	70.0
Zielonogórskie	8,868	651.4	73.5
total	**312,683**	**37,775.1**	**120.8**

* each region named by town where administration is based
Source: *Europa World Year Book 1990* (31st edition)

Births and deaths for every 1,000 population (1988)

birth rate	15.5
death rate	9.8
infant mortality per 1,000 live births	18.0
marriage rate	6.7
life expectancy (women)	75.5
life expectancy (men)	67.5
fertility rate per woman	2.2

Source: data from *Demographic Statistics 1990* (Eurostat)

Evolution of infant mortality for every 1,000 live births

	urban	rural
1970	31.6	34.8
1980	21.0	21.7
1984	18.8	19.5
1985	18.4	18.4
1986	17.3	17.3

Source: *Poland – Reform, Adjustment and Growth* (A World Bank Country Study)

Family structure by % of total families (1988)

	total	urban areas	rural areas
married couples with children	61.8	60.9	63.4
married couples without children	22.8	22.3	23.6
single-parent households headed by a woman	13.7	15.0	11.3
single-parent households headed by a man	1.7	1.8	1.7

Source: data from *Report of the Government of the Republic of Poland on the progress made in implementation of the Convention on the elimination of all forms of discrimination against women of 1979 in the period from 1 June 1988 to 31 May 1990*

LESBIAN RIGHTS

A common age of consent of 15 was introduced in 1932 (before then male homosexual acts were illegal).

WOMEN AND HEALTH CARE

The first lesbian and gay organisation was set up in 1986. Most major cities now have their own lesbian and gay groups

Health care is organised through the country's 49 voivodships. Most patients seek medical care through workplace or mobile health centres, but may be referred to a hospital or clinic for specialist treatment. All doctors must work at least 40 hours each week in the state service, though many work longer. About 12% of doctors are based in the workplace. In 1984 only 2.5% of visits to doctors were outside the free state system, but these are increasing. Roughly 10% of doctors belong to co-operatives or have private practices as well as their state jobs. Fees in private medicine are not regulated.

In 1988 there was 1 doctor for every 497 people.

Major indicators for women's health (1989)

maternal deaths (all causes) per 100,000 live births	10.67
maternal deaths (abortion) per 100,000 live births	2.31
ratio of abortions to 1,000 live births (all ages)	141.49
% of all live births to mothers under 20 (1988)	6.98
% of all live births to mothers aged 35+	8.34
deaths from cancer of the cervix (age 0–64) per 100,000 women (1988)	8.19
deaths from malignant neoplasm female breast (age 0–64) per 100,000 women	15.14
deaths from trachea/bronchus/lung cancer (age 0–64) per 100,000 women	7.54
deaths from trachea/bronchus/lung cancer (age 0–64) per 100,000 men	58.73
deaths from diseases of the circulatory system (age 0–64) per 100,000 women	83.54
deaths from diseases of the circulatory system (age 0–64) per 100,000 men	238.45
deaths from suicide and self-inflicted injury per 100,000 women	3.44
deaths from suicide and self-inflicted injury per 100,000 men	11.54

Source: data from Health for All 2000 Indicator Presentation System (World Health Organisation Regional Office For Europe)

Abortion and contraception: Abortion is available on social grounds up to 12 weeks, though women under 18 need parental consent. Available up to the second trimester on medical grounds, or in cases of rape or other sexual crimes. If required by a doctor, a woman must supply documentary evidence to support her grounds for an abortion. Abortion is free and, because of lack of contraceptives, has been widespread.

An anti-abortion film, distributed by a Roman Catholic organisation, which includes footage of an abortion being carried out, is reportedly being shown in schools to children as young as eight

A draft bill proposing major changes to abortion law has been adopted by the Senate and has been passed to the parliament, where the issue has been prolonged. The draft bill would exempt mothers of unborn children from penalty if they collaborated in an abortion, but would introduce a penalty of 2 years' 'deprivation of liberty' for anyone who causes the 'death of an unborn child'.

Under communism, the few contraceptives available were of poor quality. However, foreign contraceptives are now available though they are expensive and the supply is erratic. The Ministry of Health withdrew 2 of the 5 oral contraceptives available on medical grounds, and increased the price of the remaining 3.

In 1991 only 12% of couples used contraception and less than 5% of women used either the pill or the IUD. 76% of the population in towns and 87% in villages use 'natural' methods of contraception accepted by the Catholic Church.

PARENTAL PAY, LEAVE AND BENEFITS (1988–89)

Maternity leave and pay: 16 weeks on full pay for the first child, 18 weeks for subsequent children. 26 weeks for multiple births.

Maternity grant: Payment equal to 3 family assistance payments.

Time off to look after sick children: 60 days a year on full pay is granted to mothers with a child under 4, for up to 3 years.

Special child-care leave: Up to 6 years' leave for mothers of chronically ill, physically or mentally disabled children up until the child is 18 (extended from 10 in 1988). Mothers of children requiring special care may also retire with an age-related pension after 20 years of employment, a right which can be transferred to the father or any other carer if the mother dies or cannot look after the child.

CHILD-CARE PROVISION (1988–89)

3–6 year olds: 48.7% are in publicly funded places, 14.7% in kindergartens (przedszkola) and 34% in other pre-school education. 59% of 3–6 year olds are in pre-school education in urban areas compared with only 38% for rural areas. 98.5% of 6 year olds attend 1 year of obligatory pre-primary schooling.

Primary school (7 years up): Education is free and compulsory between ages 7 and 14. In 1988 the pupil to teacher ratio in primary schools was 16:1.

Contributions to child care: Parents pay 7% to 12% of costs.

STATE BENEFITS (1988–89)

Family assistance: Paid for children up to the age of 16, or 25 if in full-time education, and without limit for handicapped children. The level of payments depends on the number of children, but is higher for adopted children, in order to encourage adoption.

Alimony benefit: The right to benefits from the alimony fund depends on family income. In 1988 the average monthly amount of alimony payments to families, including lone mothers, was 6.3% of average pay. The amount is set by the courts but cannot exceed the upper limit for alimony benefits of 25% of average pay.

WOMEN AND EMPLOYMENT

In 1988, 45% of employees were women, with 72% of women of child-bearing age economically active. Women are most likely to be employed between the ages of 35 and 44 (they make up 84.1% of this age group, including 92.1% in agriculture and 82.4% in other industries). In 1988, 60.7% of women employed in the socialised economy worked in material production, almost half in industry and 26.6% in trade. Most working women are employed full time – in 1988 only 7.6% of women employees worked part time. 75% of working women are married.

Poland's chronic housing shortage means that growing numbers of couples cannot live together, while divorced couples are forced to continue living together

Women's share in employment in agriculture in 1988 was 27% of the workforce in state farms and 47.7% in private farms, 30% of which were run by women.

Unemployment: In July 1990 the overall unemployment rate was 5.2%: women account for 48.9% of the unemployed, up from 40.7% in January 1990. Youth unemployment was higher for young women than for young men. 41.3% of unemployed women had been out of work for 3 months or more.

At the beginning of 1990 there were 2 unemployed people for every job vacancy, but by the end of the year this had increased to 21. Women were much worse off than men with the number of unemployed for every vacancy increasing from 3 to 40 over the year, compared with 1 to 14 for men.

Women in the workforce by industrial sector (% of total) (1988)

trade	69.0
communications	58.2
industry	37.2
all material production	37.4
finance and insurance	84.2
health and social services	80.2
education	76.3
state administration and justice	63.6
culture and art	62.5
physical culture, tourism and recreation	53.4

Source: data from *Report of the Government of the Republic of Poland on the progress made in implementation of the Convention on the elimination of all forms of discrimination against women of 1979 in the period from 1 June 1988 to 31 May 1990*

The most commonly mentioned goals of feminist organisations are protecting women's rights, ending discrimination, fighting anti-abortion laws and greater accessibility of contraceptives

Women managers: Although women account for 63.6% of workers in state administration and justice, only 12.7% of managerial staff are women. Within central government in May 1990 the highest proportions of women managers were in the Ministries of Culture and Arts (35.4%), Health and Social Protection (34.6%), Labour and Social Policy (30.0%), Finance (17.7%) and National Education (17.6%). Lowest proportions of women managers were in the Ministries of Foreign Affairs (0.5%), International Economic Co-operation (2.3%), Central Planning Office (5.0%) and Justice (7.1%).

Women's earnings: Surveys in 1987 and 1988 suggest that women's earnings are 30% less than men's. Women manual workers earned 68.6% of the equivalent men's earnings in 1988, while non-manual women were earning 69.8% as much as male colleagues. Women have had the right to equal pay since 1952.

Working mothers: In 1970 75% of working women were married with children (30% in 1956).

Women's pay as a percentage of men's for the highest and lowest paid professions (May 1990)

highest paid	
lawyers	**98**
administrative and management experts	**68**
doctors	**78**
lowest paid	
social workers	**72**
storekeepers	**89**
agricultural technicians	**74**

Source: *Superwomen and the Double Burden* (ed Chris Corrin, Scarlet Press)

WOMEN AND POLITICS

Women won the vote in 1918. In June 1991, 13.5% of MPs were women. The main parties, and their percentage of the vote, in Poland are: Unified Labour Party, 37.4%; Solidarity, 35%; Peasants' Party, 16%; Democratic Party, 6%; and others 5.6%. There are no

women voivods – heads of the 49 regional state
administrations. Only 1 Polish ambassador is a woman.

WOMEN AND EDUCATION

After primary school, 98% of pupils choose to go on
to attend academic, technical or a range of vocational
secondary schools. Overall 21% of second-level
students go to academic schools, while 76% attend
vocational and technical schools. In primary and
secondary schools women fill 73% of managerial
posts and 80% of deputy directors' posts.

% of women students in education (1988–89)

second-level schools	58.3
second-level schools providing general education	72.5
post-secondary schools	76.6
third-level schools	51.8

% of women graduates in higher studies (1988)

technical studies	17.9
agricultural studies	42.5
economic studies	51.5
law and administrative studies	49.8
classical studies	80.0
mathematics and natural sciences	66.1
medical studies	67.7
art schools	53.3

Source: *Report of the Government of the Republic of Poland on the
progress made in implementation of the Convention on the elimination
of all forms of discrimination against women of 1979 in the period from
1 June 1988 to 31 May 1990*

Educational attainment by sex (%) (1985–86)

	women	men
no education	3.0	1.3
incomplete primary education	4.4	3.2
complete primary education	7.5	5.4
incomplete secondary education	45.7	41.4
complete secondary education	35.8	43.3
higher education	3.6	5.5
average number of years in education	10.2	10.7

Source: *Poland – Reform, Adjustment and Growth* (A World Bank
Country Study)

SOURCES

Abortion Laws in Europe, Planned Parenthood in Europe, Vol 18 No 1, Spring 1989 (Supplement, amended April 1990) (International Planned Parenthood Federation); *Demographic Statistics 1990* (Eurostat); *Europa World Year Book 1990* (31st edition); Health For All 2000 Indicator Presentation System (World Health Organisation Regional Office for Europe); *Out In Europe* (Peter Tatchell, for Channel 4 Television); *Planned Parenthood in Europe* (Vol 20, No 2) (International Planned Parenthood Federation); *Pocket World in Figures* (The Economist); *Poland in Figures 1991* (Central Statistical Office); *Poland – Reform, Adjustment and Growth* (A World Bank Country Study); *Poland's Next Five Years* (The Economist Intelligence Unit); *Report of the Government of Poland on the progress made in implementation of the Convention on the elimination of all forms of discrimination against women in the period from 1 June 1988 to 31 May 1990; Superwomen and the Double Burden* (ed. Chris Corrin, Scarlet Press); *Third World Guide 91/92* (Instituto del Tercer Mundo); *Women of Europe* (No 69); *Women, State and Party in Eastern Europe* (ed Sharon L Wolchik and Alfred G Meyer, Duke University Press)

LETTERS FROM POLAND

Anka Wisniewska, student, age 17, Rzeszów

Women have the same political rights as men, but don't participate because they are too busy with their jobs, running the house, cooking, taking care of children. Women are too tired to fight for change.

One of the biggest troubles now is unemployment. Offices and workplaces dismiss women first (particularly divorced and single mothers) because they often have to take sick leave because their children are ill. What often happens is that women who have just come back from maternity leave (16 weeks for first and 18 after that) or leave without pay after maternity leave (up to 3 years) are dismissed. Women get 1 day's leave, twice a year, if they have a child under 14.

Being a Polish woman isn't easy. Women are tired and have no free time. We have equality of rights, but it is a little theoretical. Women have their holiday: it is Women's Day when they are given flowers and men are nice.

Izabela Nowacka, President of the Polish Women's League, Warsaw

After the last political, economical and social changes, the position of most women also changed. Unfortunately this doesn't mean that it improved. The percentage of women in the Lower Chamber of parliament is 13 and in the Higher Chamber, 7. Women bear the consequences of this. The proposed law on protecting the unborn child is a simple example. Many Polish women are afraid that such important decisions might be made without their influence.

Anna Prochnicka, age 26, English teacher, Gdynia

Our knowledge about contraception is rather poor. We are still afraid to talk about contraception, a fear caused by the Catholic faith and its influence. Many women, even if they know, are afraid to use it. Others think their sex lives aren't part of the Church and if they are not prepared for another baby it's better to use things that prevent pregnancy, like vaginal inserts.

Our relationships are very strong. We are used to family, although we have big problems like alcoholism. Many women suffer from having drunken husbands. Some decide to divorce, but there are still problems with housing and they are forced to live in the same flat.

ADDRESSES

Embassy of the Republic of Poland, 47 Portland Place, London W1N 3AG. Tel: 071 580 4324

Women's Affairs Bureau, Ministry of Labour, Wages and Social Affairs, Ul Nowogrodzka 1/3, Warsaw

Central Statistical Office, 00-925 Warsaw, Ul Niepodlegosci 208

Towarzystwo Rozwoju Rodziny; Ul Karowa 31, Warsaw 00 324. Tel: (48 22) 26 88 25

Ogólnopolskie Porozumienie Zwiazków Zawadowych, The All Polish Trade Union Alliance, 00 924 Warsaw, Kopernika 36/40

Solidarnosc, 81-856 Gdansk, Waly Piastowskie 24

Lambda Polsce (lesbian and gay rights), c/o Slawek Starosta, 01-684 Warsaw, Ul Kludyny 16/116

Portugal

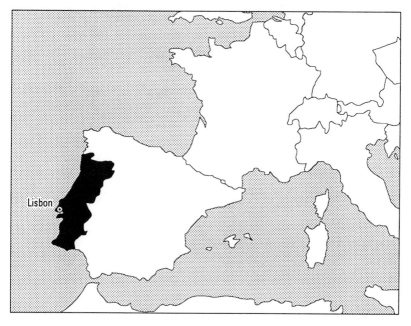

- **Population** 10.3 million, 51.7% female
- **Area** 92,390 sq km
- **Population density** 111.6 people sq km
- **GDP 1988** escudos 6,008 billion (£26 billion)
- **GDP per capita** £2,546
- **GDP per capita in purchasing power parity** (UK=100) 52
- **Public spending as % of GNP:** debts 14.3% (1987); defence 3.3% (1986); education 4.3% (1986); health 5.7% (1987)
- **Consumer price index** 1980 = 100; 1989 = 449
- **Currency is the escudo** 1989 £1 = ESC241.6; US$1 = ESC149.8

Portugal has a single-chamber parliament, the Assembly of the Republic, which has 250 members (including 4 to represent the 3.5 to 4 million Portuguese living abroad) elected for 4 years. The president is directly elected for 5 years. Madeira and the Azores are autonomous regions and the overseas territory of Macau is governed by special statute.

Most of the population is Roman Catholic. In 1987 more than 1 in 5 (21%) of the population worked in agriculture.

In 1988 Portugal had 94,453 foreign residents, 43.2% of them women. 26.8% of foreign residents were from other EC states, 2.1% from non-EC European countries, 42.6% from African countries and 28.5% from other countries.

IMMIGRATION AND RESIDENCE RIGHTS

Foreigners married to Portuguese citizens can acquire Portuguese nationality by declaration. The children of Portuguese citizens are automatically also citizens.

EQUAL RIGHTS

The Constitution guarantees equality in law to all citizens irrespective of sex, ancestry, race, language, territory of origin, religion, political or ideological convictions, education, economic situation or social condition. It also guarantees equality in a number of specific areas including civil, political, social, economic and cultural rights. The law allows temporary measures to remove existing inequalities, and specifically allows positive action with regard to employment.

When widow Dr Carolina Michaëlis de Vasconcelos demanded the right to vote in 1912 as head of her family, the law was amended specifically to bar from voting anyone other than 'masculine heads of family'

The Commission on the Status of Women (recently renamed the Commission for Equality and Rights of Women) was established in 1977 as an official department attached to the prime minister's office and is responsible for promoting equality of women and men, to encourage society to recognise the fundamental social importance of maternity and its responsibilities, and to contribute towards changing the attitudes of women and men 'so that every person may achieve full human dignity'. The commission also offers free legal information and library services.

BIRTH, LIFE AND DEATH

Breakdown of population by sex and age group (1000s) (1988)

	all		women		men		% of women in age group
	no	%	no	%	no	%	
0–14	2,267.6	22.1	1,104.2	20.8	1,163.4	23.5	48.7
15–24	1,727.7	16.8	850.8	16.0	876.9	17.7	49.2
25–39	2,177.8	21.2	1,097.1	20.7	1,080.7	21.8	50.4
40–59	2,279.2	22.2	1,207.6	22.7	1,071.6	21.6	53.0
60–74	1,302.4	12.7	723.4	13.6	579.0	11.7	55.5
75+	514.8	5.0	327.2	6.2	187.6	3.8	63.6
all	10,269.5	100.0	5,310.3	100.0	4,959.2	100.0	51.7

Source: data from *Demographic Statistics 1990* (Eurostat)

In 1987 the natural increase for every 1,000 of population was 0.6 and net migration was 6.4, giving a total increase per 1,000 population of 7.0.

Population density by region (1990)

region	area sq km	population	pop density per sq km
Aveiro	2,808	665,500	237.0
Beja	10,225	177,700	17.4
Braga	2,673	771,400	288.6
Bragança	6,608	184,700	28.0
Castelo Branco	6,675	223,700	33.5
Coímbra	3,947	446,500	113.1
Évora	7,393	174,300	23.6
Faro	4,960	341,200	68.8
Guarda	5,518	196,200	35.6
Leiria	3,515	435,900	124.0
Lisbon	2,761	2,126,400	770.2
Portalegre	6,065	137,500	22.7
Porto	2,395	1,670,600	697.5
Santarém	6,747	460,600	68.3

Population density by region (1990) (continued)

region	area sq km	population	pop density per sq km
Setúbal	5,064	779,600	153.9
Viana do Castelo	2,255	266,400	118.1
Vila Real	4,328	262,900	60.7
Viseu	5,007	423,300	84.5
total (continental Portugal)	88,944	9,744,400	109.6
autonomous regions			
The Azores	2,247	254,200	113.1
Madeira	794	271,400	341.8
total	**91,985**	**10,270,000**	**111.6**

Source: *Europa World Year Book 1990* (31st edition)

Births, deaths, marriages and divorces per 1,000 population

	1960	1970	1980	1985	1988
birth rate	23.8	19.9	16.3	12.9	11.9
% of births outside marriage	9.5	7.3	9.2	12.3	13.7
average age of mother at 1st birth	25.1	24.4	23.6	23.8	24.3
infant mortality per 1,000 live births	77.5	55.5	24.3	17.8	13.1
fertility rate per woman	3.0	2.8	2.2	1.7	1.5
marriage rate	7.8	–	7.4	6.7	6.9
average age at marriage (women)	25.3	24.8	24.3	24.6	24.9
average age at marriage (men)	27.9	27.7	27.2	27.4	27.7
divorce rate	0.1	0.1	0.6	0.9	0.9
life expectancy (women)	66.9	70.8	75.2*	–	77.7
life expectancy (men)	61.2	64.2	67.7*	–	70.6
death rate	10.6	10.3	9.8	9.6	9.6

* 1979

Source: data from *Demographic Statistics 1990* (Eurostat)

Women and men have equal rights in marriage and divorce law. Property acquired during marriage is deemed to be joint, unless specifically connected to a partner. Married parents have joint authority over children. Where parents are not married, authority is exercised by the parent caring for the child, assumed in law to be the mother. Children have had equal rights, regardless of whether they were born outside of marriage, since 1981. One-parent households in

1988 accounted for 6% of households with a child
aged 0–4 and 8% of households with a child aged 5–9.
In 1986 73.1% of all marriages were Roman Catholic.

LESBIAN RIGHTS

A common age of consent of 16 was introduced in
1852 (before then male homosexual acts were illegal).
Article 71 of the penal code which bans 'acts against
nature' has been used against lesbians and gay men.
Other legislation has been used to deny lesbian and
gay parents custody of their children after divorce.

WOMEN AND HEALTH CARE

The Portuguese Constitution states that 'everyone
shall have the right to the protection of health, and
the duty to defend and foster it'. The National Health
Service, set up in 1979, replaced an insurance-based
system. Private health care is also available. Doctors
are employed by the state and work from health
centres. Patients pay flat rate charges for prescription
medicines. 37% of doctors are women, according to
a 1989 survey by the National Order of Physicians. In
1988 there was 1 doctor for every 397 people.

Major indicators for women's health (1989)

maternal deaths (all causes) per 100,000 live births	10.12
maternal deaths (abortion) per 100,000 live births	4.22
% of all live births to mothers under 20 (1985)	10.35
% of all live births to mothers aged 35+ (1985)	8.91
deaths from cancer of the cervix (age 0–64) per 100,000 women (1988)	2.18
deaths from malignant neoplasm female breast (age 0–64) per 100,000 women	16.98
deaths from trachea/bronchus/lung cancer (age 0–64) per 100,000 women	3.05
deaths from trachea/bronchus/lung cancer (age 0–64) per 100,000 men	18.27
deaths from diseases of the circulatory system (age 0–64) per 100,000 women	40.13
deaths from diseases of the circulatory system (age 0–64) per 100,000 men	91.97
deaths from suicide and self-inflicted injury per 100,000 women	3.44
deaths from suicide and self-inflicted injury per 100,000 men	11.54

Source: data from Health for All 2000 Indicator Presentation System (World Health Organisation
Regional Office For Europe)

Abortion and contraception: Available up to 12 weeks if there is a risk to the physical or mental health of the woman, or in cases of rape or other sexual crimes, and with the agreement of two doctors after a wait of up to three days. Available up to 16 weeks on eugenic grounds. The doctor who initiates the abortion cannot perform it. Abortion is free of charge. There is a high level of refusal to perform abortions among medical staff and most are performed in private clinics, or illegally. Voluntary sterilisation is only available to over 25s.

PARENTAL PAY, LEAVE AND BENEFITS (1989–90)

Maternity leave and pay: 90 days, including 6 weeks before the birth, on full pay. 12 weeks on full pay for adoptive mothers. To qualify women must have paid at least 6 months' national insurance contributions, of which 8 days must be in the previous 3 months. In the public sector an extra 15 days on full pay is available for mothers of babies with disabilities.

Birth grant: ESC16,600 for each live birth.

Nursing mothers: A monthly allowance of ESC3,050 is paid to nursing mothers for the first 10 months, provided the child has the required monthly check-ups. Working women who are breastfeeding can reduce their daily hours by 1 hour until the child is 9 months old.

In 1867 a new civil code for the first time gave women equal parental responsibilities with their husbands

Parental and paternity leave: 24 months' unpaid leave is available, although take-up is reported to be low.

Time off to care for sick children: Up to 30 days a year to care for children under 10, and up to 15 days a year for care of a sick spouse, parents, or children over 10. Paid leave is available to government employees and low-paid lone parents; for other parents leave is unpaid. Parents of a child with a disability can work 2 hours less a day (unpaid) for up to 3 years (not available to managers).

CHILD-CARE PROVISION (1989–90)

Under 3s: 6% are in publicly funded services, most of which are run by private organisations. Almost all of these places (94%) are in nurseries, with the rest being provided in the carer's home. Between 1985 and 1988 provision for under 3s increased by 40%.

3–5 year olds: 32% have publicly funded places, half in pre-primary schooling (9.00 to 16.00 with a 2-hour lunch break) and the rest in kindergartens. 7% are in privately funded services (including schools, nurseries and kindergartens). Between 1985 and 1988, pre-primary schooling increased by almost 25%. Only 11% of the children of working mothers have daytime child-care places.

Married women were first allowed to leave the country without their husband's permission in 1969

Primary school (6 years up): Many schools operate a shift system, either from 8.15 to 13.00 or from 13.00 to 18.00. In 1985 just 40% were running from 9.15 to 16.00 with a 2-hour lunch break. The school year runs from October to June. In 1988 the pupil to teacher ratio in primary schools was 17:1.

Outside school hours care: Publicly funded places provide for 6% of 6–11 year olds, though the actual numbers attending are higher because of the school shift system. Between 1985 and 1988 outside school hours care increased by 75%.

Contributions to child-care costs: Parents contribute to the costs of all services (excluding schools) depending on income. Tax relief on a number of family expenses including child care was introduced in 1989. It is available up to a maximum of ESC90,000 for single taxpayers and ESC180,000 for married taxpayers. The loss of tax benefit to employers providing child-care services has led to a massive drop in provision (from 6,373 services in 1985 to 400 in 1988), but more employers are now providing direct financial assistance to employees with child-care costs.

STATE BENEFITS (1989–90)

Retirement pension: Normal retirement age is 62 for women and 65 for men. Pensions are paid after 120 months of contributions. Monthly pensions are 2.2% of average monthly earnings from best-paid years. The minimum per month is ESC13,000. In cases of invalidity caused by industrial injuries or specific diseases the percentage is increased to 2.5%. In addition, there is ESC2,750 for a dependent marriage partner. Pensions are normally increased each year. Workers who are unemployed can retire with an early pension, and those aged 55 and over can retire early with a pension if they are employed in heavy or unhealthy work.

Survivors' pensions: The deceased must have had 36 months' contributions. Pensions are paid to widows married for at least a year, unless they have or are carrying a child, or unless the death was the result of an accident. Widows must also be at least 35 (or their pension entitlement is limited to 5 years), unless they have dependent children or are unable to work due to incapacity. Pension is 60% of the retirement or invalidity pension of the person who has died. It stops on remarriage. A Christmas bonus equal to the December pension is paid.

Maria de Lurdes Pintasilgo became Portugal's first woman prime minister in 1979

Surviving children under 18 (or 24 if studying) qualify for 20%–40% of the pension depending on the number of children. This increases in cases where no marriage partner receives a pension.

Death grant: 6 times the average monthly wage for the best 2 years in the previous 10. It is shared in the same way as survivors' pensions except that 50% goes to the widow.

Sickness benefit: Paid at 65% of the person's average daily wage. After 365 days incapacity it is paid at 70% for up to 1,095 days (no limit for TB). Waiting period is 3 days. To qualify, workers must have been members of the social security scheme for 6 months and worked for 12 days in the previous 4 months. There are means-tested sickness allowances for single parents in

The first
Portuguese
feminist
organisation, the
National Council
of Portuguese
Women, was
founded in 1914
by Adelaide
Cabete

the case of illness of a child under 10, paid at the same rate as sickness benefit for a maximum of 30 days.

Invalidity: Paid to those with 60 months' contributions unable to earn more than one-third of a normal wage because of illness or accident. Invalidity benefit, which is paid until retirement, is between 30% and 80% of average monthly earnings during the five best-paid years from the previous 10 years, subject to a minimum of ESC17,000 a month. An extra ESC2,750 a month is paid to those with a dependent marriage partner. There is an extra ESC6,250 for those requiring constant attendance. A Christmas bonus equal to the December pension is paid.

Funeral grant: ESC19,300 is paid for each death of an insured person, or their children or equivalent dependants, or marriage partner or, in some cases, close relatives.

Family benefits: ESC1,550 is paid for each child up to the age of 14, or 25 if in further education. This can be extended for up to 3 years for children with serious infirmity. Poor families receive ESC2,350 for the third and later children.

Handicapped children qualify for an extra ESC4,100 a month up to the age of 14; ESC6,000 up to 18, and ESC8,000 up to 24. The constant care allowance is ESC6,250 a month, and there are also special educational allowances for handicapped children.

In 1910 a law
was introduced
allowing women
the same terms
for divorce
as men

Marriage grant: ESC13,800 to each person covered by national insurance.

Unemployment benefit: Insured workers receive 65% of the reference wage (up to a maximum of 3 times the minimum wage) for between 10 and 30 months. Unemployed people no longer eligible for benefit can receive 'unemployment assistance' at a rate of between 70% and 100% of the minimum wage depending on number of dependants.

WOMEN AND EMPLOYMENT

Employment and unemployment (1989)

	% women	% men
economic activity rate	46.5	70.8
employed working part time	10.0	3.1
labour force who are employers or self-employed	26.6	26.1
labour force who are family workers	4.9	2.9
unemployment rate	7.4	3.6
youth unemployment rate (age 14–24)	15.7	8.5
unemployed who have been unemployed for 12 months or more	51.8	43.1
all unemployed by sex	60.4	39.6

Source: data from *Demographic Statistics 1990* (Eurostat)

Employment by industrial sector (1000s) (1989)

	women		men		women as % of workforce
	no	%	no	%	
agriculture	433	22.8	449	16.9	49.1
all industry	483	25.4	1,097	41.3	30.6
energy and water	5	0.2	38	1.4	11.6
mineral extraction and chemicals	40	2.1	127	4.8	24.0
metal manufacturing and engineering	33	1.7	182	6.8	15.3
other manufacturing industry	394	20.7	375	14.1	51.2
building and civil engineering	12	0.6	376	14.1	3.1
all services	986	51.9	1,113	41.9	47.0
distributive trades and hotels	306	16.1	490	18.4	38.4
transport and communication	38	2.0	158	6.0	19.4
banking, finance and insurance	51	2.7	103	3.9	33.1
public administration	108	5.7	204	7.7	34.6
other services	483	25.4	158	5.9	75.4
total*	1,902	100.0	2,667	100.0	41.6

* includes 7,000 men whose industrial sector was not stated.

Source: data from *Demographic Statistics 1990* (Eurostat)

Statutory rights: The working week is limited to 48 hours, with overtime restricted to 2 hours a day, and 160 hours a year. Workers must have at least 1½ days' rest from work each week. Paid annual leave is

In July 1991,
ballerinas from
the National
Dance Company
danced in protest
outside the
presidential
palace in support
of their 5 year old
claim for equal
pay with other
companies

between 21 and 30 days, and there are 12 statutory
public holidays.

In 1991 the national minimum wage was ESC40,100
a month with the full wage being paid at the age of 20
(75% at 18–19 and 50% at 17). Wages cannot be
seized in full by creditors.

Equal rights: The Commission for Equality in Work
and Employment deals with equality cases relating to
employment and makes recommendations to the
government on measures needed to fulfil the law
of equality in the workplace.

Part-time workers: In 1989 69.9% of part-time
workers were women.

Women's and men's wages: A 1990 government
survey found that in both industry and services more
women than men (9.5% compared with 4.8%) were
being paid the minimum wage. Figures for 1989 were
10.1% for women and 5.6% for men, and for 1988
they were 12.5% for women and 6% for men.

The General
Workers' Union
has brought a
discrimination
case against the
Portuguese
Commercial
Bank to the EC
Court of Justice
because only 16
of its 2,300
employees are
women

Figures from October 1987 show that women earned
85.9% of men's salaries in credit institutions and 85.4%
in private insurance offices. Figures from the union
SITES for November 1990 for comparative salaries for
office workers suggest that women are earning more
than men in fishing (plus ESC3,000), footwear industry
(plus ESC1,000) and glass making (plus ESC12,000).
However women were earning less than men in tobacco
(minus ESC37,000), pharmaceuticals (minus
ESC36,000) and graphic art (minus ESC30,000).

Working mothers (1988): In that year 62% of women
with a child under 10 were employed (the second
highest level in the EC) compared with 95% of men.
69% of women aged 20–39 without children were
employed. 10% of employed women with a child
under 10 have part-time jobs. Levels of temporary
employment are high compared to the rest of the EC,
with 16% of mothers working in temporary jobs.

Employment rates are higher for lone mothers than all
mothers: 65% for lone mothers with a child aged 0–4

(61% for all mothers) and 68% for lone mothers with a child aged 5–9 (61%). Unemployment rates are also higher for lone mothers: 13% for those with a child aged 0–4 (6% for all mothers) and 7% for those with a child aged 5–9 (5% for all mothers).

WOMEN IN TRADE UNIONS

1988 figures show that women make up 30% of the membership of the Confederação Geraldos and 17% of the union's main bodies. The figures are 46% and 24% respectively for the Trabalhadores Portugueses – Intersindical Nacionalnião Geral dos Trabalhadores.

WOMEN AND POLITICS

In 1931 women with university degrees or secondary school qualifications won the right to vote. Men only had to be able to read and write. In 1968 women were granted the vote on the same basis as men – if they could read and write. Women won full rights to vote only in 1976 when the new constitution. In June 1991, 7.6% of MPs were women.

WOMEN AND DETENTION

In September 1988 women made up 6.5% of prisoners. Minors (age 21) and young adults made up 9.6% and foreigners 8.8%.

Of the 304 women in prison then, 1 was in part-time detention; 32 were sentenced to up to 12 months; 37 for 1–2 years; 51 for 2–4 years; 77 for 4–8 years; 64 for 8–12 years; and 42 for over 12 years.

SOURCES

Abortion Laws in Europe, Planned Parenthood in Europe, Vol 18 No 1, Spring 1989 (Supplement, amended April 1990) (published by International Planned Parenthood Federation, Europe Region); *Childcare in the European Communities 1985–90 (Women of Europe* Supplement No 51); *Comparative Study on rules governing working conditions in the member states* (Commission of the European Communities);

Demographic Statistics 1990 (Eurostat); *Employment in Europe 1991* (Commission of the European Communities); *Europa World Year Book 1990* (31st edition); *Health Care Systems and Professional Organisations in the European Community, Information note – Europe* (British Medical Association); Health For All 2000 Indicator Presentation System (World Health Organisation Regional Office for Europe); *Labour Force Survey (Results 1989)* (Eurostat); *Labour Research* September 1991 (Labour Research Department); *Les Actions Positives en Faveur des Femmes en Europe Occidentale* (Institut Syndical Europeen); *Out In Europe* (Peter Tatchell, for Channel 4 Television); *Pocket World in Figures* (The Economist); *Portugal – Status of Women* (Commission on the Status of Women); *Prison Information Bulletin* June 1990 (Council of Europe); *Positive action and the constitutional and legislative hindrances to its implementation in the member states of the Council of Europe* (Council of Europe); *Proposition de Directive Du Conseil concernant la protection au travail de la femme enceinte ou venant d'accoucher* (Commission of the European Communities); *Social Protection in the Member States of the Community* (Commission of the European Community Directorate General on Employment, Industrial Relations and Social Affairs); *Third World Guide 91/92* (Instituto del Tercer Mundo); *Women of Europe* (Nos 61, 64, 66, 67, 68, 69)

LETTER FROM PORTUGAL

Elina Guimarães, lawyer, extracted from *Portuguese Women Past and Present* (Commission on the Status of Women) – printed with her heirs' permission

A husband's right to open his wife's correspondence was abolished in 1976

In the 1920s feminism as an ideology was still only defended by the Council of Portuguese Women. This society was very active, and had organised a Feminist Convention in 1924. I became a member when still a student in 1925. The members were a great deal older than I was but afterwards many other graduates and students joined. The council had three main purposes: to obtain political rights, better family laws and better working conditions for women.

The Portuguese Council had no official support, few members, no money, not even an office or typewriter, but so much enthusiasm that we did a good deal of work and had some influence.

I was especially busy in my legal department,

answering queries, and began my special work of enlightening women about their legal position which was later to become my life's work. All seemed plain sailing for Portuguese woman. But a political event set her back for almost half a century; the military rebellion of 28 May 1926 which later emerged into a dictatorial regime. It was called the 'New State'. The 'New State' did not antagonise women. On the contrary they were greatly praised if they did what they were told and stayed in their proper place, a very subordinate one.

Democracy was restored when the government was overthrown by a military rebellion in 1974. Women took and are taking a very important part in everything from the very first days, when women of all classes and ages spontaneously carried food and coffee to the troops.

In 1975 a new constitution was voted for by everyone, men and women, over 18 years of age. It was a touching sight to see very young girls and especially careworn working women, voting with quiet dignity, many for the first time in their lives. At last women received justice on all levels.

ADDRESSES

Portuguese Embassy, 11 Belgrave Square, London SW1X 8PP. Tel: 071 235 5331/4

Comissão Para A Igualdade e Direitos das Mulheres, Presidência do Conselho de Ministros, Av da República 32 –1º, 1093 Lisboã Codex. Tel: (351 1) 77 60 81

Associaçáo para o Planeamento da Família, Rua Artilharia um 38 2º Dto, 1200 Lisboã. Tel: (351 1) 65 39 93

Confederação Geraldos Trabalhadores Portugueses – Intersindical Nacional, Rua Victor Cordon 1 2º e 3º, 1200 Lisboã

União Geral dos Trabalhadores de Portugal, Rua Buenos Aires 11, 1200 Lisboã

Gay Rights International (lesbian and gay rights), PO Box 110, 4702 Braga Codex

Romania

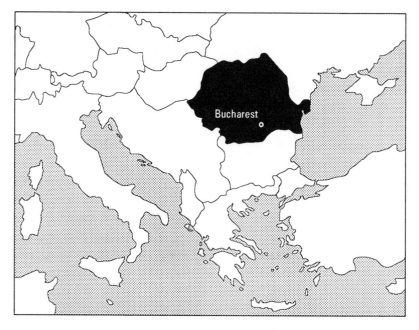

- **Population** 23 million, 50.7% female
- **Area** 237,500 sq km
- **Population density** 97.1 people sq km
- **GNP per capita** £1,587
- **Public spending as % of GNP:** defence 1.6% (1986); education 1.8% (1986); health 1.9% (1987)
- **Currency is the lei:** official exchange rate 1989 £1 = 55.5 lei; US$1 = 34.41 lei

**After the
revolution in
January 1990,
the cost of basic
foodstuffs rose
by over 180%
by October**

Legislative power is held by the 2-chamber
parliament: the Assembly of Deputies has 387
members and the Senate has 119 members, elected by
a form of proportional representation. In May 1990
the president was directly elected for a 30-month term
to coincide with the Assembly's term.

Voters must be 18 and candidates must be over 21 for
the Assembly and over 30 for the Senate. A new
constitution is being drafted and local government is
being reorganised.

At the end of 1987, 28.2% of the labour force was
employed in agriculture and 37.4% in industry.

BIRTH, LIFE AND DEATH

Population density by region (1988)

region	area sq km	population (1000s)	% of women pop (1987)	pop density per sq km
Alba	6,231	426	49.8	68.4
Arad	7,652	505	51.4	66.0
Arges	6,801	672	50.6	98.8
Bacau	6,606	718	50.5	108.7
Bihor	7,535	658	50.7	87.3
Bistrita-Nasaud	5,305	323	50.2	60.9
Botosani	4,965	460	51.6	92.6
Brasov	5,351	695	49.2	129.9
Braila	4,724	401	49.9	84.9
Buzau	6,072	523	51.2	86.1
Caras-Severin	8,503	407	49.4	47.9
Calarasi	5,074	347	49.8	68.4
Cluj	6,650	741	50.6	111.4
Constanta	7,055	726	49.1	102.9
Covasna	3,705	233	50.1	62.9
Dîmbovita	4,036	564	50.5	139.7
Dolj	7,413	772	51.0	104.1
Galati	4,425	635	49.5	143.5
Giurgiu	3,636	325	50.7	89.4
Gorj	5,641	381	50.4	67.5
Harghita	6,610	359	49.6	54.3
Hunedoara	7,016	560	49.5	79.8
Ialomita	4,449	305	50.2	68.6

Population density by region (1988) (continued)

region	area sq km	population (1000s)	% of women pop (1987)	pop density per sq km
Iasi	5,469	793	50.7	145.0
Maramures	6,215	546	50.4	87.9
Mehedinti	4,900	327	51.0	66.7
Mures	6,696	616	50.5	92.0
Neamt	5,890	570	51.2	96.8
Olt	5,507	531	50.7	96.4
Prahova	4,694	869	50.8	185.1
Satu Mare	4,405	412	50.5	93.5
Salaj	3,850	268	50.5	69.6
Sibiu	5,422	509	51.1	93.7
Suceava	8,555	686	50.6	80.2
Teleorman	5,760	505	51.1	87.7
Timis	8,692	732	51.2	84.2
Tulcea	8,430	270	50.0	32.0
Vaslui	5,297	458	51.0	86.5
Vilcea	5,705	427	51.4	74.8
Vrancea	4,863	390	51.1	80.2
Bucharest	1,695	2,298	52.0	1,355.7
total	**237,500**	**22,940**	**50.7**	**96.6**

Sources: data from *Europa World Year Book 1990* (31st edition); *Anuarul Statistic al Republicii Socialiste România 1988*

Births and deaths for every 1,000 population (1988)

birth rate	15.6
death rate	10.7
infant mortality per 1,000 live births	22.0
marriage rate	7.0
life expectancy (women)	73.0
life expectancy (men)	69.2
fertility rate per woman	2.15

Source: data from *Demographic Statistics 1990* (Eurostat)

In 1966, in an effort to raise the birth rate, the government made abortion and divorce virtually impossible and increased taxes on childless adults, whether married or not. Although the rate of population growth doubled the following year, it had declined to 1966 levels by 1983.

LESBIAN RIGHTS

Romania is the only country in Europe where all same-sex relationships are illegal. Article 200 of the penal code specifies a maximum penalty of 5 years' imprisonment. Lesbians and gay men were severely oppressed under the 1965–89 regime of Nicolae Ceausescu, and there has been no known change under the new government.

WOMEN AND HEALTH CARE

In 1988 there was 1 doctor for every 475 people.

Major indicators for women's health (1984)

maternal deaths (all causes) per 100,000 live births	148.83
maternal deaths (abortion) per 100,000 live births	128.01
ratio of abortions to 1,000 live births (all ages) (1989)	522.28
% of all live births to mothers under 20 (1985)	15.75
% of all live births to mothers aged 35+ (1985)	5.31
deaths from cancer of the cervix (age 0–64) per 100,000 women	10.51
deaths from malignant neoplasm female breast (age 0–64) per 100,000 women	13.49
deaths from trachea/bronchus/lung cancer (age 0–64) per 100,000 women	5.12
deaths from trachea/bronchus/lung cancer (age 0–64) per 100,000 men	34.01
deaths from diseases of the circulatory system (age 0–64) per 100,000 women	104.46
deaths from diseases of the circulatory system (age 0–64) per 100,000 men	192.91

Source: data from Health for All 2000 Indicator Presentation System (World Health Organisation Regional Office For Europe)

In October 1990, the cost of a decent winter coat was equal to one month's wages

Abortion and contraception: Since 26 December 1989 abortion has been available on request up to 12 weeks, and up to the second trimester when there is a risk to a woman's life, or the foetus is malformed. The charge is 30 lei. Women are given advice on contraception when they go into hospital for an abortion.

Previous abortion laws (passed in 1957 and 1985) only allowed abortions for women under 18, and those over 40 with 5 or more children under 18; on medical or eugenic grounds; or in cases of rape.

Changes to abortion law, coupled with increased access to family planning services are expected to lead to an 80% decrease in maternal mortality, which at the end of 1989 was 149 per 100,000.

Under communism, contraception was only available on prescription to women whose health was judged to be endangered by pregnancy; imported oral contraceptives and IUDs were banned and only condoms and spermicides were produced in Romania.

CHILD-CARE PROVISION

Under 6s: In 1985 77.6% of children under 6 were in kindergartens.

Primary school (6 years up): Education is compulsory between ages 6 to 16. In 1988 the pupil to teacher ratio in primary schools was 21:1.

WOMEN AND EMPLOYMENT

Statutory rights: In January 1990 the working week was cut from 40–42 hours to 35–40.

Unemployment: The official unemployment figure was expected to reach 200,000 by the end of 1991.

Employment in the state sector (1990)

	no (1000s)	%
industry	4,213.9	50.9
transport and telecommunications	721.1	8.9
agriculture	640.1	7.9
internal trade and tourism	640.1	7.9
construction	478.0	5.9
education, arts and culture	413.2	5.1
health, welfare and physical education	307.9	3.8
community services	186.3	2.3
science	105.3	1.3
other	486.1	6.0
total	8,192.0	100.0

Source: *Doing Business with Eastern Europe: Romania* (Business International)

Women's share of employment in the state sector (1990)

	%
industry	42.6
transport and telecommunications	53.9
agriculture	20.4
internal trade and tourism	61.8
education, arts and culture	65.3
health, welfare and physical education	74.7
all workers	41.3

Source: data from *Doing Business with Eastern Europe: Romania* (Business International)

Women's share in employment by industry (1977)

	women no	%	men no	%	women as % of workforce
agriculture and forestry	2,478,249	50.3	1,497,380	25.5	62.3
industry	1,196,070	24.3	2,306,488	39.3	34.1
construction	77,147	1.6	620,090	10.6	11.1
electricity, gas, water and sanitation services	26,523	0.5	89,037	1.5	23.0
commerce	322,665	6.5	252,531	4.3	56.1
transport, storage and communications	87,839	1.8	468,666	8.0	15.8
services	716,235	14.5	607,322	10.4	54.1
others	21,991	0.4	25,369	0.4	46.4
total	**4,926,719**	**100.0**	**5,866,883**	**100.0**	**45.6**

Source: data from *Europa World Year Book 1990* (31st edition)

WOMEN AND POLITICS

Women won the vote in 1946. In June 1991 women made up only 3.6% of MPs. The political parties, and their percentage of votes received in 1990, are National Salvation Front (67.5%); Hungarian Democratic Union (7.3%); National Liberal Party (6%); others (19.2%).

WOMEN IN EDUCATION

In the academic year 1989–90 a total of 164,507 students were enrolled in 133 different faculties at 44 educational institutions. 48.8% of enrolled students were women. Two-thirds of all students were studying technical subjects, 10.1% medicine, 9.4% economics, 9.6% education, 1.4% law and 0.6% arts.

SOURCES

Abortion Laws in Europe, Planned Parenthood in Europe, Vol 18 No 1, Spring 1989 (Supplement, amended April 1990) International Planned Parenthood Federation, Europe Region; *Anuarul Statistic al Republicii Socialiste România* (Directia Generalâ de Statisticâ); *Demographic Statistics 1990* (Eurostat); *Doing Business with Eastern Europe: Romania* (Business International); *Europa World Year Book 1990* (31st edition); Health For All 2000 Indicator Presentation System (World Health Organisation Regional Office for Europe); *Planned Parenthood in Europe* (Vol 18 No 2, Vol 19 No 2) (International Planned Parenthood Federation); *Third World Guide 91/92* (Instituto del Tercer Mundo); *Women of Europe,* No 68; *Women, State and Party in Eastern Europe* (ed Sharon L Wolchik and Alfred G Meyer, Duke University Press)

LETTER ON ROMANIA

Angela Lener, television researcher, from Bucharest, now living in Switzerland

To reduce energy consumption Nicolae Ceausescu limited the temperature in homes to 10°C. Between November and February a one-room apartment had a monthly quota of 22kwh, enough electricity to boil two kettles of water a day

Before the revolution there certainly didn't exist any women's organisations. Then it would have been impossible and dangerous. The only organisations which existed were Communist, where people were obliged to subscribe. The non-existence of these organisations is also due to the fact that the Marx and Engels Communist thesis gives equal rights to men and women. What the thesis says was usually not true, but on this point it happened to be so. Women really had the same salaries as men and they also could get a high or very high position following the same procedure as men followed. That meant becoming a member of the Communist Party and making a kind of activist career.

I don't really think there are any feminist women in Romania. It is a fact that women were confronted with a lot of problems, but men were also. In Romania for everyone there was a question of surviving. Men and women were obliged to have jobs (full time) to get money, which anyway was not enough to live on. They were also both obliged to go on queuing to get something to eat, wasting a lot of time and energy.

Those who were not really poor could afford buying food at the black market. But this was not very easy either. Sometimes you had to go several kilometres out of Bucharest to reach your 'contrabandist'. You had to keep good relations with him, because he had surely enough clients. Sometimes he had enough money but wanted to trade for something else, for example wine or potatoes given for oil. And to get the oil you had to queue for hours. So this was usually men's contribution.

Women used to do the cooking, washing and of course they had also to go on queuing for food. In short, both of them were wasting all their energy from morning till night.

ADDRESSES

Embassy of Romania, 4 Palace Green, London W8 4QD

National Women's Council, Office of the Chairman, Council of Ministers, Str Academiei 34, Bucharest

National Statistics Commission, Str Stavropoleos 6, Bucharest

Uniunea Generala a Sindicatelor din Romania, 71724 Bucharest, Al Stefan Gheorghie 14

Spain

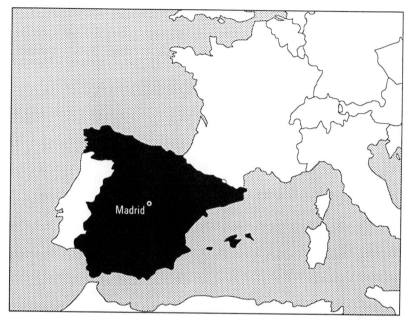

- **Population** 38.8 million, 50.9% female
- **Area** 504,879 sq km
- **Population density** 76.7 people sq km
- **GDP 1988** pesetas 39,440 billion (£210.2 billion)
- **GDP per capita** £5,374
- **GDP per capita in purchasing power parity** (UK=100) 70
- **Public spending as % of GNP:** defence 2.3% (1986); education 3.2% (1986); health 4.3% (1987)
- **Consumer price index** 1980 = 100; 1989 = 235
- **Currency is the peseta** 1989 £1 = PTA176.9; US$1 = PTA109.7

Spain is a hereditary monarchy with the monarch as head of state. The monarch appoints the prime minister, and then jointly other members of the Council of Ministers. Legislative power is held by the 2-chamber parliament, Cortes Generales, which is made up of the Congress of Deputies and the Senate. The 23-member Council of State is the supreme consultative body. The Congress of Deputies has 350 members elected by proportional representation. The territories of Ceuta and Melilla each have a deputy. The Senate has 208 elected members and 49 regional members.

The constitution recognises the right to autonomy of the nationalities and communities that go together to make up the Spanish state: Basque country (País Vasuo), Cataluña, Galicia, Andalucia, Asturias, Cantabria, Rioja, Murcia, Community of Valencia, Aragón, Castile-La Mancha, Canary Islands (Canarias), Navarra, Extremadura, Balearic Islands, Madrid and Castile-León. Each of these has their own parliament which is elected for 4 years.

While the constitution states that Spain has no official religion, the majority of people are Roman Catholics.

IMMIGRATION AND RESIDENCE RIGHTS

Residence permits are required for stays of longer than 90 days. Those planning to work in Spain need both residence and work permits which normally last for 5 years. Entertainers, journalists, members of the clergy and academic staff invited by Spanish universities are among those who do not need work permits. The availability of local labour is a factor in awarding work permits, but sympathetic consideration is given to those married to a Spaniard or who have Spanish children or who already have a work or residence permit.

In 1987 Spain had 334,935 foreign residents, 57.7% from other EC states, 6.9% from non-EC European countries, 5.5% from African countries and 29.5% from other countries.

EQUAL RIGHTS

The Spanish constitution grants equal rights to all citizens and prohibits discrimination on the grounds of birth, race, sex or religion, and calls on the public authorities to promote conditions which allow for equality between all citizens. The Institute for Women's Affairs co-ordinates information on equality, encourages positive action programmes and deals with complaints of discrimination.

BIRTH, LIFE AND DEATH

Breakdown of population by sex and age (1000s) (1988)

	all no	all %	women no	women %	men no	men %	% of women in age group
0–14	8,307.7	21.4	4,019.0	20.4	4,288.7	22.5	48.4
15–24	6,590.7	17.0	3,214.7	16.3	3,376.0	17.7	48.8
25–39	8,169.4	21.1	4,060.7	20.6	4,108.7	21.6	49.7
40–59	8,809.9	22.7	4,474.6	22.7	4,335.3	22.8	50.8
60–74	4,858.3	12.5	2,668.0	13.5	2,190.3	11.5	54.9
75+	2,000.1	5.2	1,261.9	6.4	738.2	3.9	63.1
all	38,736.1	100.0	19,698.9	100.0	19,037.2	100.0	50.9

Source: data from *Demographic Statistics 1990* (Eurostat)

Births, deaths, marriages and divorces for every 1,000 people

	1960	1970	1980	1985	1988
birth rate	21.8	19.7	15.3	11.9	10.7
% of births outside marriage	2.3	1.4	3.9	8.0	–
average age of mother at 1st birth	–	24.5[1]	24.6	25.4	–
infant mortality per 1,000 live births	43.7	28.1	12.3	8.9	8.1
fertility rate per woman	2.9	2.8	2.2	1.6	1.4
marriage rate	7.7	7.3	5.9	5.2	5.5
average age at marriage (women)	26.3	25.0	23.6	24.8	–
average age at marriage (men)	29.3	27.9	26.2	27.4	
divorce rate	–	–	–	–	0.5[2]
life expectancy (women)	72.2	74.8	78.6	79.6[3]	–
life expectancy (men)	67.4	69.2	72.5	73.1[3]	–
death rate	8.6	8.3	7.8	8.1	8.2

[1] 1975; [2] 1987; [3] 1985–86

Source: data from *Demographic Statistics 1990* (Eurostat)

Population trends by region (1987)

region	pop (1000s)	% of total pop	pop density per km	natural increase per 1,000	net migration per 1,000	total increase per 1,000
Galicia	2,845.4	7.3	96.7	-0.2	1.3	1.1
Asturias	1,134.8	2.9	107.4	-1.1	1.2	0.1
Cantabria	526.3	1.4	99.3	1.3	1.7	3.0
País Vasco	2,191.1	5.6	301.8	1.8	0.6	2.3
Navarra	518.9	1.3	49.8	1.2	1.2	2.3
Rioja	258.3	0.7	51.3	0.5	1.4	1.9
Aragón	1,210.5	3.1	25.4	-0.4	3.8	3.4
Madrid	4,893.7	12.6	612.1	4.5	1.8	6.3
Castile – León	2,620.8	6.7	27.8	0.4	1.3	1.7
Castile – La Mancha	1,687.6	4.3	21.3	2.5	0.8	3.3
Extremadura	1,093.5	2.8	26.3	3.5	0.5	4.0
Cataluña	6,079.9	15.7	190.4	1.7	1.5	3.3
Comunidad Valenciana	3,754.2	9.7	161.1	2.4	1.7	4.0
Baleares	671.2	1.7	133.9	2.5	0.6	3.1
Andalucia	6,773.4	17.4	77.6	5.9	1.4	7.3
Murcia	1,006.9	2.6	89.0	6.7	1.4	8.1
Ceuta y Melilla	125.7	0.3	4,053.6	9.5	-0.8	8.7
Canarias	1,443.0	3.7	199.2	6.3	0.8	7.1
Spain	**38,835.2**	**100.0**	**76.9**	**2.9**	**1.4**	**4.3**

Source: *Demographic Statistics 1990* (Eurostat)

Women and men have equal rights in marriage and divorce law. Divorces are granted after a judicial separation of 1 year or after living apart for 2 years, with the consent of both partners. Either partner may apply for divorce after living apart for at least 5 years. If there are children, both parents have equal rights to custody and control, though the mother is normally awarded custody of children under 7. Parents retain the right of access even if denied custody. Property acquired by either partner during the marriage is divided equally on divorce, with each partner retaining private property brought to the marriage.

One-parent households in 1988 accounted for 2% of households with a child aged 0–4 and 4% of those with a child aged 5–9, the lowest in the EC. 80% of adolescent mothers are single.

LESBIAN RIGHTS

Public morality laws, used against gay men since the late 1930s, were repealed in 1978. A common age of consent of 12 for lesbians, gay men and heterosexuals was introduced in 1822 (though male homosexual acts were illegal between 1928 and 1932). This is the lowest common age of consent in Europe.

WOMEN AND HEALTH CARE

Health care is provided through a social security system funded by contributions from employees and employers and taxation. Changes to the General Health Act in 1986 moved away from heavily tiered services which differed for urban and rural communities, towards a more integrated national service. Private health care is also available. The social security fund covers GPs' fees, dental extractions and hospital services, but there are charges for medicines except for pensioners. In 1988 there was 1 doctor for every 318 people.

Major indicators for women's health (1986)

maternal deaths (all causes) per 100,000 live births	5.4
maternal deaths (abortion) per 100,000 live births	0.68
% of all live births to mothers under 20	6.09
% of all live births to mothers aged 35+	11.21
deaths from cancer of the cervix (age 0–64) per 100,000 women (1985)	1.43
deaths from malignant neoplasm female breast (age 0–64) per 100,000 women	15.59
deaths from trachea/bronchus/lung cancer (age 0–64) per 100,000 women	2.34
deaths from trachea/bronchus/lung cancer (age 0–64) per 100,000 men	27.78
deaths from diseases of the circulatory system (age 0–64) per 100,000 women	34.74
deaths from diseases of the circulatory system (age 0–64) per 100,000 men	91.12
deaths from suicide and self-inflicted injury per 100,000 women	3.46
deaths from suicide and self-inflicted injury per 100,000 men	11.37

Source: data from Health for All 2000 Indicator Presentation System (World Health Organisation Regional Office For Europe)

Abortion and contraception: Available up to 12 weeks in cases of rape (if the rape was reported) or other sexual crime. Available up to 22 weeks on eugenic grounds with 2 medical opinions. Available without time limit if there is a risk to the woman's life, or her physical or mental health, on 1 medical opinion. Women under 18 must have parental consent. Abortion is free in the public health system; private charges range from £150 to £400. Most abortions are performed privately. Medical staff may refuse to carry out abortions on conscientious grounds. 13.2% of abortions in 1988 were carried out on women under 20, of whom 41.7% had never practised contraception.

PARENTAL PAY, LEAVE AND BENEFITS (1989–90)

In 1988 Dr German Saenz de Santamaria was sentenced to 4 years in jail for performing an abortion on a girl of 14 forced to have sex with her 55 year old cousin since the age of 8

Maternity leave and pay: 10 weeks after the birth plus 6 weeks which can be taken before or after, paid by benefit equivalent to 75% of earnings. Maternity leave was extended by 2 weeks in 1989. Adoptive mothers qualify for 8 weeks' leave for a child of less than 9 months, or 6 weeks if child is between 9 months and 5 years. To qualify women must have paid 180 days of national insurance contributions in the previous 12 months, and have been registered for national insurance at least 9 months before the birth.

Nursing mothers: Women can take time off work to breastfeed.

Parental leave: 12 months' unpaid leave was introduced in 1989. Parents of a child under 6 can reduce their working hours (unpaid).

Right of return to work: A woman can return to her previous job provided leave has been for no longer than 1 year for the care of a child under 3.

Time off to care for sick children: Unpaid leave for parents during the first 2 days of a child's illness.

CHILD-CARE PROVISION (1989–90)

Under 3s: Less than 5% are in publicly funded places (nurseries, centres for children of mixed ages and pre-primary schooling). 20% of 3 year olds are in pre-primary schooling though the government has set a target of 1992 to provide schooling for all 3 year olds.

3–5 year olds: 70% in publicly funded places, mostly in pre-primary schooling, though also in nurseries and mixed age centres. 90% of 4–5 year olds are in pre-primary schooling (9.00 to 17.00 with a 3-hour lunch break, though growing numbers of schools are providing supervision for the break).

Primary school (6 years up): 9.00 to 17.00 with a 3-hour lunch break. Growing numbers of schools are providing supervision for the break. The school year runs from September to June. In 1988 the pupil to teacher ratio in primary schools was 26:1.

Outside school hours care: No publicly funded services during term time but the number of holiday playschemes for children over 6 is growing.

Contributions to child-care costs: Parents pay for publicly funded services (excluding schools) depending on income. Tax relief was to be introduced in 1991 for 10% of the costs of care for under-3s.

STATE BENEFITS (1989–90)

Retirement pension: Normal retirement age is 65 for both women and men. Qualification depends on the contributions record of the previous 15 years, with payments ranging from 50% of a 'reference wage' for 10 years' contributions to 100% for 35 years. Annual pension is 14 times a monthly pension, subject to a minimum monthly payment of PTA39,950 (PTA47,010 for a pensioner with a dependent marriage partner) and a maximum of PTA207,152. Pensioners on the minimum qualify for a family income supplement of PTA1,050 a month for each dependent child. Pensions are adjusted with inflation forecasts. Early retirement is possible from 60 though the amount of pension is reduced. Pensions are suspended if beneficiaries have earnings from employment.

Survivors' pensions: For survivors to qualify, the deceased must have contributed to a social security scheme or had an invalidity or old age pension. They also must have lived together on a regular basis. In cases of separation or divorce, the pension is shared between beneficiaries based on the number of years the couple lived together. Pension is 45% of the reference wage used to calculate old age pension, and 14 payments of the monthly pension are made each year. Minimum pensions are PTA36,680 a month for widows over 65, PTA28,040 for widows between 60 and 65 and PTA26,290 for widows under 60. The pension stops on remarriage, though if this happens before the age of 60, a lump sum payment of 24 times the monthly pension is made. In cases where the survivor's pension is only that of the minimum retirement pension, there is a family income supplement of PTA1,050 a month.

Where a spouse survives, children qualify for 20% to 50% of the deceased's reference wage; if no spouse, they can receive beween 20% and 100%. The minimum surviving child's pension is PTA9,940 a month (14 monthly payments each year). Minimum orphan's pension is PTA11,805 plus a sum equal to PTA26,290 divided by the number of children (again 14 monthly payments per year).

Death grant: PTA5,000.

Sickness benefit: Benefit is calculated according to a reference wage and is paid at 60% of the wage for days 4–20, then at 75% from day 21 for up to 12 months. This can be extended by 6 months if the person is likely to return to work after treatment. To qualify, workers must be covered by the social security scheme and have paid 180 days of contributions in the previous 5 years. Waiting period is 3 days.

Invalidity: Provisional invalidity benefit is paid to workers who have exhausted their entitlement to sickness benefit and are expected to become fit for work. Contributions must have been paid for the previous 180 days. Benefit is payable from the day after sickness benefit stops until the person returns to work, is permanently incapacitated or after 6 years.

Permanent invalidity benefit is paid to workers with sufficient contributions who are partially or totally incapable of work because of physical or functional disabilities. The benefit for permanent partial incapacity is a lump sum equal to 24 times the reference wage used to calculate sickness benefit. For permanent total incapacity the pension is 100% of the reference wage subject to a minimum of PTA39,950 a month (PTA47,010 for those with a dependent marriage partner). In cases of severe disablement an additional 50% is paid. Maximum monthly pensions are PTA207,152.

Invalidity pensions can not be drawn with any other pensions apart from the widow's pension. All pensioners receive 14 monthly payments a year.

In 1991 the government decided not to increase child benefit because it was seen as contrary to the emancipation of women

Family benefits: PTA250 a month for each child up until the age of 18 (there is no time limit for cases of serious infirmity). Large families qualify for supplements, ranging from 25% to 35% depending on the number of children. Additional benefits include PTA3,000 a month for each handicapped child, and a special educational allowance for large families with handicapped children. The family benefit system is under review.

Unemployment benefit: 80% of earnings for 180 days, then 70% from the sixth to twelfth month and, after that, 60%. Benefit can be claimed for up to 2 years depending on the employment record. The unemployed not entitled to these benefits are paid 75% of the interprofessional minimum wage (more for long-term unemployed over 45 with large families) for up to 18 months. Extensions are possible for the long term unemployed over 45.

WOMEN AND EMPLOYMENT

Statutory rights: The working week is limited to 40 hours, with overtime restricted to 80 hours a year. However longer working days are allowed provided average hours over a specified period are maintained.

Workers must have 1½ days' rest from work each week. Paid annual leave is 30 days and there are 14 statutory public holidays.

In 1991 the national minimum wage was PTA53,250 a month, payable at 18 (60% at 17 and 40% at 15). The government is required by law to take inflation into account when setting the minimum wage. Most collective agreements include clauses allowing them to be reopened if prices increase by more than 6%. Employees are legally entitled to bonuses in May and at Christmas, normally worth one month's wages. Wages cannot be seized by creditors in full.

Employment trends (1989)

	% women	% men
economic activity rate	31.4	64.1
employed working part time	11.9	1.6
labour force who are employers or self-employed	16.7	23.8
labour force who are family workers	11.8	3.4
unemployment rate	25.3	13.1
youth unemployment rate (age 14–24)	42.6	27.5
unemployed who have been unemployed for		
12 months or more	67.3	53.5
all unemployed by sex	50.1	49.6

Source: data from *Labour Force Survey (Results 1989)* (Eurostat)

Part-time workers: In 1989 77.2% of part-time workers were women. Part-time workers have the same rights as full-time workers, though social security contributions and benefits are proportionate to the number of hours worked.

Economic activity by type of employment (1990)

	% of active women	% of active men	women as a % of total
employer	1.58	4.76	13.38
self-employed	13.82	17.54	26.91
members of co-operatives	0.57	0.83	24.04
family workers	10.54	2.98	62.30
public sector workers	20.29	14.80	39.05
private sector workers	52.93	58.85	29.59
others	0.28	0.23	35.99
total	100.00	100.00	31.85

Source: data from *La Mujer en Cifras* (Instituto de la Mujer, Ministerio de Asuntos Sociales)

Why women work seasonally (1990)

	share of seasonal employment				women as % of group
	women		men		
	no (1000s)	%	no (1000s)	%	
can't find permanent employment	873.4	87.2	1,577.4	90.2	35.6
don't want permanent employment	7.3	0.7	4.8	0.3	60.3
for other reasons	104.3	10.4	145.8	8.3	41.7
don't know why	16.7	1.7	20.7	1.2	44.7
total	1,001.7	100.0	1,748.7	100.0	36.4

Source: data from *La Mujer en Cifras* (Instituto de la Mujer, Ministerio de Asuntos Sociales)

Women's reasons for working part-time (1990)

	share of part-time employment				women as % of group
	women		men		
	no (1000s)	%	no (1000s)	%	
full-time workers	3,511.6	87.8	8,410.3	98.3	29.5
part-time workers	484.4	12.1	136.8	1.6	78.0
because of education	13.5	0.3	13.8	0.2	49.5
due to ill health	10.3	0.3	13.9	0.2	42.6
can't find full-time work	127.9	3.2	31.5	0.4	80.2
don't want full-time work	51.7	1.3	4.7	0.1	91.7
other reasons	280.9	7.0	73.0	0.9	79.4
non classifiable by hours	2.9	0.1	10.5	0.1	21.6
all economically active	3,998.9	100.0	8,557.6	100.0	31.8

Source: data from *La Mujer en Cifras* (Instituto de la Mujer, Ministerio de Asuntos Sociales)

Employment by industrial sector (1000s) (1989)

	women		men		women as % of workforce
	no	%	no	%	
agriculture	428	11.2	1,176	14.0	26.7
all industry	647	17.0	3,338	39.8	16.2
energy and water	10	0.3	134	1.6	6.9
mineral extraction and chemicals	58	1.5	375	4.5	13.4
metal manufacturing and engineering	91	2.4	795	9.5	10.3
other manufacturing industry	463	12.2	960	11.5	32.5
building and civil engineering	26	0.7	1,074	12.8	2.4
all services	2,736	71.8	3,869	46.2	41.1
distributive trades and hotels	1,015	26.6	1,671	19.9	37.8
transport and communication	81	2.1	622	7.4	11.5
banking, finance and insurance	188	4.9	458	5.5	29.1
public administration	200	5.3	457	5.5	30.4
other services	1,252	32.9	661	7.9	65.4
total	**3,811**	**100.0**	**8,384**	**100.0**	**31.3**

Source: data from *Labour Force Survey (Results 1989)* (Eurostat)

Women's share of occupational groups (1990)

	%
professional, technical and similar occupations	46.11
public administration, directors and business managers	8.45
administrative staff and similar	48.13
traders, retailers and similar	43.87
hotel, domestic service and other personal services staff	57.33
agriculture, forestry and fishing workers	27.01
miners, textile workers, transport and construction workers	12.36
armed forces	0.25
total	**31.85**

Source: data from *La Mujer en Cifras* (Instituto de la Mujer, Ministerio de Asuntos Sociales)

Women's monthly earnings compared to men's (1989)

	non-manual workers %	manual workers %
industry	63.0	66.2
construction	61.2	95.3
services	64.4	69.0
all workers	62.8	69.1

Women's hourly earnings compared to men's (1989)

	non-manual workers %	manual workers %
industry	63.7	67.8
construction	61.2	99.3
services	66.8	76.7
all workers	64.6	72.8

Source: data from *La Mujer en Cifras* (Instituto de la Mujer, Ministerio de Asuntos Sociales)

In 1990 Marisa Tejedor Salguero became the first woman rector of a Spanish university at the Universidad de la Laguna, Santa Cruz de Tenerife

Working mothers (1988): In that year, 28% of women with a child under 10 were employed (one of the lowest levels in the EC) compared with 89% of men. 44% of women aged 20–39 without children were employed, the lowest in the EC.

15% of employed women with a child under 10 had part-time jobs. Spain has the highest level of temporary employment in the EC; 19% of employed mothers were in temporary jobs.

Employment rates were almost twice as high for lone mothers than all mothers, because of greater levels of full-time employment; 50% for lone mothers with a child aged 0–4 (28% for all mothers) and 50% for lone mothers with a child aged 5–9 (26%).

Unemployment rates are also nearly twice as high for lone mothers: 18% for those with a child aged 0–4 (10% for all mothers) and 14% for those with a child aged 5–9 (7% for all). Spain has the highest EC unemployment rate for women with a child under 10.

WOMEN AND POLITICS

Women won the vote in 1931.

In the 1989 election, women were elected to 13.4% of the seats in the Congress of Deputies and 11.2% of those in the Senate. The next general election will be in 1993.

Women in the Congress of Deputies (after 1989 election)

political party	total no of seats	no of seats held by women	% of seats held by women
Socialist Workers' Party (PSOE)	175	32	18.3
People's Party (PP)	107	10	9.3
Centre Democratic Union (CDS)	14	0	0.0
Union of the Centre (CIU)	18	1	5.6
Basque Nationalist Party (PNV)	5	0	0.0
United Left (IU)	17	2	11.8
others	14	2	14.3
total	**350**	**47**	**13.4**

Source: data from *La Mujer en Cifras* (Instituto de la Mujer, Ministerio de Asuntos Sociales)

Women in the Senate (after 1989 election)

political party	total no of seats	no of seats held by women	% of seats held by women
PSOE	128	20	15.6
PP	90	7	7.8
CDS	7	0	0.0
CIU	11	1	9.1
PNV	6	0	0.0
others	9	0	0.0
total	**251**	**28**	**11.2**

Source: data from *La Mujer en Cifras* (Instituto de la Mujer, Ministerio de Asuntos Sociales)

After the 1987 local elections, 8.3% of local councillors, 6.7% of deputy mayors and 3.1% of mayors elected were women.

None of Spain's 143 ambassadors is a woman.

WOMEN AND EDUCATION

Most university students are women, but a breakdown
of subjects they studied in 1987–88 shows that many
continue to cluster in subject areas that have been
traditionally female.

	%
university faculties	
fine arts	60.2
mathematics	52.2
economics and business studies	34.0
pharmacy	70.6
philology	71.0
geography and history	63.8
psychology	72.3
veterinary medicine	36.6
medicine	50.0
all university students	54.4
technical schools	
architecture	23.6
agronomy	20.4
telecommunications	5.82
chemistry	26.0
all technical school students	16.2
university schools	
architecture and technical engineering	12.7
business studies	48.3
teacher training	77.8
nursing	82.1
social work	87.6
all university school students	64.7

Source: data from *La Mujer en Cifras* (Instituto de la Mujer, Ministerio de
Asuntos Sociales)

WOMEN AND DETENTION

In September 1988 6.8% of all prisoners were
women; 7.7% were minors (age 21) or young adults;
and 15.1% were foreigners.

SOURCES

Abortion Laws in Europe, Planned Parenthood in Europe, Vol 18
No 1, Spring 1989 (Supplement, amended April 1990);
Bargaining Report 101 (Labour Research Department);
*Childcare in the European Communities 1985–90 (Women of
Europe* Supplement No 51); *Comparative Study on rules
governing working conditions in the member states* (Commission
of the European Communities); *Demographic Statistics 1990*
(Eurostat); *Europa World Year Book 1990* (31st edition); *Labour
Research* September 1991 (Labour Research Department);
*Health Care Systems and Professional Organisations in the
European Community, Information note – Europe* (British
Medical Association); Health For All 2000 Indicator
Presentation System (World Health Organisation Regional
Office for Europe); *La Mujer en Cifras* (Instituto de la Mujer,
Ministerio de Asuntos Sociales); *Labour Force Survey (Results
1989)* (Eurostat); *Les Actions Positives en Faveur des Femmes en
Europe Occidentale* (Institut Syndical Europeen); *Out In Europe*
(Peter Tatchell, for Channel 4 Television); *Pocket World in
Figures* (The Economist); *Positive action and the constitutional
and legislative hindrances to its implementation in the member
states of the Council of Europe* (Council of Europe); *Proposition
de Directive Du Conseil concernant la protection au travail de la
femme enceinte ou venant d'accoucher* (Commission of the
European Communities); *Prison Information Bulletin* June 1990
(Council of Europe); *Rights of Women in Spain* (Embajada de
España en Londres); *Social Protection in the Member States of
the Community* (Commission of the European Community
Directorate General on Employment, Industrial Relations and
Social Affairs); *Spain 1989* (Ministerio del Portavoz del
Gobierno); *Spanish Constitution*; the Spanish Embassy; *Third
World Guide 91/92* (Instituto del Tercer Mundo); *Women of
Europe* (Nos 61, 66, 67, 68)

ADDRESSES

Spanish Embassy, 24 Belgrave Square, London SW1X 8QA.
Tel: 071 235 7537

Insituto de la Mujer, Almagro 36, Madrid.
Tel: (34 1) 347 00 00

Federacíon de Planificacíon Familiar de España (family
planning), Almagro 28, 28010 Madrid. Tel: (34 1) 319 92 76

FAGC (Front d'Alliberament Gai de Catalunya) (lesbian and gay
rights), Calle Villarol 62, 3er 1a, 08011 Barcelona.
Tel: (34 3) 254 63 98

Sweden

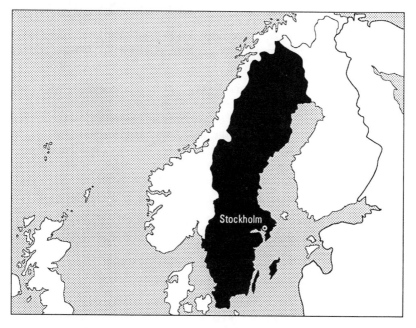

- **Population** 8.5 million, 50.6% female
- **Area** 449,964 sq km
- **Population density** 18.9 people sq km
- **GDP 1988** krona 1097 billion (£111 billion)
- **GDP per capita** £13,116
- **GDP per capita in purchasing power parity** (UK=100) 117
- **Public spending as % of GNP:** defence 2.9% (1986); education 7.6% (1986); health 8.0% (1987)
- **Consumer price index** 1980 = 100; 1989 = 193
- **Currency is the krona** 1989 £1 = SEK10; US$1 = SEK6.23

Sweden is a hereditary monarchy with the monarch as head of state. Legislative power is held by the single-chamber parliament, the Riksdag, which has 349 members elected by proportional representation for 3 years. Executive power is held by the cabinet and the prime minister is appointed by the speaker and confirmed by the full parliament. Voting is at 18.

Forest covers half of Sweden's land surface, with less than 10% farmland. 85% of the population lives in the southern half of the country. All citizens become members of the State Lutheran Church at birth, provided 1 parent is a member, but can leave upon application. While 85% are church members, only an estimated 5% attend church weekly.

37% of the labour force works in the public sector and 22% in industry (which is overwhelmingly private). While the country is more than 80% self-sufficient in agriculture, only 4% of people work in that area. Industrial growth is mainly concentrated in engineering chemicals and forestry.

Since the Second World War immigration of roughly 700,000 has accounted for more than half of the population growth. About 1 in 10 people was born abroad or has at least one foreign-born parent. In 1989 the largest categories of foreign residents were Finnish (124,000), Yugoslavian (39,600), Iranian (35,100), Norwegian (35,000), Danish (28,000), Turkish (24,100), Chilean (19,000), Polish (14,700) and German (12,000). There are also 15,000–17,000 Sami (Lapp) people in Sweden (roughly 0.2% of the population).

IMMIGRATION AND RESIDENCE RIGHTS

During the 1970s and 1980s much tougher restrictions were introduced covering those looking for work who had no family or other ties in Sweden. Only citizens of Denmark, Finland, Iceland and Norway can settle in Sweden without residence permits. Others coming to work or study must have permits before arriving.

In 1989 only 160 citizens from non-Nordic countries who came to Sweden to work were granted permanent residence permits. As a result political refugees now account for a larger proportion of recent immigrants. In 1989 24,900 people were granted residence on refugee or similar grounds, an increase of 55% on the previous year.

Qualification for citizenship is normally 5 years' residence (2 for citizens of other Nordic countries). Foreigners who marry Swedes do not automatically become citizens. 'Aliens' living in Sweden have the same rights to education, state benefits and so on, but may only vote and run for office if they have lived there for 3 years.

EQUAL RIGHTS

The Swedish constitution safeguards against discrimination on the grounds of sex. Overall responsibility for equality lies with the Minister of Equality Affairs (who is also the Deputy Minister of Public Administration). The Equality Affairs Division develops and co-ordinates policy, and initiates practical measures to improve the conditions of working women. The Council on Equality Issues, which includes representatives of women's groups, political parties, trade unions and employers, acts as an advisory body. There is also a Commission for Research on Equality Between Men and Women.

The Office of the Equal Opportunities Ombudsperson works to promote equality in employment, but its main function is to ensure compliance with the 1980 Equal Opportunities Act. There is also an Ombud against Ethnic Discrimination.

BIRTH, LIFE AND DEATH

Breakdown of population by sex and age group (1000s) (1989)

	all		women		men		% of women in age group
	no	%	no	%	no	%	
0–14	1,508.1	17.8	734.7	17.2	773.4	18.5	48.7
15–24	1,183.0	14.0	577.1	13.5	605.9	14.5	48.8
25–39	1,745.1	20.6	852.6	19.9	892.6	21.4	48.9
40–59	2,078.8	24.6	1,028.6	24.0	1,050.1	25.1	49.5
60–74	1,278.7	15.1	679.2	15.9	599.5	14.4	53.1
75+	665.2	7.9	410.8	9.6	254.4	6.1	61.8
all	8,458.9	100.0	4,283.0	100.0	4,175.9	100.0	50.6

Source: data from The Swedish Institute

Population by county (December 1990)

Stockholms län	1,641,669
Uppsalas län	268,835
Södermanlands län	255,636
Östergötlands län	403,011
Jönköpings län	308,290
Kronobergs län	177,882
Kalmars län	241,102
Gotlands län	57,108
Blekinges län	150,564
Kristianstads län	289,278
Malmöhus län	779,309
Hallands län	254,725
Göteborgs o. Bohus län	739,945
Älvsborgs län	441,391
Skaraborgs län	276,830
Värmlands län	283,110
Örebros län	272,513
Västmanlands län	258,487
Kopparbergs län	289,067
Gävleborgs län	289,294
Västernorrlands län	261,155
Jämtlands län	135,726
Västerbottens län	251,968
Norrbottens län	263,735
total	**8,590,630**

Source: *Europa World Year Book 1990* (31st edition)

Births and deaths per 1,000 population

birth rate (1988)	13.3
death rate (1988)	11.5
infant mortality per 1,000 live births (1988)	6.0
marriage rate (1989)	4.9
life expectancy (women) (1990)	80.1
life expectancy (men) (1990)	74.2
fertility rate per woman (1990)	2.0

Source: data from *Demographic Statistics 1990* (Eurostat); the Swedish Institute

Men lost the legal right to hit their wives in 1864

Women have had equal inheritance rights since 1845. Swedish family law treats women and men equally in marriage, and protects the financially weaker partner after divorce or death. 80% of all cohabiting couples were married in 1989.

A couple without children under 16 are entitled to a divorce if both agree. In other cases there is a compulsory 6-month deliberation period. Although children may only live with one parent after divorce, both parents have equal legal responsibility unless they request otherwise. Parents who do not live with their children must pay maintenance according to their means.

65% of all weddings take place in churches

In 1987, 50% of children were born outside of marriage. 81% of children under 18 live with both parents and 12% with a lone parent, mainly the mother. Married couples, heterosexual couples living together and single people are entitled to adopt children, though in practice it is reportedly extremely difficult for single people to adopt.

LESBIAN RIGHTS

Same-sex relationships were illegal until 1944. A common age of consent was introduced in 1978. Under a 1987 law, businesses are prohibited from discriminating on the grounds of a person's 'homosexual inclinations'. Making insulting remarks about a person's sexual orientation is also a criminal offence.

The 1987 Homosexual Cohabitees Act legally recognises gay and lesbian relationships, and gives cohabitees equal rights to inheritance, taxation and property rights. Individual gays and lesbians, but not same-sex couples, can adopt children. Sex education in schools must present homosexuality as a positive lifestyle. In 1990 the government gave £100,000 in grants to lesbian and gay organisations.

The foreign partners of lesbians and gay men in long-term relationships have the right of residence. Cohabitees must apply for permits before going to Sweden, making it clear they are eligible for residence because of a loving lesbian or gay relationship. Previously lesbians and gays at risk of persecution because of their sexual orientation were granted similar status to refugees, but the rules were tightened in 1990 and in practice this has stopped.

Lesbians are not allowed to marry, but the government is considering introducing a 'registered partnership' along the same lines as Denmark, which would give homosexual couples the same legal rights as married couples.

The practice of restricting adoption means it is virtually impossible for lesbian couples to adopt, but the Swedish Federation for Gay and Lesbian Rights reports that more and more lesbian women are conceiving children through self-insemination with sperm donated from a gay male friend, and with joint custody of the child.

WOMEN AND HEALTH CARE

All Swedish residents (excluding the self-employed who pay into a separate scheme for all health and other state benefits) are covered by the national health insurance scheme, which provides medical and dental care, sickness and parental benefits, pharmaceuticals and other services. Payment is required for medical or dental care, or hospital treatment. Examples of 1990 fees include SEK105 a day for hospital treatment, SEK70 to see a doctor and a maximum of SEK75 for a prescription. More than half of all visits to doctors (53%) take place in hospitals. 30% are to district doctors and 17% to private doctors.

76% of 1 year olds had been immunised in 1987. In 1988 there was 1 doctor for every 380 people.

Major indicators for women's health (1987)

maternal deaths (all causes) per 100,000 live births	4.78
maternal deaths (abortion) per 100,000 live births	0.00
ratio of abortions to 1,000 live births (all ages) (1986)	324.90
% of all live births to mothers under 20	3.11
% of all live births to mothers aged 35+	11.64
deaths from cancer of the cervix (age 0–64) per 100,000 women	3.05
deaths from malignant neoplasm female breast (age 0–64) per 100,000 women	15.56
deaths from trachea/bronchus/lung cancer (age 0–64) per 100,000 women	7.67
deaths from trachea/bronchus/lung cancer (age 0–64) per 100,000 men	14.70
deaths from diseases of the circulatory system (age 0–64) per 100,000 women	31.61
deaths from diseases of the circulatory system (age 0–64) per 100,000 men	108.23
deaths from suicide and self-inflicted injury per 100,000 women	10.16
deaths from suicide and self-inflicted injury per 100,000 men	24.75

Source: data from Health for All 2000 Indicator Presentation System (World Health Organisation Regional Office For Europe)

Abortion and contraception: Available on request up to 12 weeks on consultation with a doctor, between 12 and 18 weeks on consultation with a doctor and a counsellor (though in practice counselling takes place in less than half of cases), and after 18 weeks with the approval of the National Board of Health and Welfare. Approval may not be granted after the 18-week limit if the foetus is viable. Although the Act only applies to Swedish citizens and residents, permission to have an abortion may be granted in special circumstances to foreigners. Abortion, which cost SEK105 in 1990 (standard charge for hospital treatment), is freely available and there are no illegal abortions.

Contraception was legalised in 1938. Family planning legislation from the mid 1970s, which includes the Abortion Act and the Sterilisation Act, aims to allow women to decide freely the number and spacing of children, and to give every child the right to be wanted.

Family planning is state funded through the county councils. Consultation (at maternity clinics, doctors' surgeries, two special clinics for sexual information and about 130 clinics for young people), diaphragms and IUDs are free. Condoms and spermicides may be dispensed free, and oral contraceptives are subsidised. Midwives are trained to give contraceptive advice and carry out about 70% of public health consultations on contraception.

Anyone who is over 25 and a Swedish citizen or legal resident can be sterilised on request. Sterilisation is not common as a method of birth control. Around two-thirds of sterilisations are performed on women.

PARENTAL PAY, LEAVE AND BENEFITS (1989–90)

Maternity and parental leave and pay: A total of 450 days of parental benefit can be shared between parents. It must be used before the child's eighth birthday or the end of the first year of school and is not paid for children over the age of 10. Pregnant women qualify for benefit from 60 days before the expected birth. Adoptive and foster parents qualify for parental benefit, which is paid at roughly 90% of income for the first 360 days, then at a basic flat rate (SEK60 in March 1990) for 3 months. The final 3 months is unpaid. In addition to being shared between parents, the benefit can be used for part-time working so that the parent receives a combination of pay and benefit; in most cases it is the mother who takes parental leave. Proposed changes would extend the period to 18 months at 90% of normal earnings. In 1989, only 1 in 5 of fathers took parental benefit during the child's first year (taking an average of 41 days).

'Women's pay' was abolished in 1960 when women won the right to equal pay for equal work

Paternity leave: In addition to parental leave, fathers are entitled to 10 days' benefit which can be taken up to 60 days after the mother returns from hospital. Benefit is extended to 20 days for twins or the adoption of 2 children. 72% of fathers take paternity leave, using an average of 9 days.

Reduced hours: Since 1979 parents of small children have the right to a 6-hour working day.

Time off to look after sick children: Temporary parental benefit is paid to parents, adoptive parents and guardians when a child is sick, for up to 90 days a year for each child up to the age of 12. In cases of severe illness or disability this is paid up to the age of 16. In practice this provision is shared equally between mothers and fathers.

Other leave: Parents of children aged 4–12 receive 2 days' leave on parental benefit for each child every year, for visits to the child's school, or for parental education. Both parents can use this benefit at the same time.

CHILD-CARE PROVISION (1989)

0–6 year olds: 58% were cared for outside the home in 1989, most in municipal day-care centres (32%) and by municipal childminders (17%) with only 9% in private care. 42% were cared for by parents: 17% by mothers or fathers on parental leave, 9% by a parent working from home, 9% by couples who are employed/studying, 5% by a parent who is a municipal childminder and 1% by a parent who is unemployed. Just over 98% of all 6 year olds have a place in a part-time group or day-care centre.

Primary school (7 years up): Compulsory schooling is 9 years from the age of 7. The school year runs from August to June. In 1988 the pupil to teacher ratio in primary schools was 16:1.

Outside school hours care: Leisure time centres (fritidshem) are open before and after school and during the school holidays. In 1989 places were available for 45% of 7–9 year olds and 7% of 10–12 year olds. Under 'home language support' all children who speak a language other than Swedish at home are offered instruction in that language (about 60 languages are offered). Municipalities receive state subsidies for pre-school children for up to 4 hours' home language support a week (though not for children who attend pre-school groups, which operate only in Swedish).

Care for sick children: The Social Services Act entitles children in hospital to play activities corresponding to those offered in pre-school or leisure time centres.

Contributions to child-care costs including tax relief: Fees paid by parents account for 11%–15% of child-care places depending on income. Pre-school and part-time groups for 6 year olds are free. State subsidies range from 13% of part-time group costs to 44% of day-care centre costs. Municipal authorities pay the remaining costs of child care, ranging from 44% of day-care centres to 87% of part-time groups.

STATE BENEFITS (1989–90)

Pensions: Basic old age pension plus an income-related supplementary pension (funded by employers through the state) is paid to everyone from the age of 65, the normal retirement age for both women and men. These two pensions amount to two-thirds of average real earnings during the pensioner's 15 best paid years. However a growing number of people are using private pensions to supplement their state pensions which are increasingly being seen as inadequate. In 1984 55% of women pensioners lived on the basic state pension compared with 9% of men.

Housing benefits: Low-income families and pensioners are paid housing allowances.

Unemployment: Most Swedish workers have unemployment insurance through their trade unions. Benefits can be up to 90% of previous income, or a daily maximum of SEK495 (1990). Unemployment benefit cannot be claimed for more than 300 days in a row, though the limit rises to 450 days for those aged 55–64. Those who are not covered by a union insurance scheme receive a smaller state benefit of

SEK174 a day. Unemployment benefit is taxed.

Sickness benefits: Paid by health insurance at 90% of income up to a ceiling.

Child allowances: SEK5,820 per child per year (March 1990) plus a supplementary allowance for three or more children.

WOMEN AND EMPLOYMENT

Equality: The 1980 Equal Opportunities Act forbids discrimination on the grounds of sex and requires employers to promote equality at work, within specific planned targets. However, in practice, most active measures to promote equality at work are covered by trade union agreements. The ban on discrimination does not apply if the employer can show a decision was made to promote equality in the workplace or in other cases of special interest. Employers who fail to comply with the Act can be made to pay compensation. Individuals pursuing cases of discrimination receive legal help, either from their trade unions or the government.

Women in employment (1989)

	women		men	
	no (1000s)	%	no (1000s)	%
labour force participation	2,057.0	85.0	2,251.0	90.4
employed	2,030.0	83.9	2,221.0	89.2
employees who are part time	837.0	41.2	137.0	6.2
employees who are				
self-employed	104.0	5.1	289.0	13.0
unemployed	22.6	1.1	24.8	1.1
% of total unemployed by sex	–	47.7	–	52.3

Source: data from *Women and Men in Sweden – Equality of the Sexes 1990* (Statistics Sweden)

Employment by industrial sector (1989)

	women		men		women as % of workforce
	no (1000s)	%	no (1000s)	%	
agriculture and forestry	10	1	38	2	21
all private sector	872	43	1,544	76	36
construction	17	1	197	10	8
transport and communications	36	2	103	5	26
mining and manufacturing	273	13	683	34	29
banking and insurance	128	6	157	8	45
commerce, hotels and catering	285	14	270	13	51
other services	123	6	96	5	56
all public sector	1,154	57	489	24	70
teaching and health care	932	46	200	10	82
admin and emergency services	99	5	104	5	49
transport and communications	57	3	87	4	40
other public services	66	3	98	5	40
total	2,026	100	2,033	100	50

Source: data from *Women and Men in Sweden – Equality of the Sexes 1990* (Statistics Sweden)

Statutory rights: All workers have statutory paid holidays of 5 weeks.

Women spend 15 hours more than men on household work and child care and 4 hours less on repairs per week, a household study found in 1984–85

Part-time work: In 1987, 85.9% of part-time workers were women. They have the same rights as full-time workers.

Average earnings: In 1988 women's average earned income was 68.9% that of men's. In the civil service women's average pay compared with men's rose from 80% in 1973 to 91% in 1985; in municipal councils it rose from 74% to 87% in the same period; but in county councils in 1985 women's average pay was 75% of men's (a gap largely accounted for through job segregation).

In the private sector between 1973 and 1985, women non-manual workers' pay rose from 63% to 73% of men's pay, and from 84% to 91% for women manual workers.

Working mothers: In 1986 85.6% of women with a child under 7 belonged to the labour force.

Taxation: Uniform tax allowances of SEK6,720 for each child are granted until the child is 16.

Occupations: 58% of women work in the 30 most common occupations for women compared with 40% of men in their most common occupations.

Most common occupations by sex (1985)

women	%
1 secretaries and typists	89.5
2 nursing assistants	93.8
3 shop assistants	76.0
4 cleaners	89.0
5 children's nurses	96.8
6 home-care workers	97.7
7 accountants and cashiers	98.5
8 kitchen assistants	91.6
9 nurses	94.1
10 class teachers	80.6

Most common occupations by sex (1985)

men	%
1 mechanical engineers and technicians	96.6
2 fitter-assemblers and repairers	98.5
3 farmers and foresters	73.1
4 drivers of motor vehicles and trams	97.3
5 salespeople and purchasers	85.5
6 architects, building technicians	93.2
7 carpenters	99.6
8 machine tool operators	89.8
9 stock and store workers	80.8
10 electricians (machine operation and installation)	98.4

Source: data from *Women and Men in Sweden – Equality of the sexes 1990* (Statistics Sweden)

WOMEN IN TRADE UNIONS

85% of non-manual and 90% of manual workers belong to trade unions.

Women's participation in the main trade union organisations (1990)

	PTK	MIA	KTK	KA	TCO-S	SF
% of women members	40	21	82	81	60	35
% of women delegates to congress	33	9	58	48	43	16
% women on exec committee	0	15	30	62	24	19

PTK = Federation of Salaried Employees in Industry and Service
MIA = Metalworkers' Union
KTK = Federation of Salaried Local Government Employees
KA = Municipal Workers' Union
TCO-S = The Section for State Employees
SF = National Union of State Employees

Source: data from *Women and Men in Sweden – Equality of the Sexes 1990* (Statistics Sweden)

WOMEN AND POLITICS

Women won the right to vote in both local and parliamentary elections in 1919. The first woman was elected to parliament in 1921 and the first woman cabinet member appointed in 1947.

In 1921 Kerstin Hesselgren was the first woman elected to parliament

Electoral turn-out is high for women (87% in the 1988 general election) and men (84%). The number of women MPs has doubled since 1971, with 38% of parliamentary seats and 35% of standing (government) committee seats held by women. One-third of the 21 members of the government are women, and women ministers have responsibility for labour, immigration, equality, environment and energy, foreign trade, international aid and justice.

Women in parliament (after 1988 election)

party	no of seats	no of women	% of women
Moderate	66	18	27
Centre	42	16	38
Liberal	44	19	43
Social Democratic Labour	156	63	40
Left Party Communist	21	8	38
Green Party	20	9	45
total	349	133	38

Source: data from *Women and Men in Sweden – Equality of the sexes 1990* (Statistics Sweden)

42% of county councillors and 34% of municipal councillors are women. There are 25 county administrations and 284 municipal districts.

WOMEN AND EDUCATION

From 1980 the law has required universities to monitor the gender balance of students and staff and to draw up proposals to correct imbalance.

Sex education in schools became compulsory in 1956

Courses in women's studies are available at the Universities of Göteburg, Linköping, Luleå, Lund, Stockholm, Umeå and Uppsala, and at Örebro College.

% of women students in higher education (1987–88)

undergraduate studies

technical professions	24
administrative, economic and social work professions	55
health professions	81
teaching professions	78
information, communication and cultural professions	62
other courses	61
postgraduate training	31

Source: data from *Higher Education in Sweden – Fact Sheets on Sweden,* April 1990 (The Swedish Institute)

Overall in 1987–88, women made up 58% of enrolled undergraduates. 35% of students who complete compulsory (9 years) and upper secondary schooling go on to higher education. Young people who continue their education after the age of 16 receive study allowances. At university level funding is by means-tested study assistance, made up of a grant (29% of total) and a loan. The loan must be repaid within six months of a student receiving the final assistance payment, and instalments are 4% of annual income. Interest rates on student loans are fixed by the government.

Visiting students must have a residence permit before arriving in Sweden, and must be prepared to complete a 1-year course in Swedish in addition to their chosen course.

WOMEN AND DETENTION

In 1988, 4.6% of prisoners were women; 3.5% were minors and young adults and 22.3% were foreigners.

Women as a % of those found guilty of crimes (1989)

Crimes against the person	7
murder/manslaughter	11
assault	7
causing another's death	16
rape	1
Crimes against property	23
shoplifting	41
Crimes against the general public	28
Crimes against the state	8

Source: data from *Women and Men in Sweden – Equality of the Sexes 1990* (Statistics Sweden)

SOURCES

Abortion Laws in Europe, Planned Parenthood in Europe, Vol 18 No 1, Spring 1989 (Supplement, amended April 1990) (International Planned Parenthood Federation, Europe Region); *Demographic Statistics 1990* (Eurostat); *Economic Equality for Swedish Women – Current Situation and Trends* (Inga Persson-Tanimura – Tvärsnitt No 1, 1988); *Equality in the Labour Market* (National Labour Market Board 1989); *Europa World Year Book 1990* (31st edition); *Fact Sheets on Sweden* (The Swedish Institute) [Child Care in Sweden, Equality Between Men and Women in Sweden, General Facts on Sweden, The Swedish Population, Primary and Secondary Education, Higher Education in Sweden, Adult Education in Sweden, Geography of Sweden, Swedish Government, Labor Relations in Sweden, Swedish Labor Market Policy, Immigrants in Sweden, Family Planning in Sweden, The Swedish Economy, Health and Medical Care in Sweden]; Health for All 2000 Indicator Presentation System (World Health Organisation Regional Office For Europe); *Immigration for gays and lesbians – Sweden and immigration* (RFSL); *Les Actions Positives en Faveur des Femmes en Europe Occidentale* (Institut Syndical Europeen); *On Sweden* (Stig Hadenius and Ann Lindgren – The Swedish Institute); *Out In Europe* (Peter Tatchell, for Channel 4 Television); *Parental Benefit in Sweden* (Embassy of Sweden, London); *Pocket World in Figures* (The Economist); *Prison*

Information Bulletin June 1990 (Council of Europe); RFSL,
Stockholm; Riksförbundet för Sexuell Upplysing (Swedish
Association for Sex Education); The Swedish Institute; *Women
and Men in the Nordic Countries* (Christina Österberg
and Birgitta Hedman, Nordic Council of Ministers); *Women and
Men in Sweden – Equality of the Sexes 1990* (Statistics Sweden);
*Women's Studies and Research on Women in the Nordic
Countries* (ed. Mie Berg Simonson and Mona Eliasson for
Nordic Forum)

LETTERS FROM SWEDEN

Inga Britt Larsson, Swedish Trade Union Confederation

We are sometimes criticised for not having special
rules to protect women, but we have chosen another
way and have general rules for both women and men.
In Sweden women and men have the same rights and
obligations on the labour market. In many countries
there is a prohibition of nightwork for women in
industry. In Sweden that was removed in 1978.
We have a general prohibition of nightwork and, if
needed, the employer must apply for an exemption
after having negotiated with the trade union. There
is only one special exception made for women in the
Working Hours Act – women of fertile age (under 45)
must not work with lead.

All professions are open to women except smoke-
helmeted firefighter and deep sea diver. Regarding
these professions, researchers maintain that women's
lungs do not have the same capacity of absorbing
oxygen under high pressure. The same thing was said
about female war pilots, but in that field the first
woman has been employed recently.

The parental insurance and parental leave are very
flexible. You are also entitled by law to have time
off work for study, for instance to improve your
education or attend training courses. You can be away
from your job for several years and still keep it. This is
very important for women, particularly since there is
financial support from the government for
educational leave.

Charlotte Cederschiöld, MP for Stockholm City of the Moderate Coalition Party

All measures encourage women to work, which is necessary if the family is to have a normal standard of living. It is almost impossible to live on one salary. A few years ago the newspapers showed that even the prime minister couldn't support a family of three to four children if his wife were not gainfully employed. I normally have time to sleep three to four hours a night and so has my husband. We have been working for years like this. What many Swedish women long for is not more work but less work, a chance to spend some time with the family.

The percentage of sick leave for women has risen by 50% in the 1980s. Swedish women want to keep their independence, which probably is more developed than in many Western countries. They want to have their work, but they also need more freedom. It is important not to forget the freedom of choice and the fact that family-raising takes time. As I see it there ought to be economic support of some kind for the time women give to raise new taxpayers.

ADDRESSES

Embassy of Sweden, 11 Montagu Place, London W1H 2AL. Tel: 071 724 2101

National Immigration and Naturalisation Board, Statens Invandrarverk, PO Box 6113, 600 06 Norrköping. Tel: (46 11) 15 60 00

Jämo (Equal Opportunities Ombudsman), Birger Jarls Torg 7, Riddarholmen, 103 33 Stockholm. Tel: (46 8) 24 36 90

Swedish Institute, PO Box 7434, 103 91 Stockholm

Riksförbundet för Sexuell Upplysing (family planning), Rosenlundsgatan 13, Box 17006, 104 62 Stockholm. Tel: (46 8) 668 09 40

Landsorganisationen i Sverige (Swedish Trade Union Confederation), Barnhusgt 18, 105 53 Stockholm. Tel: (46 8) 796 25 00

RFSL (lesbian and gay rights), PO Box 350, 101 24 Stockholm. Tel: (46 8) 736 6217

Switzerland

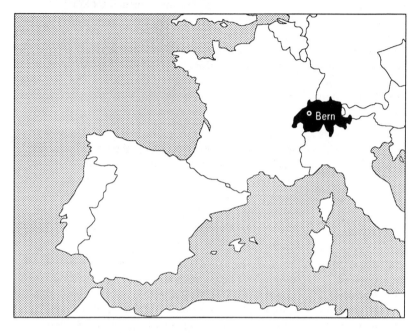

- **Population** 6.67 million, 51.1% female
- **Area** 41,293 sq km
- **Population density** 161.6 people sq km
- **GDP 1988** Swiss francs 270 billion (£114.1 billion)
- **GDP per capita** £17,204
- **GDP per capita in purchasing power parity** (UK=100) 132
- **Public spending as % of GNP:** defence 1.9% (1986); education 4.8% (1986); health 6.8% (1987)
- **Consumer price index** 1980 = 100; 1989 = 137
- **Currency is the Swiss franc** 1989 £1 = SFR2.5; US$1 = SFR1.55

Sophie Taueber-Arp, a founder of the Dada movement who died in 1943, became the first woman to appear on a Swiss bank note in the mid-1980s

The Swiss Confederation is made up of 20 cantons and 6 half-cantons. Legislative power is held by the 2-chamber Federal Assembly, made up of the 46-member council of states and the 200-member national council. The former has 2 members for each canton and 1 for each half-canton who are elected for 3 to 4 years. National council members are elected for 4 years by proportional representation. The assembly elects the president, who is head of state for 1 year at a time.

The cantons are autonomous and hold all power not specifically laid down as a federal responsibility. Each has its own constitution and government. National and canton-wide referenda are held to decide a variety of issues. In some cantons all legislation must be accepted by a majority of voters. A national referendum must be held if it is asked for in a petition of 50,000 voters.

On 14 June 1991 an estimated 500,000 Swiss women at home and work went on strike in support of equality. Four men set up an emergency open-air ironing service in Bern

Since almost two-thirds of Switzerland is uninhabitable, being mountains, lakes or forest, the population density in inhabited areas is approximately 250 people per sq km. In 1980 65% of the population spoke German as their first language, 18.4% French, 9.8% Italian, 0.8% Rhaeto-Romansch and 6% another language. 47.6% were Roman Catholic, 44.3% Protestant, 3.2% followers of other religions, and 4.9% without religion.

Highest incomes in 1989 compared with a national index of 100 were in Zug (170), Basel City (146) and Geneva (129). Lowest were in Appenzell Inner-Rhoden (75), Valais and Obwalden (both 76).

IMMIGRATION AND RESIDENCE RIGHTS

Foreigners married to Swiss citizens can apply for citizenship after 3 years of marriage and 5 years' residence. Marriage partners qualify for permanent residence permits immediately. Otherwise, permits are granted after 10 years' residence (5 for citizens of Belgium, Denmark, Finland, France, Iceland, Ireland, Norway, Sweden and the UK).

In August 1989 the public service union (SSP) launched a campaign against sexual harassment, estimating that 20,000 women in Switzerland each year lose their jobs because of it

A limited number of temporary residence permits are issued each year. They must be renewed every 12 months. Short-term residence permits for stays of up to 12 months are granted for specific projects, including training.

Temporary work permits are applied for by prospective employers, who must show that vacancies cannot otherwise be filled. If granted, a temporary residence permit is issued to cover the employee's spouse and children, though partners are not usually allowed to work. For the first year foreign residents may not normally move to another canton or change jobs or employers.

At the end of 1989 there were over 1 million foreign residents in Switzerland, accounting for 16% of the population. 72.4% of these were permanent foreign residents, 25.2% foreign residents with annual permits, and 2.4% were international officials.

EQUAL RIGHTS

The constitution guarantees the principle of equality for all citizens, and specifically gives a mandate to the legislature to ensure equal rights between women and men. It makes no reference to positive action.

The Bureau for Equality Between Women and Men, which is part of the federal Culture Office, was set up in 1988. It is responsible for implementing equality policy and advises the federal and cantonal governments. The federal Commission for Women's Affairs has no specific duties but works to formulate policy.

BIRTH, LIFE AND DEATH

In 1989 17.8% of live births were to foreign residents, who also accounted for 6.1% of deaths. 68.8% of marriages were between Swiss women and men, 7.7% between Swiss women and foreign men, 14.9% between foreign women and Swiss men, and 8.5% between foreign women and men.

Population and population density by canton (1989)

region	area sq km	population	% change in pop 1988–89	pop density per sq km
Zurich	1,729	1,144,900	0.3	662.2
Berne	6,049	937,400	0.5	155.0
Lucerne	1,492	314,800	1.0	211.0
Uri	1,076	33,500	-0.1	31.1
Schwyz	908	108,100	1.6	119.1
Obwalden	491	28,300	1.5	57.6
Nidwalden	276	32,000	1.3	115.9
Glarus	685	37,300	0.8	54.5
Zug	239	84,000	0.7	351.5
Fribourg	1,670	204,300	2.1	122.3
Solothurn	791	223,500	0.9	282.6
Basel (city)	37	190,400	-0.3	5,145.9
Basel (county)	428	229,000	0.4	535.0
Schaffhausen	298	71,000	0.9	238.3
Appenzell Ausser-Rhoden	243	50,900	1.1	209.5
Appenzell Inner-Rhoden	72	13,500	1.3	78.5
St Gallen	2,014	414,700	1.0	205.9
Graubünden	7,106	169,000	0.7	23.8
Aargau	1,405	490,400	1.3	349.0
Thurgau	1,013	201,600	1.6	199.0
Ticino	2,811	283,000	0.9	100.7
Vaud	3,218	572,000	1.2	177.8
Valais	5,226	243,700	1.9	46.6
Neuchâtel	797	158,600	0.7	199.0
Geneva	282	373,000	0.4	1,322.7
Jura	837	65,000	0.4	77.7
Switzerland	**41,293**	**6,673,900**	**0.8**	**161.6**

Source: data from *Statistical Data on Switzerland 1991* (Swiss Federal Statistical Office)

Age structure of the population (1987)

	women (%)	men (%)	all (%)
0–19	24	26	25
20–39	30	32	31
40–64	30	30	30
65–79	12	10	11
80+	4	2	3
total	100	100	100

Source: data from *Statistisches Jahrbuch der Schweiz 1990/Annuaire statistique de la Suisse 1990* (Bundesamt für Statistik/l'Office fédéral de la statistique)

Breakdown of population by sex and age group (1000s) (1988)

	all		women		men		% of women in age group
	no	%	no	%	no	%	
0–14	1,221.6	19.2	595.9	18.3	625.7	20.1	48.8
15–24	995.2	15.6	487.4	15.0	507.8	16.3	49.0
25–39	1,468.1	23.1	719.7	22.1	748.4	24.0	49.0
40–59	1,515.3	23.8	769.6	23.7	745.7	23.9	50.8
60–74	811.2	12.7	449.2	13.8	362.0	11.6	55.4
75+	354.6	5.6	229.4	7.1	125.2	4.0	64.7
all	6366.0	100.0	3251.2	100.0	3114.8	100.0	51.1

Source: data from *Femmes et hommes: faits, perspectives, utopies* (Rapport de la Commission fédérale pour les questions féminines)

Births, deaths, marriages and divorces per 1,000 population

	1980	1987	1988	1989
birth rate	11.6*	11.7	12.2	12.2
% of births outside marriage	5.4*	6.2	6.5	–
infant mortality per 1,000 live births	9.1	6.8	6.8	7.3
marriage rate	5.6*	6.6	6.9	6.8
divorce rate	1.8*	1.8	1.9	1.9
life expectancy (women)	78.8	–	80.7	81.0
life expectancy (men)	72.3	–	73.9	73.9
death rate	9.4*	9.1	9.2	9.2

* 1981

Sources: data from *Demographic Statistics 1990* (Eurostat); *Statistical Data on Switzerland 1991* (Swiss Federal Statistical Office); *Statistisches Jahrbuch der Schweiz 1990/Annuaire statistique de la Suisse 1990* (Bundesamt für Statistik/l'Office fédéral de la statistique)

LESBIAN RIGHTS

Male homosexuality was illegal until between 1937 and 1942 (the Swiss cantons legislate separately). The common age of consent is now 16. The government has recently repealed a law against homosexual seduction of a 16 to 20 year old, which was used against lesbians and gay men. Lesbian and gay sex with someone under 16 will not be subject to prosecution provided there is no more than 3 years' age difference between the partners. Homosexual prostitution, which unlike heterosexual prostitution, was illegal, has also been legalised.

WOMEN AND HEALTH CARE

Apart from hospital treatment, health care is dominated by the private sector. Treatment is paid for through health insurance, which covers hospital expenses up to 720 days. Cantons regulate private doctors' fees.

62.1% of homes in Switzerland have 4 or more rooms

In 1989 the federal tribunal overturned the canton of Vaud, where legislation did not allow in-vitro fertilisation for unmarried couples, saying this infringed personal liberty.

In 1988 there was 1 doctor for every 401 people.

Major indicators for women's health (1989)

maternal deaths (all causes) per 100,000 live births	3.70
maternal deaths (abortion) per 100,000 live births	0.00
% of all live births to mothers under 20 (1986)	1.97
% of all live births to mothers aged 35+	8.61
deaths from cancer of the cervix (age 0–64) per 100,000 women (1988)	2.28
deaths from malignant neoplasm female breast (age 0–64) per 100,000 women	19.42
deaths from trachea/bronchus/lung cancer (age 0–64) per 100,000 women	6.16
deaths from trachea/bronchus/lung cancer (age 0–64) per 100,000 men	27.99
deaths from diseases of the circulatory system (age 0–64) per 100,000 women	22.43
deaths from diseases of the circulatory system (age 0–64) per 100,000 men	76.78
deaths from suicide and self-inflicted injury per 100,000 women	11.96
deaths from suicide and self-inflicted injury per 100,000 men	30.99

Source: data from Health for All 2000 Indicator Presentation System (World Health Organisation Regional Office For Europe)

Abortion and contraception: Available until the foetus is viable, if there is a risk to the woman's physical or mental health. The consent of a second doctor with a special permit is required. Charges for abortions depend on health insurance cover. Most abortions are carried out on psychiatric grounds. There are wide regional differences in services available.

PARENTAL PAY, LEAVE AND BENEFITS

Although the law offers some employment protection to women before and after childbirth, including

In the two months after the Chernobyl nuclear disaster, miscarriages in Ticino increased by 34% (to 114). Radiation in the south of the Alps was higher because of heavy rainfall

against dismissal and loss of holiday entitlement, there is no statutory right to maternity leave, as such.

Women who interrupt their employment because of maternity are treated on the same basis as employees who cannot work because of illness, accident, and legal or public duty. This places an obligation on an employer to pay compensation to employees equivalent to the loss of salary for a limited period, provided their period of employment has lasted for more than 3 months.

In practice industrial tribunals (tribunaux de prud'hommes) have established maximum periods of salary entitlement. In the early 1980s the 2 most important were Berner-Tabelle, which set entitlement at between 1 month in the second year of service and 4 months for service of between 10 and 14 years; and Zürcher-Skala, which set an alternative scale of 4 weeks after 2 years of service, 5 weeks after 3 years, 6 weeks after 4 years and so on.

CHILD-CARE PROVISION

0–6 years old: In the school year 1985–86 there were a total of 123,128 places in pre-school education, 598,48 of them for girls (48.6%). 15% of 4 year olds and 65.2% of 5 year olds had pre-school places. In 1989–90 this had risen to 24.9% of 4 year olds and 75% of 5 year olds.

Primary school (age 7 and up): Children begin primary school at age 7 and the school year runs from August/September to June/July.

STATE BENEFITS (1989–90)

Social security insurance is compulsory. Most western and northern European nationals who are insured in their own countries are covered by benefits through bilateral agreements.

Retirement pension: Normal retirement age is 62 for women and 65 for men. Pensions are made up of a benefit, based on insurance contributions, and a pension-fund payment. The benefit depends on earnings at retirement and number of contributions. In 1990 maximum benefits were SFR19,200 a year for a single person and SFR28,800 for a married couple. Pension fund payments increase with earnings up to a fixed maximum. The entire pension should equal 60% of earnings on retirement up to a maximum of SFR54,000 each year.

In 1991 the Swiss voted against introducing VAT. It is the only country in the world where taxation is decided directly by the electorate

Disability pension: Depending on the level of disability, a proportion of retirement pension (up to a full pension) is paid until the person qualifies for retirement pension.

Survivors' pensions: In 1990 pension benefits paid to widows ranged from a minimum of SFR7,680 to a maximum of SFR15,360. Orphans' benefits ranged from SFR3,140 to SFR11,520.

Child benefits: Family allowances are administered by cantons and funded by employers who pay contributions of 1.2% to 2.25% of their payrolls. Monthly payments depend on the age of the child and vary according to canton but are usually SFR100–200.

Unemployment benefit: Paid through insurance contributions as a daily allowance equal to 70% of insurable earnings (80% for married people) for 250 days. Maximum insurable earnings are SFR81,600.

WOMEN AND EMPLOYMENT

Statutory rights: There is no legal minimum wage. Annual paid leave is 4 weeks (5 weeks for those under the age of 20). Some collective agreements provide for 5 weeks for employees over the age of 50. Overtime is restricted to 260 hours a year.

Part-time work: Part-time workers do not have the same rights as full-time workers. For example, the right to accident insurance depends on working 12 hours a week.

Employment and unemployment (1989)

	% women	% men
economic activity rate	37.5	62.8
unemployment rate	0.6	0.4
all unemployed by sex	44.5	55.5

Source: data from *Statistical Data on Switzerland 1991* (Swiss Federal Statistical Office)

> Unemployment: Highest unemployment rates in 1989 were in cantons Ticino (1.5%), Basel city (1.4%) and Neuchâtel and Geneva (both 1%).

WOMEN IN TRADE UNIONS

> Overall 32% of workers are members of trade unions. Highest levels of union membership are in public administration (46%). In private-sector industry union membership averages 30%. Low levels of trade union membership among women are blamed on their higher level of home responsibilities. However, since 1975 the Société Suisse des Employés de Commerce has seen its proportional female membership grow from 24% to 31% in 1984. Among young members of the association the percentage of women increased from 30.5% in December 1977 to 37.6% in March 1985.

WOMEN AND POLITICS

> Women won the right to vote in parliamentary elections in 1971. The last all-male bastion cracked on 27 November 1989 when the council of Appenzell Rhodes-intérieures proclaimed itself, without discussion, in favour of introducing the right of women to vote.

> 15.9% of the Federal Assembly (made up of the national council and the council of states) are women.

Women in the national council (after the October 1991 election)

political party	total no of seats	no of seats held by women	% of seats held by women
Radical Democrats	44	5	11.4
Christian Democrats	36	4	11.1
Socialists	42	13	31.0
Swiss People's Party	25	3	12.0
Liberal-Democrats	10	1	10.0
Environmentalists	14	8	57.1
Landesring	6	1	16.7
Evangelical People's Party	3	0	0.0
Swiss Democrats	5	0	0.0
Automobile Party	8	0	0.0
Workers' Party	2	0	0.0
others	5	0	0.0
total	**200**	**35**	**17.5**

Source: data from the Swiss Embassy, London

Women in the council of states (after the October 1991 election)

political party	total no of seats	no of seats held by women	% of seats held by women
Radical Democrats	18	1	5.6
Christian Democrats	16	2	12.5
Socialists	3	0	0.0
Swiss People's Party	4	0	0.0
Liberal-Democrats	3	0	0.0
Landesring	1	1	100.0
others	1	0	0.0
total	**46**	**4**	**8.7**

Source: data from the Swiss Embassy, London

After the May 1990 canton elections, women won 419 (14%) of the 3,003 council seats. In 1989, 33 out of 100 elected deputies to the Geneva canton parliament were women, after the Association of Women's Rights launched a 'Vote for Women' campaign.

WOMEN AND EDUCATION

Girls and women as a % of pupils and students (1989–90)

pre-school education	48.5
compulsory education	48.7
secondary education	45.0
tertiary education	34.1
teacher training	72.4
higher vocational education	24.4
university	37.7

Source: data from *Elèves et étudiant-e-s – Année scolaire 1989/90* (Office fédéral de la statistique Suisse)

Women as a % of university and vocational training students (1989–90)

university	**37.7**
humanities and social sciences	44.5
pure and natural sciences	24.1
medicine and pharmacy	44.3
technical sciences	15.5
law school	**42.0**
professional federal law	38.6
other legal studies	58.7
vocational training	**42.0**
agriculture	27.7
engineering	8.7
technical studies	24.2
business and administration	66.8
transport	43.8
hotel trade and home economics	61.6
public health and hygiene	90.7
security and police	11.7
nursing and medical care	91.8
arts	55.9
welfare and social work	98.7
other professions	16.8

Source: data from *Elèves et étudiant-e-s – Année scolaire 1989/90* (Office fédéral de la statistique Suisse)

The proportion of women students is dramatically lower for the longest educational courses. Women accounted for 63.1% of students on courses of 1 year, 54.6% on courses of $2^{1}/_{2}$ to 3 years, but only 10.9% on courses of $3^{1}/_{2}$ to 4 years.

WOMEN AND DETENTION

In September 1988 women made up 5.6% of all prisoners, with minors (age 18) and young adults making up 3.8% and foreigners 36%.

SOURCES

Abortion Laws in Europe, Planned Parenthood in Europe, Vol 18 No 1, Spring 1989 (Supplement, amended April 1990); *Aide-mémoire concernant la protection des travailleuses en cas de maternité* (Office fédéral de l'industrie, des arts et métiers et du travail); *Annuaire statistique de la Suisse* 1990 (Bundesamt für statistik/Office Fédéral de la Statistique); *Demographic Statistics 1990* (Eurostat); *Doing Business in Switzerland* (Price Waterhouse); *Elèves et étudiant-e-s – Année scolaire 1989–90* (Office Fédéral de la Statistique Suisse); *Europa World Year Book 1990* (31st edition); *Femmes et hommes; faits, perspectives, utopies* (Rapport de la Commission fédérale pour les questions feminines); Frauenfragen 1/90; Health For All 2000 Indicator Presentation System (World Health Organisation Regional Office for Europe); *Les Actions Positives en Faveur des Femmes en Europe Occidentale* (Institut Syndical Europeen); OECD *Economic Surveys Switzerland 1990/1991* (OECD); *Out In Europe* (Peter Tatchell, for Channel 4 Television); *Pocket World in Figures* (The Economist); *Positive action and the constitutional and legislative hindrances to its implementation in the member states of the Council of Europe* (Council of Europe); *Prison Information Bulletin* June 1990 (Council of Europe); *Statistical Data on Switzerland 1991* (Swiss Federal Statistical Office); the Swiss Embassy, London; *Third World Guide 91/92* (Instituto del Tercer Mundo)

ADDRESSES

Embassy of Switzerland, 16/18 Montagu Place, London W1

Alliance de Sociétés Féminines Suisses, Altikofenstrasse 182, Postfach 101, 3048 Worblaufen. Tel: (41 31) 58 48 48

Schweizerischer Gewerkschaftsbund, Swiss Confederation of Trade Unions, Monbijoustr 61, 3007 Berne

LOS/OSL (Swiss organisation for lesbians), c/o La Maison, 30 av Peschier, 1206 Genève

United Kingdom

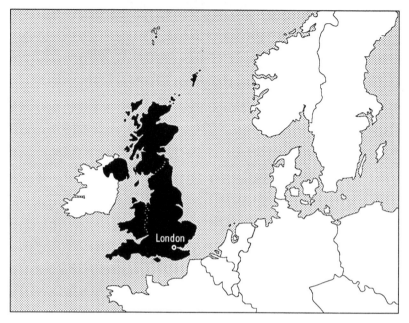

- **Population 56.9** million, 51.3% female
- **Area** 244,755 sq km
- **Population density** 233.2 people sq km
- **GDP 1988** £464 billion
- **GDP per capita** £8,976
- **GDP per capita in purchasing power parity** (UK=100) 100
- **Public spending as % of GNP:** defence 5.0% (1986); education 5.35% (1986); health 5.3% (1987)
- **Consumer price index** 1980 = 100; 1989 = 178
- **Currency is the pound.** 1989 £1 = US$0.62

The United Kingdom of Great Britain and Northern Ireland is an hereditary monarchy with the monarch as head of state. The parliament has 2 chambers – the House of Commons whose 650 members are elected for 5 years on single-member constituencies, and the House of Lords, which is made up of hereditary and life peers. The Lords can amend and delay legislation but cannot prevent any bill passed by the Commons. Executive power is held by the cabinet, which is led by the prime minister.

While the United Kingdom has no written constitution, it is regarded as having a number of constitutional principles. The right to vote and stand in elections is at age 18.

IMMIGRATION AND RESIDENCE RIGHTS

EC citizens do not require visas, but all visitors to the United Kingdom can be asked to show that they can find accommodation and maintain themselves during their stay. Visits are not normally for longer than 6 months.

The 1380 poll tax return for Oxford lists 12 trades out of a total of 93 which had women members, including: washerwomen, peddlers, shoemakers, tailors, innkeepers, brewers, net makers, chandlers, spinners and wool combers

Spanish and Portuguese citizens do not require work permits from 1 January 1993; all other EC citizens do not require them. Commonwealth citizens aged between 17 and 27 can come for a 'working holiday' of up to 2 years, provided they can show that their work is 'incidental to their holiday', that they will not have to rely on public funds, and that they can pay for their return journey. Public funds are defined as income support, family credit, housing benefit (see section on State Benefits) and the need to be rehoused as homeless.

Marriage partners and fiances/fiancees, dependent children, dependent parents and grandparents of EC nationals settled in the UK have residence rights. Children born from 1983 of someone born in the UK or who became a UK citizen before the child was born are automatically UK citizens and have residence rights. This also applies to childen who are Commonwealth citizens. Children born before 1983 can only inherit UK citizenship through their father, provided their parents were married.

Between 1985 and 1987 the UK had 1,785,000 foreign residents, 51.6% of them women. 42.9% of foreign residents were from other EC states (more than two-thirds of these from Ireland), 6.7% from non-EC European countries, 5.3% from African countries and 45% from other countries.

EQUAL RIGHTS

The UK has no constitution. However, the Sex Discrimination Act 1975 prohibits discrimination based on sex and marital status in employment. Positive action is confined to training programmes.

The Equal Opportunities Commission provides the institutional machinery for promoting equality between women and men. It co-ordinates information on equality issues and has numerous equality programmes including positive-action schemes.

BIRTH, LIFE AND DEATH

Breakdown of population by sex and age group (1000s) (1988)

	all		women		men		% of women in age group
	no	%	no	%	no	%	
0–14	10,754.3	18.9	5,236.3	17.9	5,518.0	19.9	48.7
15–24	9,069.5	15.9	4,436.0	15.2	4,633.5	16.7	48.9
25–39	12,200.7	21.4	6,068.0	20.8	6,132.7	22.1	49.7
40–59	13,163.3	23.1	6,604.5	22.6	6,558.8	23.6	50.2
60–74	7,995.8	14.0	4,351.1	14.9	3,644.7	13.1	54.4
75+	3,814.1	6.7	2,526.9	8.6	1,287.2	4.6	66.3
all	56,997.7	100.0	29,222.8	100.0	27,774.9	100.0	51.3

Source: data from *Demographic Statistics 1990* (Eurostat)

Population, population density and increase by region (1987)

region	pop	% of total pop	pop density per sq km	natural increase per 1,000	net migration per 1,000	total increase per 1,000
North	3,076.8	5.4	199.8	1.0	-2.1	-1.1
Yorks & Humberside	4,900.2	8.6	317.8	1.8	-1.7	0.2
East Midlands	3,942.1	6.9	252.2	2.4	3.2	5.6
East Anglia	2,013.7	3.5	160.2	2.0	9.0	11.0
South East	17,317.5	30.4	636.2	3.2	-0.2	3.1
South West	4,588.3	8.1	192.4	0.6	9.2	9.8
West Midlands	5,197.7	9.1	399.4	3.2	0.0	3.2
North West	6,370.3	11.2	869.0	1.9	-2.5	-0.6
Wales	2,836.2	5.0	136.6	1.4	4.0	5.4
Scotland	5,112.3	9.0	64.9	0.8	-2.5	-1.7
Northern Ireland	1,575.2	2.8	111.6	8.0	-2.6	5.3
United Kingdom	**56,930.3**	**100.0**	**233.2**	**2.3**	**0.6**	**2.9**

Source: data from *Demographic Statistics 1990* (Eurostat)

Births, deaths, marriages and divorces per 1,000 population

	1960	1970	1980	1985	1988
birth rate	17.6	16.3	13.4	13.3	13.8
% of births outside marriage	5.2	8.0	11.5	18.9	25.1
average age of mother at 1st birth	24.8	23.9	25.1	25.9	26.6
infant mortality per 1,000 live births	22.5	18.5	12.1	9.3	9.0
fertility rate per woman	2.7	2.4	1.9	1.8	1.8
marriage rate	7.5	8.5	7.4	6.9	6.9
average age at marriage (women)	25.2	24.6	26.5	27.3	28.1
average age at marriage (men)	28.1	27.0	29.2	30.2	30.7
divorce rate	0.5	1.1	2.8	3.1	2.9
life expectancy (women)	73.7	75.0	76.2	–	77.5*
life expectancy (men)	67.9	68.7	70.2	–	71.1*
death rate	11.6	11.8	11.8	11.9	11.4

* 1984–86

Source: data from *Demographic Statistics 1990* (Eurostat)

Marriage: Between 1971 and 1989 the proportion of all first marriages in England and Wales that were first marriages for both partners dropped from 79% to 63%.

Marital status in Great Britain (%) (1988)

	women aged 16+	men aged 16+	women aged 65+	men aged 65+
single	18	24	8	6
married	58	64	39	72
not married but living with a partner	4	4	–	–
widowed	14	4	50	20
divorced/separated	7	4	3	2

Source: data from *The Family Today* (Family Policy Studies Centre, Fact Sheet 1)

Northern Ireland has the highest birth rate in the EC with 16.5 live births for every 1,000 population

Single parents: In 1988 single parents headed 12% of households with a child aged 0–4 and with a child aged 5–9 (together with Denmark the highest level in the EC). 88.7% of lone parents were women. Divorced women were the largest single group (33%) followed by single mothers at 31.3%.

Main source of income for 1- and 2-parent families in Great Britain (%) (1987)

	1-parent families	2-parent families
earnings	27	86.0
maintenance	4	0.4
social security benefits	67	12.6
other	2	1.0

Source: data from *Family Finances* (Family Policy Studies Centre, Fact Sheet 4)

LESBIAN RIGHTS

The age of consent is 16 for lesbians and heterosexuals, compared with 21 for gay men. Male homosexuality was illegal until 1967 in England and Wales (1980 in Scotland and 1982 in Northern Ireland). Despite changes in the law, more gay men are being prosecuted for their sexuality than before the 1967 Sexual Offences Act. In individual judgements, lesbian and gay parents have been denied custody of their children on divorce.

Section 28 of the Local Government Act prohibits local authorities from 'intentionally promoting homosexuality' or promoting teaching of 'the acceptability of homosexuality as a pretended family relationship' in schools. The 1986 Sex Education Act says sex education lessons must encourage 'due regard to moral considerations and the value of family life'.

WOMEN AND HEALTH CARE

The National Health Service was established in 1946 to provide free health care for all residents. There are no fees for consultations with doctors, hospitals or other medical treatment though patients pay a standard charge for prescription drugs, unless they are under 16, aged 16–19 and in full-time education, women aged 60 and over (65 for men), pregnant women, mothers of a child aged less than 12 months, or receiving Income Support or Family Credit. The housebound and those with specified chronic diseases are also exempt from prescription charges.

In the 17th century 45% of English noblewomen died before the age of 50, a quarter of them in childbirth

Dental treatment charges are 75% of the cost up to a maximum of £150. There is no charge for expectant mothers, mothers of children aged less than 12 months, those in full-time education until age 18, and those on Income Support or Family Credit. Those on low incomes either are not charged or are given help with payment. In 1988 there was 1 doctor for every 691 people.

Major indicators for women's health (1989)

maternal deaths (all causes) per 100,000 live births	7.72
maternal deaths (abortion) per 100,000 live births	0.77
ratio of abortions to 1,000 live births (1988)	227.48
% of all live births to mothers under 20	8.13
% of all live births to mothers aged 35+	6.46
deaths from cancer of the cervix (age 0–64) per 100,000 women	4.69
deaths from malignant neoplasm female breast (age 0–64) per 100,000 women	26.48
deaths from trachea/bronchus/lung cancer (age 0–64) per 100,000 women	14.08
deaths from trachea/bronchus/lung cancer (age 0–64) per 100,000 men	30.65
deaths from diseases of the circulatory system (age 0–64) per 100,000 women	48.47
deaths from diseases of the circulatory system (age 0–64) per 100,000 men	133.26
deaths from suicide and self-inflicted injury per 100,000 women	3.59
deaths from suicide and self-inflicted injury per 100,000 men	11.32

Source: data from Health for All 2000 Indicator Presentation System (World Health Organisation Regional Office For Europe)

Abortion and contraception: Available on social grounds up to 24 weeks with the consent of 2 doctors. Available without time limit if there is risk of grave injury to a woman's physical or mental health, or to foetal health or of foetal handicap. In practice, women under 16 have to involve their parents or guardians, or social workers if they are in care. Abortions performed under the National Health Service (about 40% of total) are free.

PARENTAL PAY, LEAVE AND BENEFITS (1989–90)

Maternity leave and pay: 11 weeks before plus 29 weeks after the birth, for women who have worked for the same employer for at least 2 years (for at least 16 hours a week) or 5 years (for less than 16 hours a week). Although this is the longest period of leave granted in the EC, the UK applies the strictest qualifying rules. Leave is paid at 90% of earnings for 6 weeks (the shortest earnings-related period of payment in the EC), then a flat-rate payment for 12 weeks, with the remaining 16 weeks unpaid.

Birth grant: A one-off maternity payment of £100 is available for mothers receiving income-related benefits.

CHILD-CARE PROVISION (1989–90)

There is a great deal of regional variation in child-care provision, with highest levels in cities, particularly inner London. Local authorities must review services for children under 8 every 3 years, though the only services they have to provide are for children deemed to be 'in need'.

Under 3s: 2% are in publicly funded places, mainly provided by local authorities, which are normally for disadvantaged children rather than children with employed parents.

3–4 year olds: 37% are in full-time schooling or other publicly funded places and, after including children in part-time places, 45% of children are at school. 2% are in centres providing mixed-age care, or in private care that is publicly subsidised. 50% of this age group go for a limited time to playgroups – one-third of which receive public funding – that provide for more children under 5 than any other service.

In 1988 the proportion of 3–4 year olds in primary school was 31.4% in Northern Ireland, 20.5% in England, 7.5% in Scotland and 30.6% in Wales.

A National Children's Home study found that 1 in 10 children under 5 in low-income families does not eat enough at least once a month because their parents cannot afford to buy food

Under 5s: 1% are in private nurseries with an estimated 1%–2% looked after at home by a paid carer. 5% of under 4s are looked after by a paid carer in the carer's home.

Primary school (5 years up): Normally from 9.00 to 15.30 with a supervised lunch break, though some education authorities have reduced the school day. Most schools provide meals. The school year runs from September to July. In 1988 the pupil to teacher ratio in primary schools was 22:1.

Outside school hours care: Provides for less than 0.5% of 5–10 year olds, in schools or other centres. One-third are in London.

Contributions to child-care costs: School-based provision is free, but parents contribute to all other services. In 1990 taxation of workplace child-care subsidies was abolished (from 1984 employees had been taxed on the value of any child-care subsidy provided by employers).

STATE BENEFITS (1989–90)

Retirement pension: Normal retirement age is 60 for women and 65 for men. Employers may not legally require a woman to retire at an earlier age than a man. While there must be equal access to pension schemes, there is no requirement that equal benefits be paid to men and women.

State pensions are made up of a flat-rate pension, a graduated pension and the State Earnings Related Pension (SERPS). To qualify for a flat-rate pension you must have paid at least 50 weekly flat-rate

contributions in any tax year before 1975, or 50 times
the minimum weekly contributions for 1975 in any
tax year between 1975 and 1978, or 52 times the
minimum in any tax year from 1978. There are no
conditions for a graduated pension, but to qualify for
SERPS people must have contributed more than the
minimum rate.

The flat-rate pension is £46.90 a week. Graduated
pension is £0.0614 a week for each £9 contributed
(£7.50 contributed for men) up to £4.42 a week
(£5.28 for men). The earnings-related pension is
based on 1.25% of each year's revalued earnings
between upper and lower earnings limits. There is an
additional £28.20 for a dependent spouse and £9.65
for a child. Pensions are adjusted each year. State
pensions are not affected by earnings.

Survivors' pensions: For a wife to qualify for a
widow's pension and a widowed mother's allowance,
the husband must have paid at least 50 weekly flat-rate
national insurance contributions before 6 April 1975,
or have paid contributions after then of at least 50 times
the lower weekly limit for that year. He must have paid
enough national insurance to qualify for full benefit.

For a wife to qualify for a widow's pension only, the
husband must have paid 25 flat rate contributions
before 6 April 1975, or have paid contributions after
then of at least 25 times the lower weekly limit for
that year.

A wife must be over 50 when her husband dies to
qualify for a full widow's pension, which is paid at
age 55 and is £46.90 a week. A reduced pension is
payable to widows aged 45–55 (40–50 if the death
was before 11 April 1988). Widows may also qualify
for an earnings-related pension depending on their
husband's earnings from April 1978.

A widow's payment of £1,000 is paid on the
husband's death if the widow is under 60, or if her
husband was not getting retirement pension when he
died. The husband must also have paid 25 times the
lower weekly earnings limit in any tax year since 1975.

The widowed mother's allowance of £46.90 a week is paid as long as a woman has a qualifying child in her care. Plus £9.65 for each child who qualifies for child benefit. Families who take in orphans are entitled to a guardian's allowance of £9.65 a week provided they are receiving child benefit for that child, and one of the child's parents fulfilled a residence condition.

Sickness benefit: Statutory Sick Pay (SSP) is paid by the employer for 28 weeks at the weekly rate of £39.25 for those earning between £46 and £124.99 a week (£52.50 for those earning more than £125). Those earning below £46 do not qualify.

Sickness benefit is paid for up to 168 days (after this invalidity benefit applies) at the flat rate of £35.70 a week (more if over pension age). There are extra payments of £22.10 for a dependent adult and £9.65 for a dependent child. To qualify you must have paid enough national insurance contributions to give a total of at least 50 times the weekly contributions payable on earnings at the lower earnings limit in the 2 previous tax years.

More people live in poverty in the UK than in any other EC state, the European Commission says. Almost 1 in 4 of all households defined as poor in the EC is in the UK

Invalidity benefit and allowance: Paid to those incapable of work because of physical or mental illness or disability who have exhausted their sickness benefit entitlement. Invalidity benefit and invalidity allowance are paid until retirement age, but to receive the allowance, incapacity must begin at least 5 years before retirement age.

Invalidity benefit is £46.90 a week (reduced if the claimant stays in hospital for more than 8 weeks). Invalidity allowance is £10 a week for those under 40, £6.20 for those aged 40–49 and £3.10 for women aged 50–54 (and men aged 50–59). Plus 1.25% of earnings after 6 April 1978 between upper and lower earnings limits. There is also £28.20 a week for one adult dependant, and £9.65 for each child for whom child benefit is received.

A severe disablement allowance can be paid to those who do not qualify for invalidity benefit. The allowance is £28.20 a week plus £16.85 for one adult

Conservative Employment Secretary Michael Howard opposed an EC directive to improve the rights of pregnant women at work on the grounds it would discourage employers from taking them on

dependant and £9.65 for each child for whom child benefit is received.

In addition, there is a day-and-night attendance allowance of £37.55 a week (less if constant care is not required) and a mobility allowance of £26.25 a week for those who are unable to walk.

Those who care for a relative receiving an attendance allowance may qualify for an invalid-care allowance (£28.20 a week plus £16.85 for one adult dependant plus £9.65 for a child).

Family benefits: A monthly benefit of £31.42 for each child up to the age of 16, or 19 if in vocational training. Single parents qualify for an extra allowance of £24.26 a month for the first child.

Unemployment benefit: A flat-rate benefit of £37.35 a week (£46.90 if over pension age) paid for up to 312 days for any period of interruption of employment. There is an extra 312 days if a claimant has worked for an employer for 13 weeks, for more than 16 hours a week within a given period.

WOMEN AND EMPLOYMENT

Statutory rights: There is no general legislation governing the working week, overtime, annual leave or statutory public holidays.

A 1991 Labour Party survey found the UK's unemployment benefit was the lowest in the EC – 12% of average male earnings, compared with 90% in Denmark, 70% in the Netherlands and 63% in Germany

Minimum levels of pay which are legally binding are set for some trades by wages councils, and in agriculture by agricultural wage boards. These rates no longer apply to young people below the age of 21. An estimated 2.5 million workers are covered by minimum wages set by wages councils.

Manual and non-manual: Female employment increased by 17% from 1979 to 1989 with all of that increase occurring in non-manual employment. The number of women in manual jobs fell by 183,000 in the same period. Non-manual women workers are more likely to work full time – 63% compared with only 41% of women manual workers.

Employment and unemployment (1989)

	% women	% men
economic activity rate	51.4	73.3
employed working part time	42.9	4.9
labour force who are employers or self-employed	7.3	17.7
unemployment rate	7.1	7.6
youth unemployment rate (age 14–24)	9.3	11.2
unemployed who have been unemployed for 12 months or more	28.1	48.6
all unemployed by sex	41.3	58.7

Source: data from *Labour Force Survey (Results 1989)* (Eurostat)

Part-time work: In 1989 71.2% of part-time workers were women. Most social security benefits depend on working at least 16 hours a week, some on working at least 8.

Employment by industrial sector (1000s) (1989)

	women		men		women as % of
	no	%	no	%	workforce
agriculture	115	1.0	478	3.2	19.4
all industry	2,008	17.6	6,599	44.0	23.3
energy and water	88	0.8	490	3.3	15.2
mineral extraction and chemicals	200	1.8	622	4.1	24.3
metal manufacturing and engineering	575	5.0	2,013	13.4	22.2
other manufacturing industry	961	8.4	1,538	10.2	38.5
building and civil engineering	184	1.6	1,936	12.9	8.7
all services	9,258	81.4	7,933	52.8	35.0
distributive trades and hotels	2,874	25.3	2,552	17.0	53.0
transport and communication	393	3.5	1,272	8.5	23.6
banking, finance and insurance	1,380	12.1	1,443	9.6	48.9
public administration	644	5.7	940	6.3	40.7
other services	3,967	34.9	1,727	11.5	69.7
total	11,431	100.0	15,125	100.0	43.0

* includes 51,000 women and 115,000 men whose industrial sector was not stated.

Source: data from *Labour Force Survey (Results 1989)* (Eurostat)

% of women workers who are part time, by industry in Britain (1989)

industrial sector	%
agriculture, forestry and fishing	36.3
energy and water supply	17.6
extraction of minerals, manufactured metals	13.9
metal goods, engineering etc	17.1
other manufacturing industries	22.6
construction	40.4
retail distribution	56.3
hotels and catering	67.6
transport and communications	21.9
banking, finance etc	22.8
other services	49.3
total	**41.6**

Source: *Some Facts About Women* (Statistics Unit, Equal Opportunities Commission)

Women's share of occupational groups in Great Britain, and average earnings compared to men's (1988)

	women workers as % of occupational group	women's weekly earnings as a % of men's
professional and related supporting management and administration	25.7	74.0
professional and related in education, welfare and health	67.0	71.1
literary, artistic, sports	39.8	73.8
professional and related in science, engineering and technology	10.6	67.8
managerial	26.5	68.7
clerical and related	76.3	77.5
selling	58.3	58.0
security and protective service	11.2	90.9
catering, cleaning, hairdressing and other personal services	80.0	73.5
farming, fishing and related	21.0	–
processing, making and repairing (excluding metal and electrical)	29.2	62.4
processing, making and repairing (metal and electrical)	47.2	58.1
painting, assembly, packing and related	41.1	62.8
construction and mining	0.5	–
transport operating, materials moving and stores	6.0	67.6
miscellaneous	9.9	–

Source: *Some Facts About Women* (Statistics Unit, Equal Opportunities Commission)

Women's earnings as a % of men's in industry (1987)

	manual hourly earnings	non-manual monthly earnings
chemical industry	70.7	80.6
all metal manufacture and engineering	73.8	–
mechanical engineering	77.5	72.4
electrical engineering	76.4	79.4
food, drink and tobacco	77.0	53.9
clothing and footwear manufacture	76.9	–
printing and publishing	62.4	58.7
all manufacturing industry	68.0	54.5
all industry	68.9	54.5

Source: data from *Earnings in Industry and Services* (Eurostat)

Women's share of high- and low-paid jobs (%) (1989)

high paid

surgeons	2
electrical engineers	I
dentists	19
solicitors	15
architects	7
accountants	9
financial managers	10

low paid

nurses	92
telephone operators	90
electrical assembly	78
typists/secretaries	98
shop assistants	84
domestic staff	98
clerks	70

Source: *Women at Work* (Equal Opportunities Commission)

Working mothers in Great Britain (1988)

age of youngest child no of children	% who work	% of these who work part time
0–2		
I child	32	50
2 children	33	76
3 or more children	29	83
total	**32**	**66**
10 or over		
I child	71	58
2 children	77	62
total	**73**	**59**
all ages		
I child	57	58
2 children	60	72
3 or more children	46	72
total	**56**	**66**

Source: data from *The Family Today* (Family Policy Studies Centre, Fact Sheet 1)

The UK has the highest proportion of households with a microwave (35%) according to a 1991 survey by Euromonitor. The lowest was in Spain and Italy, both with less than 2%

Working mothers (1988): In that year, 46% of women with a child under 10 were employed compared with 88% of men. 83% of women aged 20–39 without children were employed, the highest level in the EC. 8% of both women and men with a child under 10 were unemployed.

Women with a child aged 5–9 are much more likely to be employed (53%) than women with a child aged 0–4 (37%), the greatest difference in employment levels in the EC.

In the UK, a high level of working mothers are employed part time: the rate is 70% for those with a child under 10. Single mothers, however, do not work part time as much as married mothers and this affects the employment rate: 18% for lone mothers with a child aged 0–4 (37% for all mothers) and 37% for lone mothers with a child aged 5–9 (53%).

Single mothers have a higher unemployment rate: 10% for those with a child aged 0–4 (9% for all mothers) and 11% for those with a child aged 5–9 (7% for all).

WOMEN IN TRADE UNIONS

Women in trade unions (1990)

	NUPE	NALGO	GMB	USDAW	TGWU
number of women members	430,000	398,660*	267,894	251,371	210,758
% of women members	71.3	53.1*	30.8	61.7	16.9
% of women on national executive committee	46.1	42.0	29.4	31.3	7.7
% of women among delegates to annual conference	33.3	–	17.4	27.1	–
% of women on TUC delegation	36.1	41.7	19.8	26.9	20.6
% of women full-time national officers	38.5	31.6	11.8	20.0	3.4
% of women full-time regional officers	11.0	13.4	3.6	18.6	–

NUPE – National Union of Public Employees
NALGO – National and Local Government Officers' Association
GMB – GMB (general workers' union)
USDAW – Union of Shop, Distributive and Allied Workers
TGWU – Transport and General Workers' Union
*1989
Source: data from *Women in Trade Unions – Action for Equality* (Labour Research Department)

Women as a % of trade unions members in Northern Ireland (1989)

trade union	no of women members	% of women members
Northern Ireland Public Service Alliance	18,198	54.0
Confederation of Health Service Employees	16,200	81.0
Amalgamated Transport and General Workers' Union	12,100	24.2
National Union of Public Employees	10,486	87.2
Royal College of Nursing	10,000	100.0

Source: data from *Where do Women Figure?* (Equal Opportunities Commission for Northern Ireland)

WOMEN AND POLITICS

Women over 30 won the vote in 1918, and those aged 21 and over in 1928.

Women in the House of Commons (December 1991)

political party	total no of seats	no of seats held by women	% of seats held by women
Conservative	372	17	4.6
Labour	230	24	10.4
Liberal Democrat	20	1	5.0
Scottish National	5	1	20.0
Plaid Cymru	3	0	0.0
Others	20	1	5.0
total	650	44	6.8

Source: data from *Labour Research* January 1992 (Labour Research Department)

The UK is the only EC country where weekly periods of rest from work are not provided for in law and where there is no statutory right to paid annual leave

In 1991 there were no women in the cabinet, and the 4 women members in the government are all in junior posts. A general election was called for April 1992.

The Labour Party has pledged to set up a Ministry for Women with an automatic seat in the cabinet, and a House of Commons Select Committee for Women. 40% of both Labour Party executive committee seats and policy forum seats are to be reserved for women by 1996.

In Northern Ireland 11.2% of local government district councillors were women in 1990. None of Northern Ireland's MPs to the UK or European parliament is a woman.

WOMEN AND EDUCATION

Destination of female school leavers in England and Wales (1987–88)

	% of female school leavers	female school leavers as % of all school leavers
degree or teacher training courses	8.6	46.1
other full-time further and higher education courses	27.2	59.5
employment/unemployment	64.2	45.6
all school leavers	100.0	48.7

Source: data from *Some Facts About Women* (Statistics Unit, Equal Opportunities Commission)

Percentage of women students at universities in Great Britain by subject studied (1987–88)

languages and related	70.7
social sciences	47.1
multi-disciplinary studies	47.4
medicine and dentistry	45.4
biological sciences	54.7
humanities	47.2
physical sciences	26.3
studies allied to medicine	67.7
mathematical sciences	23.9
business and financial studies	40.2
engineering and technology	10.9
veterinary science, agriculture and related	46.7
creative arts	60.0
education	77.3
architecture and related	28.1
librarianship and information science	50.0
all subjects	43.1

Source: data from *Some Facts About Women* (Statistics Unit, Equal Opportunities Commission)

Percentage of women students in further education in Northern Ireland by subject and vocational training (1988–89)

medicine, dentistry and health	91.7
engineering and technology	6.5
agriculture, forestry and veterinary science	12.6
science	56.5
social administration and business studies	72.8
miscellaneous professional studies	60.1
education, language and other arts	55.2
music, drama and visual	54.5
total	**51.8**

Source: data from *Where do Women Figure?* (Equal Opportunities Commission for Northern Ireland)

Percentage of women students at universities in Northern Ireland by subject studied (1988–89)

medicine and dentistry	64
biological sciences	58
veterinary science, agriculture and related	39
physical sciences	39
mathematical sciences	33
engineering and technology	9
architecture and related studies	22
social sciences	57
business and financial studies	58
librarianship and related studies	72
language and related studies	70
humanities	37
creative arts	64
education	78
multi-disciplinary studies	57
total	**49**

Source: data from *Where do Women Figure?* (Equal Opportunities Commission for Northern Ireland)

WOMEN AND DETENTION

In September 1988, 3.4% of all prisoners were women, 23.7% were minors (age 21) and young adults, and 1.3% were foreigners. In 1989 2,017 women were sentenced to prison, with the average length of sentence of more than 14 months.

Offences for which women were imprisoned in 1989 (%)

theft, handling, fraud, forgery	44.0
other offences	19.8
drugs offences	18.4
violence against a person	10.2
burglary	4.6
robbery	2.0
sexual offences	1.0
total	**100.0**

Source: data from Prison Reform Trust

The UK imprisons a higher proportion of citizens than any other western European country, according to 1991 figures from the National Association for the Care and Resettlement of Offenders

Women sent to prison have far fewer previous convictions than men, and are less likely to be sentenced after being held on remand. A study by the National Association for the Care and Resettlement of Offenders found that in 1984 17% of women given immediate sentences had no previous convictions, compared with only 6% of men. 56% of women given immediate sentences had only 1 or 2 previous convictions compared with 22% of men.

38% of women remanded in custody in 1984 were later given prison sentences compared with 62% of men. 21% of women prisoners were on remand. 16% of women in prison were there for their first offence.

Women are allowed to wear their own clothes but are restricted to 3 sets at any one time. There are 39 places in 3 units where mothers can be with their babies in prison. Two of the units only allow babies until they are 9 months old, and the third until 18 months. Women are punished twice as often as men for breaking prison rules.

SOURCES

Abortion Laws in Europe, Planned Parenthood in Europe, Vol 18 No 1, Spring 1989 (Supplement, amended April 1990); *Caring for children – the 1990 report* (Family Policy Studies Centre); *Childcare in the European Communities 1985–90* (Women of Europe Supplement No 51); *Comparative Study on rules governing working conditions in the member states* (Commission of the European Communities); *Demographic Statistics 1990* (Eurostat); *Earnings in Industry and Services* (Eurostat); *Employment in Europe 1991* (Commission of the European Communities); *Europa World Year Book 1990* (31st edition); *Family Finances* (Family Policy Studies Centre, Fact Sheet No 1 and 4); *The Family Today* (Family Policy Studies Centre, Fact Sheet No 1 and 4); *A History of Their Own – Women in Europe from Prehistory to the Present, Volumes I and II* (Bonnie Anderson and Judith Zinsser, Penguin); Health For All 2000 Indicator Presentation System (World Health Organisation Regional Office for Europe); *Immigration Fact Sheets 1–5* (Joint Council for the Welfare of Immigrants); *Labour Force Survey (Results 1989)* (Eurostat); *Labour Research* January 1992 (Labour Research Department); *Les Actions Positives en Faveur des Femmes en Europe Occidentale* (Institut Syndical Européen); *Out In Europe* (Peter Tatchell, for Channel 4 Television);

People, Parity and Pensions (Equal Opportunities Commission and Age Concern); *Positive action and the constitutional and legislative hindrances to its implementation in the member states of the Council of Europe* (Council of Europe); *Prison Information Bulletin* June 1990 (Council of Europe); Prison Reform Trust; *Proposition de Directive Du Conseil concernant la protection au travail de la femme enceinte ou venant d'accoucher* (Commission of the European Communities); *Social Protection in the Member States of the Community* (Commission of the European Community Directorate General on Employment, Industrial Relations and Social Affairs); *Some Facts about Women* (Statistics Unit, Equal Opportunities Commission); *Third World Guide 91/92* (Instituto del Tercer Mundo); *Where do Women Figure?* (Equal Opportunities Commission for Northern Ireland); *Women and Men in Britain 1991* (Equal Opportunities Commission); *Women at Work* (Equal Opportunities Commission); *Women in Trade Unions – Action for Equality* (Labour Research Department); *Women of Europe* (No 68, 69)

LETTER FROM BRITAIN

Althea Efunshile, education office (youth and community) for the London borough of Harrow, extracted from 'Notes of a Black Woman Manager' in *The Journal: Women in Organisations and Management*, December 1991 (Newcastle upon Tyne)

In these times of numerous statements of commitment to equal opportunities, public sector organisations tend to be pleased, even delighted, to have a non-white female on board. It is less clear, however, the extent to which this delight has extended to a willingness to systematically alter the organisational structure and climate to reflect a real commitment to equality.

In one job, for example, the first staffing appointment that I made soon after I took up my post was to a black female. The remark was made to me by one of my male white managers that 'it was a pity that my first appointment was a black woman because of how that might be perceived'.

While on the one hand this same manager and others in the organisation had professed a keenness to have the benefit of my 'different perspective', the implications for the organisation of that perspective were not so welcome.

Some of the other factors which have affected me have been to do with my outside commitments as a mother. In a predominantly male environment and culture, care of dependants is not an issue. The fact is that it is still women who have the main responsibility for looking after children and elderly relatives. While I would like changes to this situation, the reality now for women managers, as they juggle with baby-sitters, childminders and 7pm meetings, is still nightmarish and decidedly stressful.

I don't think of myself as a 'disadvantaged person'. I believe that everyone has some measure of power and that it is important to use this power either collectively (preferably), or individually towards change. To be a black or white woman is not inherently to be a victim. We should not, on the other hand, underestimate the tensions which go hand in hand for the woman manager who is attempting to manage change towards a more equitable and equal system. Our challenge is to find even more effective strategies in order to reach this goal.

ADDRESSES

Equal Opportunities Commission, Overseas House, Manchester M3 3HN

EOC (NI), Chamber of Commerce House, 22 Great Victoria Street, Belfast BT2 2BA

Family Policy Studies Centre, 231 Baker Street, London NW1 6XE

British Refugee Council, 3 Bondway, London SW8 1SJ

Child Poverty Action Group, 4th Floor, 1–5 Bath Street, London EC1V 9PY

Family Planning Association, Margaret Pyke House, 27–35 Mortimer Street, London W1N 7RJ. Tel: 071 636 7866

Organisation for Lesbian and Gay Action, Room 3, 38 Mount Pleasant, London WC1X 0AP. Tel: 071 833 3860

Yugoslavia

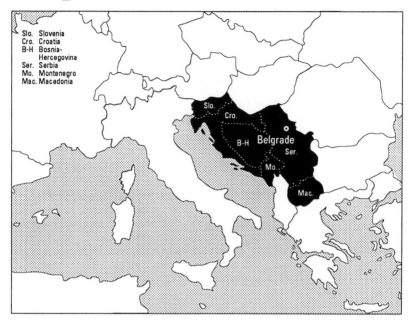

Slo. Slovenia
Cro. Croatia
B-H Bosnia-Hercegovina
Ser. Serbia
Mo. Montenegro
Mac. Macedonia

- **Population** 23.6 million
- **Area** 255,804 sq km
- **Population density** 92.6 people sq km
- **GDP 1988** £33.5 billion
- **GDP per capita** £1,413
- **GDP per capita in purchasing power parity** (UK=100) 44
- **Public spending as % of GNP:** defence 4.0% (1986); education 3.8% (1986); health 4.3% (1987)
- **Consumer price index** 1980 = 100; 1989 = 270,830
- **Currency is the dinar:** official exchange rate 1989 £1 = YUD190,238; US$1 = YUD118,160

Yugoslavia consisted of 6 republics (Serbia, Croatia, Macedonia, Montenegro, Slovenia and Bosnia-Herzegovina) and 2 autonomous Serbian provinces of Kosovo and Vojvodina. The republics of Croatia and Slovenia declared their independence in 1991 amid a civil war between the Croats and the Serbian-dominated Federal Army. The EC recognised Croatia and Slovenia in January 1992.

The governmental structures are in flux now, but federal Yugoslavia has been ruled by a presidency consisting of an 8-member collective (representating republics and provinces) with the posts of president and vice president rotating each year. The 2-chamber parliament was made up of the 220-member Federal Chamber and the 88-member Chamber of the Republics and Provinces; the parliament elected the presidential collective.

Official languages are Serbo-Croat, Macedonian and Slovenian, but Albanian and Hungarian are also spoken. The main language of Serbo-Croat has two forms: Serbian which uses the Cyrillic alphabet and Croatian which uses the Roman.

The 1981 census showed 24 different national and ethnic groups, with the major groups consisting of Serbians (36.3%), Croatians (19.8%), Muslims (8.9%), Slovenes (7.8%), Albanians (7.7%), Macedonians (6.0%), Montenegrins (2.6%), Hungarians (1.9%), Romanians (0.8%) and Turkish (0.4%).

40% of the population belong to the orthodox churches and about one-third are Roman Catholics. There is also a large number of Muslims, mainly among Albanians, Turks, Bosnians and Herzegovinians.

BIRTH, LIFE AND DEATH

Population density by republic (1000s) (1989)

republic	area sq km	population (1000s)	pop density per sq km
Bosnia-Herzegovina	51,129	4,479	87.6
Montenegro	13,812	639	46.3
Croatia	56,538	4,683	82.8
Macedonia	25,713	2,111	82.1
Slovenia	20,251	1,948	96.2
Serbia*	55,968	5,840	104.3
Kosovo	10,887	1,939	178.1
Vojvodina	21,506	2,051	95.4
Total Yugoslavia	**255,804**	**23,690**	**92.6**

*excluding Kosovo and Vojvodina

Source: data from *Statistical Pocket Book of Yugoslavia '90* (Federal Statistical Office)

Births and deaths for every 1,000 population (1989)

Federal Republic of Yugoslavia
birth rate	14.3
death rate	9.1
infant mortality rate per 1,000 live births	24.3
marriage rate	6.7
life expectancy (women) (1980–82)	73.0
life expectancy (men) (1980–82)	68.0

Republic of Bosnia-Herzegovina
birth rate	14.5
death rate	6.5
infant mortality rate per 1,000 live births	16.3
marriage rate	7.8
life expectancy (women) (1980–82)	73.0
life expectancy (men) (1980–82)	68.0

Republic of Montenegro
birth rate	14.8
death rate	5.8
infant mortality rate per 1,000 live births	14.9
marriage rate	6.3
life expectancy (women) (1980–82)	76.0
life expectancy (men) (1980–82)	72.0

Republic of Croatia

birth rate	12.2
death rate	11.3
infant mortality rate per 1,000 live births	11.3
marriage rate	6.3
life expectancy (women) (1980–82)	74.0
life expectancy (men) (1980–82)	67.0

Republic of Macedonia

birth rate	17.4
death rate	7.1
infant mortality rate per 1,000 live births	42.0
marriage rate	7.6
life expectancy (women) (1980–82)	72.0
life expectancy (men) (1980–82)	68.0

Republic of Slovenia

birth rate	13.1
death rate	10.0
infant mortality rate per 1,000 live births	10.0
marriage rate	5.1
life expectancy (women) (1980–82)	75.0
life expectancy (men) (1980–82)	67.0

Republic of Serbia (excluding Kosovo and Vojvodina)

birth rate	11.7
death rate	10.4
infant mortality rate per 1,000 live births	21.4
marriage rate	6.3
life expectancy (women) (1980–82)	74.0
life expectancy (men) (1980–82)	69.0

Province of Kosovo

birth rate	28.4
death rate	5.2
infant mortality rate per 1,000 live births	52.1
marriage rate	7.4
life expectancy (women) (1980–82)	72.0
life expectancy (men) (1980–82)	68.0

Province of Vojvodina

birth rate	10.7
death rate	12.2
infant mortality rate per 1,000 live births	12.6
marriage rate	6.7
life expectancy (women) (1980–82)	74.0
life expectancy (men) (1980–82)	68.0

Source: data from *Statistical Pocket Book of Yugoslavia '90*
(Federal Statistical Office)

LESBIAN RIGHTS

Same-sex relationships are illegal in the republics of
Bosnia-Herzegovina, Macedonia and Serbia. Until
1977 they were illegal throughout Yugoslavia.
Slovenia has a common age of consent of 16. The new
constitution adds sexual orientation to the grounds on
which it is illegal to discriminate against a person. In
Croatia and Montenegro the homosexual age of
consent is 18 compared with 14 for heterosexuals.
(For more information, see Suzana Tratnik's
contribution at the end of the chapter.)

WOMEN AND HEALTH CARE

In 1988 there was 1 doctor for every 549 people.

Major indicators for women's health (1988)

maternal deaths (all causes) per 100,000 live births	16.28
maternal deaths (abortion) per 100,000 live births	3.93
ratio of abortions to 1,000 live births (all ages) (1987)	1,015.40
% of all live births to mothers under 20	10.22
% of all live births to mothers aged 35+	6.46
deaths from cancer of the cervix (age 0–64) per 100,000 women (1987)	4.59
deaths from malignant neoplasm female breast (age 0–64) per 100,000 women	15.43
deaths from trachea/bronchus/lung cancer (age 0–64) per 100,000 women	5.93
deaths from trachea/bronchus/lung cancer (age 0–64) per 100,000 men	41.50
deaths from diseases of the circulatory system (age 0–64) per 100,000 women	78.08
deaths from diseases of the circulatory system (age 0–64) per 100,000 men	161.64
deaths from suicide and self-inflicted injury per 100,000 women	10.32
deaths from suicide and self-inflicted injury per 100,000 men	25.79

Source: data from Health for All 2000 Indicator Presentation System (World Health Organisation
Regional Office For Europe)

10.8% of adolescents use abortion as a method of birth control. 15% of women who had abortions in 1986 had had four or more abortions

Abortion and contraception: Available on request up to 10 weeks, though minors require parental consent. Available after 10 weeks on social, medical and eugenic grounds or in cases of rape or other sexual crime, with the consent of a committee. Abortion is free on medical grounds, failure of IUD or if a woman is on social security. Otherwise charges are the equivalent of around UK£15.

In 1976 47% of women between 15 and 49 were not using contraceptives. Overall 53% of married women used contraceptives; 69.5% in Croatia, 66.8% in Macedonia, 65.9% in Slovenia, 59.2% in Vojvodina, 55.6% in Serbia (excluding Kosovo and Vojvodina), 46.6% in Bosnia-Herzegovina, 40.7% in Montenegro and only 9% in Kosovo.

The survey found that overall 66.7% used withdrawal, 7.7% hormonal methods, 7.2% a combination of methods; 5.7% chemical methods, 5.6% the rhythm method, 4% condoms and 3.1% IUDs.

PARENTAL PAY, LEAVE AND BENEFITS (1989)

Maternity leave and pay: A total of 270 days' paid leave.

Parental leave: Between 105 and 210 days which can be shared between women and men.

Time off to look after sick children: Women are entitled to work shorter hours when their children are sick.

CHILD-CARE PROVISION

Primary school (7 years up, but 6 in Croatia): Education is compulsory between the ages of 7 (6 in Croatia) and 15. The school year runs from September to June.

Primary pupil to teacher ratio by republic and provinces (1988–89)

Bosnia-Herzegovina	24
Montenegro	18
Croatia	19
Macedonia	21
Slovenia	17
Serbia	19
Kosovo	22
Vojvodina	18
Yugoslavia	**20**

Source: data from *Statistical Pocket Book of Yugoslavia '90* (Federal Statistical Office)

STATE BENEFITS

Retirement pension: Normally paid at 85%–87% of average monthly income over the 5 years prior to retirement.

WOMEN AND EMPLOYMENT

Abroad: Between 500,000 and 700,000 Yugoslavs work abroad, accounting for an estimated £1 billion remittances sent back each year.

Statutory rights: All workers are entitled to between 18 and 36 days leave each year.

Unemployment: At the end of 1989 653,000 women were unemployed, accounting for 54.4% of all unemployed. In 1989 highest total unemployment was in Kosovo at 57.2%, the lowest in Slovenia at 1.8%.

Women in workforce: In 1988 women accounted for 39.3% of the workforce in the socialist sector in Yugoslavia, a proportion which ranged from 34% in Slovenia and 31% in Croatia to 14% in Kosovo.

Women's share of employment by industrial sector throughout Yugoslavia (1988)

	%
industry and mining	37.5
textiles	81.2
trade	51.1
education	60.9
catering	60.9
communal services	16.9
financial services	52.3
health	74.6

% of women employed in the socialist sector

	1986	1987	1989
Bosnia-Herzegovina	34.6	35.5	36.2
Montenegro	35.8	36.8	38.7
Croatia	41.2	41.7	42.7
Slovenia	45.9	45.9	46.5
Macedonia	34.9	35.5	37.3
Serbia*	37.2	37.9	38.9
Kosovo	22.3	22.6	23.4
Vojvodina	38.7	39.3	40.1

*excluding Kosovo and Vojvodina

Source: *Superwomen and the Double Burden* (ed Chris Corrin, Scarlet Press)

Employment by groups of occupations (1000s) (1986)

	women		men		women as % of workforce
	no	%	no	%	
agricultural and related	24	0.9	118	2.9	16.9
miners, industrial and related	698	27.5	2,296	56.9	23.3
sales	233	9.2	293	7.3	44.3
service	376	14.8	160	4.0	70.2
security and protective	3	0.1	141	3.5	2.1
clerical, administrative	614	24.2	338	8.4	64.5
managerial	28	1.1	158	3.9	15.1
professionals and artists	539	21.2	462	11.4	53.9
other occupations	–	–	2	–	–
workers without an occupation	24	0.9	69	1.7	25.8
total	2,539	100.0	4,037	100.0	38.6

Source: data from *Statistical Pocket Book of Yugoslavia '90* (Federal Statistical Office)

Women as a percentage of the workforce by age (1986)

15–27 years	43.4
28–34 years	42.1
35–44 years	41.1
45–54 years	30.8
55 and over	16.8

Source: data from *Statistical Pocket Book of Yugoslavia '90* (Federal Statistical Office)

Women's income as a % of total monthly average by level of education (1986)

higher professional qualifications	90.5
secondary professional qualifications	94.7
lower professional qualifications	96.8
highly skilled workers	87.6
skilled workers	86.5
semi-skilled workers	94.6
unskilled workers	93.8

Source: data from *Statistical Pocket Book of Yugoslavia '90* (Federal Statistical Office)

Earnings comparison: In 1986 throughout Yugoslavia women's earnings were 86.9% of men's. This ranged from a small number of managerial women workers in Kosovo who earned 93.7% of men's wages, to manual women workers in Bosnia-Herzegovina who earned 69.3% compared to men.

Household spending excluding housing, loans and savings (%) (1988)

Federal Republic of Yugoslavia	100.0
Bosnia-Herzegovina	78.1
Montenegro	77.7
Croatia	105.4
Macedonia	75.0
Slovenia	183.1
Serbia*	88.5
Kosovo	74.8
Vojvodina	95.9

*excluding the provinces of Kosovo and Vojvodina

Source: data from *Statistical Pocket Book of Yugoslavia '90* (Federal Statistical Office)

WOMEN AND POLITICS

Women won the vote in 1946 after Communist rule was established. In June 1991, 17.7% of MPs of federal Yugoslavia were women.

WOMEN AND EDUCATION

Women as a % of students in higher education throughout Yugoslavia (1988–89)

natural science and mathematics	62
mechanical engineering	18
mining, geology and metallurgy	29
medicine	57
agriculture	42
economics	60
tourism, catering and foreign trade	56
law	57
philosophy and philology	74
teacher training	86
physical culture	27
total	**49**

Source: data from *Statistical Pocket Book of Yugoslavia '90*
(Federal Statistical Office)

Women as % of specialists, masters and doctors of science by republic (1988)

republic/provinces	specialists	masters of science	doctors of science
Bosnia-Herzegovina	–	27	16
Montenegro	–	50	–
Croatia	40	36	32
Macedonia	–	29	29
Slovenia	55	34	20
Serbia	45	41	25
Kosovo	53	36	40
Vojvodina	–	30	4

Source: data from *Statistical Pocket Book of Yugoslavia '90* (Federal Statistical Office)

SOURCES

Abortion Laws in Europe, Planned Parenthood in Europe, Vol 18 No 1, Spring 1989 (Supplement, amended April 1990); *Europa World Year Book 1990* (31st edition); Health For All 2000 Indicator Presentation System (World Health Organisation Regional Office for Europe); *Out In Europe* (Peter Tatchell, for Channel 4 Television); *Planned Parenthood in Europe* (Vol 19 No 2) (International Planned Parenthood Federation); *Pocket World in Figures* (The Economist); *Superwomen and the Double Burden* (ed. Chris Corrin, Scarlet Press); *Statistical Pocket Book of Yugoslavia '90* (Federal Statistical Office); *Third World Guide 91/92* (Instituto del Tercer Mundo)

LETTERS FROM YUGOSLAVIA

Vlasta Jalusic, political scientist and sociologist, Ljubljana, January 1992

'Nobody cares about anything in the case of women in Serbia,' a woman friend of mind said. 'Not even in the sense of trying to eliminate women's formal rights, because they are lost in any case.'

When asking myself how to grasp the 'position of women in Yugoslavia' a few years ago, I would be confronted with one difficulty: namely that it is impossible to write about women in Yugoslavia as a unique field. I would start by describing the broader historical, political, cultural, economic and other differences that resisted 45 years of a unifying socialist system. I would speak about six republics and two autonomous provinces, about big differences not only between men and women but also among women of different republics, nationalities, religions and regions. For instance, the gap between women from the south and north: in the republic of Slovenia 0.9% of women are illiterate but in Kosovo, the ex-autonomous province with an Albanian majority population where the Serbian regime destroyed all legal Albanian institutions, the figure is 23.3%.

Anyway I have much bigger troubles now. As I am writing this, there exists no Yugoslavia as a common state of six republics and two autonomous provinces. There has been a war in the republic of Croatia. Some parts of the former Yugoslavia are proclaiming themselves independent states, some are trying to preserve 'the rest' as something they want to call Yugoslavia.

I cannot offer any certain new statistics. My starting point is somewhere between the past and the future, where everything is difficult to define.

After the Second World War, the legal position of women became quite good. This occurred not because of women's politics, however, but because of the special ideological premise of the 'role of women in socialism'. Socialist 'state feminism' succeeded in forming a relatively equalising system for women. The main achievements were in such areas as employment, social care, public care for children, parental leave, reproductive rights.

For example, reproductive rights were founded in the constitution from 1974 as a paragraph about the 'human right to decide over the birth of one's own children'. In the republic of Slovenia, for example, this right included not only abortion rights (on demand until the tenth week of pregnancy) but, first of all, the social, health and other facilities to make it possible to give birth to desired children. This included the whole network of women's health centres, accessible (free) contraception, abortion on demand paid out of the health insurance.

Then in the Eighties, there were growing economic difficulties and the whole system – and society – began to change. Nearly 40 years of the absence of an organised women's network had tragic consequences on the legal and empirical position of women after the first post-socialist elections in different republics. The old socialist legislative came 'from above' and was not the result of a long lasting political battle by women 'from below'. The political issue was reinterpreted as a question of 'the social' and covered by imposing social solutions without raising the question of women's position as a political issue. And, when the power changed, there was no powerful basis in the form of women's groups to influence the new law.

In the mid-Eighties we could see women from Macedonia fighting for bread at the door of a shop. We can hardly imagine the Kosovo situation in 1991 where no schools in the Albanian language exist any more (and where even before in the early Eighties only 46% of girls finished primary school), where women give birth either without professional help or must pay large amounts of hard currency.

After more or less democratic elections in the single republics, fewer women were elected (under socialist conditions, women made up 10% to 25% of various assemblies). In Slovenia, women made up 11%; in Croatia 4% and elsewhere less than 4%. In most republics, the reproductive rights were left out of the constitutions. In Croatia a very strong anti-abortion campaign, which took place before the war, meant the abolition of the individual right to decide over the birth.

In Slovenia, reproductive rights were left in the new constitution as a 'freedom' but only after long campaigns by women's groups. In Serbia, Montenegro, Macedonia, Bosnia and Herzegovina, there is no discussion about the position of women at all.

The common question I see for women is how to come to terms with the situation where women in a few years changed from being a semi 'social subject' (women workers) to the 'natural ferment' of reproduction of life (national mothers). Namely, in a society where only the question of survival appears, there is no real space to make politics.

Tanja Rener, assistant professor of family sociology, University of Ljubljana, January 1992

An enormous anxiety and a pressing anger are the feelings we are seized with daily. What can I do, what must we do, as women and pacifists, to fight against these feelings of impotence? And why, even before this war, was it so difficult to think and to act as women? While understandable during the socialist/communist regime which repressed all unguided social and political expressions 'from below', why haven't things changed in 'the new democratic' political system?

I believe the reasons are to be found in three spheres of everyday life: economics, political and cultural/ideological. The economics of the transition to a market economy and the demolition of the social state have affected women in mostly two ways: the substantial growth of domestic and household work and the enormous growth of the so-called grey/black economy. The result is that the great majority of women are overloaded and chronically exhausted.

The political system is regulated strictly as a multi-party system for political parties only. In this sense, the political sphere is closed to women's independent political organisations, which depend on volunteers. Parties in power ignore women's issues, except for emphasising women's maternity role.

Ideologically, the former social collectivism has been replaced by a new one that strongly appeals to homogeneity and national unity. There was simply not enough time or a big enough chance for women to articulate their own interests and demands: we were once again regarded as mothers and wives (of the nation) before we were able to open our mouths as individuals. All those not willing to subordinate to the so-called 'Blut und Boden' ideology are simply thrown out of the system. In the new constitutional draft, women are mentioned twice as persons to be protected because of their maternity; the civil rights movements' proposal to equalise gay people's rights was abolished.

In this period of senseless war, when women's words, gestures and activities are politically instrumentalised, will we find the necessary strength to speak, write, act and demonstrate, or will we once again be mute?

Suzana Tratnik, member of the Lesbian Section, written in 1989

If we had written about lesbian life and politics in

Yugoslavia 3 or 4 years ago, there would have been nothing to write about. We still know nothing about Yugoslav lesbians in the past. In September 1987, 6 women of the women's group Lilit decided to organise a lesbian group. In January 1988 it separated from Lilit, taking the name Lesbieka Sekcija (the Lesbian Section). We organised many activities and published the bulletin called *Lesbozine*. We were associated with the gay group, but figured out that it is much better to work separately and make common events from time to time (like demanding equal rights for homosexual couples and the equality for all citizens irrespective of one's sexual orientation).

Homosexuality is legal in the republics of Slovenia, Croatia, Montenegro and the autonomous province Vojvodina – the age of consent is 16, the same for heterosexuality. Homosexuality is illegal in Serbia, Macedonia, Bosnia and the province of Kosovo. The punishment is 1 year of prison. Of course, it concerns male homosexuality only. The Penal Code doesn't mention lesbianism except in Croatia which labels lesbianism (when the person is not 16) as a 'sick act between women'.

For the time being, the group is not very active. Perhaps many events in the past and the small reaction from lesbians have exhausted us.

ADDRESSES

Embassy of the Socialist Federal Republic of Yugoslavia, 5 Lexham Gardens, London W8 5JJ. Tel: 071 370 6105

Feministicka grupa zena i drustvo (feminist organisation), SKC Marsala Tita 48, 1100 Belgrade

Family Planning Council of Yugoslavia, c/o Danica Sasic, Brace Jugovica 13, 11000 Belgrade

Vece Saveza Sindicata Jugoslavije (federation of Yugoslav trade unions), 1100 Belgrade, trg Marska i Engelsa 5 (Dom Sindikata)

Club Magnus/Lilit Lesbozine (lesbian and gay rights), SKUC Studentski Kulturni Centre, Kersnikkova 4, 61000 Ljubljana. Tel: (38 61) 31 9662

Comparative tables

Population

78,200,000	Germany (totalled)
57,398,100	Italy
56,997,700	United Kingdom
55,750,400	France
38,736,100	Spain
37,850,000	Poland
23,560,000	Yugoslavia
23,050,000	Romania
15,640,000	Czechoslovakia
14,714,900	Netherlands
10,450,000	Hungary
10,269,500	Portugal
9,988,900	Greece
9,875,700	Belgium
8,990,000	Bulgaria
8,458,900	Sweden
7,596,100	Austria
6,673,900	Switzerland
5,129,500	Denmark
5,109,200	Finland
4,230,000	Norway
3,539,300	Ireland
3,210,000	Albania
371,700	Luxembourg
352,400	Malta
253,785	Iceland

Area in sq km

543,965	France
504,879	Spain
449,964	Sweden
356,910	Germany (totalled)
338,144	Finland
323,895	Norway
312,683	Poland
301,270	Italy
255,804	Yugoslavia
244,755	United Kingdom
237,500	Romania
131,990	Greece
127,900	Czechoslovakia
110,994	Bulgaria
103,000	Iceland
93,030	Hungary
92,390	Portugal
83,853	Austria
70,282	Ireland
43,075	Denmark
41,864	Netherlands
41,293	Switzerland
30,519	Belgium
28,748	Albania
2,586	Luxembourg
316	Malta

Population density per sq km

1,115.2	Malta
350.3	Netherlands
323.6	Belgium
233.2	United Kingdom
219.1	Germany (totalled)
190.5	Italy
161.6	Switzerland
143.7	Luxembourg
122.2	Czechoslovakia
121.1	Poland
119.1	Denmark
112.3	Hungary
111.6	Portugal
110.7	Albania
102.3	France
97.1	Romania
92.1	Yugoslavia
90.6	Austria
81.0	Bulgaria
76.7	Spain
75.7	Greece
50.4	Ireland
18.9	Sweden
15.1	Finland
13.1	Norway
2.5	Iceland

Living standards adjusted for cost of goods and services: GDP per capita in purchasing power parity (UK = 100) (1988)

132	Switzerland
127	Norway
117	Sweden
112	Denmark
112	West Germany
106	Finland
103	France
103	Netherlands
100	Austria
100	Italy
100	United Kingdom
98	Belgium
70	Spain
62	Ireland
52	Portugal
55	Greece
47	Hungary
44	Yugoslavia
38	Poland

Consumer price index (1989) (1980 = 100)

103	Malta
113	Czechoslovakia
125	Netherlands
137	Switzerland
138	Austria
149	Luxembourg
153	Belgium
176	Denmark
178	United Kingdom
180	France
185	Finland
193	Sweden
203	Norway
206	Ireland
224	Hungary
235	Spain
242	Italy
449	Portugal
515	Greece
1,711	Iceland
2,756	Poland
270,830	Yugoslavia

Public spending on defence as % of GNP (1986)

12.0	Luxembourg
5.7	Greece
5.0	United Kingdom
4.9	East Germany
4.1	Czechoslovakia
4.0	Albania
4.0	Yugoslavia
3.9	France
3.6	Bulgaria
3.5	Iceland
3.3	Poland
3.3	Portugal
3.2	Norway
3.1	Belgium
3.1	Netherlands
3.1	West Germany
2.9	Sweden
2.4	Hungary
2.3	Italy
2.3	Spain
2.1	Denmark
1.9	Ireland
1.9	Switzerland
1.7	Finland
1.6	Romania
1.3	Austria

Public spending on education as % of GNP (1986)

7.6	Sweden
7.5	Denmark
6.9	Ireland
6.8	Norway
6.6	Netherlands
6.0	Austria
5.9	Finland
5.9	France
5.6	Belgium
5.3	United Kingdom
4.8	Switzerland
4.5	West Germany
4.5	Poland
4.4	Bulgaria
4.3	Portugal
4.0	Italy
3.8	East Germany
3.8	Hungary
3.8	Yugoslavia
3.7	Iceland
3.6	Czechoslovakia
3.6	Malta
3.2	Spain
2.6	Luxembourg
2.5	Greece
1.8	Romania

Public spending on health as % of GNP (1987)

8.0	Sweden
7.8	Ireland
7.5	Netherlands
6.9	Iceland
6.8	Switzerland
6.6	France
6.3	West Germany
6.0	Finland
5.7	Portugal
5.6	Belgium
5.5	Norway
5.3	Austria
5.3	Denmark
5.3	United Kingdom
4.5	Italy
4.3	Spain
4.3	Yugoslavia
4.2	Czechoslovakia
4.0	Poland
3.5	Greece
3.2	Bulgaria
3.2	Hungary
2.6	East Germany
2.3	Albania
1.9	Romania

Fertility rate per woman

1.3	Italy
1.4	West Germany
1.4	Spain
1.43	Austria
1.5	Luxembourg
1.5	Greece
1.5	Portugal
1.54	Belgium
1.6	Denmark
1.6	Netherlands
1.65	Finland
1.7	East Germany
1.8	France
1.8	United Kingdom
1.88	Hungary
1.9	Norway
2.0	Sweden
2.0	Bulgaria
2.0	Czechoslovakia
2.05	Iceland
2.15	Romania
2.2	Ireland
2.2	Poland
3.0	Albania

Birth rate for every 1,000 people

9.9	Italy
10.7	Spain
10.8	Greece
11.1	West Germany
11.4	Austria
11.4	Hungary
11.5	Denmark
11.9	Portugal
12.0	Belgium
12.2	Switzerland
12.4	Luxembourg
12.7	Finland
12.7	Netherlands
13.0	East Germany
13.0	Bulgaria
13.3	Sweden
13.6	Norway
13.8	Czechoslovakia
13.8	France
13.8	United Kingdom
14.3	Yugoslavia
15.1	Malta
15.3	Ireland
15.5	Poland
15.6	Romania
16.1	Iceland
24.7	Albania

Infant mortality rate for every 1,000 live births

39.0	Albania
24.3	Yugoslavia
22.0	Romania
18.0	Poland
16.0	Bulgaria
15.8	Hungary
15.0	Czechoslovakia
13.1	Portugal
11.0	Greece
9.5	Italy
9.2	Ireland
9.1	Belgium
9.0	East Germany
9.0	Malta
9.0	United Kingdom
8.7	Luxembourg
8.0	Norway
8.1	Spain
7.8	France
7.6	Denmark
7.5	West Germany
7.3	Switzerland
6.8	Netherlands
6.0	Finland
6.0	Sweden
5.0	Iceland

Maternal deaths for every 100,000 live births

148.83	Romania
18.70	Bulgaria
16.28	Yugoslavia
15.41	Hungary
11.56	East Germany
11.06	Finland
10.67	Poland
10.12	Portugal
9.64	Netherlands
9.59	Czechoslovakia
9.34	France
7.89	Austria
7.72	United Kingdom
7.63	Italy
5.58	Greece
5.40	Spain
5.28	West Germany
4.78	Sweden
3.70	Switzerland
3.48	Norway
3.42	Belgium
3.40	Denmark
1.83	Ireland
0.00	Iceland
0.00	Luxembourg
0.00	Malta

Ratio of abortions to 1,000 live births

1,015.40	Yugoslavia
988.90	Bulgaria
769.30	Czechoslovakia
734.00	Hungary
522.28	Romania
360.26	Denmark
351.75	Italy
324.90	Sweden
275.56	Norway
227.48	United Kingdom
217.20	Finland
210.00	France
146.93	Iceland
141.49	Poland
134.63	West Germany
96.40	Netherlands
95.82	Greece

No abortion in Ireland or Malta

Number of people for every doctor (1988)

304	Hungary
318	Spain
323	Bulgaria
327	Czechoslovakia
333	Belgium
344	Greece
380	Sweden
381	Germany (totalled)
394	Denmark
397	Portugal
401	Switzerland
425	Iceland
428	Finland
428	Netherlands
433	France
448	Norway
475	Romania
497	Poland
517	Austria
549	Yugoslavia
554	Luxembourg
671	Albania
689	Ireland
691	United Kingdom
706	Italy
829	Malta

Deaths from breast cancer (age 0–64) per 100,000 women

13.49	Romania
14.72	Greece
15.08	Bulgaria
15.14	Poland
15.43	Yugoslavia
15.56	Sweden
15.59	Spain
16.29	East Germany
16.65	Finland
16.98	Portugal
17.19	Czechoslovakia
17.59	Norway
17.80	France
19.02	Austria
19.25	Italy
19.42	Switzerland
20.27	Iceland
20.76	West Germany
20.86	Hungary
22.21	Luxembourg
23.71	Netherlands
23.71	Malta
24.94	Belgium
26.11	Denmark
26.48	United Kingdom
26.70	Ireland

Deaths from cancer of the cervix (age 0–64) per 100,000 women

0.89	Italy
0.94	Finland
1.10	Greece
1.43	Spain
1.50	Malta
1.79	France
1.89	Luxembourg
2.18	Portugal
2.26	Belgium
2.28	Switzerland
2.33	Netherlands
2.72	Iceland
2.88	West Germany
3.05	Sweden
3.15	Ireland
3.18	Austria
4.28	Bulgaria
4.29	Norway
4.59	Yugoslavia
4.69	United Kingdom
5.43	Denmark
5.44	East Germany
5.91	Czechoslovakia
6.35	Hungary
8.19	Poland
10.51	Romania

Women's life expectancy

73.0	Romania
73.0	Yugoslavia
74.0	Czechoslovakia
74.0	Hungary
75.0	Bulgaria
75.5	Albania
75.5	Poland
76.2	East Germany
76.7	Ireland
76.8	Belgium
77.5	United Kingdom
77.6	Denmark
77.6	Greece
77.6	Malta
77.7	Portugal
77.9	Luxembourg
78.1	Austria
78.4	West Germany
78.8	Finland
78.9	Netherlands
79.1	Italy
79.6	Spain
79.9	Norway
80.0	France
80.1	Sweden
80.4	Iceland
81.0	Switzerland

Deaths from suicide and self-inflicted injury per 100,000 women

2.02	Greece
2.74	Malta
3.44	Poland
3.44	Portugal
3.46	Spain
3.59	United Kingdom
3.81	Italy
4.84	Ireland
5.15	Iceland
7.28	Netherlands
8.19	West Germany
8.39	Bulgaria
8.60	Czechoslovakia
9.20	Luxembourg
9.22	Norway
10.16	Sweden
10.32	Yugoslavia
10.99	France
11.30	Finland
11.96	Switzerland
12.49	Austria
13.29	Belgium
13.29	East Germany
17.52	Denmark
20.40	Hungary

Marriage rate for every 1,000 people

4.0	Iceland
4.8	Greece
4.9	France
4.9	Sweden
5.0	Norway
5.1	Ireland
5.3	Finland
5.5	Luxembourg
5.5	Italy
5.5	Spain
6.0	Belgium
6.0	Netherlands
6.2	Hungary
6.3	Denmark
6.5	West Germany
6.7	Poland
6.7	Yugoslavia
6.8	Switzerland
6.9	Portugal
6.9	United Kingdom
7.0	Romania
7.1	Bulgaria
7.8	Czechoslovakia
8.5	East Germany
8.6	Albania
10.1*	Austria
14.5	Malta

*   1987 figure which was inflated by the abolition of the marriage allowance

Divorce rate for every 1,000 people

0.5	Italy
0.5	Spain
0.8	Albania
0.9	Greece
0.9	Portugal
1.9	France
1.9	Netherlands
1.9	Switzerland
2.1	Belgium
2.1	West Germany
2.1	Luxembourg
2.3	Hungary
2.9	Denmark
2.9	United Kingdom
3.2	Czechoslovakia

No divorce in Ireland or Malta

Date of women's suffrage

1906	Finland
1907	France
1913	Norway
1915	Denmark
1915	Iceland
1918	Austria
1918	Poland
1919	Czechoslovakia
1919	Germany
1919	Luxembourg
1919	Netherlands
1919	Sweden
1928	United Kingdom
1931	Spain
1935	Ireland
1938	Bulgaria
1945	Hungary
1945	Italy
1946	Romania
1946	Yugoslavia
1947	Malta
1948	Belgium
1958	Albania
1971	Switzerland
1976	Portugal

Percentage of women in national parliaments

38.5	Finland
38.1	Sweden
36.0	Norway
33.0	Denmark
27.3	Netherlands
23.8	Iceland
21.9	Austria
20.5	Germany
17.7	Yugoslavia
15.9	Switzerland
13.5	Poland
13.3	Luxembourg
12.5	Spain
10.6	Italy
9.4	Czechoslovakia
9.4	Belgium
8.7	Ireland
8.5	Bulgaria
7.6	Portugal
7.3	Hungary
6.8	United Kingdom
5.3	Greece
5.0	France
3.6	Albania
3.6	Romania
2.9	Malta

Pupil : primary teacher ratio (1988)

11	Austria
11	Denmark
14	Finland
14	Hungary
14	Italy
15	Belgium
16	Norway
16	Poland
16	Sweden
17	Germany (totalled)
17	Netherlands
17	Portugal
18	Bulgaria
19	France
20	Albania
20	Yugoslavia
21	Czechoslovakia
21	Romania
22	United Kingdom
23	Greece
26	Spain
27	Ireland

Number of tv sets for every 1,000 people (1987)

83	Albania
159	Portugal
166	Romania
175	Greece
175	Yugoslavia
189	Bulgaria
228	Ireland
249	Luxembourg
257	Italy
263	Poland
285	Czechoslovakia
297	Iceland
320	Belgium
333	France
348	Norway
368	Spain
374	Finland
386	Denmark
387	Malta
395	Sweden
402	Hungary
405	Switzerland
434	United Kingdom
464	Germany
469	Netherlands
480	Austria